Orde Wingate

Unconventional Warrior

From the 1920s to the Twenty-First Century

Simon Anglim

Pen & Sword
MILITARY

First published in Great Britain in 2014 by
Pen & Sword History
an imprint of
Pen & Sword Books Ltd
47 Church Street
Barnsley
South Yorkshire
S70 2AS

Copyright © Simon Anglim 2014

ISBN 978 1 78346 218 6

The right of Simon Anglim to be identified as the Author of this Work has been asserted by him in accordance with the Copyright, Designs and Patents Act 1988.

A CIP catalogue record for this book is available from the British Library

All rights reserved. No part of this book may be reproduced or transmitted in any form or by any means, electronic or mechanical including photocopying, recording or by any information storage and retrieval system, without permission from the Publisher in writing.

Typeset in Ehrhardt by
Mac Style Ltd, Bridlington, East Yorkshire
Printed and bound in the UK by CPI Group (UK) Ltd, Croydon, CR0 4YY

Pen & Sword Books Ltd incorporates the imprints of Pen & Sword Archaeology, Atlas, Aviation, Battleground, Discovery, Family History, History, Maritime, Military, Naval, Politics, Railways, Select, Transport, True Crime, and Fiction, Frontline Books, Leo Cooper, Praetorian Press, Seaforth Publishing and Wharncliffe.

For a complete list of Pen & Sword titles please contact
PEN & SWORD BOOKS LIMITED
47 Church Street, Barnsley, South Yorkshire, S70 2AS, England
E-mail: enquiries@pen-and-sword.co.uk
Website: www.pen-and-sword.co.uk

Contents

Acknowledgements		iv
Introduction: Orde Wingate and the Twenty-First Century		1
1.	Genius or Madman?	5
2.	Winning Small Wars – Wingate's Army	18
3.	Before Palestine, 1923–36	29
4.	Wingate and Counter-terrorism in Palestine, 1937–39	46
5.	Wingate in Ethiopia, 1940–41	94
6.	Wingate in Burma (1) – The Origins of the Chindits, 1942–43	136
7.	Wingate In Burma (2) – Operation *Longcloth* And Its Consequences	163
8.	Wingate In India – Go Ye To The Stronghold	183
9.	Wingate In Burma (3) – Operation *Thursday*, 1944	191
10.	Orde Wingate and the Twenty-First Century Refined	205
Notes		209
Bibliography		242
Index		249

Acknowledgements

First and above all, my eternal gratitude to Professor Martin Alexander for his supervision of the doctoral thesis which parented this book: his support then and since has been unstinting, his advice impeccable and always constructive. My thanks also to my original supervisor, Professor Colin McInnes, for suggesting most of the main themes investigated here. Credit also to their colleague Dr Peter Jackson and the anonymous consultant editors of *Intelligence and National Security*, whose response to a paper extracted from the thesis suggested new themes which redirected it onto a stronger and more interesting path, as well as Dr Paul Rich and his consultant editors at *Small Wars and Insurgencies*, who did likewise at a later stage. Another such was the late Sir Douglas Dodds-Parker, who spent a day in August 2004 answering my questions on his acquaintance with Orde Wingate (it could never be called friendship) and his experiences with MI(R) and the Special Operations Executive; I am grateful also to the various Chindit veterans who have answered my enquiries and who, along with Sir Douglas, did so much to bring the documents to life. My thanks also to the staff at the Department of Documents of the Imperial War Museum, the National Archives at Kew, the British Library, the Liddell Hart Centre for Military Archives, the Churchill Archives at Cambridge and John Montgomery at the RUSI Library, all of them unfailingly helpful. My thanks also to Mrs Holly Wingate for granting me permission to quote from her late father-in-law's papers, and for her interest in this project. Finally, I acknowledge all those friends and colleagues who have provided me with advice, constructive criticism and opportunities to give my findings an audience: Mark Baillie, Dr William Bain, Eila Bannister, Colonel David Benest, Dr Tim Benbow, Professor Brian Bond, Colonel Hugh Boscawen, the late Dr David Chandler, Commander Michael Codner, Professor Christopher Dandeker, Nathan Finney, the late Dr David Fisher, Professor Yo'av Gelber, Euan Grant, Professor Colin Gray, the late Professor Richard Holmes, Dr Matthew Hughes, Colonel John Hughes-Wilson, Frank Ledwidge, Dr Terry MacNamee, William F. Owen, Professor Bill Philpott, Major Dan Simmons, Colonel Michael (Coyote) Smith USAF, Professor Hew Strachan, Adam E. Stahl, Dr Danny Steed, Colonel Jim Storr, Dr Frank Tallett and Colonel John Wilson.

Finally, all my thanks to my mother for supporting and sometimes driving me through this project, and to my father for instilling me with his enthusiasm for military history and his admiration for people who 'don't mess around'.

Introduction

Orde Wingate and the Twenty-First Century

There was a man of genius, who might well have become also a man of destiny.
Winston Churchill[1]

Much of what he preached strategically, operationally, and tactically, was flawed, and some of it was downright nonsense.
Major General Julian Thompson[2]

Two quotations, five decades apart, providing but a tiny sample of opinions of Major General Orde Charles Wingate (1903-44), a controversial figure in Britain and Israel to this day. This controversy, and Wingate's popular image, stem from three episodes occurring late in a military career beginning with his passing out from the Royal Military Academy, Woolwich, in 1923 and ending in his death in an air crash in Burma in 1944. During the Palestine Arab uprising of 1936–39, Wingate, a captain on the Staff of General Headquarters in Haifa, was authorised by two British General Officers Commanding (GOC) Palestine, General Sir Archibald Wavell and General Sir Robert Haining, to train Jewish policemen, in British-organised irregular units known as the Special Night Squads (SNS), in his own personal brand of counter-insurgency. Wingate, a passionate Zionist, politicised this mission, turning it into the backbone of a personal campaign for a Jewish state: Moshe Dayan and Yigal Allon were among the young men he trained; both rose to become generals in the Israel Defence Force and both identified Wingate as a major influence upon Israeli military thought, as did Ariel Sharon later on.[3] Wingate roused strong feelings even then, deploying his Jewish Night Squads, in majority Arab areas, in politically explosive pre-emptive and reprisal attacks on Arab villages believed to be hiding insurgents, as well as using some 'robust' methods to extract intelligence from prisoners.[4] Despite this – or perhaps because of it – Wingate was summoned by Wavell, now Commander in Chief, Middle East, in late 1940 to take over an operation organised by G(R) – an offshoot of the MI(R) covert warfare branch of the British War Office – aimed at escalating and steering guerrilla resistance in Italian-occupied Ethiopia. Wingate succeeded far beyond G(R)'s ambitions, raising and training 'Gideon Force', a purpose-organised regular formation for operations deep inside hostile territory, which cooperated with local tribal irregulars in the Gojjam region of western Ethiopia to defeat an Italian force at least ten times its size, and participated directly in restoring the Emperor Haile Selassie to the throne taken from him by the Italians five years before.[5] It was after Ethiopia that Wingate began to advocate what he claimed was a new form of warfare, which he called Long Range Penetration (sic), based upon his interpretation of his operations in Gojjam and which he argued held the key to victory against the Axis.[6] Wingate is best remembered in Britain for the third episode, his command of Long Range Penetration Groups, light infantry formations ostensibly using 'guerrilla' methods, supplied and supported by air, in two major operations deep inside Japanese-occupied Burma, Operations *Longcloth*, of February-May 1943, and *Thursday* of March-August 1944, during which he was killed in an air crash.[7]

So what? Why should anyone interested in military affairs post-1945 want to know of somebody who died during the Second World War after a life spent defending the British Empire? What follows is not a biography of Orde Wingate, as that has been done very well by others at least twice before. Rather, it is an attempt to answer this 'so what' question, and to present an argument that one major reason why we should be interested in Orde Wingate now is that he pioneered some of the methods utilised in more recent operations.[8] Mention of the Night Squads, their organisation and ethos can draw parallels with Allied Tier One Special Forces' offensives against the Iraqi insurgents in 2007–10 and the Afghan Taliban in 2011–13, or indeed, the US Navy SEAL (SEa Air Land) operation to assassinate Osama bin Laden in April 2012. Wingate proposed what twenty-first-century soldiers might identify as 'enemy-centric counterinsurgency', or, as he put it more bluntly, a 'counter-gang' strategy, referring explicitly in official papers to 'government gangs' hunting insurgent gangs on their own territory and using their own methods against them. Moreover, he insisted from the very beginning that his Night Squads should include personnel from the Jewish Settlement Police (JSP, *Notrim* in Hebrew), a part-time volunteer force formed to protect Jewish settlements from the terrorists, and should operate from Jewish settlements likely to come under attack. Because of this, the squads were infiltrated thoroughly by the Jewish underground militia, the *Haganah*. This raises issues for those hoping to enlist participants in inter-communal conflicts or resistance movements as allies, the most important being how far they might bring their own agenda with them. How much this affects the aims and methods of the outsiders soliciting their support, Wingate recognised with his *Haganah* allies, as did his distant (and much-loathed) relative, T.E. Lawrence, with the Bedu of the Hejaz twenty years before: both argued that the locals' programme should be recognised, accommodated and turned into a cause to fight for, although in both cases there were political repercussions later on.

Beyond insurgency there is the use of certain types of unit against more conventional foes. In March 2011, a British 'diplomatic team', incorporating personnel from the Secret Intelligence Service (MI6) and E Squadron, 22 Special Air Service Regiment (22 SAS), was detained while contacting rebels fighting the regime of Colonel Gadafi in Libya, the most violent expression of that year's 'Arab Spring'. By April, reports emerged that 'former' SAS men and 'Private Military Companies' were 'advising' the rebels and providing forward air control for North Atlantic Treaty Organisation (NATO) airstrikes.[9] September brought official admission of the reality: D Squadron, 22 SAS, had coordinated Libyan rebel ground offensives with NATO airstrikes, most notably in the liberation of Colonel Gadafi's home town of Sirte, while Special Forces from France and Qatar operated anti-tank guided missiles for the rebels and guided airstrikes elsewhere in Libya.[10] Ten years before, US Special Operations Forces (SOF) deployed into Afghanistan alongside the Northern Alliance as part of Operation *Enduring Freedom*, the invasion of al Qaeda's sanctuary following the mass terror attacks on the USA of 11 September 2001. These provided a degree of coordination among anti-Taliban forces which was lacking previously and also controlled US Air Force (USAF) heavy bombers and US Navy F-18s for battlefield close air support; in 2003, US Special Forces working alongside the Kurdish *Peshmerga* defeated Iraqi regular troops and Iranian-backed irregulars alike, taking Mosul, Kurdistan's biggest city.[11] Military and paramilitary operations supporting armed uprisings appear a growingly important component of twenty-first-century warfare and provide means of achieving strategic aims cost-effectively and with a low political footprint: the Libyan episode saw the rapid removal of a forty-year-old regime still considered by some to be a regional power, while in 2001, US SOF plus airpower plus the Northern Alliance toppled the Taliban regime in a matter of weeks in lieu of a conventional invasion. It is unsurprising, therefore, that some countries have entire 'fourth forces' devoted to such activity, such as the Iranian Revolutionary Guard Corps al Quds Force or the US Central Intelligence Agency's (CIA) Directorate of Operations Special Activities Division, and one of the earliest examples was the Military Intelligence (Research) branch of the British War Office, created in 1938. MI(R) and its sub-branch at General Headquarters (GHQ) Middle East, G(R), from 1940 to 1941, executed successful paramilitary support operations against the Italians in Ethiopia and Somalia and Vichy French in Lebanon and Syria. As touched on already, their biggest operation, in Gojjam, Western Ethiopia, from December 1940 to May 1941, involved the then Colonel Wingate being ordered to divert Italian forces away from the main British offensive into Eritrea, which drew into a major battle around the fortified town of Keren; some 18–20,000 Italian troops, which might have reinforced the defenders of Keren or elsewhere, were pinned in Gojjam by Wingate's 'Gideon Force', which numbered at most 800 men (mainly British-trained Ethiopians and Sudanese) plus variable numbers of local guerrillas; eventually an Italian force of 14,000 surrendered to 150 British, Ethiopians and Sudanese.[12] Wingate therefore bears study here also: not only did he plan and command successful paramilitary support operations, but also put opinion to paper, arguing they were the wave of the future (in 1942) and advocating what current soldiers identify as 'manoeuvre warfare' carried out by specially-trained regular troops alongside local irregulars and supported by air, as seen with Gideon Force in Gojjam in 1941 and the Chindit operations in Burma of 1943 and 1944. Orde Wingate might, therefore, have things to say to twenty-first-century warriors.

However, another reason Wingate might reward a deeper look is what he tells us about some of the controversies pertaining to those very methods, some of which are still heard today. To begin with, there were many distinguished figures, from Wingate's time and since, who would argue that Wingate's type of operation is not only an unsound means of attaining strategic aims, but also wasteful of lives and resources. The opinions cited most often in support of this argument are those of the authors of two widely-read works from the decade after Wingate's death, Volume III of the British Government's *Official History of the War against Japan*, authored largely by the former Director of Staff Duties, India, Major General S. Woodburn Kirby, and Field Marshal Lord Slim's personal memoir of the Burma campaign, *Defeat into Victory*, which remains in print to this day.[13] Kirby and Slim questioned not only Wingate's professional abilities, but also his mental stability.[14] They are not alone: adjectives applied to Wingate most glibly and often by many other authors tend to be variations on 'eccentric' or 'mad'. He was certainly 'different': brought up in the Plymouth Brethren, he regarded the Old Testament as literal history and political tract and laced his speeches, and sometimes his official writings, with portentous, Biblical rhetoric; in an army which still makes a fetish of conformity, smartness and 'grooming standards', he was often scruffy and fully bearded, and on operations wore a filthy uniform and old-fashioned solar topee helmet; he ate six raw onions a day, and ordered all his officers to eat at least one; he often carried out business in the nude, brushing himself vigorously with a wire brush instead of washing, sometimes during official briefings and press conferences, and carried an alarm clock to time his meetings and show those around him that 'time was passing'.[15] Even Wingate's admirers agree that he could be a bloody-minded and disputatious individual of strong and frequently unorthodox opinions on many matters, who apparently went through life seeking out feuds, and was unafraid to 'name and shame' those he saw as thwarting him, including senior officers, in official documents using the most vitriolic language.[16] He could also be brittle: he attempted suicide in 1941, after the Ethiopian operation, due to a combination of depression, exhaustion and dementia arising from cerebral malaria, and accounts of him are full of anecdotes of tantrums, sulks and occasional physical assaults on soldiers and even subordinate officers.[17] More sinister allegations have been made: in the late 1990s, an Israeli journalist, Tom Segev, suggested that Wingate committed atrocities in Palestine, a claim taken up with some enthusiasm by Israeli revisionist historians, anti-Zionist websites and, predictably, Palestinian nationalists.[18] These allegations centred upon claims that Wingate, and others acting on his orders, had physically abused captured or suspected insurgents ostensibly to extract information from them, but also with an element of 'encouragement of others' about it; there are echoes of abuses made by US and Allied forces in Iraq since 2003 here, as well as of allegations made against Israeli forces in their occupied territories, and this opens up debate as to how these things happen, in particular whether they form part of premeditated strategy in counterinsurgency.

In order to assess Wingate's real status as a military figure it will be necessary to address these issues and also to tease out the reality of the man from the many myths which have grown up around him, many of which have come to be accepted as reality since his time. This work has done this by looking at what Wingate himself and his contemporaries said about these issues in their own words, and has been worth doing, as a far more interesting figure has emerged from behind the myths. However, those myths seem an appropriate starting point.

Chapter One

Genius or Madman?

He was a military genius and a wonderful man.
General Moshe Dayan[1]

Personally I doubt if [Wingate] was a genius except for short intervals, even though he had what most people consider a qualification for the role in that he crossed the border line of lunacy...more than once.
Field Marshal Lord Slim[2]

The Case Summarised

Wingate's Long Range Penetration Groups are better remembered as the *Chindits*, a propaganda name derived from Wingate's mispronunciation of *Chinthey*, the stone griffin-figures which guard Buddhist temples in Southeast Asia; as part lion, part dragon, they seemed an apt symbol for an air-land force, and their mythical significance to the people of the region was not lost on Wingate, either.[3] Many were arguing over the military legacy of the Chindit operations within five years of Wingate's death. Among friends and supporters, Wingate is remembered as a military genius of the highest order whose brilliant ideas played a decisive part not only in defeating Japan in Southeast Asia, but also in earlier operations in Palestine and Ethiopia. Churchill made his 'man of genius' statement shortly after Wingate's death, and the Supreme Allied Commander in Southeast Asia, Admiral Lord Louis Mountbatten, wrote to the Chief of Staff of the United States Army Air Force, General 'Hap' Arnold: 'In him I lost not only a personal friend but a forceful and dynamic leader who helped immensely in getting a move on in the war in Burma', while Wavell reflected 'I have better cause than anyone to recognize his genius, and to be grateful for it'; among Wingate's former subordinates, Sir Robert Thompson, who served as a Royal Air Force (RAF) Liaison and Forward Air Control Officer on both Chindit operations and later became a globally-respected authority on guerrilla warfare, described Wingate as 'one of the great men of the century' while Moshe Dayan's thoughts are summarised succinctly at the head of this chapter.[4] To Wingate's detractors, the Chindit operations were the brainchild of a madman, militarily unsound, wasteful of lives and resources and an unnecessary diversion from the 'real war' – the destruction of Japanese formations in main-force battle. Moreover, they argue, this was known at the time: Lieutenant General Sir Ernest Down, the tough old paratrooper who commanded a British airborne division in the Far East, commented of Wingate, 'I thought that his administration was a little "airy-fairy"… Had it not been for Derek Tulloch, his Chief of Staff, his venture [Operation *Thursday*] would have been a failure' or General Sir Henry Pownall, writing in February 1944, 'I shouldn't be at all surprised if within the next few months it is proved that Wingate is bogus; at any rate he is a thoroughly nasty bit of work' or, perhaps most damning of all, the words of the supreme hero of Britain's war in Burma, Field Marshal Lord Slim: 'I do not believe that the contribution of Special Force [the Chindits] was either great in effect, or commensurate with the resources it absorbed.'[5]

The controversy therefore revolves partially around whether or not the kind of operations Wingate planned, led and advocated were a sound means of attaining British aims in the theatres in which he served, and solidified in the 1950s around two books, Volume III of the British Government's *Official History of the War against Japan*, authored largely by the former Director of Staff Duties, India, Major General S. Woodburn Kirby, and Slim's personal memoir of the Burma campaign, *Defeat into Victory*, which remain at the heart of the case against him.[6]

Prosecution – Wingate the Charlatan

It would be no exaggeration to divide published works on Wingate into pre-Kirby and post-Kirby eras, as the controversy arising from the *Official History*'s judgment of Wingate has touched, at least indirectly, every work published on Wingate since Volume III, covering the second Chindit operation, was released in 1961. However, a number of other works had appeared by the mid-1950s, suggesting not only that Wingate had made numerous powerful enemies long before Burma, but also giving the impression of a rather unhinged character, most notably *Wingate's Phantom Army* by Wilfred Burchett and *Gideon Goes to War* by Leonard Mosley. It would be well-advised to take both these authors with the proverbial pinch of salt. Burchett's politics, and a lifetime of problems with the truth, mean that any reading of *Wingate's Phantom Army* must be done with care. A war correspondent and devout Marxist, Burchett reported from the war in Asia and the Pacific – and interviewed Wingate – before spending most of the 1950s and 60s in North Korea and North Vietnam, culminating in him being effectively exiled from his native Australia for tricking Australian prisoners of war in the Korean and Vietnam Wars into participating in enemy propaganda through combining blackmail, promises of special treatment, or posing as a supposedly neutral journalist conducting 'interviews' wherein they were steered into condemning their government or confessing to bogus 'war crimes'. He remained an apologist for the Stalinist regimes in North Korea and Bulgaria until his death in Sofia in 1983, and there is still some debate as to the extent of his control by the KGB.[7] *Wingate's Phantom Army* portrayed Wingate as a kindred spirit, anti-imperialist and anti-British, engaged in a quasi-revolutionary crusade framing his military operations. In Palestine, Burchett alleged, Wingate almost single-handedly turned the tide of the Arab revolt, against obstruction from an anti-Semitic British High Command; later, Wingate saved Ethiopia from 'international sharks… racketeers and stock market strategists' by overcoming British attempts to stimulate guerrilla warfare in Ethiopia, which Burchett implied were set up deliberately to fail.[8] Some of Burchett's assertions will be contrasted with the reality later on, and not only do they come off worse, but a degree of gratuitous calumny against numerous British officers and officials is soon apparent. The same can be said of Mosley for somewhat different reasons. Mosley published *Gideon Goes to War* in 1955: the first real Wingate biography, this was as controversial as the *Official History* was to be later. Mosley was an American journalist based in Cairo during the war, during which time he met Wingate on several occasions, and was present when he crossed the border into Ethiopia in 1941. As with Burchett, Mosley was fascinated by Wingate's character, particularly his sense of historical mission, his religiosity and the struggle against depression which culminated in his suicide attempt in 1941. Mosley's approach was therefore psychological-anecdotal, some aspects of Wingate's character being emphasised and probably over-emphasised in pursuit of colourful stories, the better to sell the book. Like Burchett, Mosley dwelt throughout on Wingate's Zionism: however, while Burchett approved, Mosley suggested that Wingate's fanatical devotion to the Jewish cause clouded his professional and moral judgment more than once, having him dismiss General Headquarters, Jerusalem, as 'a gang of anti-Jews', and railing at the passivity of timid Jewish politicians and the Islamophilia of British officials, which was condemning Jewish settlers on the frontiers of Palestine, 'with nothing but a few rook rifles per settlement' to massacre until Wingate galvanised them onto the offensive and shamed the British authorities into supporting them.[9] His account of Wingate's leadership of the Night Squads was fictionalised heavily, including two lurid incidents which appear to be embellished if not completely fabricated. The first has Wingate ordering the murder of an Arab prisoner in order to terrify others into giving information, an incident in which Dayan was also supposedly involved, but for which Mosley did not give a date; there was no corroboration for these incidents and they were not repeated in any subsequent works until Segev's in 1999. Mosley's second allegation was that Wingate was prepared to commit treason against the British Crown, offering to desert the Army and lead a Jewish sabotage campaign in Palestine following the publication of the 1939 MacDonald White Paper on Palestine's future.[10] Also echoing Burchett, Mosley portrayed Wingate as rescuing Ethiopia from a British colonial establishment which half-welcomed the Italian occupation and treated the Emperor-in-exile, Haile Selassie, with supercilious dismissiveness until Wingate launched a one-man assault upon the staff in Khartoum.[11] The image emerging of Wingate so far was of a man engaged in a private war not only against the British Army, but also against the British Government and the 'establishment' behind it, and was capable of reaching such extremes of fanaticism that he was happy to risk his career and his very life against them.

This leads neatly to the two 'star witnesses' for the prosecution. Field Marshal Lord Slim of Burma's *Defeat into Victory*, his memoir of his command of the British 14th Army during the Burma Campaign, published in 1956, discussed Wingate's military ideas and his character at length, and found them wanting, and coming from a figure still revered in the British Army decades after his death in 1970, and still seen by many as the final authority on the British campaign in Burma, this must be taken seriously indeed. Slim surprised many, given the magnanimity he showed towards almost everyone else, and in 1944 he had written an entirely complimentary eulogy for Wingate for a South East Asia Command (SEAC) pamphlet on the Chindits. According to this, when Slim first met Wingate in Abyssinia in 1940: 'I regarded him then as one of the several daring young soldiers who were showing themselves to be outstanding guerrilla leaders... I then learned that, added to the tactical daring of the guerrilla leader, were a wealth of vision and a depth of imagination that placed him far above his comrades.'[12] This made *Defeat into Victory*'s portrayal of Wingate all the more surprising. The Wingate presented in *Defeat into Victory* was a paradox, a highly strung *prima donna* who was also a calculating political operator, Slim recalling a 'strange, excitable, moody creature' and offering the reader several opportunities to contrast Wingate's histrionics with his own calm self-assurance.[13] He opened by dismissing Gideon Force – which had consisted of regular troops commanded by British officers – as '*Shifta* or brigands' and by doubting whether a repeat in Burma would work 'against a tougher enemy and in country not so actively friendly.'[14] Slim later described Wingate as 'strangely naive when it came to the business of actually fighting the Japanese', an enemy which would not be scared into retreating by threats to their rear, but would have to be defeated in battle, the Chindits being too outnumbered and lightly-equipped to do this.[15] *Longcloth* exemplified this, an operation in which several hundred men died, but which had 'no immediate effect on Japanese dispositions or plans' and provided a 'costly schooling' in jungle fighting: its only tangible value being as propaganda and a slight rise in British confidence in fighting the Japanese in the jungles of Burma.[16] Wingate would not accept this, however, and – two ranks subordinate to Slim, a full general – repeatedly threatened to report Slim to Churchill.[17] In his chapter on 'lessons learned' from the Burma campaign, Slim berated the plethora of special forces formed by the British in the Second World War, claiming that 'Any well-trained infantry battalion should be able to do what a commando can do; [in Burma] they could and did', and arguing that special operations in future should be limited to small parties carrying out sabotage, subversion and assassination, on the lines of the Special Operations Executive (SOE): 'Private armies... are expensive, wasteful and unnecessary', a drain on manpower leeching the best personnel away from units having to fight the enemy's main armies in battle.[18]

The impact of all this is increased by Slim being the only British senior commander of the Second World War whose reputation has not undergone any serious historical revision or reassessment, and he remains a figure of semi-divine reverence in some circles. This seems to include most British military historians, historical study of Slim being dominated by a small group of well-published but mainly 'popular' authors, most prominently Ronald Lewin, Duncan Anderson and Robert Lyman, who treat him unquestioningly and view *Defeat into Victory* as the infallible final source not only on the war in Burma – far more so, it seems, than contemporary documents and testimony – but also on many aspects of modern warfare in general. Wingate does not get an easy ride from this group, needless to say: Lewin's biography of Slim contrasts Wingate's approach to fighting the Japanese with Slim's unfavourably throughout, and describes Wingate as 'untruthful', 'disloyal' and 'highly wrought, almost manic in his oscillations between euphoria and pessimism', while Wingate's defenders, principally Derek Tulloch and Michael Calvert, are accused of 'special pleading'.

Kirby is viewed widely as the 'Godfather' of this group, and Volumes II and III of *The Official History of the War against Japan* took the Wingate debate to its highest pitch. Given its impact, it would be no exaggeration to claim that, whatever its flaws, real and perceived, the *Official History* is the most important work ever published on Wingate. The passages in question, including the assessment of Wingate in Volume III causing greatest animation, were drafted initially not by Kirby, but by Miss R.J.F. Hughes, an assistant historian in the Cabinet Office, and, like the rest of the *Official History*, were based upon narratives written by Colonel J.E.B. Barton and Brigadier M. Henry, both working in the Cabinet Office Historical section. Passages involving Slim read similarly to those in *Defeat into Victory*, while Volume II's rationale of the Chindit operations paraphrased Wingate's official report on *Longcloth* almost verbatim.[19] Volume II of the *Official History*, released in 1958, contained little hint of the furore to come. Wingate was criticised for his tactical handling of *Longcloth*, but the volume corroborates the argument of Brigadier Michael Calvert, who commanded a Chindit column on *Longcloth* and a brigade on *Thursday*, that *Longcloth* convinced the Japanese that their previous defensive strategy was flawed, leading to a new offensive policy 'which was eventually to lead them to disaster' at the battles of Imphal and Kohima.[20] It was Volume III, published four years later, which contained the passages that have offended so many former Chindits. These centre on the 'Assessment of Wingate', which closes its narrative of Operation *Thursday*, Wingate being the only Allied commander in Southeast Asia to have such, not even Slim warranting such analysis in detail. Kirby attributed Wingate's success as much to the patronage of Wavell and, later, Churchill, 'who claimed Wingate as a genius', as to the validity of his ideas.[21] Moreover, 'Whether his theories were sound or unsound, he appeared as a "doer" at a time when something desperately needed to be done [about the dire predicament the Allies faced in Southeast Asia].'[22] Kirby then implied that Wingate's success owed more to force of argument and skilful self-publicity than to any intrinsic merit, leading, as he became more ambitious, to megalomania:

> The way in which his ideas on the use of long-range penetration forces grew in Wingate's fertile imagination would form an interesting psychological study. From his early conception of lightly armed troops penetrating behind the enemy lines and attacking communications as part of a larger operation by conventional forces, the operations of [the Chindits] clearly became in his mind the only means by which northern Burma could be dominated. Subsequently, much increased in numbers, the force would become the spearhead of a victorious advance through southern Burma, Siam and Indo-China to win the war against Japan.[23]

Wingate was so determined to demonstrate this model that 'his handling of his forces became unsound', Kirby listing a series of perceived mistakes from both Chindit operations to support this claim, the most egregious of which echoed an accusation thrown at all Special Forces until recently, that the Chindits leeched the best soldiers away from 'real' units which needed them more.[24] Kirby then presented his own view of 'sound' warfare: Wingate was 'so obsessed by his theories that he forgot that victory in Burma could be achieved only by the defeat of the enemy's main forces' and, in his belief that lightly-equipped columns could defeat the Japanese, he underestimated them as an enemy.[25] However, Wingate's influence on Churchill resulted in one-sixth of all British infantry in Southeast Asia being 'locked up in LRP formations suitable only for guerrilla [sic] warfare.'[26] To Kirby, Wingate's ideas represented an egregious misdirection of manpower and resources, based upon shaky concepts, imposed upon the army in Southeast Asia largely by Churchill. However, the *Official History* was not entirely the 'hatchet job' that some in the pro-Wingate camp claim; Kirby did express admiration for Wingate's imagination, energy and ability to inspire, and prior to the personal assessment in Volume III, Wingate emerged with more credit than in *Defeat into Victory*. Yet Kirby did question the validity of many of Wingate's ideas, and certain passages of the *Official History* might be interpreted as a polemic about one particular model of warfare, officially approved, versus another, radical model. In asserting that victory came only through the destruction of the main Japanese armies in main-force battles involving conventional formations, and that the Chindit operations reduced the capacity of 14th Army to do this, Kirby and Slim might have been revealing either their own thoughts on war, or those of the institution which they served.

Defence – Wingate the Genius

That the *Official History*'s comments on Wingate have angered many is indisputable. Some of these angry people saw conspiracy: David Rooney recounted that, in 1947, Calvert – a close friend of Wingate as well as his subordinate commander – then working on Field Marshal Montgomery's planning staff, discovered an Army Council minute stating 'Wingate was a divisive influence in the British Army, and we do not want every company commander thinking he is a Wingate... Therefore we must write down Wingate...' and went on to quote Kirby's subordinate author, Colonel J.E.B. Barton, as referring to 'the vile accusations emanating not only from the Establishment, but also from high-ranking officers in all branches of the services.'[27] The notion of a British 'military establishment' objecting to Wingate's personality and ideas ran through work on him from the beginning. Charles Rolo, an American journalist and literary critic, produced *Wingate's Phantom Army*, an anecdotal narrative of *Longcloth*, in 1944, shortly after Wingate's death. Much of *Wingate's Phantom Army* reads like twenty-first-century tabloid journalism, full of hyperbole of the 'they said it couldn't be done' variety: 'The more conventional military leaders were aghast... Wingate was an upstart, a madman. Certainly it was not "pukka war" as they or anyone else knew it' and he later commented that: 'Wingate's fixity of purpose led to countless clashes with brass-hats and complacent officials, outraged by his forthright methods and assaults on red tape.'[28]

Such 'countless clashes' run like a thread through the two memoirs by Major General Sir Bernard Fergusson, who features prominently in what is to come. An old Etonian and officer of the Black Watch, Wavell's old regiment, and the Field Marshal's former aide de camp, Fergusson was serving on Wavell's Staff at General Headquarters (GHQ) India when Wingate put out a call for volunteers for the first Chindit operation in 1942. Dropping two ranks and a comfortable headquarters job, Fergusson commanded a Chindit column on *Longcloth* and went on to lead a brigade on *Thursday*, the earlier operation producing the best, and best-known of all Chindit memoirs, *Beyond the Chindwin*, Fergusson's account of *Longcloth*, published in 1945.[29] In 1946, at the behest of the Commandant of Police in the British Mandate in Palestine, the then Brigadier Fergusson raised two undercover units to fight Jewish insurgents: these may have been rooted at least partially in Wingate's ideas on counterinsurgency, as they bear a superficial resemblance to his Special Night Squads. After taking charge of psychological operations against Egypt in the Suez crisis of 1956, Fergusson served as Governor-General of New Zealand (a post held also by his father and grandfather) from 1962 to 1967. Besides *Beyond the Chindwin*, Fergusson also published a memoir of *Thursday*, *The Wild Green Earth*, in 1946, which took up a theme first presented at a lecture to the Royal United Services Institute (RUSI) in March 1946, that Wingate's ideas were a source of friction with certain others: 'On the whole [Wingate] failed to convert current military thought to his belief in deep penetration. He certainly convinced his lieutenants; but deprived of his fiery leadership and teaching, I cannot hope to succeed where he failed.'[30] Fergusson also felt strongly enough about the accusations evidently mounting by 1946 to include a defence of Wingate ('Some of those who now whisper that he was not all that he was cracked up to be remind me of the mouse who has a swig of whisky, and then says: "Now show me that bloody cat"') but, unfortunately for the historian, was not specific then about what these accusations might be or from whom they were coming.[31] Yet Fergusson made no secret of his own clashes with Wingate, and his often critical opinions will inform what follows.

The figure arguing longest and most vociferously for the existence of an anti-Wingate conspiracy was Michael Calvert, beginning with *Prisoners of Hope*, his memoir of commanding 77th Brigade on Operation *Thursday*. Calvert was an interesting commentator upon Wingate: an experienced Special Forces soldier and thinker on such matters in his own right long before meeting Wingate, following his three-year association with the Chindits, in January 1945, he took over command of 1 SAS Brigade for the closing stages of the war in Europe, carried out operations ahead of the main British and Canadian armies in Holland, and oversaw the early stages of the surrender of German forces in Norway. In 1949 Calvert went to Malaya, where he played a part in devising the strategy masterminded by General Sir Harold Briggs, the Director of Operations in Malaya, for countering the communist insurgency there. In 1951 he raised and commanded the Malayan Scouts (SAS), a specialist counter-insurgency unit formed partially from veterans of the Chindits and other British and Commonwealth special forces that formed the kernel of today's 22 SAS. Before and since his death in 1999, Calvert was revered by former Chindits second only to Wingate himself, and was consulted by almost every author writing on Wingate, thereby playing a major part in shaping posthumous perceptions of

Wingate and those around him. There is some compelling evidence to suggest that leaning so heavily on Calvert's testimony may have been unwise.

It is clear why Calvert was remembered with such awe by so many who served with him: not only did he oversee much of the Chindits' selection and training, but he was also one of the greatest battlefield leaders the British Army has ever produced. Such was his thirst for action that in 1939 he resigned his commission in the Royal Engineers to enlist as a private soldier in the 5th Battalion Scots Guards, then earmarked as part of a potential British intervention force in the 'Winter War' between Finland and the USSR. He claimed to have killed a Japanese officer with his bare hands during the retreat from Burma in 1942, and on *Thursday* – as a brigadier – he personally led a Gurkha bayonet and kukri charge against Japanese prepared positions at Pagoda Hill, the same action in which Lieutenant George Cairns of the South Staffordshire Regiment won a posthumous Victoria Cross. This might have been sufficient to assure his legendary status, but throughout the operation he would also often get close enough to the Japanese to be able to throw grenades at them, and he had his Brigade Major carry a bagful just in case.[32] He was just as fierce about the welfare of his men, coming within a hairsbreadth of mutiny in the months after Wingate's death when the American General, Joseph Stilwell, ordered 77th Brigade, already depleted by exhaustion, disease and casualties from months of fighting the Japanese in the hills of Burma, to assault fortified Japanese positions at Mogaung, a role for which the Chindits were not trained or organised. Combine this with an endearing propensity to credit the soldiers under his command with any success and there is little wonder that he seems to have been liked as well as admired by those who served with him.[33] Calvert also wrote extensively on guerrilla warfare and special operations, demonstrating a grasp of the subject and knowledge of military history to match many professors.[34]

All this is apparent in *Prisoners of Hope*, an important source on Operation *Thursday*, written while Calvert was still a serving officer. Calvert's assessment of Wingate was at this stage relatively balanced; he for instance holding Wingate largely responsible for the debacle suffered by Fergusson's 16th Brigade at Indaw, and alluding to how the difficulties of commanding Chindit columns led to him converting 77th Brigade from columns back to more orthodox battalions for the attack on Mogaung.[35] However, while most of this work is a detailed personal narrative, that it is also intended as a defence of Wingate is indicated by a lengthy appendix giving testimony from the postwar interrogations of senior Japanese officers on the impact of *Thursday* on their operations in 1944, Calvert's reasons for including this being:

> Two of the most controversial aspects of the campaign in Burma were the two Wingate operations and the results they achieved. Could the thirteen British... five Gurkha and three West Africa battalions and their attendant ancillary forces, bases, and RAF and USAAF effort [which made up Wingate's forces on *Thursday*] have been of greater use to the Burma campaign if employed elsewhere in a more stereotyped role?[36]

Calvert went beyond Rolo's and Fergusson's allusions to state explicitly that Wingate faced deliberate obstruction from the British military authorities in India, claiming that they were obtuse about Wingate's military ideas and did not plan seriously for the second Chindit operation, that Brigadier WDA ('Joe') Lentaigne, the Gurkha officer who succeeded Wingate in command of Special Force was unsuitable because he was 'too orthodox', a Staff College-trained plodder, and that the Chindits had greater sympathy and cooperation from the Americans and the Royal Air Force, this being Calvert's first serious accusation laid against the rest of the British Army, or at least the first on the record.[37]

It was after the publication of *Prisoners of Hope* in 1952 that the demons Calvert had been fighting for years finally destroyed him. Anyone who has served in the British forces will recognize a particular 'type', the charismatic 'roughy-toughy soldier' who revels in his hard-living, hard-fighting persona, expects everybody around him to behave likewise and can react badly when they don't. Given the 'macho culture' of most militaries, such traits can be essential in winning the confidence of troops one may have to lead into battle, but can be potentially catastrophic under other circumstances, particularly at higher levels of command. Calvert seems to have taken this 'type' to extremes, a surprise for such a highly intelligent man. Throughout his career, he was an enthusiastic 'hell raiser', preferring to socialise with junior officers and his soldiers rather than his peers, frequently drinking too much when doing so, and when drunk could become extremely foolish and occasionally violent.[38] This escalated in the aftermath of *Thursday*, probably exacerbated by the boredom of the return to peacetime routine after 1945, which might explain why, contrasting with his superb command and leadership during the Chindit operations, Calvert's Malayan Scouts developed an abysmal reputation not only for incompetence on operations, but also for violent, booze-fuelled indiscipline extending to the attempted 'fragging' of unpopular officers and, indeed, of visiting personnel they took a dislike to.[39] Calvert's subordinate officers, while admiring him as a military thinker, were shocked by his carelessness in welcoming all comers to the unit – including some who had purportedly deserted from the French Foreign Legion in Indochina – the contrast between his martinet-like behaviour with junior officers and indifference to serious insubordination from the soldiers and, indeed, his apparent encouragement of some of the more open excesses. It may be that his posting home in June 1951, purportedly due to exhaustion and illness, was done in order to spare him the embarrassment of being relieved of command; it is worth noting that the Malayan Scouts' performance improved beyond all recognition under his successor, Lieutenant Colonel John Sloane, who almost immediately kicked out the sixteen biggest drunks and introduced a rigorous selection process which evolved into that used by UK Special Forces to this day.[40] Worse was to come: in July 1952, Calvert was court martialled and dishonorably discharged from the Army following a conviction for gross indecency, three German youths having claimed that in May that year he had twice invited them to his flat in the Officer's Mess at Soltau and then made sexual advances on them. Not only was homosexuality illegal at the time, but it is worth recalling that the KGB were making use of homosexual 'honey-traps' to entangle the likes of Tom Driberg and John Vassall: and a Brigadier with Special Forces experience would have been a bigger catch than either of these, so there was the potential for Calvert to have developed into a major security risk. Calvert never recovered from this episode: his binge-drinking escalated into full-blown alcoholism, and the number of jobs from which he was sacked for drunkenness during his seven-year self-imposed exile in Australia following the court martial seem to have run into the dozens.[41] However, by the 1960s he was back in England, had his drinking under control, and for five years was in charge of recruiting engineers for the Greater London Council. In 1970 he quit this post to spend the rest of his life effectively in genteel poverty as a freelance writer and expert on guerrilla warfare, and, more significantly for what we are investigating here, on Orde Wingate and the Chindits. Even at this mature stage there were spectacular lapses of judgment, such as his gate-crashing a Sinn Fein press conference in Belfast in 1971 (while wearing his SAS regimental tie), endangering himself and every journalist present.[42]

Calvert seems to have remained deeply embittered and somewhat paranoid throughout his life, his interest in subversive operations leading him to see 'reds under the bed' everywhere in British society, his politics moving further and further rightwards and his public writings and speeches often featuring broadsides against the 'useful idiots' in the British establishment who were allowing a gradual communist takeover of British society to happen.[43] This was echoed in his memories of his military career, a claim repeated time and again being that his and Wingate's attempts to drag the British Army into the modern age were met with resistance at every turn from a complacent and reactionary 'military establishment' which seems at times to have been far more of a menace than the Japanese. The theme of 'Orde Wingate and Michael Calvert versus the British Army' runs not only through his memoirs, *Fighting Mad*, but also David Rooney's biography of him (although Rooney seems to have taken it all with increasingly large pinches of salt): his downfall was blamed variously on Royal Military Police entrapment, the anti-Chindit conspiracy among the Army's high command alluded to already or, most interestingly, Brigade of Guards retaliation for an incident which he claims took place shortly after his arrival in Malaya.[44] In this case, Calvert claimed that the Commanding Officer of 2nd Battalion Scots Guards, Lieutenant Colonel David Sanderson, was sacked and sent home by the General Officer Commanding (GOC), General Sir John Harding, after telling Calvert that he was not going to retrain his battalion 'to chase bare-arsed niggers around the jungle', an allegation which is quoted as fact by Rooney and, later, Colonel John Nagl in his influential work on guerrilla warfare, *Learning to eat Soup with a Knife*.[45] This is interesting, given that official records indicate that Sanderson remained in command of 2nd Scots Guards until mid-1950, at least a year after his alleged clash with Calvert, during which time he executed a highly effective programme of jungle training followed by successful operations in the Selangor region, and, upon reposting, was awarded the Distinguished Service Order on the recommendation of the aforementioned General Harding. Calvert also claimed to have 'talent spotted' General Sir Gerald Templer as a potential GOC Malaya when Templer was acting as Vice Chief of the Imperial General Staff in the late 1940s.[46]

Calvert's veracity as a witness was coloured further by his fanatical devotion to Wingate: when, in 1970, Fergusson included some passing critical remarks about Wingate in his autobiography, Calvert wrote to him stating that 'First you forsook all and followed him; now you have denied him thrice!' and their correspondence indicated that Calvert had major fallings-out with several other ex-Chindit commanders over their perceived lack of loyalty to 'the Leader'.[47] This perhaps explains why what at the time were petty clashes and quarrels, and Kirby's slanted assessment of Wingate, were turned in Calvert's mind into a vast anti-Wingate conspiracy which, via Calvert's treatment as an authoritative source by certain previous authors, has come to be taken for granted by so many.

However, he was not alone in this view. That the 'establishment' might be steering the record was argued in the 1960s and 70s by other former senior Chindits, Derek Tulloch, Peter Mead and Sir Robert Thompson. Tulloch was a close friend of Wingate's since their time together as Gentlemen Cadets at the Royal Military Academy, Woolwich, in 1920-22, and he served as Wingate's Brigadier, General Staff (Chief of Staff) on *Thursday*, and unsurprisingly his work is as deeply personal as Calvert's: 'Since the war... people in this country have expressed less flattering views on Wingate both as a man and a soldier. Hopefully my account of this controversial figure will help in the task of setting the record straight...'[48] He had been consulted by the authors of the *Official History* in the 1950s, and, according to Mead, became increasingly disturbed by the tone of the drafts he read, particularly after Kirby became involved.[49] After the war he took home with him a large body of Wingate's official papers – which he held illegally and are now added to those in the Imperial War Museum. Tulloch produced his own account of Wingate in Burma, *Wingate in Peace and War*, based on these papers, in 1972. *Wingate in Peace and War* revolves partially around a perceived conspiracy to cancel *Thursday*, instigated by the Supreme Allied Commander, Southeast Asia, Admiral Lord Louis Mountbatten, who allegedly preferred amphibious attacks directed at Singapore and Sumatra.[50] Once *Thursday* was launched, Tulloch claimed, Wingate planned to divert Chindit columns away from their initial mission – supporting Chinese forces under Stilwell, advancing into central Burma in an attempt to restore land communications with China – and redirect them towards attacking the communications of the Japanese 15th Army, then engaged in its offensive against Imphal and Kohima, in what Tulloch called Wingate's 'Plan B.'[51] Tulloch therefore developed further the notion of 'Wingate versus the British Army' and suggested also that his military prescience may have impacted upon the decisive battle of the Burma campaign. Tulloch asked Peter Mead to assist him with research and 'advise what more could be done to correct the *Official History*'s assessment of Wingate' in 1972.[52] Mead was a Royal Artillery officer who had served with Tulloch on Wingate's staff on *Thursday* and had met Wingate several times, Wingate befriending him as he often did with junior officers he considered worth his time. Mead later transferred to the Army Air Corps, finishing his career in 1964 as its Director, with the rank of brigadier. Tulloch died in 1974, and Mead continued his task of rebutting the *Official History*'s perceived calumnies against Wingate, producing *Orde Wingate and the Historians* in 1987. Much of this was a deliberate counterblast against the *Official History*, which led to Mead, upon reading it in the late 1970s, dedicating himself 'to unbend[ing] a piece of bent history.'[53] Mead centred his work on the existence of an official anti-Wingate 'line to take' originating shortly after Wingate's death. He presented extensive evidence for this, but much of it was anecdotal, circumstantial and uncorroborated: for instance, Calvert's assertions about official 'lines to take', and what Mead interpreted as derogatory comments made about the Chindit operations in Sandhurst and British Army Staff College training literature.[54] Mead's overview of the existing published work was thorough but slanted, with anything less than hagiography being viewed as under the influence of the 'conspiracy', even broadly sympathetic works by Christopher Sykes and Shelford Bidwell.[55] Some interesting original research went alongside this, however, Mead demonstrating from documentary evidence that some senior officers were, indeed, obtuse about Wingate's ideas and also discovering the testimony of certain Japanese senior officers to the impact of *Thursday* upon their Imphal-Kohima offensive, apparently available to Kirby and his co-authors and, apparently, ignored by them.[56]

Mead also enlisted the support of perhaps Wingate's highest-placed and most powerful posthumous supporter – Sir Robert Thompson. Thompson served throughout the Second World War with the Royal Air Force (RAF), including as an air liaison and forward observation officer on both Chindit operations, and later became a globally respected expert on counterinsurgency, in which capacity he advised the administration in Malaya during the communist guerrilla insurgency of 1948-60 and the Nixon White House in the latter stages of the Vietnam War. His *Defeating Communist Insurgency* is still regarded as a seminal work in this field.[57] Thompson wrote the foreword to Tulloch's book, but did not, apparently, read the *Official History* until 1977, at Mead's suggestion, and he seems to have been enraged:

> Of the hundreds of Generals on all sides mentioned in the British Official History of the War against Japan it is significant that Wingate was the only one who rated a separate individual assessment. Even two of his outline plans of early 1944 for future operations are included… Their inclusion was intended to show the wildness of Wingate's ideas… The whole assessment was no more than a hatchet job by little men who could not have competed with Wingate either in military argument or in battle. Not only has it failed but it has made him such a controversial figure that his reputation will live on for ever.[58]

Thompson accepted Mead's argument that official recognition and, by implication, correction of perceived inaccuracies in the *Official History* would be the only means of settling the controversy. Thompson and Mead subsequently presented the Cabinet Office with a suggested appendix, drafted by Mead, pointing out the alleged errors in the *Official History* and referring the reader to Sykes, Tulloch or Mead for guidance: their request that this be pasted into all copies of Volume III of the *Official History* has yet to be granted.[59] Thompson, thereafter, was an outspoken defender of Wingate in print and on television, and his memoirs, *Make For the Hills*, published in 1989, contained five chapters – nearly a quarter of the book – devoted to the Chindit operations and an extended assessment of Wingate. Thompson claimed that Wingate was first to realise that air supply could grant British forces superior relative mobility to the Japanese in the jungle and also, more contentiously, that he advocated close air support of troops fighting on the ground in the face of some apparent resistance from the Royal Air Force (RAF). He also claimed that Wingate was alone in advocating an overland offensive into northern Burma from India. Thompson then argued that resentment against Wingate, culminating in the 'hatchet job' of the *Official History*, was largely in reaction to Wingate's unsettling personality and the radicalism of his military ideas, which others in India simply did not understand.[60] Thompson was unequivocal about Wingate's historical significance: after presenting his assessment of the Chindit contribution to Imphal and Kohima – that it was a key factor in the Japanese defeat, and might have been greater, with more resources – Thompson commented that every time he saw the photograph of Slim and his Corps Commanders being knighted on the field of Imphal after the battle, 'I see the ghost of Wingate present.'[61]

The field is therefore divided. Several key previous books on Wingate have the theme of Wingate taking on a perceived 'military establishment', which, by the 1960s, was personified by S. Woodburn Kirby. Moreover, this 'establishment's' principal objection to Wingate was that he presented new forms of warfare that challenged accepted ideas, a view confirmed, apparently, by Kirby and Slim. So, in order to assess these arguments it is therefore vital to begin by establishing just how 'new' or 'radical' Wingate's ideas were to the British Army of the time: once this is done, we can assess how valid those ideas were in meeting the aims set by Wingate and his superiors, and so how valid they might be as guides for action in later military operations. Even a cursory overview of how the British Army fought its wars from the 1920s to the 1940s presents a more complex picture than might be presumed.

Chapter Two

Winning Small Wars – Wingate's Army

[T]o most officers there was no such thing as 'doctrine', only 'pamphlets' – and they were, at best, a basis for discussion, and for quoting in promotion exams. Instead there was an ethos... which viewed tactics as being the opinion of the senior officer present: an agreeable state of affairs (for the senior officer, at least).
Major General John Kiszely, 1997[1]

[I]f an Army is to succeed, everyone in it must know the class of action other people on their right and left, or in front of or behind them, will take under certain circumstances. It is fatal not to work to a common doctrine...
General Sir Philip Chetwode, 1923[2]

Introduction – Orde Wingate and the British Army

Wingate was commissioned in 1922 into an army reverting to its pre-1914 role as a colonial police force. This policing role was likely to expand, given that, under the terms of the 1919 peace settlements, Britain added to an already global Empire colonial territory of the defeated powers, mandated under the League of Nations. Indeed, after 1918, the idea grew within the Army that the First World War had been an aberration, a distraction from 'real soldiering' in the Empire, unlikely ever to be repeated. Practice reflected this: the 'Cardwell System' of infantry organisation was reintroduced after 1918, each regular infantry regiment consisting of two battalions, one for home service, the other for the Empire, with drafts passing regularly between them. The 'overseas' battalion could expect to be abroad for up to sixteen years, six to ten of them in India, with at least a year in the Covering Troops Districts on the Northwest Frontier where they would almost certainly see action against the Pathan tribesmen who dominated the area.[3] Likewise, units based in Egypt or Sudan would be highly likely to be called out against hostile tribesmen in their region at some point during their posting.

The British Army therefore knew all about 'insurgency' (armed rebellion by an activist minority) and 'out of area' operations (military operations in regions other than Europe or North America) long before these terms became fashionable. Those interested in these themes would be wise, however, to remember that Wingate and his contemporaries operated before the 1950s, since when three generations of 'experts' have muddied the waters by insisting that 'war' and 'insurgency' are different and separate phenomena, insurgency being more 'complex' than 'war' and therefore requiring a more 'sophisticated' response than simply defeating the opposing force, an assumption shaping 'counterinsurgency', at least as practised by Western liberal democracies, into the twenty-first century. True, while British authorities of Wingate's time hoped always to address reasonable grievances in negotiation with any rebels, they had little compunction about using force to get them to listen. To the Army, armed rebellion was war, pure and simple, and to be treated as such, many British Army officers advocating aggressive and sometimes ruthless responses to organised dissent, the most notorious being the Amritsar incident of April 1919, when Brigadier General Reginald Dyer ordered Gurkha troops to open fire on Indian rioters, killing 379.[4] The claim that insurgencies persisted because the authorities were not aggressive enough was recurrent, even after the shock-wave of Amritsar, being made not only by Wingate in Palestine, but also by several others, many officers apparently holding the Hobbesian view that anti-British insurgency constituted a criminal revolt against lawful authority – dismissed variously as 'banditry', 'dacoity' and, later in the period, 'terrorism' – arising from ignorant, excitable natives coming under the malign influence of populist agitators such as the Mahdi of Sudan, the 'Mad Mullah' of Somaliland, Saya San in Burma in or Haj Amin al-Husseini, the Mufti of Jerusalem.[5]

Such attitudes were expressed most lucidly in Major General Charles Callwell's *Small Wars: Their Principles and Practice*, published in three editions between 1896 and 1906.[6] This work seems to have influenced at least two generations of colonial soldiers: it formed part of the curriculum of the Army Staff Colleges at Camberley and Quetta and the RAF Staff College at Andover, and the chapter on 'Warfare in Undeveloped and Semi-Civilised Countries' in the 1929 edition of *Field Service Regulations*, the closest the British Army of the time had to a codified doctrine for war fighting, appears to be an unattributed, semi-plagiarised summary of chapters VI-VIII of the 1906 edition of *Small Wars*.[7] Callwell intended to provide a digest of colonial warfare, reflecting prevailing opinion in the Army as much as influencing it, and many of the tactical and operational methods he recommended can be observed in practice in Imperial operations in 1918-39. Many of these are described also in *Imperial Policing*, published in 1934 by Major General Charles Gwynn, who had been commandant of the Staff College at Camberley from 1926 to 1930; Gwynn not only provided narratives of colonial operations in the interwar period, but also offers a useful digest of prevailing British Army thought in this field as it stood at the end of this period. Perhaps the major evolution from Callwell's work is that Gwynn argued that Callwell's model of 'small wars' – military campaigns aimed at defeating rebel forces in battle – now represented but one end of a spectrum also comprising the restoration of civil order under martial law, or supporting police in the face of the kind of civil disobedience, sabotage and general low-level disturbance practised by the Egyptian nationalist *Wafd* movement in the years immediately after the First World War, and the Indian National Congress from the 1920s onwards: Gwynn opened the main body of his text with a case study of the Amritsar episode as 'how not to do it', wherein he made little attempt to conceal his disgust at what had happened there, and his loathing of Dyer.[8] Another officer appreciating that times were changing was Lieutenant Colonel H.J. Simson, who, in *British Rule, and Rebellion*, of 1937, introduced what he called 'sub-war', '[A]n organised use of force, partly under arms, designed to get something against the will of the properly constituted Government', which Simson saw as happening in Ireland in the early 1920s and India and Palestine at the time he published.[9] 'Sub-war' involved a militant, organised minority pursuing a radical nationalist agenda via coercive pressure via targeted, exemplary violence aimed at intimidating the police, local administration and opposing elements of the public mixed with propaganda and ostensibly 'peaceful' political and legal action to undermine efforts to counter this violence, erode faith in the colonial government and further subvert the civilian populace, a strategy Britain would face all too often from Simson's time into the twenty-first century.[10]

However, all these authors agreed that insurgency was still 'war', and the answer to it lay with the military. In particular, there was the belief that military action should be aimed at crushing the insurgent leadership's will under that of the British commander, a common theme in British 'small wars' thought, from Callwell to Wingate, being that their opponents were unsophisticated and excitable 'savages' or criminal miscreants who could be overawed or, if necessary, terrorised into recognising the folly of defying the Empire. There were cultural and institutional reasons for this. Belief in 'national characteristics', that those of a certain ethnicity or culture think, behave and react in certain, predictable ways, ran through British political and military thought of the time. Wingate, like most Europeans of this time, took this for granted, there being several examples of his beginning or resting a case on the assumed national characteristics of the enemy and claims that his methods met or exploited them. He was not alone, a factor in Slim's prescribed tactics against the Japanese, for instance, being his interpretation of their previous behaviour in battle.[11] Adapting operational and tactical methods to suit the perceived 'character' of the enemy was common in 'small wars' and counterinsurgencies outside Europe, and Callwell discussed the different types of opponent faced in such conflicts and how tactics should be adapted to suit their favoured fighting style, and touched frequently upon 'national characteristics', for instance in discussing intelligence gathering ('The ordinary native found in theatres of war peopled by coloured races lies simply for the love of the thing, and his ideas of time, numbers and distance are of the vaguest…'), the world view and favoured tactics of hill tribesmen ('He is a fighter the world over, and always has been…[A]lthough once beaten, they take it like good sportsmen, hoping for better luck next time') and those living in jungles ('[T]hey have not the love of war for its own sake nor the sporting instincts… of the hill man… [I]t would be absurd to place the races of West Africa on the same platform as warriors with the Pathans and Gurkhas…').[12] 'National characteristics' also influenced recruitment, the Indian Army, at least in its combat arms, being confined to so-called 'martial races', such as Sikhs and Gurkhas, deemed to possess the appropriate innate soldierly qualities.[13] Some argued that national characteristics applied also to major wars. In 1933, Wavell, then commanding 6th Infantry Brigade, suggested that such influences should be recognised through creating a new branch of the War Office 'to study ourselves, our national characteristics and our reactions as a nation to military matters' in the same way the Intelligence Branch studied those of other countries, so they could form the basis of a coherent recruiting and training programme.[14]

Callwell was firm that 'boldness and vigour' were essential because 'The lower races are impressionable. They are greatly influenced by a resolute bearing...', the 'natives' interpreting restraint as weakness being another recurring claim throughout this period.[15] Callwell advocated a swift offensive, aimed at bringing the insurgents to battle, shattering their resolve and deterring would-be allies and imitators, as 'the impression made upon semi-civilised races... by a bold and resolute procedure', was always great.'[16] Simson explicitly blamed the caution and willingness to compromise of British politicians for the Palestine Arab revolt of 1936–39, as well as for previous 'sub-wars', particularly in Ireland from 1916 to 1921.[17] Firm, rapid action also reduced the risk of becoming involved in 'desultory' and protracted operations involving guerrilla warfare, assassination and sabotage, in which the locals had the advantage.[18] Emphasis upon will and resolve was redoubled in dealing with 'insurrections' – politically motivated urban uprisings, distinct from 'open' warfare against tribal warriors or Boer guerrillas, Simson's 'sub-wars' – 'where [according to Callwell] the object is not only to prove to the opposing force unmistakably which is the stronger, but also to inflict punishment on those who have taken up arms.'[19] Wholesale destruction of villages and hostage-taking were warranted and, although Callwell recommended such measures be sparing and targeted carefully, he tacitly acknowledged that 'severity' was sometimes necessary *pour encourager les autres*: 'Unciviliced races attribute leniency to timidity... fanatics and savages... must be thoroughly brought to book and cowed or they will rise again.'[20] Gwynn was less sanguine than Callwell, but was also clear that swift, decisive action represented an economy of effort, his ideal also being to bring a situation under control before it could dissolve into guerrilla warfare, and that threatened rather than overt violence minimised the need for higher levels of force. Gwynn, however, while unequivocal that captured insurgents should be dealt with severely, was less enthusiastic than many about collective punishments and reprisals against the communities supporting them, arguing that these could harden resistance to lawful authority.[21]

Boldness, aggression and 'severity' recurred in practice throughout this period. Martial law was enforced in rebel areas of Ireland in 1920-21, twenty-one death sentences being passed upon Irish Republican Army (IRA) members and sympathisers by courts martial, rebel houses being blown up and the Army's official *Record* of operations referring openly and with undisguised approval to unauthorised reprisals by troops in Cork in May–June 1920, placing Sinn Fein leaders in convoys to forestall ambush, and atrocities committed against prisoners and civilians by the 'Black and Tans', the mainly British volunteers in the Royal Irish Constabulary who were already becoming a metaphor for crass, self-defeating brutality on both sides of the Irish Sea. Moreover, the *Record*, an official War Office document authored by serving Army officers, expressed its contempt for political authorities throughout, judging the effectiveness of some actions by the strength of the outcry in the English press and Parliament, which the authors seem to have viewed as a nest of IRA sympathisers.[22] Simson was equally blunt, arguing that the institutionalised divisiveness of parliamentary democracy could prevent effective reaction to 'sub-war' and even create sympathy for the rebels in high places, while insistence on due process of law mutated the government and judiciary from participants in the counterinsurgency to 'referees' between rebels and security forces, the police and Army simply being reduced to another armed faction or, as he put it 'another dog in the dog-fight'.[23] His answer was unrestricted martial law, including powers of summary execution, administered by the GOC as plenipotentiary of the British Crown, with the colonial government and police reduced to offices on his staff.[24]

'Severity' was conspicuous in Imperial operations of the time: martial law, including extensive use of the death penalty, and punitive measures, including the destruction of hostile villages and the confiscation of crops and livestock, featured prominently in the suppression of the Iraq revolt in 1920-21, the Moplah rebellion in India in 1921-22, and the Burma rebellion of 1931.[25] Reprisals were discussed even in the official press of the Indian Army: General Sir Andrew Skeen's *Passing it On: Short Talks on Tribal Fighting on the North-West Frontier of India* was, on the orders of the Commander in Chief India, issued to all units serving in India, and contains an entire chapter devoted to 'foraging' – forcibly seizing food and other goods from the locals in a hostile area – and the punitive demolition of hostile villages, which included destroying food supplies.[26] An unattributed article in the *Journal of the United Services Institute of India* discussed how operations could be executed on the Northwest Frontier 'against a village... which has misbehaved itself, with the object of doing as much damage as possible', to capture 'outlaws' and destroy houses sheltering them, or to carry off livestock, and also included the following advice:

> It is...a good plan when searching houses to send a couple of villagers into every house immediately in front of the search party. Should the inmates prove truculent their own friends will get the benefit of the first shot and the troops will know what to expect.[27]

The Army on the Northwest Frontier kept a 'hostage corps' of relatives of known hostiles, to be thrown into houses where tribesmen where known to be hiding, ahead of search parties, or placed in the front lorries of convoys to prevent ambush, as late as 1938.[28]

However, by the 1930s, new means of countering rebellion were being introduced, Burma in 1931 seeing the introduction of the system of 'Military Control' applied later in Palestine.[29] Military Control represented a mean between civilian control and martial law; the Civil Administration, represented by the Viceroy or High Commissioner, remained supreme, but devolved all responsibility for public security and order on the GOC of the region, who controlled the Army and police. The GOC and High Commissioner were supposed to confer regularly on policy, as were local commanders and District Commissioners. Troops and police were empowered to arrest and search without warrant, but civilian law remained in force – captured insurgents were entitled to a trial, for instance – reinforced by emergency measures.[30]

Tactical methods remained more consistent. Imperial operations centred on all-arms columns advancing on broad fronts, with aircraft acting in observation or in lieu of artillery, harrying the enemy, keeping him on the move and, once he was engaged, outflanking him, cutting or threatening his lines of supply and retreat in an attempt to 'turn' him out of his position before driving him onto a cordon established across his line of retreat.[31] This open, mobile warfare differed from the tightly controlled and concentrated European battlefields seen in the First World War and envisaged for future wars in *Field Service Regulations*. Colonial operations of the British and other armies traditionally centred upon such columns, sometimes purpose-organised for various missions, but more often comprising whatever troops could be scraped together in theatre.[32] Callwell discussed column organisation for different types of 'small war', and contended that separate, but cooperating columns could produce the desired effect from the confusion they instilled about British objectives, the intimidatory effect of apparent British ubiquity and the subsequent panic-diffusion of enemy strength as native commanders tried to confront every column.[33] *Passing it On* details the organisation of a column, and the duties of officers within it, in homely second person.[34] While reading Callwell alone can give an impression of high speed and mobility, Skeen's description of a column on the move in enemy territory suggests something more deliberate: a screen of infantry picquets, van-, flank and rear guards rolling forward systematically around a slow-moving artillery and baggage train still reliant on pack animals, and beyond them, 'floater' platoons patrolling the surrounding countryside in order to pre-empt any would-be ambushers and hit them as they tried to attack the main column.[35]

Most contemporary writers were still confident that the British would have superior mobility relative to the insurgents. Callwell's ideal pattern was to pin the enemy with a small force in front while larger columns turned his flanks: while an irregular enemy was unlikely to have any lines of communication to threaten, the appearance of large forces in his rear was likely to panic him into retreat from his position, the outflanking columns then destroying him in detail on the move. Emphasis throughout was upon speed, aggression and flexibility rather than weight of numbers, Callwell believing that such characteristics allowed small forces to overcome larger numbers of poorly-led natives through surprise and 'moral force' (it is unlikely that Callwell read Sun Tzu).[36] Columns should carry their supplies with them, removing the need for lines of communication, and there should be extensive devolution of command authority and tolerance of initiative, Callwell quoting Field Marshal Lord Roberts' – an experienced 'Imperial Warrior' if ever there was one – instructions that column commanders should be allowed the 'utmost latitude of movement', arguing that such was essential in hill and jungle warfare with poor or nonexistent communications between columns.[37]

The period 1919-39 saw the melding of twentieth-century technology with these nineteenth-century techniques. In Ireland in 1919-21, units of the Army and the Royal Irish Constabulary patrolled the countryside in columns of armoured lorries, escorted by armoured cars, regularly employing 'cordon and search' techniques, sealing off areas in which the IRA were believed to be active, while other columns, or cavalry units, 'drove' the IRA onto the cordon; although of limited use in actually catching IRA men, these methods were deemed threat enough to force the IRA, on several occasions, to break down its large 'Flying Columns' into smaller, less effective units.[38] Aircraft were used for spotting, although this was hampered by the small number of machines available, inability to tell IRA from civilians, and the lack of wirelesses capable of communicating from air to ground.[39] In the Iraq rebellion of 1920-21, Baghdad and other towns were fortified while small columns, heavy in artillery and engineers, carried out punitive counter-attacks against rebel villages; later, larger columns, consisting of two squadrons of cavalry, an artillery brigade and six battalions of infantry, were used to establish a permanent presence in outlying areas.[40] In the 1921 Moplah rebellion in southern India, columns of lorry-borne infantry occupied villages by surprise and cordoned rebels in inhospitable areas where they had the option of surrender or starvation. Interestingly, Captain Carpendale, writing on the Moplah campaign for the United Services Institute of India, had clearly read Callwell, as he cites the same historical sources in support for these methods.[41]

On the Northwest Frontier from the 1920s, 'frontier columns' included tanks, armoured cars and towed artillery, and experimented with night operations.[42] Skeen noted that the advantages of armoured fighting vehicles, even in hill warfare, came from their speed, protection and firepower, and that the tribesmen of the Northwest Frontier, with no recourse against them other than home-made mines, became notably less aggressive when they were in the area.[43] The inter-war period saw the use of aircraft in support of such operations become standard practice. In the 1920 Iraq rebellion, outlying British Army garrisons, their ground lines of communication cut by the rebels, were resupplied by aircraft, dropping ammunition and medical supplies.[44] Following the suppression of the rebellion, at the behest of the Colonial Secretary, Winston Churchill, the RAF took over responsibility for keeping order in Britain's mandated territories in Iraq, Transjordan and Palestine. The subsequent policy of 'Air Control' centred on RAF bombers, operating from defended bases, supporting fast-moving units of RAF armoured cars, and, later, ground columns of Army troops, a technique employed on numerous punitive operations in the region from the 1920s through to the mid-1960s.[45] In 1931, eleven years before Wingate presented similar ideas as his own, Major L.V.S. Blacker of the Guides Infantry was arguing that columns operating on the Northwest Frontier of India could be resupplied by airdrop or air landing, thereby removing the need for large numbers of slow-moving pack animals (Wingate used both animal and air supply), and increasing their firepower through allowing greater numbers of automatic weapons to be carried, as well as improving morale through speedy casualty evacuation.[46] Skeen noted, in 1932, that the main uses of aircraft in support of ground troops included spotting, attacking targets of opportunity, and bombing and strafing tribesmen flushed into the open by ground action.[47] The Mohmand operation of July-October 1933 saw RAF aircraft attached to columns in order to bomb snipers and, later, 'any enemy seen.'[48] The second Mohmand operation, two years later, saw Brigadier Claude Auchinleck use aircraft to 'weaken the resistance' of the Mohmands ahead of the advance of his ground forces, and support battalion columns used during the advance to outflank and 'turn' the Mohmands out of strong defensive positions; moreover, increasing use was made of wireless to coordinate the movement of columns – presented by some authors as another Wingate innovation – although this was undone frequently by degradation of high frequency signals in the mountainous terrain.[49] Between larger engagements, ambushes were set along snipers' favourite paths, which were also bombed to prevent tribesmen returning to the sanctuary of their villages.[50] Tactics evolved further by the Waziristan operation of 1937, consisting now of driving or turning tribesmen out of strong positions into the open, where they could be bombed or shelled without any cover, infantry columns often moving large distances by night to achieve this.[51]

Another method used extensively was the creation of specialist units, raised and trained on the initiative of individuals or small groups of relatively junior officers, circumventing approved 'chains of command', and intended to carry out tasks deemed beyond the capability of regular troops – not quite 'Special Forces' as understood in the twenty-first century, but with some of the characteristics evident already. Callwell recommended that every force should have a 'Corps of Scouts', reconnoitering, raiding and ambushing ahead of the main advance, consisting of purpose-trained and organised units answering directly to the force commander, made up either of Gurkhas – used for this role on the Northwest Frontier for ninety years – natives armed with British weapons and commanded by British officers, or second and third-generation white settlers familiar with the geography of the area of operations.[52] An apparent forerunner of Wingate's Special Night Squads was the Corps of Gurkha Scouts formed by captains N.H. Edwards and G.G. Rogers of the Northwest Frontier Force (NWFF) in 1919. This consisted of two platoons drawn from all Gurkha units in the NWFF and directed by the Force HQ, organised specifically for night-time ambush work inside hostile tribal territory on the Northwest Frontier – the same role the Night Squads would fulfill in Palestine – and used continuously from May to August 1919, during which time it carried out one successful ambush of a large Pathan force.[53] Such forces were seen in other theatres. The Royal Irish Constabulary, its morale collapsing in the face of IRA terrorism directed at officers and their families, began raising its Auxiliary Division in September 1920. The 'Auxies' consisted of independent, lorry-borne companies of ex-British Army officers, and, although technically police, they received little police training, being in actuality an armed paramilitary force trained by the Army and intended to react swiftly to IRA activity in a given area. 5th Division, for instance, trained 'Black and Tans' and Auxiliaries in counter-ambush drills and night raiding in rebel areas under its remit.[54] Indeed, Professor Charles Townshend, a globally respected expert on both the history of terrorism and the British Army in the inter-war period, identifies the Auxiliaries explicitly as 'the nearest approach to a specialist counterinsurgency force so far', although poor discipline and a culture of heavy drinking created a reputation for wildness and thuggery to equal the Black and Tans.[55] Likewise, in Burma in 1931, British troops cordoned rebels in inhospitable areas, allowing 'packs' of Burmese irregulars – presumably under British officers – to hunt them down.[56] Simson wrote admiringly of the US Federal Bureau of Investigation's 'G' men, presented by him as 'an organised body of government servants, armed and authorised to shoot, without trial, outlawed citizens' (the FBI might disagree with this description) and implied that such a body might be required to bring in 'gunmen' 'dead or alive' should 'sub-war' go beyond certain levels of violence.[57] The Night Squads, therefore, could be viewed as part of the continuum of established British Imperial military thought and practice, not a new and dramatic departure from it.

Callwell versus the Italians

Many of these methods were carried into the Second World War, in operations against the regular forces of the Italians, Germans and Vichy French in North Africa and the Middle East in 1940-41. The November 1941 edition of *Notes from Theatres of War*, the Army's official digest of lessons learned from operations, argued that 'Mobile desert warfare appears to be largely a matter of columns of all arms, which may work over long distances very widely separated', and a key feature of British operations of this period was such columns moving through desert or mountain to bypass enemy positions and either cut their communications or line of retreat or surprise them with attack from the rear, as recommended by Callwell. This was exemplified by actions during Operation *Compass*, Wavell's offensive against the Italians in Cyrenaica in December 1940, in particular XIII Corps' devastating attacks on the Nibeiwa-Sidi Barrani camps on 9-11 December 1940, and 7th Armoured Division opening the attack on Bardia in mid-December by cordoning off the road between Bardia and Tobruk before advancing upon the town from behind.[58] This also happened in Italian East Africa: in April 1941, 24th Gold Coast Brigade made a 25-mile march through the Somali bush to occupy the road and river crossings north of Jelib on the Juba River, which was taken by the brigade's parent formation, 12th African Division, advancing 'from three directions' the following day, the Italian garrison surrendering without a fight.[59] Ad hoc task forces were also used extensively for operations against the enemy rear. In Eritrea, General Sir William Platt, GOC East Africa, formed Gazelle Force, commanded by Brigadier Frank Messervy and consisting of an Indian armoured car regiment, a motor-machine-gun group of the SDF, and attached artillery, to harry Italian communications north and east of Kassala, a factor in the Italian withdrawal from Sudan; Gazelle Force then cut roads around Agordat, causing another Italian retreat, and then sought, unsuccessfully, to 'turn' the Italians out of their main defensive position, the fortress at Keren, by threatening their line of retreat.[60] In Iraq, Habforce (Habbaniyeh Force, consisting of 4th Cavalry Brigade, reinforced by the Arab Legion, some RAF armoured cars and a battery of 25-pounder field guns) was not intended as a manoeuvre force, but as something with an older pedigree, a 'flying column' relieving beleaguered British garrisons; however, in June 1941, following the resolution of the Iraq crisis, Habforce operated from Mosul against Vichy communications in Syria, to the west of Palmyra, assisting in the Allied occupation of the town and destroying several German airfields.[61] 'Task forces' were soon being used at lower levels. 'Jock Columns', named for Colonel 'Jock' Campbell VC of the Royal Horse Artillery, who first devised them in December 1940, were created from 7th Armoured Division's artillery support group, and consisted of a battery of 25-pounders, a company of lorry-borne infantry and some armoured cars, executing harassing attacks on advancing Italian and German formations and lines of supply, sometimes at some distance behind the front.[62] They were used initially as a 'makeshift', a means of sustaining offensive action when the remainder of the division was weakened by its logistical state: yet their use proved popular, as by November 1941 *Notes from the Theatres of War* was extolling their use and recommending they be strengthened by adding tanks.[63]

Another 'small wars' practice continued into the Second World War was the use of small, specialist units to wage war deeper in enemy-occupied territory. Although the continuous fronts of Europe made such operations difficult, the wider spaces and open flanks of the desert war were ideal for them. In June 1940, Wavell accepted a proposal from the desert explorer Major Ralph Bagnold to create long-range motor patrols capable of crossing the sand sea to the south of the main operational area to reconnoitre Italian positions and force the Italians to divert troops from the Egyptian frontier by raiding targets of opportunity inside Libya.[64] Bagnold's Long Range Desert Group (LRDG) took its orders directly from Wavell himself at GHQ Middle East, and during Operation *Compass* distracted Italian attention via raids on key airfields and supply roads. Wavell noted in official reports that Bagnold's attacks resulted in Italian supply convoys ceasing altogether in some areas and their forward troops becoming even more cautious than previously.[65] May 1941 brought the debut of the best-known penetration force of all, as L Detachment, Special Air Service (SAS), initially a small unit of volunteers raised by Captain David Stirling of the Scots Guards, carried out its first airborne raid on an Italian airfield in Cyrenaica; following the failure of this mission, the SAS switched to long-range lorry and jeep-borne raids, focusing upon Axis airfields and operating initially alongside the LRDG.[66] Wingate's operations in Ethiopia and, initially, in Burma, therefore came at a time when the British Army already made extensive use of scratch-assembled mobile columns and special forces, intended to harry enemy communications, and can be viewed as a continuation of established British practice.

The proliferation of such forces in the British army of this time has been attributed to, amongst other things, a 'cavalry' culture in 7th Armoured Division, officers' reading of the works of Basil Liddell Hart, or the influence of Brigadier Eric Dorman-Smith, former commandant of the Staff College at Haifa and Auchinleck's roving 'tactical consultant', a fanatic for mobile operations and a figure as loathed as Wingate in many quarters (and probably with greater reason).[67] However, Wavell had been GOC Palestine, from where Lieutenant General Sir Richard O'Connor came directly to take command of Western Desert Force (XIII Corps) in 1939. O'Connor and many other officers, particularly those in the Indian Divisions, had served on the Northwest Frontier, where similar methods had been applied for decades. Indeed, a pioneer of their combination with tanks, wireless and aircraft was Claude Auchinleck, who succeeded Wavell as CinC Middle East in June 1941; Auchinleck and Dorman-Smith were both officers of the Indian Army.[68] British methods in Africa in 1940–41 might, therefore, be interpreted as an evolution from small war 'doctrine', consisting of using trusted pre-war tactical and operational methods to fulfill the strategic mission of destroying the Italian armies in North and East Africa.

Geography was another shaping factor, the Libyan Desert and savannah of southern Ethiopia being particularly suitable for mobile forces. In Eritrea, however, mobile operations were precluded by the mountainous, heavily-wooded terrain, in which any advance had to be along the few roads, passing through easily defended defiles.[69] Italian resistance in Eritrea was broken not via manoeuvre, but by the seven-week siege and assault of the fortified town of Keren from February to March 1941. Lieutenant General Sir William Platt, GOC Sudan and British commander at Keren, acknowledged methods used elsewhere in describing his own: '[A] certain amount of the lessons of Frontier warfare had to be unlearnt due to the influence of artillery, mortars, LMGs and aircraft on mountain warfare.'[70] Platt's methods involved a steady build-up of supplies, ammunition in particular – Platt would not begin an attack until his artillery had 600 rounds per gun – prior to deliberate, timetabled divisional assaults built around the artillery fire plan, based on 'the maximum number of guns', with tanks reverting to their 'traditional' role of 'shooting in' the infantry, the intention being to weaken the enemy methodically over time, rather than smash him with a single blow.[71] Likewise, during the invasion of Syria in June 1941, a combination of hilly terrain crossed by rivers and unexpectedly tough resistance from the Vichy French defenders resulted in 8th Australian Division executing deliberate assaults in which firepower was prioritised over mobility.[72] In these battles, Commonwealth forces fought in brigades and divisions, not columns. Different methods of fighting, therefore, were emerging in this single theatre over a short period.

Wingate's operations from 1940 to 1943 thus took place within an army where some senior commanders used mobility to reach and target key points in the enemy infrastructure. Some formations were organised to maximise their ability to do this, and permanent units and organisations specialising in this role, such as the LRDG, were emerging to fit 'troops to task'. Although Wingate would later employ all-arms columns, supported by air and coordinated by wireless, in mobile operations, aimed at manoeuvring his opponents into difficult or impossible positions, it is clear that these units were not 'new' other than in their existence. The Chindits seem, when placed in the context of British Army operational practice of Wingate's time, to share ancestry with other methods. It therefore remains to explore Wingate's experience in 'small wars' and its impact on his ideas on warfare, beginning with his time as a subaltern in the 1920s, this being made easier by his putting his thoughts on paper from the earliest stages of his career.

Chapter Three

Before Palestine, 1923–36

[P]ossession of the interior lines gives a priceless advantage to the possessor... [and] although it may be possible to derive special advantages from exterior lines... he who deliberately divides his forces in order unnecessarily to assume them is a pedant with little knowledge of war.
Lieutenant Orde Wingate, 1926[1]

[C]olumns achieve their results by skilful concentration at the right time and in the right place, where they will deliver the maximum blow against the enemy. The essence of LRP is concentration, the method of dispersal is only a means to achieve ultimate concentration.
Brigadier Orde Wingate, 1942[2]

A formative period

Wingate was gazetted a second lieutenant in the Royal Artillery in 1923 and arrived in Palestine in 1936. The key episode in this thirteen-year period appears to be the four years he spent on attachment to the Sudan Defence Force, 1928-33, which may have exerted more influence upon his subsequent military ideas than appreciated previously. Moreover, it was during this time that Wingate first encountered the ideas of his distant relative, T.E. Lawrence, which exerted a powerful influence upon his own – in some cases, through determination to demonstrate that he and Lawrence were *not* alike.

Wingate's First Promotion Paper

In 1926, Lieutenant Wingate produced an essay on 'Strategy in Three Campaigns' – the Russo-Japanese War, the German invasion of France in 1914 and Allenby's Palestine Campaign of 1917, as part of the examination for promotion from lieutenant to captain, one of the earliest instances of him committing his views to paper. He opened with an attack on the idea of fixed rules of strategy, stating that, if Napoleon had revealed 'the science of war' (familiarity with the works of Clausewitz and Jomini might be presumed, but is unprovable) then surely fewer military blunders would be evident since his time. Instead, 'we see generals making the same old mistakes, ignoring even their own maxims and failing to recognise the blunders of others' – powerful stuff from a twenty-two-year-old subaltern.[3] It might be possible to derive principles from 'intermingling causes with effects', but Napoleon said he learned nothing from the sixty battles he fought and so, on that evidence alone, the reader should 'cease to talk of "principles of strategy"'; the best that could be hoped for was to examine common conditions between battles and campaigns and draw conclusions from those.[4]

A propensity shared with others of the time was resting his case on 'national characteristics'. For instance, on the Schlieffen Plan, with which Germany hoped to overwhelm France in 1914 by marching around to the north of Paris to get behind the main French armies, Wingate wrote:

> Envelopment as strategy is folly, unless used to round up uncivilised or guerrilla enemies… But as in [Napoleon's] day, so today the Teuton loves envelopment. He is never happy unless his armies are scattered over vast tracts of territory, all approaching his concentrated enemy from different directions.[5]

While, on Russian popular attitudes to the expansion of their empire:

> The Russian people…knew little and cared less for the emperor's ambition to extend his domains. They were content to remain in their own country and could not see that any useful purpose was to be served by enslaving the Manchu. Their attitude was typical of the Slav race…[6]

Wingate suggested that such national characteristics could lead to strategic blunder. Germany invaded France in 1914, attacking her strongest enemy, not her weakest – Russia – and Schlieffen's plan to envelop the French army was undone by adjustments made after his death and by the French moving their reserves inside the converging German columns to halt the German offensive at the Marne.[7] In the chapter on the Russo-Japanese War, which is incomplete, Wingate berated the Japanese for adopting 'the absurd idea of envelopment for envelopment's sake' from their officers' staff training in Germany – presumably how the Japanese overcame this to win the war was in the missing passages.[8] Wingate concluded 'it is not possible to cut your enemy's communications at theatre level': by 1944 he would not only be saying the diametric opposite, but proposing a complete new model of warfare centred on this very aim.

Wingate obtained a mark of 78 per cent for this paper, two marks short of a distinction.[9] Its analysis was puerile in places, but it did indicate what was to come: firstly, recognition that speed and skill could compensate for numbers; secondly, belief in national characteristics as a basis for military style, something shared with many other officers; and thirdly, it showed that the pontificating and sometimes scabrous literary style which got Wingate into trouble several times later on developed early.

The Sudan Defence Force

The examination for captain came while Wingate was a subaltern in the Royal Garrison Artillery, stationed at the Royal Artillery Centre at Larkhill, and all his biographies focus more on his social activities – hunting to hounds in particular – than his military interests at this time. Wingate's hunting ended temporarily in autumn 1926, when the Army sent him on an Arabic language course at the School of Oriental Studies of the University of London. A keen student, Wingate obtained a mark of 85 per cent on his preliminary examination after just four and a half months and was encouraged by his tutor, Sir Thomas Arnold, to seek a posting to the Middle East or North Africa with a view to qualifying as an interpreter.[10] Wingate had been interested in serving in Egypt or Sudan since 1924, when he began regular correspondence with his father's first cousin, General Sir Reginald Wingate. 'Cousin Rex' had been Kitchener's Director of Intelligence during the Omdurman campaign of 1898, Governor General of the Sudan, *Sirdar*, or commander in chief of the Egyptian Army from 1899 to 1916 and British High Commissioner in Cairo from 1916–19. Sir Reginald used these posts to exert his influence over British strategy in the Middle East from the 1890s to the First World War, in particular being a powerful and enthusiastic supporter of undermining the Turkish position in the region by encouraging the aspirations of the Hashemite clan of the Hejaz, in particular Hussein, the Sherif and Emir of Mecca, to create an independent Arab nation-state on the Arabian peninsula, and supporting Lawrence and others materially in fomenting the Arab revolt of 1916-18.[11] He stood down as High Commissioner in Egypt in 1919 largely in the face of his inability to deal with the rise of the *Wafd* and its use of riots and mass civil disobedience rather than armed force to achieve its aims, something of which the British had little previous experience; in particular, he had been in favour of a gradual transfer of political power to Egyptians with whom the British could 'do business', while the Foreign and Colonial Office wished to see Britain remain in control in Egypt, apparently in perpetuity. This is an interesting contrast with the attitudes his younger relative would later express.

Sir Reginald encouraged Orde to continue his Arabic studies in Sudan, by attending the language classes run by the Sudan Agency, the colonial 'government' of Sudan, and also suggested that he should apply for a posting with the Sudan Defence Force (SDF), producing a letter of introduction to the SDF's commander, Major General Sir Hubert Huddleston.[12] Sir Reginald's backing overcame the younger Wingate's not meeting the criteria to join the SDF – he had been commissioned fewer than five years and would normally require a recommendation from a serving officer of the SDF, which he did not have – and exemplifies one of the most significant factors in Wingate's career: his cultivation of powerful patrons to whom he could appeal outside the formal chain of command.[13]

Orde Wingate served with the SDF from 1928 to 1933, the last four years as a *Bimbashi*, or acting local major. For an officer in his mid to late twenties, this marked a considerable promotion and the granting of independent command he certainly would not have had at home. He was engaged on small operations throughout this time, his longest continuous period of command, yet previous references to its possible impact upon his subsequent military practice are passing. According to Mosley, 'Orde Wingate regarded the Ethiopian frontier as a training ground upon which he could work out the theories of guerrilla [sic] warfare which were already working in his brain',[14] while Trevor Royle commented that Wingate learned three lessons in Sudan:

The first was that, properly trained and motivated, small groups of men could learn to survive in a hostile environment. Second, they could operate in isolation far from home base provided they were properly led and had faith in their commanders. Third, they had to be kept up to the mark and galvanized by constant training...[15]

Wingate also suffered his first major attack of depression during this time, arising from a combination of too much time in the hot and monotonous Sudanese desert, his first sight of death – a man killed by his soldiers – the sudden death of his sister and a major crisis in the religious faith on which much of his self-image rested.[16] Yet the length of his experience in the Sudan would suggest some impact upon Wingate's professional and intellectual development, and his *protégé*, Moshe Dayan, stated explicitly that Wingate put the lessons of Sudan into practice in Palestine later on.[17] Wingate's SDF period therefore demands more attention that it has had previously.

The SDF was founded in 1924, when Egyptian troops were withdrawn from Sudan following the assassination of the *Sirdar*, General Sir Lee Stack, and the revelation of widespread agitation in the ranks by the *Wafd*.[18] In 1928, it consisted of the Camel Corps (a mixed force of mounted infantry), a motor transport and machine-gun battalion and three infantry 'corps' (actually battalions), the Equatorial Corps, the East Arab Corps and the West Arab Corps, Wingate being posted, in June 1928, to the East Arab Corps, stationed along the border with Eritrea.[19] He was made *Bimbashi* of Number 3 *Idara*, an Arab infantry company based at Gedaref; the majority of his 375 troops were Arabs, but there was a large minority of black Africans, a mixture of ethnic Somalis from southern Sudan and Muslim immigrants from elsewhere in Africa who settled in Sudan following their *Haj*.[20] British officers had a very high level of independence: each *Bimbashi* was responsible for enlisting his own recruits, devising a training programme, promoting and discharging his soldiers, and for administering military law among them.[21] Training was realistic, desert conditions allowing free use of live ammunition during exercises, and route marches of 5-600 miles were carried out regularly in remote areas in order to 'show the flag'; each *Idara* carried its own supplies on these marches, supplemented by game shot by the *Bimbashi*. Each February, the SDF would concentrate for combined exercises with 47(B) Squadron RAF, the unit responsible for air control of remoter regions of the Sudan, and Wingate participated in operational experiments in air-ground cooperation while in Sudan.[22] So, a number of characteristics of forces Wingate commanded subsequently were evident, most obviously the raising and training of forces by their own commanders for long-distance operations in rough country involving possible cooperation with aircraft.

Missions varied. A revival of Mahdism was a serious threat into the 1930s and resulted in uprisings in the majority Arabic provinces of Kordofan and Darfur in 1916, 1921 and 1928; more frequent were small-scale police actions against tribal chiefs resisting Government control, particularly among the hill tribes of southern Sudan.[23] However, the problem with which Wingate was concerned for most of his time at Gedaref was *Shifta*, gangs of Ethiopian bandits crossing the border from

Ethiopia and Eritrea to poach ivory, skins and meat or kidnap slaves from the non-warlike *Nuba* tribes of the border area.[24] Many of these slaves were girls, intended to be sold into prostitution or domestic service across the Red Sea in Arabia: slavery had been gradually dying out in Ethiopia, due mainly to the rise of cash farming, when Ras Tafari, Regent of Ethiopia and the future Emperor Haile Selassie, issued an edict banning the slave trade in 1918, while the British had used a series of treaties with local rulers to eradicate the slave trade in East Africa and the Indian Ocean in the nineteenth century.[25] Nevertheless, while the trade was banned, slavery itself survived in Ethiopia, Ras Tafari – an extremely cautious ruler throughout his long life – hoping to avoid any trouble arising from a direct assault on the institution by allowing it to wither over time, and it also remained legal across most of the Arabian Peninsula into the 1960s and Muscat and Oman up to 1970. Slaving and ivory poaching were therefore highly lucrative illegal businesses, and raids by *Shifta* into Sudan, some of which could involve parties of several hundred, were such a nuisance to the British colonial authorities that many in Khartoum welcomed the Italian invasion of Ethiopia in 1935 as likely to put a stop to their activities – which, indeed, it did.[26]

This was not insurgency, but criminality, although it had characteristics in common, in particular its centering on small bands of irregulars using superior mobility and knowledge of the ground to evade retribution. For guidance on how to deal with this problem, the SDF had Callwell's recommendations upon 'Bush Warfare' and the *Field Service Regulations* chapter on 'Warfare in Undeveloped and Semi-Civilised Countries', which leaned heavily upon Callwell. Indeed, the 1929 edition semi-plagiarised Callwell, opening by stating that the principles of war still applied in campaigns in such countries, and the aim should be to break down enemy resistance through forcing them to concentrate for battle by threatening their capital, their sacred sites or their wells and crops, as recommended by Callwell.[27] An alternative course of action which Callwell could not have anticipated, writing, as he was, in the 1900s, was 'Air Control' – 'an interruption of normal life… enforced by properly directed air attack until the enemy is ready to make terms' as *FSR* put it.[28] However, aircraft were less effective when dealing with an opponent operating in small, dispersed parties in close or broken country (such as the Sudanese-Ethiopian border), where friendly and hostile tribes were mixed, and who could retreat to an inviolable sanctuary across the border: 'In such circumstances the best chance of success lies in a well-planned combination of the action of aircraft with that of troops' which, in desert areas, should be mounted or supported by armoured cars.[29] As noted previously, the SDF exercised annually with the Fairey IIIFs of 47(B) Squadron RAF, and operated with them under joint command of the *Kaid all'Am*, the GOC Sudan, Major General Huddleston; the RAF provided close support for the SDF's Camel Corps during the attempted Mahdist uprising in Nuer in 1928 and a *Nuba* revolt in the Eliri Jebel in 1929, and resupply and reconnaissance for a number of long-range patrols during a border dispute with Italian Libya in 1931.[30]

It would be best to prevent *Shifta* getting into Sudan in the first place, and control of the border was maintained through infantry or police patrolling.[31] Douglas

Dodds-Parker, who served as a District Commissioner – responsible for policing – in the Sudan-Ethiopia border region in the late 1930s, and was also attached to the SDF, recalled that the standard technique for dealing with *Shifta* involved SDF or police patrols pushing inwards from the border along the bandits' favourite tracks, forcing them deeper into Sudan where they could be caught more easily.[32] Wingate's operations were no major departure from this, as illustrated by the patrol in April 1931, pursuing two gangs of *Shifta* poaching in game reserves in the Dinder and Gallegu country. Each gang was around a dozen strong, half of them slaves, and had not crossed the border to fight; Wingate therefore ordered that fire was to be opened only if they resisted arrest or seemed on the point of getting away.[33] He arranged his route of patrol to get between the gangs and their sanctuary and take them by surprise. On 11 April, he took two sections of the Eastern Arab Corps out of Singa, on the Blue Nile, announcing that his destination was the town of Roseires to the south: instead, they headed for the island of Umm Orug on the River Dinder.[34] Two poachers were captured there on 19 April, and released upon condition they disclosed where the main party was operating. Wingate was able to surround a band of nine poachers near Ras Amer shortly after, and in the subsequent fight one of the poachers, evidently a former soldier of the SDF, wearing the remains of his uniform, was killed, this being the incident contributing to Wingate's depression. Wingate's patrol again surrounded and surprised a band of eleven poachers on 21 April, killing one and arresting the rest.[35] Wingate aimed at using cover and concealment to surround the gangs stealthily, and then surprise them with attack from all sides: this made sense, as *Shifta* could out-run even a man on horseback in the rough country of the Dinder, and could get clean away if alerted.[36] Patrol tactics, therefore, depended upon deception, surprise and careful selection of the areas of operation, all things Wingate would stress later.

These became more apparent still in Wingate's report of a patrol the following February. He chose to march on a route going from point-to-point along the frontier, including stretches of open desert, reasoning:

(1) That the approach of the patrol would be unexpected at almost every point of descent on poaching areas, since by cutting across long stretches of waterless country each line… would be out of reach of warning by fleeing poachers.
(2) That should Abyssinians be poaching on GALLEGU-DINDER the patrol would be between them and their base. This had special value in view of possible air cooperation.[37]

Wingate aimed, therefore, to surprise and possibly ambush the *Shifta* as they tried to retreat to sanctuary in Ethiopia, a pattern in accordance with SDF and police procedures as described by Dodds-Parker and which Wingate later hoped to repeat in counter-terrorist operations in Palestine.

A subsidiary aim was experimenting with cooperation between patrols and spotter planes: in the event, Wingate noted:

[P]oachers associate the appearance of aircraft with the approach of soldiery and are on their guard. As the only chance of catching them lies in achieving a complete surprise this would not seem an advantage... With the legitimate presence of honey gatherers, etc, and the apparent very great difficulty in seeing anything in the densely bushed areas it is very unlikely that aircraft would be able to detect anything but a very considerable party of Abyssinian poachers, and even in that event it would be impossible to see them once they had broken up.[38]

In the earliest traceable example of his differing from institutional 'accepted wisdom', Wingate concluded that the SDF's existing approach, based on 'drives' by foot patrols, limited its efficacy in dealing with poachers. In a note on game protection in the Dinder area, he argued that while this deterred some poaching:

Owing to expence [sic] the measures taken against the poachers are limited to the maintenance of highly mobile patrols operating at irregular intervals and in various directions; and it should be plainly understood that such wide toothed and occasional combing has not the smallest chance of success in inhabited country.[39]

This arose from a common problem in counterinsurgency: inability to distinguish insurgents from civilians, SDF patrols relying upon following the tracks of poacher gangs in areas crossed regularly by nomads and their herds.[40]

Whatever his criticisms of SDF procedures, there is no recorded evidence that Wingate tried to change them. Indeed, there was just one minor confrontation during Wingate's time in Sudan when, shortly after arrival, he was warned by the Commanding Officer of the Eastern Arab Corps about discussing religion and politics – including Marxism – in the officers' mess.[41] This aside, he seems to have been liked by his fellow officers in the SDF and respected for his prowess on the polo field.[42]

It would appear that it was in Sudan that Wingate developed his skill – and taste – for training and leading forces 'in his own image', free of intervention from above, as the Special Night Squads, Gideon Force and the Chindits were all to be. Moreover, Wingate was evidently beginning to think critically about tactics, and was becoming confident enough to question accepted wisdom in official reports. This period is also of interest in that some of the counterinsurgency practices Wingate applied in Palestine seem to have been learned from the SDF, in particular concentration upon insurgent entry and exit points and the use of deceptive movement to achieve surprise.

Wingate contra Lawrence

By 1936, and Wingate's arrival in Palestine, other influences were apparent. One seems unlikely, given it was that of an individual whom Wingate apparently detested and never missed an opportunity to disparage – T.E. Lawrence 'of Arabia'. Lawrence and Wingate appear never to have met, although Lawrence's parents were guests at the Wingate family home in Reigate in the 1900s, and Wingate was stationed at Larkhill in 1923–27 while 'Trooper Shaw' of the Royal Tank Corps – the pseudonym under which Lawrence sought escape from the attention his own myth had created – was stationed close by at Bovington.[43] However, there were connections between them. Lawrence's father was Wingate's great-uncle, thrice-removed on his mother's side, and many who knew both men, including Churchill, Wavell, Basil Liddell Hart, Chaim Weizmann, Leo Amery and Field Marshal Sir Edmund Ironside detected similarities in appearance and personality between them.[44] As noted already, Sir Reginald Wingate was a driving force behind the Arab revolt and Lawrence's operational commander in 1917 and provided the 'Baksheesh and rifles' with which Lawrence enlisted the support of the Arab chiefs, almost bankrupting the Egyptian treasury in doing so.[45] Wingate's other two great benefactors, Wavell and Churchill, knew Lawrence well. In 1920, Churchill invited Lawrence to join the Colonial Office's recently formed Middle Eastern Department as Advisor on Arab affairs, and remained in contact with Lawrence until Lawrence's fatal motorcycle crash in 1935.[46] Wavell met Lawrence while a staff officer in Egypt in 1917 and was assigned by Allenby to stop him entering Syria in 1920, when the French feared he might aggravate the revolt which was already brewing there, and in the 1920s and 1930s Lawrence was an infrequent but welcome guest at Wavell's house in England. Wavell liked Lawrence personally, but was unsure whether his reputation as a soldier was justified, and implied that at least some of it was self-created: 'His name will live for his words and spirit more than for his wars.'[47]

That Lawrence was perhaps more capable as a man of letters than as a soldier also lay at the heart of Wingate's assessment of him. Lawrence is today best known partially via David Lean's film of 1962, in which he was portrayed by Peter O'Toole, and partially via *The Seven Pillars of Wisdom*, his personal account of the Arab revolt, published posthumously in 1935. Both revolve around the notion that Lawrence was the principal driving force behind the Arab revolt of 1917–18, an event which saw the Bedouin, a race of noble warriors, liberate themselves from the Turkish yoke in a brilliant guerrilla campaign devised, commanded and led by Lawrence, only to then be betrayed by the imperialist ambitions of Britain and France. It seems to have been in the wake of Lawrence's death in 1935 that Wingate became interested in him, and he was apparently familiar with the contents of *Seven Pillars* by the time of his arrival in Palestine sixteen months later. He was unimpressed with what he read, perhaps disgusted by some of it – particularly Lawrence's romanticisation of Bedouin pederasty – and allusions to Lawrence and *Seven Pillars* in reports and correspondence indicated consistently Wingate's view that Lawrence was grossly overrated as both thinker and commander, his Arab desert bandits little different from the *Shifta* he had chased in Sudan.[48] Worst of all, Wingate argued, the 'Lawrence Myth' was exerting a malign influence on British policy in the Middle East, giving the Arabs authority and influence they did not deserve. In his paper, 'Palestine in Imperial Strategy', written in 1939, Wingate commented on 'that unfortunate masterpiece', *The Seven Pillars of Wisdom*:

The vanity of the principals plus a great amount of romantic dust has been allowed so far to obscure what really did happen. A ragged horde of at most a few thousand and often only a few hundred Bedouin, paid in gold for approximately two days' fighting per month... caused the Turks a certain amount of embarrassment and anxiety... In return for the highly paid assistance of this small rabble of Hejazi Bedouin, we have handed over to the 'Arabs' the whole of Saudi Arabia, and the Yemen, Iraq, Trans-Jordan and Syria. A more absurd transaction has seldom been seen.[49]

In his written Appreciation of the analogous situation in Abyssinia in 1941 Wingate took pains to emphasise the differences between Lawrence's methods and his own, treating the words 'Lawrence' and 'wrong' as interchangeable.[50] Most significantly, Wingate developed a vitriolic anti-Arabism and anti-Islamism, impacting upon his actions in Palestine. There is little evidence of Wingate holding any opinion on Middle Eastern politics before 1935; it is unclear whether his opinion of Lawrence was a cause or a product of his Zionism and anti-Arabism, and other reasons suggest themselves. For instance, Sir Reginald, about whom Lawrence was patronizing in *Seven Pillars*, provided an alternative – and more authoritative – source of information on the Arab Revolt from most of Lawrence's hagiographers, at least two of whom, Robert Graves and Basil Liddell Hart, were close friends of their subject and took the 'Lawrence Myth' at face value, as did Sir David Lean, many of Lawrence's subsequent biographers and three generations of writers on the history of guerrilla warfare.[51]

Wingate's attitude to Lawrence is relevant here for reasons beyond his politics. On the broadest level, the two men represent possibly the best-known examples of yet another distinctive British 'type': the romantic misfit compensating for perceived rejection and 'outsider' status among their own people by taking up another people as their personal cause. This other people is idealised sometimes beyond recognition, becoming less a group of individual human beings than a construct onto which are projected dreams of changing the world or escaping from it, and what they are like, individually and collectively, is less important than what their self-appointed saviour believes about them. Ninety years before Lawrence, Lord Byron appointed himself the rescuer of the Greeks from the Ottoman Empire; Lawrence had as contemporaries James Bourchier (Bulgarian nationalist and apologist for King Ferdinand, an ally of the Kaiser during the First World War) and large numbers of Christian Zionists, while Wingate's included Harry St John Philby (the Bedouin, particularly the Saudis of Nejd) and Frank Thompson (Bulgaria again); one could also cite any number of 'useful idiots' recruited by communist secret services in Britain and elsewhere during the Cold War period, including Wilfred Burchett. This is relevant here because Lawrence and Wingate both sought to further their chosen peoples' cause via military means, which had a major bearing both on their ideas about warfare and how they presented them; the possible relationship between Wingate's Zionism and the military methods of the Night Squads are to be discussed in pages to come.

Moreover, and ironically, it somewhat refutes the 'Orde Wingate versus the British Establishment' myth, as it seems that almost no one in that 'establishment' bought into the Lawrence Myth at the time. The anonymous author of a Colonial Office memorandum from 1938 echoed Wingate, complaining of the distorting effect of the myth of the Arab Revolt upon British policy in Palestine; in actuality, he claimed, the Arabs had to be bribed constantly and provided no more than 'nuisance value.'[52] Lawrence himself warranted just two mentions in the official British summary of the Arab revolt, one in a footnote; this document presents Lawrence as just the best-known of several staff officers of the British Military Mission to the Arabs, commanded in actuality by Lieutenant Colonel S.F. Newcombe.[53] British official documents from 1917-18 were sceptical about the cost-effectiveness of the revolt, which was conditional upon British financial and logistical support throughout – particularly rifles and ammunition, of which the Arabs were constantly demanding more – and, in March 1918, faced extinction as funds began to run out.[54] Field Marshal Lord Robertson, the Chief of the Imperial General Staff in 1917, had opposed the diversion of resources on this scale to the Hejaz as undermining Allenby's effort at the main front in Palestine, echoing arguments directed at Wingate in 1943-44 and after his death.[55] Replying to Wingate sending him a draft of 'Palestine in Imperial Strategy' in 1939, General Sir Edmund Ironside – who knew Lawrence and was himself no stranger to covert operations[56] – endorsed Wingate's views on the Arab revolt and referred to Lawrence as an 'unfortunate charlatan... such an impossible creature that I cannot understand how this wretched myth has sprung up around him... Had it not been for men like Liddell Hart he might have been forgotten'.[57] Expressing general disdain for covert operations and irregular forces, General Sir William Platt, Commander of the British advance into Eritrea in 1941 (and no friend of Wingate's either), pronounced, 'The curse of this war is Lawrence in the last.'[58]

This makes another factor linking Lawrence with Wingate all the more surprising. Not only is there a detectable resemblance between Lawrence's military organisation and Wingate's, but an overview of Lawrence's military philosophy, laid out as Wingate would have read it, in *Seven Pillars*, Lawrence's earlier work, *Revolt in the Desert*, and the entry on 'Guerrilla Warfare' (sic) Lawrence authored for the 1929 edition of *Encyclopaedia Britannica*, reveals several other concepts which may have influenced Wingate, perhaps unconsciously. First was the idea of directing effort against enemy supplies and communications, rather than armies, with the aim of forcing the enemy to disperse to protect them. The blockading of Mecca by the Bedouin tribal forces of Emir Faisal, at the outset of the Arab revolt in 1916, resulted in the Turks withdrawing on Medina, which was linked by railway with their garrison in Syria; the Turks were reinforced by a corps from Syria and began an offensive to retake Mecca. In the way was a small range of hills held by more Bedouin tribesmen and a small regular force made up of Arabs recruited mainly from deserters from the Turkish Army. The Turks broke through easily, and Lawrence took this as evidence for the inferiority of 'orthodox' methods to his own: 'Military opinion was obsessed by the dictum of [Marshal] Foch that the ethic of modern war is to seek for the enemy's army, his centre of power, and destroy it in battle. Irregulars would not attack positions and so they were regarded is incapable of forcing a decision.'[59] However, Lawrence noticed that the Turkish offensive followed a lengthy period of inertia, and pondered that maybe this was due to the threat posed by the tribesmen in the countryside around Mecca:

> [P]erhaps the virtue of irregulars lay in depth, not in face, and that it had been the threat of attack by them upon the Turkish northern flank which had made the enemy hesitate for so long. The actual Turkish flank ran from their front line to Medina, a distance of some 50 miles, but if the Arab force moved towards the Hejas [sic] railway behind Medina, it might stretch its threat... as far, potentially, as Damascus, 800 miles away to the north.[60]

Lawrence contended that such a move – directed at the Turks' critical vulnerability – would enable the Arabs to eject the Turks from Hejaz without the need for major battles.[61] As if to prove Lawrence's point – he appeared to be taking credit for it in his writings – in January 1917, Faisal moved the bulk of his tribal forces to Wejh, 200 miles north of the Holy Cities, and the Turks in response aborted their offensive towards Mecca, falling back on Medina and spreading the rest of their forces along the railway to Syria, where they remained until the end of the war in 1918.[62]

To continue the offensive against the Turks, Lawrence advocated forcing an enemy wedded to decisive battle to disperse his strength; from *Seven Pillars*:

> And how would the Turks defend [the Hejaz railway]? No doubt by a trench line across the bottom, if we came like an army with banners; but suppose we were... an influence, an idea, a thing intangible, invulnerable, without front or back, drifting about like a gas?... .It seemed a regular soldier might be helpless without a target, owning only what he sat on, and subjugating only what, by order, he could poke his rifle at.[63]

The war could be won, Lawrence argued, not by *beating* the Turks, but by *containing* them:

> [The Arabs] were in occupation of 99% of the Hejaz. The Turks were welcome to the other fraction till peace or doomsday showed them the futility of clinging to the window pane. This part of the war was over, so why bother about Medina? The Turks sat in it on the defensive, eating for food the transport animals which were to have moved them to Mecca... They were harmless sitting there; if taken prisoner, they would entail the cost of food and guards in Egypt; if driven out northward into Syria, they would join the main army blocking the British in Sinai. On all counts they were best where they were, and they valued Medina and wanted to keep it. Let them![64]

The Bedouin could achieve this via superior mobility in the desert beyond the railway, allowing constant hit and run attacks upon key points in the Turkish supply infrastructure, the railway in particular, the Bedouin emerging from the desert, destroying their assigned targets, then melting back into the vast, empty wilderness before the Turks could react. These attacks should be directed not at the Turks' armed strength, but at their supplies:

> We were to contain the enemy by the threat of a vast unknown desert, not disclosing ourselves until we attacked. The attack might be nominal, directed not against him but his stuff; so it would not seek either his strength or his weakness, but his most accessible material. In railway-cutting it would be usually an empty stretch of rail; and the more empty, the greater the tactical success.[65]

This was expeditious for two reasons. First was the Hashemite policy aim (which Lawrence took upon as his own) of establishing an independent, Hashemite-ruled Arab kingdom stretching north from the Hejaz into Syria and the Levant; to secure this, the Hashemites' Bedouin warriors would have to be seen as playing the major part in driving the Turks out. Secondly, and more prosaically, it was more suitable for tribal warriors from a culture as intensely individualistic as that of the Bedouin:

> The Arab army just then was equally chary of men and materials: of men because they being irregulars were not units, but individuals, and an individual casualty is like a pebble dropped in water: each may make only a brief hole, but rings of sorrow widen out from them. The Arab army could not afford casualties.[66]

This was hardly some great original strategic insight, but a harnessing of one of the eternals of Bedouin culture, the *Ghazu* or raiding party. Beyond the few towns, central and southwestern Arabia was a true anarchy, and in the absence of any government, the Bedouin supplemented their frugal existence by stealing livestock, slaves and other goods from their neighbours and trade caravans, a man's standing among his peers hinging on his bravery in battle and what he took in plunder. This was supplemented by *khuwwa* or 'brotherhood tribute', protection money paid by settlements and trade caravans to Bedouin tribes to avert further raiding, the proceeds being divided among the Bedouin concerned. 'Warfare' among the Bedouin effectively consisted of constant raiding of neighbours until they agreed to pay *khuwwa*, or, in the case of more ambitious rulers – such as the Hashemites or the al Sauds of Nejd, already a major power in the areas east of Hejaz – they agreed to become vassals of the raiding tribes.[67] What Lawrence was advocating was that the *Ghazu*, or something like it, could be directed against a large regular army. The Bedouin's greater mobility, based on the ability of camels to cover up to 75 miles per day in the desert, their familiarity with the terrain and experience of a lifetime of raiding combining with the reliance of modern armies upon a complex supply infrastructure would allow a campaign of incessant 'tip and run' attacks with the Turks unable to launch any effective response: '[N]ot pushes, but strokes. The Arab Army never tried to maintain or improve an advantage, but to move off and strike again somewhere else. It used the smallest force in the quickest time at the farthest place.'[68]

The mindset of the *Ghazu* was never far below the surface. Whatever the political ambitions of the leaders of the Arab revolt, the motivation of individual

Bedouin warriors to carry out Lawrence's offensive was more traditional and more pragmatic: from autumn 1917, a policy of giving them an incentive to attack Turkish trains on the Hejaz railway by allowing them to keep all they plundered from the wreckage was adopted. This may have been at Lawrence's suggestion, he being candid about the Bedouin's motivation in his published works.[69] He also stressed a need to understand the mores of tribal warriors: the very irregularity of such forces was an advantage, as it made them unpredictable in terms of size, organisation and tactics, and it meant they did not depend on the cumbersome lines of supply and communication which were the very weakness he purported to be exploiting. However, idiosyncrasies came too: certain tribes were traditional enemies, so could not operate together, and taking warriors of one tribe onto another's territory, even to strike at a common enemy, could be asking for trouble. Lawrence's suggested solutions to this included the attachment of officers with a degree of local cultural knowledge (like himself) and increasing the fluidity of operations so the Turks were hit in a different district each day of the week, resulting in the maximum number of men from each region joining in.[70]

Constant *Ghazu* raiding would stretch Turkish forces in space to where they were so dispersed they would no longer be effective strategically or even tactically. Lawrence's long-term aim was psychological, however, as he put it, 'arrang[ing] the mind of the enemy... then the minds of the enemy nation making the verdict', reflecting the common British belief in will as the decisive factor in war.[71] Given its liberationist aim, moreover, a rebellion such as the one he envisaged should have a local population, if not actively friendly, then at least sympathetic to the point of not betraying rebel movements to the enemy; 'Rebellions can be made by 2% active in a striking force, and 98% passive sympathetic'; a rebellion should therefore win popular support through an attractive political aim or what Lawrence called 'doctrine (the idea to convert every subject to friendliness)'.[72] This 'doctrine' was the political 'message' aimed at promoting popular support for the Allied cause in enemy-occupied territory. This form of 'doctrine' featured prominently in Wingate's writings on 'penetration warfare', particularly from the Ethiopia period and afterwards. However, Wingate felt always that the role of local allies should be confined to providing information via scouting and liaison with the local civilian community, rather than fighting, echoing Lawrence's belief that guerrilla warfare centred on an active minority. These will be discussed in context below but at this stage, given the similarity between Lawrence's 'doctrine' and Wingate's, and their views on the role of the general population in guerrilla warfare, it is difficult not to detect some influence of one on the other.

However, while Lawrence's abstractions may have been pondered upon by Wingate, it would be rash to search for any direct link in tactical or operational thought. Lawrence was sceptical about the role of 'decisive battle' in war (and was perhaps justified within the times, given what was happening in Europe), and his mode of warfare aimed at victory through pure manoeuvre: striking at the enemy infrastructure would force him to disperse his forces and eventually break his will to fight through frustration and exhaustion, without the need to risk battle:

Most wars are wars of contact, both forces striving to touch to avoid tactical surprise. Ours should be a war of detachment. We were to contain the enemy by the silent threat of a vast unknown desert, not disclosing ourselves until we attacked. The attack might be nominal, directed not against him, but his stuff... We might turn our average into a rule... and develop a habit of never engaging the enemy... Battles in Arabia were a mistake, since we profited in them only by the ammunition the enemy fired off. Napoleon said that it was rare to find generals willing to fight battles; but the curse of this war was that so few would do anything else... We had nothing material to lose, so our best line was to defend nothing and to shoot nothing.[73]

Wingate was vitriolically dismissive of this approach, and along with it, the entire concept and philosophy of 'People's War'.[74] He had a point: floating around like a gas is all very well, but it is rarely sufficient to meet policy aims on its own – Lawrence and his ally, the Hashemite Emir Faisal (the future King Faisal I of Iraq), to achieve their Hashemite kingdom, would eventually have to seize and control territory in the manner of the regular armies that Lawrence so despised. Lawrence was aware of British and French post-war plans for the region and, to forestall these, he intended to present the Great Powers with a political *fait accompli*, and so the real usefulness of Bedouin desert mobility came not via pin-prick raids on the railway, but crossing areas of wilderness rapidly to carry out the *coup de main* seizure of fixed objectives, mainly towns along the Turkish lines of communication, beginning with the port of Aqaba in June 1917 and culminating in Damascus – which Lawrence was determined the Arabs should liberate themselves – on 1 October 1918. Taking such objectives, and so achieving the policy aim, might necessitate hard fighting, and against the popular myth of 'Lawrence of Arabia', forces involved in the Hejaz operations never consisted of just Bedouin warriors: the Arabs were supported by British armoured cars, the Anglo-Egyptian Camel Corps and regular air-raids from January 1918 and the force jointly commanded by Faisal and Lawrence in Syria in September 1918 resembled less a guerrilla band than a 'Jock Column' of twenty-three years later, including as it did 450 Egyptian-trained Arab regulars, elements from the British Army's Camel Corps, an armoured car troop, a battery of 65mm French mountain guns, and Gurkha and Egyptian demolition parties, all resupplied partially by air.[75] Wingate seems to have appreciated from a far earlier point in his development that winning the 'armed struggle' in reality – even in insurgencies – necessitated success in battle, requiring disciplined, well-trained and well-armed professional guerrilla forces, the opposite of anarchic tribesmen like Lawrence's Bedouin: 'If you have a just cause you will get support only by appealing to the best in human nature; down at heel spies and pretentious levies are worse than useless'.[76] Moreover, those guerrillas would require technical, logistical and firepower support from regular forces to be fully effective. Wingate, as will be shown, always stressed defeating the enemy in battle and saw the aim of his operations as forcing battle under the most advantageous circumstances. If Wingate adopted some of Lawrence's concepts, beyond 'doctrine', he applied them within a different model of warfare.

However, the balance of evidence indicates that Lawrence did have some indirect effect on Wingate. Firstly, alongside Mao and Che, Lawrence was one of the godfathers of the myth of 'the invincible guerrilla', which shapes official and academic thought, and media reportage on insurgency and counterinsurgency into the twenty-first century, much of which presumes that every glorified bandit or misfit with a grudge is the reincarnation of one of these three. Wingate was never taken in by this myth at any point, and offered a number of means by which it might be punctured. Secondly, through his writing and personal connections, Liddell Hart in particular, and against the background of growing popular revulsion at the 'slaughter' of the Western Front, Lawrence created enthusiasm in both the British Army and the British political establishment for what, in his and Wingate's day, was called 'Scallywagging', later 'covert operations'; the use of small specialist units or individual agents to sow and direct rebellion in enemy territory. In 1939, Colonel J.C.F. Holland, commanding MI(R), put *Seven Pillars* on his essential reading list for all MI(R) personnel and referred to the Arab revolt frequently in his official writings, while Wavell was firm that operations inside occupied Ethiopia in 1940-41 should conform with the model practiced by Lawrence.[77] Wingate executed covert operations in Ethiopia under the auspices of both Wavell and MI(R) and so it seems Lawrence may have created, indirectly, an environment sympathetic to his model of warfare.

Wingate's Staff College Papers

Wingate read *Seven Pillars* after his return from Sudan, while Adjutant of 71st Territorial Army Artillery Brigade in 1935-36. Administrative and training duties aside, he concerned himself with entry to the Staff College at Camberley, without which it was unlikely he would reach senior rank. He sat the entrance examination twice, in February and June 1936, passing on the second attempt. He next had to achieve nomination by a selection committee chaired by the Chief of the Imperial General Staff (CIGS). He was rejected at this stage, prompting the much-recounted incident of his introducing himself to the CIGS, Field Marshal Sir Cyril Deverell, during an exercise and presenting a copy of his article in the *Journal of the Royal Geographical Society* on his solo expedition to find the 'lost oasis' of Zerzura, with which he had closed his service in Sudan, with the implication that Deverell should reconsider. Deverell, apparently impressed by both Wingate and the article, promised to find Wingate a staff job appropriate to his rank and experience, and Wingate was assigned as an Intelligence Officer in HQ 5th Division, in Haifa, in September 1936.[78]

What appear to be two of Wingate's examination papers, or at least papers done in preparation for the exam, survive. These demonstrate the development of Wingate's ideas at this time, and provide evidence that two key passions developed earlier than previous works have detected. Firstly, Wingate appears to have had an academic interest in Palestine some months before going there, suggesting, combined with his attitude to Lawrence, that he arrived with many of his opinions on the region forming already. The second paper shows that he did, indeed, hold a low opinion of staff officers from an early stage in his career.

Wingate's interest in the Middle East may have been inspired by Sir Reginald, as his exam answer, 'The importance of Palestine and Trans-Jordan to the Empire' concentrated entirely upon imperial geopolitics, without mentioning the ethno-nationalist issues which shape much of the politics of the region and which became his obsession. He opened by outlining how the situation in the region had changed since 1914; previously, the region had been controlled by Turkey, no threat to 'our [British] communications with the east for the reason that she was not strong enough'; the situation would be different were the region controlled by a rival European power. 'The necessary measures for the defence of the Suez Canal and Egypt would have cost immense sums of money and would not even then have afforded real security.'[79] Once Turkey disappeared from the scene after 1918, however, Palestine became vital to the British Empire's interests for several reasons. First was oil from Iraq and Persia; Britain could not rely upon sources of oil in the hands of other European countries, 'The pipeline to Haifa is already of considerable military importance to our fleet… We must, therefore, control the territory through which it runs. So long as Iraq is not controlled by any other power, we… control the oil supplies from her oil fields'. Wingate would soon be controlling the territory around that pipeline in his own personal way. Secondly was air communications to India: were a foreign power to control Trans-Jordan, it would soon dominate Iraq as well, and be in a position to menace the air route across northern Arabia. Thirdly was British influence: 'To cede the control of these territories to a strong, expanding and propagandist power would be to deal a decisive blow to our influence in the Near East. Egyptians, Arabs, Iraqis and Persians, would all conclude that the domination of Great Britain was over…'[80] The paper indicates how far Wingate's opinions were to evolve over the next three years, as he became an advocate of a 'strong, expanding and propagandist' Jewish state in the region, concluding that Arab opinion – and oil – was unimportant in the face of its development.

The question Wingate answered on the second paper has not been found, but appears to have concerned sources of military inefficiency. Wingate argued that the higher the rank, the greater the damage arising from narrow-mindedness, beginning with a rather good definition of narrow-mindedness which provides also an excellent example of his style:

> Anyone who accepts this phrase without definition is guilty of slovenly thinking. In the last analysis it means that mental quality that clings to a particular view in disregard of facts and opinions that are opposed to it. It is always given a bad sense in use, and here means clinging to views from stupidity or obstinacy when intelligent thought and admission of all the facts would compel a departure from them… It has to be admitted that staff officers are peculiarly prone to this fault.[81]

This was because 'their long and arduous training tends to make them prize the ideas and opinions they have imbibed from their teachers. The learning has cost them many pains [sic] and the thought that those pains, in some cases, have been thrown away is unacceptable to many of them.'[82] Their belief in the set systems was such that they 'would prefer failure along the right lines to success along the wrong ones.'[83] Wingate then illustrated his point with a hypothetical account of a campaign in East Africa; the commander of a 'native corps' complains that the rigid march timetable drawn up by the staff actually stifles the main advantages of his troops, their ability to march across country at three times the rate of British troops and to live off the land:

> The staff officer regards the native corps commander as an old-fashioned soldier who does not know how to conduct a modern operation. He prefers to believe, without investigation, the civil authorities' view of the resources available. He resents the tone adopted and the implication that he and the rest of the staff are making a blunder. In short, he refuses to face the facts, convinces himself that he is justified in dismissing his critic as an ignoramus, and suppresses his evidence.[84]

It might be that this little polemic stemmed from first-hand experience, and Wingate was certainly to accuse staff officers of all these sins in the future. Wingate's conclusion is interesting in that, at this time, he was apparently still an advocate of concentration of effort, blaming on the German General Staff in 1914 'the pig-headed worship of the envelopment theory of strategy… which led directly to disaster.'[85] The examiner complimented Wingate's style and his ideas, and awarded him a 'VG+' grade. This is in contrast to his mark on the tactics paper, where, Tulloch recalled, instead of answering the question, Wingate 'content[ed] himself with writing a thesis proving that the examiner did not know his subject', this presumably being Wingate's earlier, unsuccessful attempt.[86]

Wingate appears, therefore, to have arrived in Palestine with many of the opinions which were to shape his subsequent relationship with his peers already developing, if not yet set firmly in his psyche. This reverses previous opinion of Wingate, influenced mainly by some of his biographers, which argues that his Zionism, which arose from his personal opinions and early experiences, was the major influence upon his view of imperial strategy and the role of force within it.[87] Even a brief overview of Wingate's intellectual interests in this period suggests that the actuality was more complex and deeper rooted.

Chapter Four

Wingate and Counter-terrorism in Palestine, 1937–39

I cannot speak too highly... of the Special Night Squads... organized and trained by Captain OC WINGATE, Royal Artillery, from my Staff, who has shown great resource, enterprise and courage in leading and controlling their activities. These Squads have been supplemented by Jewish supernumeraries who have done excellent work in combination with the British personnel. The story of the inception and gradual development of this form of activity, and its successful results, provide a great tribute to the initiative and ingenuity of all concerned.

General Sir Robert Haining, 1938[1]

[Captain Wingate's] tendency... to play for his own ends and likings instead of playing for the side... has become so marked... as to render his services in the Intelligence Branch nugatory and embarrassing. His removal to another sphere of action has been timely.

General Sir Robert Haining, 1939[2]

Wingate and the Jews

Almost every previous account of Wingate's actions in Palestine makes two claims. Firstly, that they stemmed from his fanatical Zionism, and secondly, that they made him a pariah in the British Army. This passage comes from a work on Special Forces, by an American academic, from 2006:

Wingate was drawn to Zionism by his Christian fundamentalism and genuine admiration for the accomplishments of the persecuted Jews of Eastern and Central Europe...He offered his services to Chaim Weizmann, the great chemist turned prophet, to organize underground forces for the quietly forming framework of a Jewish state. Given the British position, this bordered on mutiny, if not subversion.[3]

Here is the popular image of Wingate in Palestine encapsulated: *Hayedid*, the Friend, helping the Jews in their righteous struggle for nationhood and thereby casting himself out from the British 'establishment', anti-Semites to a man. Indeed, one can find militant Zionist and American 'Neo-Conservative' sources who argue seriously that Wingate's fatal plane crash was arranged by the 'British establishment' for daring to support the Jews in achieving their 'historical destiny'.[4] The most extravagant – and least reliable – accounts of his time in Palestine come from contemporary Zionist sources, most of them portraying Wingate as Zionism's 'man of destiny', pursuing a lifelong mission, set by the Almighty, to secure the Promised Land from heathen Arab terrorists. According to Yigal Allon, Wingate 'absorbed the tales of the Bible with his mother's milk [and] regarded the message of Prophesy not as the mummified stuff of books, but as the plain and simple truth.'[5] Indeed, following Wingate's death, several Hebrew newspapers reported earnestly in their obituaries that Wingate's mother, Ethel, rather than the gentle, modest colonel's lady found in every other account, was actually a religious mystic, a practitioner of the Kabala, and a fire-breathing Zionist who had instilled her spiritual and political agenda in her son.[6] This, in turn, shaped Wingate's military thought, *Ha'aretz* proclaiming 'Read the Book of Judges and you will read the theory of military science as understood by Wingate', whilst according to the obituarist Joseph Nadwa, 'the Modern Gideon' treated the Old Testament as the literal truth on all matters and 'repeatedly quoted Biblical texts in his secret military dispatches'.[7] The newspaper *Hazman* not only contained the seeds of a number of myths, but gives an excellent taster of many of the posthumous Jewish tributes to Wingate:

> In the years of blood in Palestine Wingate compacted a covenant of blood with the defenders of Israel. He marshaled the youth of Jewry around him and welded them into the 'Special Night Squads' which... effected a revolution in warfare against the savage brigands. He was the first in Palestine to point the way to the correct method of fighting with fast units of irregulars... By shifting the centre of gravity from a defence system frozen to its post to one of incursive action on the part of mobile units, trained to circulate and manoeuvre, he enhanced the power of the Hebrew defences immeasurably.[8]

Other tributes abound: a ship bringing illegal immigrants to Palestine in 1946 was called *Orde Wingate*, a unit fighting in the 1948 War of Independence called itself the Wingate Brigade, and in 1953, Lorna Wingate, a guest of the Israeli government, opened the *Yemin Orde* national youth centre near Haifa, this later becoming an international educational centre; there is a Wingate street in Tel Aviv, and a Wingate Square in Jerusalem, appropriately at the junction of Balfour and Jabotinsky streets. Until 1999, all government-sponsored school textbooks in Israel covered Wingate's contributions to Zionism without qualification or criticism.[9]

The commonest impression is that Wingate single-handedly turned the tide of the Arab revolt against obstruction from a British 'military establishment' institutionally Islamophile and anti-Semitic, abetted by timid Jewish politicians. Burchett, in 1946, suggested that 'The Arab revolt was an *ersatz* production foisted on Palestine by the Axis, and more or less winked at by the British [therefore] we [sic] allowed Axis money and Axis arms to pour into Palestine to be used against the people we had lawfully permitted to settle there.'[10] Wingate, 'after a lot of trouble', obtained authority to form 'special light squadrons' [sic] and in a few weeks, 'squashed' the rebels in his operational area; however:

Many of the General Staff officers, in accordance with the fashion of the day, had become anti-Semitic, and Wingate's exploits were not looked upon favourably… The special squads were disbanded and after waiting around with nothing to do Wingate left for England…[11]

Mosley dwelt also upon the attitude of British authorities (having Wingate describe General Headquarters, Jerusalem, as 'a gang of anti-Jews') and the passivity of the Jewish leadership which condemned Jewish settlers in Galilee 'with nothing but a few rook rifles' per settlement, to massacre, it only being after galvanisation by Wingate that the Jews went on the offensive.[12] Other authors have quoted Wingate's disparagement of British tactics at length, and Wingate's criticism of the British Army is taken at face value by those concerning themselves more directly with his military ideas.[13] In a previous study of Wingate as military commander, Luigi Rossetto claimed that the Jews 'never managed to form a common front with the British and preferred to follow a policy of strict self-defence' against Arab guerrillas; the British reliance on motorised transport and heavy weaponry allowed the rebels to hit, run and then melt back into the countryside.[14] British action was sporadic and timid, the rebels always being warned by the locals in time to either lay ambushes or escape: this situation was rectified only when Wingate – and Wingate alone – realised the need to form 'small squads' to meet the rebels on their own terms, principally operating by night, something which the British Army had, according to Rossetto, avoided previously.[15]

Another side to the story has emerged since the 1950s. Claims of frequent serious breakdowns in discipline among Wingate's Special Night Squads have emerged, along with evidence that Wingate's brand of 'personal leadership' sometimes ran to enforcing discipline with his fists and boot.[16] The Night Squads sometimes seemed dangerously amateurish, their first large action, at Dabburiya in July 1938, seeing one Jewish policeman killed and Wingate seriously wounded by fire from their own side.[17] Most serious are allegations that the Squads acted as Jewish 'death squads', a local version of Simson's 'G men', fighting terror with terror. The sources of some of these are predictable, Wingate being loathed by self-styled 'freedom fighters' the world over: a pro-*Hamas* website, muddling Orde with Cousin Rex, describes him as 'a professional secret agent who was responsible for killing the successor of the Mahdi' who was 'attached to the command of the Jewish paramilitary units' to assist 'the forcible eviction of Arabs from their ancient lands'; Irish Republicans accuse Wingate of originating the 'assassination policy' applied allegedly by the British in Ulster in the 1970s, while an American 'survivalist' website claims Wingate 'was sent to Palestine to train Jewish leaders in terror tactics against the Arabs, a tradition which directly produced Ariel Sharon.'[18] However, the most serious allegations have come from Israelis. The post-*Intifada* period has seen the emergence of the so-called 'New Historians', a group of Israeli writers including Benny Morris, Avi Shlaim, Tom Segev and Gideon Levy, using previously closed Hebrew and Arabic sources to argue that the Jewish State has been neither as innocent nor as defenceless as the Zionist version of history claims.[19] In 1999, Segev published a history of the British

Mandate containing allegations that Wingate not only tortured Arabs in reprisal for terrorist attacks, but also personally murdered several.[20] Segev gave no dates for these incidents and located only one, but his claim that some in the Zionist leadership viewed Wingate as more trouble than he was worth was corroborated by David Ben-Gurion, Israel's first Prime Minister, who had personal dealings with Wingate throughout the period 1937–44.[21] Segev has something of a following, particularly in Israel: reviewing Segev's book for the Israeli newspaper *Ha'aretz*, Levy praised Segev's exposure of the 'dark side' of the Wingate 'myth', described Wingate as an 'oddball with sadistic tendencies' who tortured Arabs, and demanded the inclusion of Segev's findings in the Israeli school curriculum. In a letter responding to Benny Landau's positive review of John Bierman and Colin Smith's 2000 biography of Wingate, *Fire in the Night*, in *Ha'aretz*, Dan Yahav of Tel Aviv University described Wingate as 'view(ing) reality through the sight of a gun' and 'deal[ing] in collective punishments, in harming innocent people, in looting, in arbitrary killing... and in unrestrained degradation.'[22] British historians have joined in, Hew Strachan describing Wingate's methods as 'state terrorism', while Charles Townshend saw the Night Squads as a 'still more dubious' version of the Black and Tans.[23]

Official papers of the time and the testimony of Jewish leaders and some of Wingate's colleagues suggest many of these arguments need to be revised heavily if not ditched altogether. Indeed, many of them are preposterous. In reality, the Night Squads operated within a British counterinsurgency strategy derived from established 'small wars' practice and effective enough to force several changes in strategy upon the insurgents, in which there were atrocities committed by all participants – although the Jews really were more blameless in this case than others – and involving Anglo-Jewish and Anglo-Arab cooperation at several levels. Moreover, Wingate's use of Jewish policemen and volunteers in counterinsurgent operations had the blessing of senior commanders and the British High Commissioner in Palestine. Claims he was 'subversive' or 'mutinous' are therefore faintly ridiculous, as an overview of the insurgency will show.

The Development of the Arab Revolt

The Palestinian Arab revolt of 1936–39 arose from a long historical process. The Ottoman Empire collapsed at the end of the First World War, after which its former province, Palestine, was administered by the British Colonial Office acting under a Mandate from the League of Nations. This was never easy politically, because the Balfour Declaration of 1917 committed the British to 'use their best endeavours' to assist the creation of a Jewish national homeland in Palestine, while the 'civil and religious rights of existing non-Jewish communities' – Arabs making up 90 per cent of Palestine's population in 1917 – would not be prejudiced.[24] The Declaration was made in pursuit of Allied war aims, and was shaped more by the careful lobbying of the British government by Chaim Weizmann, President of the International Zionist Organisation, and popular perceptions about the power of 'International Jewry', than the realities of geography or demographics in Palestine, there being a fear that Jews

N
W
E
S
0
40 miles
0
40 km
Litani
Tyre
Metulla
LEBANON
Hanita
Mediterranean
Sea
Safed
SYRIA
Acre
Majd el Krum
Sea of Galilee
Haifa
Tiberias
Mitzpa
Nazareth
Ramat David
Dabburiya
Yarmuk
Mishmar Ha-Emek
Balfouriya
Ein Harod
Zikhron Yaakov
Irbid
Beit Alpha
Karkur
Beit Shean
Hadera
Jenin
TRANS-
Hogla
Jordan
Tulkarm
Netanya
Anabta
Tel Mond
Nablus
JORDAN
Zarqa
PALESTINE
Jaffa
Petah Tikva
Ramla
Amman
Ataroth
Jerusalem
Ashdod
Soreq
Motza
Bethlehem

around the world, particularly in the USA, might rally behind the Kaiser against Britain's ally, Russia, the land of pogroms and forced conversion.[25] Transjordan, although previously part of Palestine and incorporated into the Mandate, was formed into a separate Arab Emirate, and Palestine, Transjordan and Iraq took on vital strategic importance for the Empire, not only as a buffer zone protecting Egypt and the Suez Canal and an aerial artery between Britain and India, but principally because of the pipeline bringing oil from northern Iraq to Haifa.[26] The first British High Commissioner for Palestine, Sir Herbert Samuel, inadvertently set the policy agenda shaping the 1936–39 uprising. In 1920, he passed an Immigration Ordinance removing restrictions on all Jewish immigration to Palestine, and created the tripartite system by which Palestine was governed until the late 1930s, with the Zionist executive (later the Jewish Agency) and the Supreme Muslim Council representing their respective communities to the High Commissioner and other outside bodies.[27] The Immigration Ordinance resulted in Arab rioting and consequently Samuel not only suspended it temporarily, but also allowed the riots' main agitator, the Muslim cleric Haj Amin al Husseini, to be elected Grand Mufti of Jerusalem in 1921 and President of the Supreme Muslim Council in 1922, making him both spiritual and secular leader of Palestine's Arabs.[28]

Apart from occasional outbreaks of sectarian rioting, there was relative peace until 1929, mainly because Jews remained a minority in Palestine, and a Jewish national homeland there seemed a remote prospect. However, the mid-1920s saw Europe begin its greatest spasm of anti-Semitism, beginning in Poland in the 1920s and moving to unprecedented levels with the rise of the Nazis in the early 1930s. The USA restricted all immigration in 1924, so Palestine now fulfilled the role Theodor Herzl, the founder of modern political Zionism, envisaged for it – more than a homeland, it was to be a Jewish national sanctuary. Jewish migration to Palestine, encouraged by the Nazis, rose from 4,000 arrivals per year in 1931 to over 61,000 in 1935, plus perhaps 5–6,000 illegal immigrants smuggled in per year.[29] The perceived existential threat to the Palestinian Arabs posed by this explosive and apparently never-ending increase in the Jewish population produced a violent Arab nationalist response sharpened by militant Islam. The Mufti was, at heart, an opportunist politician who used his religious office to build a secular power base for himself and his Husseini clan; indeed, Simson saw a major contributing factor in the rebellion as the number of Arab leaders whose families had enjoyed power and privilege under the Turks and lost them thanks to the British, Palestinian Arab politics being dominated by a number of powerful families, principally the Husseinis and the Nashashibis, and the vast patronage networks centred on them.[30] Indeed, the subsequent insurgency saw something of a 'war within the war' as the Husseinis and Nashashibis fought it out for dominance within the Arab community, the Nashashibis generally cooperating with the British authorities against the Husseinis, particularly by passing on intelligence gleaned by their own extensive network of spies and agents.[31]

These elites found their status under threat from within the Arab community in the early 1930s due to the emergence of grass-roots militants. A number of guerrilla gangs formed in northern Palestine following the 1929 disturbances, most notably the 'Green Hand Gang' which carried out rather desultory attacks on the Jewish Quarters of Safad and Acre in November–December 1930.[32] The most prominent of the new militants was Sheikh Muhammad Izz al-Din al-Qassam, a Syrian cleric who had been preaching anti-colonial *jihad* since 1911, and who organised armed cells in Haifa and other northern towns with the apparent backing of Fascist Italy.[33] None of these 'cells' appears to have been larger than five men, and while Qassam's 1935 'revolt' was built up to epic proportions in post-1948 Palestinian propaganda, it was in reality a rather gimcrack affair; leaving Haifa with twenty-five followers in November 1935, hoping to provoke a mass uprising among the peasants around Jenin, Qassam clashed accidentally with a police patrol, his little band was isolated and scattered rapidly and he was killed seven days later. His funeral was a major public event, however, and, reacting to his 'martyrdom', from early 1936 Muslim clerics began to demand resistance to any Jewish takeover of Palestine, the most prominent now being the Mufti.[34]

This played nicely with another aggravating factor – land ownership. Aware that any future political settlement in Palestine would depend on demographics, the Zionist leadership aimed to establish a Jewish presence in every part of the Mandate by purchasing land in Arab majority areas, in the disputed northern area of Galilee in particular. There were 673 such transactions in 1933, and this shot up to 1,178 the following year.[35] This was called, cynically but accurately, 'establishing facts', and was summarised by Ben-Gurion:

> We... wanted to strike roots in new areas where there was still no Jewish settlement. This would prevent, as far as possible, fixed boundaries being imposed on the National Home, and expand the territory of the Jewish State that was yet to arise – whether the Mandatory Government liked it or not.[36]

Absentee Arab landlords living in Jerusalem, Damascus or Beirut were often keen to sell to Jews, who paid generously, but their Arab tenants were not consulted, and were often evicted forcefully from land their families had lived on for generations.[37] Once this happened, there followed a set of drills devised by the Jewish underground militia, the *Haganah*, volunteers moving in immediately to erect pre-fabricated fortified outposts to prevent Arab smallholders from returning: fifty-five such 'settlements' were established in 1936–39.[38] Although they were cloaked as ordinary agricultural settlements, the British knew their true nature: in 1938, the High Commissioner, Sir Harold MacMichael, reported back to London that 'establishing facts' stemmed from:

> The desire to press on with the establishment of a National Home all over Palestine and to show the world, in particular the Arab world, the violence and danger would not be a deterrent... [and] The desire to extend settlements in... Galilee in general so that the Jewish 'claim' to this district will be more easily established.[39]

'Establishing facts' was soon a major nuisance to the British Colonial Office. From 1935, cases grew of Arab tenants resisting eviction forcefully, requiring deployment of police, and official correspondence indicated a fear that the previously apolitical *fellahin* were becoming radicalised.[40] The Jews pressed on regardless, greatly encouraged by the Peel Report of July 1937 (see below) which recommended that *Eretz Israel* should include as many of the Jewish Settlements and as much Jewish-owned land as possible. After this, the strategy was escalated, supported by the 'Redemption of Galilee' charity which raised funds in Britain and the USA to support the settlements, one of whose organisers was the Conservative MP, Victor Cazalet, later a close friend of Wingate's.[41] In November 1938, as violence escalated, the District Commissioner for Galilee reported to MacMichael that 'Dr Weizmann's fait accompli policy' had resulted in three new settlements being established in this volatile area since his previous report, 'one disguised as a labour camp', and that his queries met with 'a conspiracy of silence'.[42] MacMichael – generally sympathetic towards the Jews – was so perturbed by the level of Army and police resources redirected to the new settlements that he requested the Privy Council to pass an Order giving him authority to ban all new settlements unless permitted specifically by himself.[43]

Phase One of the Revolt

The subsequent insurgency fell into four broad phases, the first lasting from autumn 1935, when Qassam's followers began attacks on Jewish settlements in Galilee, until the convening of the Peel Commission in November 1936. The British traced the beginning of the revolt to 19 April 1936, when the Supreme Muslim Council called a general strike of Arab workers with the tacit backing of the Arab Higher Committee, an unofficial Arab 'government' created in Palestine to represent Arab interests, chaired by the Mufti, allegedly showing solidarity with a similar strike in French-mandated Syria. The strike lasted six months, accompanied by rioting – targeting mainly Jewish businesses – sabotage, murders of civilians from both communities, and, in the summer, the formation of large guerrilla bands in the countryside.[44] These guerrillas fell into two broad types: *Mujahedeen*, who carried out guerrilla attacks on Jewish settlements and ambushed traffic on major roads, and *Fedayeen*, who were saboteurs: the British referred to the insurgents collectively as 'Oozlebarts', a corruption of *Ursabat*, another Arabic term.[45] The British noted early that *Mujahedeen* bands in particular centred upon 'volunteers' from Syria and Iraq, many of them apparently with regular army training; these were reinforced by larger numbers of local Palestinian Arabs, notably less aggressive and less disciplined.[46] Indeed, British official reports indicated that, apart from a period in late 1938, the rural Arab population was lukewarm towards the rebellion and, unless coerced directly by the guerrillas, was generally law-abiding; in the later stages of the campaign many cooperated actively with the British while a number turned violently upon the guerrillas. Consequently, the 'revolt' resembled less an insurgency than an invasion, using guerrilla methods, in support of an elite of urban agitators centred on the Husseini family and its network.

The military direction of the guerrilla campaign was initially in the hands of Fawzi al-Quwuqji, a Syrian Druze and former officer in the Ottoman Army, who had led a revolt against the French in 1925 before being appointed Commandant of the Iraqi Army Military Training College.[47] Quwuqji had visited Palestine secretly several times before 1936, giving credence to British allegations that the rebellion had been planned for some time, and was enlisted by the Higher Arab Committee to give the insurgency direction and discipline. This he did, among other things producing a simple codified doctrine for guerrilla warfare dubbed the 'Damascus *Field Service Regulations*' when copies fell into British hands; other veteran rebel leaders from Syria and Lebanon also infiltrated into Palestine to command guerrilla gangs.[48] This was one expression of the Arab Higher Committee's policy of turning the insurgency into a pan-Arabic and pan-Islamic issue; from May 1931, British authorities were tracking information that the Mufti and others were extending their existing networks to the wider Islamic world – including India – as part of a pan-Islamic plan to 'deliver' Palestine from both the British and the Jews, while sounding out the various Arab kings for potential support.[49] Iraq, which had received nominal independence from Britain in 1932, and was now the most pro-Axis of the Arab states, not only provided Quwuqji and volunteers for the guerrilla bands but also spoke internationally on behalf of the Higher Arab Committee and pressured British policy – not very convincingly – with vague threats of escalation to a general confrontation in the Middle East.[50] Contrary to Burchett's claims, Nazi Germany seems to have offered little more than propaganda support, most insurgent weapons being leftovers from 1914–18 or previous rebellions. The Mufti met with Italian diplomats in the mid-1930s, but any potential support foundered on his anger at Italian brutality against the Arab population of Libya; he was, however, happy to receive financial donations from the Italian Foreign Ministry, which the Foreign Minister, Galeazzo Ciano, considered to be money poorly spent.[51] Indeed, Burchett seems to have been unaware of – or more likely, ignored – the extent to which Fascist Italy was encouraging *Jewish* aspirations in Palestine, to undermine the British position in the eastern Mediterranean, for instance running training courses for the *Haganah* at La Spezia in 1935–37.[52]

The British Response

With just two infantry battalions and two RAF armoured car squadrons in Palestine, the British could not carry out the vigorous response a Callwell or Simson might recommend. However, Brigadier John Evetts, Commander of Troops, Palestine, took precedents from 'frontier warfare' in devising *Operations Instructions*, an ad hoc 'doctrine' for dealing with the insurgency, recommending bringing the guerrillas to battle by tempting them to attack convoys accompanied by armoured cars and lorries mounted with Royal Navy pom-pom guns, by occupying villages and waterholes they might contest, and aggressive 'cordon and sweep' operations intended to kill or capture rebel leaders.[53] At the political level, the British Government announced in August 1936 that a Royal Commission, under Lord Peel, would go to Palestine to investigate Arab and Jewish grievances and ascertain if the Mandate was being implemented satisfactorily; however, before it could convene, law and order should be restored.[54] In the biggest movement of British troops since the First World War, two infantry divisions, the 5th and the 8th, were formed into the Palestine Expeditionary Force, under Lieutenant General J.G. Dill, thereby raising the garrison to 80,000, alongside four squadrons from RAF Bomber Command.[55]

On 7 September 1936, the Army Council issued a secret instruction to Dill:

His majesty's government has resolved:

A) To reaffirm their previous decisions that order must be restored and British authority restored in [Palestine]
B) That intensive measures designed to crush that resistance should be taken and for this purpose... martial law should be applied either to the whole country or to selected parts.[56]

Further orders in Council were passed authorising severe measures: martial law was imposed, allowing the death penalty for saboteurs, those illegally wearing British uniform or carrying concealed firearms and life imprisonment for those supplying the rebels willingly.[57] Collective punishments of communities supporting the insurgency were also allowed, including fines, demolition of houses, and curfews enforced at gunpoint.[58]

The British Army went on the offensive, buoyed by this massive reinforcement. The experience of 'frontier warfare' runs through everything they did: infantry columns, small enough to tempt the guerrillas to try their chances and mobile enough to converge rapidly upon 'the sound of the guns' swept rebel areas on a wide front, with task forces made up of tanks, armoured cars and pom-pom lorries held in reserve. Upon encountering a guerrilla band, standard procedure was to send a 'GG' wireless call for tanks to 'fix' the gang in position before 'shooting in' an infantry counterattack, tactics almost identical to those used in Waziristan at the same time.[59] The ideal was to get into bayonet and grenade range: Callwell was enthusiastic about the bayonet, believing that native irregulars had a terror of cold steel, and documents based on what was happening in Palestine suggest this sentiment was common:

Infantry finding itself within 200 yards of the rebels should go straight in with bayonets and butts... Nine times out of ten the enemy will fire a few rounds wildly and try to run away. If encountered at longer range efforts should be made to pin the enemy to the ground with fire while lightly equipped troops try to get round the flanks and behind him.[60]

However, the most notable feature of these operations was support by aircraft, the RAF carrying out reconnaissance for army columns, 'pinning' insurgents in villages while columns moved up, and providing close air support in response to 'XX' wireless calls.[61] Methods applied by British forces in 'small wars' elsewhere were therefore continued in Palestine.

The Arab Higher Committee feared the insurgents would indeed be crushed, and also that the citrus crop, on which the entire Palestinian economy depended and which needed to be tended from October to March, would suffer. Consequently, on 10 October 1936 they issued a joint instruction with the Kings of Saudi Arabia and Iraq, and Emir Abdullah of Transjordan, calling off the revolt, citing the impending Peel Commission as the reason.[62]

Phase Two of the Revolt

This began in September 1937 with the breakdown of the truce pending the report of the Peel Commission, marked by the assassination of the British District Commissioner for Galilee, and ended with the defeat of the major guerrilla forces in early 1938. Three developments contributed to the Army's success. The first was Sir Arthur Wauchope's replacement as High Commissioner by the more hawkish Sir Harold MacMichael in February 1937, removing a previous disjunction between military and political aims in Palestine; second was the employment by the Palestine Government of Sir Charles Tegart, former Commissioner of Police in Calcutta, as an advisor on police organisation and methods from December 1937 to June 1938; and third was the refinement of Army tactical and operational methods. Tegart recommended that the northern border, with Lebanon and Syria, be closed by a barbed wire fence, covered by concrete blockhouses (the 'Tegart Line') and the forming of specialist counterinsurgency units.[63] Such a 'Third Force', partway between army and police, had been used in Palestine before: in 1921, the Palestine Gendarmerie had been formed by Colonel Wyndham Deedes, at the behest of the High Commissioner, in response to an outbreak of sectarian rioting. Although initially recruited on a 'mixed' basis, issues of reliability led to it becoming 'all-white'; its members included large numbers of former Black and Tans and 'Auxies' who seem to have brought many of the 'methods' they had applied in Ireland with them.[64] Now, Tegart called for the raising of 'Rural Mounted Police', from 'the tough type of man, not necessarily literate, who knows as much of the game as the other side', and composed 'partly of British and Palestinians [from which ethnicity Tegart did not specify, although he was a known Zionist]'.[65] These would patrol the countryside, gathering information on gangs and attacking any they encountered, freeing the Palestine Police for more orthodox police work.[66] Tegart's proposal was rejected on the grounds stated by a senior government official that 'In effect this will be rather like the "Black & Tans" with some of the original personnel of that body and might easily supply material for the same kind of reputation as they, rightly or wrongly, obtained in the Irish troubles.'[67] Wingate, therefore, was far from first to suggest forming specialist counterinsurgent units in Palestine.

Wavell succeeded Dill as GOC Palestine on 12 September 1937. Martial law was lifted at the end of the general strike, and the resumption of hostilities in September 1937 was met with imposition of 'Military Control'.[68] Operations now consisted of action against guerrilla bands smaller than before, confining themselves largely to robbing Arab villages and ambushing small police and Army patrols and, when engaged, preferring brief, long-range fire-fights before making swiftly for the hills.[69]

The Army responded by refining the system of mobile columns, with ten per brigade, now with mules, allowing them to pursue rebels into the hills, use superior mobility to harry the gangs, and if possible cut a gang's routes of retreat and then 'drive' in upon them, the Army destroying a number of large gangs in this way in early 1938.[70] Twice in the space of a fortnight in November 1937, Evetts, now commanding 16th Brigade in Galilee, destroyed rebel gangs, one action involving a column of 2nd East Yorkshires climbing a mountain several thousand feet tall in darkness to attack a rebel base, capturing its leader and an arsenal of weapons, earning Evetts one of several mentions in dispatches.[71] In March 1938, 16th Brigade fought the largest engagement of the rebellion, at Jenin, inflicting heavy rebel casualties; in the following fortnight, the Brigade destroyed the biggest guerrilla band in Galilee, killing its leader.[72] There was also extensive 'severity': villages were searched frequently for weapons and suspects, and searches were often accompanied by the systematic vandalisation of property for 'punishment' and intimidation.[73] British tactics, therefore, proved effective long before Wingate's involvement. However, they forced a change in operational method upon the rebels that did, temporarily, nullify the British tactical advantage and provided Wingate with an opportunity.

Phase Three of the Revolt – From Guerrilla Warfare to Terrorism

Phase three lasted from March to December 1938, during which Wingate created and led the Night Squads, which can now be seen not as a reaction to the inadequacy of British counterinsurgency techniques, but as a shift in insurgent strategy. In early 1938, the rebels, reduced to around 1,000 over the whole of Palestine, switched to terror attacks on the rural Arab population, murdering or kidnapping Arabs known to have moderate views or suspected of supplying information to the government, or coercing villagers into acts of sabotage. The terrorist offensive was concentrated upon Galilee, southern Palestine being relatively peaceful until late in this period.[74] Quwuqji's authority had by now given way largely to that of two rival Palestinian bandit chieftains: Abdul Rahim al Haj Muhammad (who also only obeyed the Mufti when it suited him) and Arif Abdul Razzik, whose followers came close to fighting each other at times, mainly, it appears, over control of the lucrative weapons and hashish smuggling rackets which were part-funding the revolt. Another bandit *cum* guerrilla, Kamal Hussein, alternated between smuggling in weapons, drugs and Jewish illegal immigrants as it suited him.[75] This created a dangerous situation for the British, with echoes of the situation in Iraq or Afghanistan in the mid-2000s: Lieutenant General Sir Robert Haining, who succeeded Wavell as GOC in April 1938, reported that the rebels now had no 'centres of gravity' against which the Army could concentrate:

> [T]here are practically no major leaders controlling a number of gangs, and the various minor leaders are practically independent and often at open enmity with each other. Thus, in addition to there being no standing armed rebel force against which the troops can act, there is no central organisation whose destruction would cause the rebellion to collapse.[76]

This was compounded by the gangs' ability to hide themselves in Arab villages, intimidating citizens into concealing them, their weapons and supplies, and 'taxing' them to support the insurgency. Alongside this stick were the kind of 'carrots' found in most insurgencies, such as threatening and assassinating unpopular government officials, and the setting-up of rebel 'courts' to arbitrate disputes and pass 'justice' on 'criminals' (particularly those smuggling or enforcing for rival gangs).[77] The British responded from May 1938 by billeting platoon-sized detachments of troops in villages in terrorist-affected areas, protecting law-abiding Arabs and patrolling the surrounding area, an approach not dissimilar to the 'platoon houses' adopted by the British Army in Northern Ireland in the 1970s and 80s and Helmand in 2006, and a cornerstone of the 'population centred' approach to counterinsurgency favoured after 1945.[78] However, unlike Afghanistan in the 2000s, much of this patrolling was at night, Haining emphasising the need to be 'top-dog' by night some time before Wingate began raising the Night Squads.[79] Twenty-five villages were occupied by June, as the Tegart line was completed, and there was nightly patrolling of the northern frontier until early December, when it was suspended following a temporary resumption of the rebels assembling in large gangs.[80] This represented something of a departure from the previous approach of having British units return to barracks in the large towns between 'sweeps', thereby allowing the gangs to disperse, then regroup after their departure.[81] The gangs, from late May, switched their activities in response to sabotage and attacks on Jewish settlements, the situation Wingate's counterterrorist operations were intended to resolve.[82]

Haining was forced to admit, in his monthly Official Report for November 1938, that due to overstretch arising from the billeting of small detachments in villages and the need to meet these incessant small-scale attacks, he had cancelled all offensive operations and: 'The situation at this time was such that civil administration and control of the country was, for all practical purposes, non-existent. The number of troops in the country was still insufficient to do more than hold down the essential localities and communications.'[83] Stuart Emeny of the *News Chronicle*, who died in the same air crash as Wingate in 1944, reported that the British had lost control over Palestine outside Haifa and Tel Aviv.[84] Moreover, it was feared that the rebels were winning 'hearts and minds', Haining noting that:

> [T]he steadily increasing number of... incidents, and the damage and dislocation caused to government property and communications forbids their dismissal as trivial. They are, in fact, symptomatic of what is now a very deep-seated rebellious spirit throughout the whole Arab population, spurred on by the call of a Holy War. The rebel gangs have now acquired, by terrorist methods, such a hold over the mass of the population that it is not untrue to say that every Arab in the country is a potential enemy of the government... He dare not be otherwise, if called upon by the rebels to give his physical or financial aid to their cause.[85]

The Army was hampered further by circumstances. Firstly, the Munich crisis in September resulted in reinforcements earmarked for Palestine being held in England

and Egypt.[86] Secondly, and another echo of Iraq and Afghanistan after 2001, was the growing uselessness of the Palestine Police, resulting from widespread bribery and intimidation of its 1,500 Arab officers (out of a total strength of around 2,300), and from incompetence, insubordination, racism and crass, self-defeating brutality among its British elements, which, as noted already, included many former Black and Tans picking up from where they left off in Ireland.[87] From July to September 1938 there were widespread thefts of weapons from police stations, culminating in an attack on Beersheba police station on 9 September, when a British sergeant was killed and seventy-five rifles, a Lewis gun and 10,000 rounds of ammunition were stolen with no opposition from the Arab police whatsoever, and Haining commented that by October the Palestine Police was 'little more than an easy source of supply for rifles and ammunition to the rebels.'[88] On 12 September, Haining took the Palestine Police under his direct command, Tegart was summoned from England for further consultations, and the force was 'purged.'[89] The other response was to allow Wingate to raise the Night Squads, something he had been badgering GHQ in Jerusalem about for several months.

Jewish responses

Jewish action took two broad forms, overt and peaceful versus covert and aggressive. Despite Weizmann's aim, stated in 1919, 'To make Palestine as Jewish as England is English', the Zionist leadership aimed at reaching this goal organically via immigration and settlement under British protection. Weizmann and Ben-Gurion, then Chairman of the Jewish Agency, advocated initially a policy of *Havlagah*, or restraint, while looking for a political solution, believing that maintaining the moral high ground was essential to retain international sympathy.[90] Yet by 1939, Ben-Gurion, the Head of the Jewish Agency and *de facto* leader of Palestine's Jews, having had several peace overtures to the Arabs snubbed, was expressing in public the anti-Arabism and Islamophobia he had long nursed in private, stating that Islam was a 'violent doctrine', that Arabs were instinctively truculent and intolerant, and peace between the two peoples was impossible, while Weizmann originated a staple of Zionist propaganda, suggesting in public statements that Palestine was witnessing a struggle 'between the forces of the desert' on one side and 'the forces of civilisation' on the other.[91]

This had long been the stance of the most uncompromising Zionist leader of all, the Polish-born former British Army officer, Vladimir Jabotinsky, President of the New Zionist Organisation, known more commonly as the 'Revisionists'. Jabotinsky argued that it was a natural instinct for any native people to resist foreign settlement and so a violent clash between Arabs and Jews over the future of Palestine was inevitable. If Zionism was 'moral and just', then justice had to prevail, leaving Jews with no option but to build up an 'Iron Wall' of invincible military force to convince the Arab world of the futility of armed struggle, inducing more moderate voices to prevail and a permanent peace settlement to be reached.[92] Jabotinsky was an Anglophile, and his actions and correspondence indicate that he saw his 'Iron Wall' as an Anglo-Jewish project. In a memorandum he wrote to the Colonial Office in early 1937, he pressed for the *Haganah* to be legalised and placed under British command and training, and for the British to raise a Jewish Legion consisting of three infantry battalions recruited from Palestine and supplemented by volunteers from the Diaspora.[93] Ben-Gurion recalled Jabotinsky arguing persistently that all armed Jews in Palestine should be under British command, contradicting the policy of Ben-Gurion's own Labour movement, that the Jewish community in Palestine should retain control over its own defence policy and facilities.[94] Moreover, from 1936, the Revisionists maintained their own militia, *Irgun Bet*, a splinter group from the *Haganah* which slowly drifted out of even Jabotinsky's control and became the most violent Jewish group.[95] *Irgun Bet*, soon retitled the *Irgun Zva'i Leumi* (National Military Organisation), from 1937 initiated a terrorist campaign against Arabs and moderate Jews and demanded guerrilla warfare against the British, bringing condemnation from Ben-Gurion – who viewed them as a mixture of posturing adolescent radicals and outright fascists – and Jabotinsky, who was adamant there should be no action against Britain.[96]

Therefore, the Zionist leadership, Labour and Revisionist, accepted the possibility of escalating inter-communal violence before Wingate's arrival, and were taking steps to fight for their community on their own terms. This increased the importance of the *Haganah*. Although illegal, the British Army tolerated the *Haganah*'s existence and appreciated its military potential, as both Ben-Gurion and Jabotinsky were aware.[97] By 1938, it had 50,000 men under arms, was being financed extensively and efficiently by the *Kofer ha-Yishuv*, an unofficial (and illegal) tax paid by Palestine's Jewish population, which provided some 70 per cent of its funding, much of the other 30 per cent coming from donations raised by the International Zionist Organisation, and had offices overseeing strategy and training and intelligence and counter-intelligence departments more efficient than those of many states.[98] It was also well-armed: far from the 'few rook rifles' per settlement claimed by Mosley, by 1939 it had 6,000 rifles, 600 machine guns and 24,000 grenades.[99] Saul Avigur, who took over command of the *Haganah* in 1931, not only founded the offices mentioned already, but imposed a chain of command and a codified system of discipline (both frequently ignored in practice), as well as a training programme which may have influenced Wingate as much as he influenced it.[100] The *Haganah* took approximately 120 hours to turn a recruit into a trained man, the process involving drill, fieldcraft, weapons handling and small unit tactics, the latter often being instilled and tested via 'hikes', lengthy cross-country speed marches usually simulating rushing to the rescue of a beleaguered settlement, with practice ambushes and attacks along the way.[101]

Moreover, bolstered by the arrival of large numbers of male Jewish refugees with military experience, from the early 1930s the *Haganah* not only expanded, but became more offensively minded. Twelve-man *Nodedot* ('Wanderers') patrols were raised in some areas with the specific intention of manning defensive positions around Jewish majority urban neighbourhoods and settlements; by 1936, the *Nodedot*, which numbered 400 men, were operating in uniform and carrying out regular patrols, some on armoured lorries, in the hills around Jerusalem with the British Army usually looking the other way.[102] Local *Haganah* commanders pressured Ben-Gurion to authorise reprisal attacks from early 1936, and occasional unauthorised revenge attacks against Arab villages happened before Wingate's arrival.[103] The most aggressive *Haganah* commander was the former Russian Army sergeant-major, Yitzhak Sadeh, an advocate of pre-emption and reprisal since mid-1937, when he began ambushing Arab insurgents in the area around Jerusalem.[104] In late 1937, Sadeh was placed in command of an elite unit within the *Haganah*, the Field Companies, intended as a mobile strike force and better known by the Hebrew acronym FOSH. FOSH consisted of some 300 men, drawn mainly from the *Nodedot*, divided into six regional companies, but operating in platoon strength. Operationally, its activities centred on ambushing incoming insurgent gangs on the Palestine-Lebanon border and, occasionally, pre-emptive attacks on villages believed to be harbouring terrorists.[105] FOSH – whose members included Moshe Dayan, Yigal Allon and Yigal Yadin – therefore operated not only in the same period as Wingate's Night Squads, and in neighbouring areas, but also to a similar operational model.

Wingate and Anglo-Jewish cooperation

Not only were well-organised and armed Jewish militias going on the offensive before Wingate arrived in Palestine, but Anglo-Jewish military cooperation was also extensive before his arrival, Wingate being far from the only Zionist in the British Army. Haggai Eshed, the biographer of Reuven Shiloah, founder of *Mossad*, the Israeli Secret Service, has revealed the extent to which intelligence officers of the *Haganah* found sympathisers among their counterparts in the British Army and RAF, among them Captain Alan Strange, a strong critic of 'pro-Arab British policy' prior to Wingate's arrival, and Lieutenant Anthony Simonds.[106] Simonds, an officer of the Royal Berkshire Regiment, was to become a close friend of Wingate's and served under him in Ethiopia. He is often portrayed as an affable lightweight, taken seriously by neither the Jewish leadership nor his colleagues in the Army, and there is, indeed, a Wodehousian air to his correspondence with 'My Dear Old Orde'.[107] However, Simonds emerges from these same letters and his memoirs as a strong idealist, a natural sympathiser with 'underdogs', and a man who loathed any form of racialism; he pointedly lived in the Jewish quarter of Jerusalem, was critical of the rampant anti-Semitism in the Palestine Police, and was deemed worthy of cultivation by Shiloah himself as early as 1934; in his own words, 'My personal sympathies were with the Jews', with no further explanation required.[108] He was also regarded highly enough by his superiors to be placed in charge of all political intelligence in Palestine from August 1937, although still a subaltern, and by 1945 was a lieutenant colonel and senior operative of MI9, aiding the escape of shot-down Allied aircrew from occupied Europe.[109] There was, therefore, a body of vociferously pro-Jewish British officers serving in Palestine before Wingate's arrival.

Nor did the Army go as easy on the Arab insurgents as many suggest. Not only did Dill and his successors take the Army Council's initial instruction to 'crush' the rebellion very seriously, and argue consistently, on 'Callwellian/Simsonian' lines, for greater 'severity', but they were also prepared to enlist Jewish support for this.[110] In his first dispatch, of October 1936, Dill argued that: '"[D]efensive duties" and dispersal do not work, & repressive measures, including martial law, resulted in a decrease in violence in early September. Martial law would ensure that gang leaders were caught & punished, & the military could go on the offensive.'[111] This was necessary because of Arab 'national character'. '[T]he Arabs respect strength and regard forbearance as weakness, which they despise', Dill claiming that Arabs respected British authority most in those areas where measures were harshest.[112] Likewise, the Air Officer Commanding, Palestine and Transjordan, from 1938–39, Air Commodore Arthur Harris, advocated bombing rebel villages, as the RAF had done in Iraq and on the Northwest Frontier.[113]

It was perhaps inevitable that arming the Jews would be seen as part of this. Jews formed part of the Palestine Police and all of the irregular Supernumerary Police (JSP), which enlisted 3,000 volunteers between April and October 1936.[114] The JSP was confined initially to protecting settlements and sections of railway running through majority Jewish areas, but it is evident that Dill not only wanted to expand their numbers, but also to use them offensively against the insurgents.[115] Nor was he alone: the unnamed author (possibly Evetts) of the 'Military Lessons of the Arab Rebellion in Palestine' of 1938, advocated using a legalised *Haganah*:

> There is little doubt that in the end the authorities benefited by the subterranean defence organizations which their policy had forced underground, and it might perhaps have been better to have legalised and controlled at an earlier period the very natural activities which developed below the surface.[116]

Wauchope opposed this vociferously, writing to Dill in December 1936 that '[T]he formation of armed Jewish units, or offensive action by Jews against Arabs [w]as a grave danger to the future of this country' and to the Secretary of State for the Colonies, a month later, 'If Jewish units are allowed to act offensively against Arabs in Palestine, I fear the chances of the two people [sic] ever living together amicably will vanish for generations.'[117] The status of Jewish units was raised in a secret dispatch of 26 January 1937 from Wauchope to the Colonial Office, prompting a conference in London in March, involving Wauchope, the CIGS, Deverell, other senior service officers and representatives of the Foreign Office, aimed at fixing policy on these issues. The policy agreed is worth dwelling on, as it stood until 1939 and so provided the political context for Wingate's Night Squad operations. It was agreed to follow Wauchope's line that, prior to the imposition of military control, 'Jews should be employed for defensive purposes only, and only in areas mainly Jewish', restricting them to defending their own settlements: yet, they could receive appropriate training 'in limited numbers', pending their use for railway protection work.[118] However:

> Any such training should… be carried out with the utmost discretion, in order to avoid giving the impression… that His Majesty's Government already foresee that after the publication of their decisions upon the Report of the Royal Commission [the Peel Commission] a state of affairs will inevitably prevail in

which the forces of authority will be ranged against the Arab population. *As regards the employment of Jews even for defensive purposes in predominantly Moslem areas, it was agreed that this would be politically most undesirable.* [italics mine][119]

Once military control was authorised, decisions on the military employment of Jews would rest with the GOC, under the advice of the High Commissioner, who was authorised to report his objections to London if the GOC decided to employ Jewish units 'for purposes or in circumstances to which there might appear to be grave political objection.'[120] In particular:

It was... agreed that in view of the possibly serious reactions which might thereby be provoked in neighbouring Arab countries, the General Officer Commanding should not, in any circumstances, decide to use Jews for offensive purposes, without the prior authority of His Majesty's Government.[121]

'Offensive purposes' were never defined, and, in practice, what was offensive and what was not seemed to depend on the 'the senior officer present.' From March 1937, JSP were authorised to carry out 'hot pursuits' of fleeing gangs, and in summer that year they were placed formally under British Army command and training.[122] Ben-Gurion recalled that by then, both the Jews and the British Army accepted the JSP as 'legal *Haganah*' and the best available source of military training for young Jewish men.[123] Wingate, therefore, became involved in counterterrorist operations in Palestine at a time when Jewish militias and the British Army were already escalating the level of force used against the insurgents and beginning to cooperate in its application, even while theoretically constrained by British Government policy.

The genesis of the Special Night Squads

Intelligence in Palestine was the responsibility of the RAF Intelligence Organisation, Jerusalem, reporting directly to the GOC: it was established practice to attach an Army subaltern, such as Simonds, but unusual for a captain of fourteen years' service, like Wingate, to be assigned, and it is possible that this was arranged by Deverell.[124] The Intelligence Organisation operated up to six regional Special Service Officers (SSOs), whose duties were 'to procure information of a military, political and topographical nature and to keep in touch with the feeling in the country by touring their districts'; each SSO employed agents and was required to 'maintain close liaison with their district commissioner, police and... military commanders.'[125]

It was as an SSO that Wingate first visited Jewish settlements in Galilee, ordered by Wavell in February 1938 to discover the routes by which gun-runners were entering Palestine from Syria and Lebanon.[126] Wingate led several JSP patrols in April and May, carrying out unauthorised nighttime recces and setting ambushes on fords across the Jordan and tracks leading from them, and from this concluded that static ambushes were 'useless' under these circumstances, the maze of tracks leading from the Jordan combining with the sound of the river and civilian activity to mean that any successful ambush would be down to sheer luck.[127] More effective, Wingate opined, would be small but well-armed patrols who knew the ground sweeping known infiltration routes, as was practiced in the SDF. Wingate backed this up with action, and approached the local commander, Evetts, in early June proposing to raise specialist patrol units to secure the areas around the northern settlements at night.[128] An appreciation written on 5 June 1938 indicates that Wingate was firm that JSP should participate: units could be British, with Jewish policemen acting as guides and interpreters, or British-trained JSP, 'ideal for this task, as possessing expert local language both of area, and character and language of Arabs. There is ample evidence of their courage and they are intensely keen and eager to learn'; conversely, 'Arab police are useless, being both sympathetic towards, and in awe of, the gangs… Trust will become appropriate after, and not before, the Government has scotched the terror.'[129]

Wingate and Wavell

Wingate owed his success in getting his scheme implemented to his cultivation of Evetts and Wavell. Whatever any author's personal view of Wingate, there is consensus among all that he was a masterly practitioner of what later generations call 'networking': gaining the trust, patronage and, occasionally, protection of powerful figures, often going a long way outside the chain of command to do so. These would run eventually to the British Prime Minister and the American President, but the most long-term and significant was Wavell, who was willing to give Wingate his head as a military thinker and practitioner, and, as theatre commander, would summon him to East Africa in 1940 and Burma in 1942.

Wavell and Wingate seem to have been 'kindred spirits', the future Field Marshal having a lifelong predilection for irregular forces and fast-moving mobile warfare which he was sure was inherited, his father having commanded irregular forces in South Africa in the 1880s while a cousin raised an irregular corps of local Arabs to fight in East Africa in the First World War. Wavell himself had observed such forces at first hand: as a Brigadier, General Staff in the Middle East in 1917–18, he participated in the planning of Allenby's offensive into Palestine and the Levant, which saw cavalry used to 'turn' Turkish flanks, threaten their communications and seize objectives ahead of the main advance, with Lawrence's Arabs attacking deeper in the Turkish rear. In 1932, Wavell, now commanding 6th Infantry Brigade at Aldershot, oversaw experiments in mechanisation of infantry and its use in mobile operations. However, Wavell was no Liddell Hart, advocating victory through clever movement alone: rather, he saw increased mobility as the most efficient means of pursuing his view of strategy, 'the art of bringing forces to the battlefield in a favourable position', and so wearing down the enemy more cost-effectively. In particular, Wavell favoured the use of mobile and 'extraordinary' forces to induce the enemy to disperse, affecting his planning process, and shared with Callwell a belief that superior speed and mobility should be used to hit the enemy, by surprise, from unexpected directions. Wavell was struck particularly by the Red Army's large formations of parachute troops while observing their exercises on behalf of the British Army in 1936 (where he met the great Soviet advocate of 'deep operations', Marshal Mikhail Tukachevsky, and took a strong dislike to him) but felt that the perceived threat they posed was more significant than anything arising from their actual use, in that troops would be tied up protecting communications from potential airborne attack. However, this can be taken too far: Wavell can best be described as 'pragmatic' rather than 'maverick', in that he accepted the unorthodox and radical when he deemed it necessary, rejected it when not, for instance maintaining that the Infantry (which he always spelt with a capital 'I'), organised through the regimental system, should remain the backbone of the British Army, and his writings contain some criticism of the Army's tank zealots and the authors they were reading. Likewise, he was suspicious of 'Commandos' formed from volunteers, believing that existing units should receive specialist training and reorganisation, a view shared by Wingate.

Another popular Wingate myth has it that Wavell and Wingate first met when Wingate waved down and jumped into Wavell's car as the GOC was on a tour of inspection in Galilee and sold him the concept of the Night Squads in a short conversation as they drove around.[130] While in character for Wingate, the reality is that Wavell first encountered Wingate when he took over as GOC in 1937, Wingate serving already in the GHQ Intelligence Staff, had probably heard of him already via Sir Reginald, an old colleague from the First World War, and first met Wingate and Lorna for certain at a lunch given by the Weizmanns.[131] He left Palestine some time before Wingate formed the Night Squads, but 'carried away in a corner of my mind an impression of a notable character who might be valuable as a leader of unorthodox enterprise in war, if I should ever have need of one.'[132] Interestingly, when the future Conservative minister, Enoch Powell, jumped into Wingate's car in Cairo in 1943, pursuing a place on Wingate's staff for Operation *Thursday*, he was conspicuously unsuccessful.[133]

Evetts was also a fortuitous contact, being something of a rising star at the time. He had contributed majorly to the tactics which had defeated the larger guerrilla gangs, and his command of 16th Brigade had earned him several mentions in dispatches from Wavell, who told him 'I always felt perfectly happy as regards northern Palestine so long as I knew you were there.'[134] Evetts was to command a division in the invasion of Syria in 1941 and finish his career as a lieutenant general and first commandant of the missile testing facility at Woomera in Australia.[135] Wingate offered a solution for problems vexing Evetts since 1936. The rebellion entered its third phase – night-time terrorism by small bands – in March 1938 and the British response of village occupation and night-time patrolling of the surrounding countryside was proving of limited effectiveness. The official digest of lessons of the rebellion, of 1938 noted that:

> [A]ny engagement at night inevitably favoured an enemy who was usually met behind good cover in a carefully chosen position with a well-reconnoitred line of retreat behind him. To carry out offensive night operations of any extent was therefore to invite casualties from an opponent more at home at night than the

British soldier, whom night deprived of most of the advantages of his superior weapons.[136]

In his 1936 'doctrine', Evetts criticised British night-time tactics in a series of passages that apparently influenced Wingate's organisation and training for the Night Squads. He commented upon the standard reaction to coming under fire at night:

> There is a tendency at the moment for troops when sniped merely to return the fire with their rifles in the hope of silencing it. Such action is not only bad for training, morale and discipline, but in a very large number of cases is a waste of ammunition. Hostile night snipers...undoubtedly gain a moral uplift, a great deal of amusement, and practically no casualties from the bulk of our return rifle fire. In addition...unaimed rifle fire at night is likely to be a danger to our own troops and civilians...[137]

Evetts' solution came straight from 'hill warfare' – parties of picked men locating, outflanking and attacking ambush positions from higher ground, with cold steel if need be, Evetts agreeing with Callwell on the efficacy of the bayonet, for its terror effect and the lesser risk of British troops shooting each other in the dark:[138] 'The aim of infantry is to close with the enemy and kill him at short range with fire or the bayonet. This principle... if applied correctly will have far more effect on enemy snipers than hundreds of unaimed rounds at long range.'[139] Ambushes and snipers should, ideally, be dealt with by:

> [O]ffensive action of small patrols consisting of a few lightly clad men carrying the minimum of equipment necessary, and if possible wearing rubber-soled shoes, either in ambush positions or working around the flanks or rear of the snipers' positions.[140]

Despite Evetts' recommendations, the Army confined its night-time activities largely to ambushes or to using darkness to cover approach marches or the setting up of cordons.[141] Evetts had embarked on a programme of night-time fighting patrols in 16th Brigade, but this had been suspended temporarily prior to Wingate's arrival.

Wingate and the Haganah

While lobbying his superiors in the British Army, Wingate also made himself useful to the Jewish leadership. This began shortly after Wingate arrived in Haifa in September 1936, when, via Simonds, he met with David Ha'Cohen, a former officer in the Ottoman Army and now head of *Solel Boneh*, the Jewish national construction company engaged in building the Tegart line. Ha'Cohen was shocked when Wingate opined that the Old Testament was the only true authority on Zionism, and then launched a vitriolic attack on Islam and the Koran, claiming that the latter was almost entirely derivative of the Hebrew Scriptures.[142] Not only was this of questionable accuracy, but it challenged Weizmann's policy of showing respect for Islam and Arab culture, and even went beyond Jabotinsky's stated attitude of 'polite indifference' to Arabs who did not resist the creation of a Jewish state. The conversation ended with Wingate pledging his support for Zionism: 'Whether it is because of envy, ignorance and distorted teaching that the neighbouring people decided to fight you and your enterprise, and if because of "political calculations" they find supporters amongst my people – I shall fight with you against them all'.[143] Wingate met subsequently with Emanuel Wilenski, the *Haganah's* chief intelligence officer, who was harangued on the folly of restraint, Wingate echoing Jabotinsky – and what Ben-Gurion was saying in private – in arguing that Islam and Zionism were now at war, and what was required was the creation of a Jewish army, which Wingate would train and lead.[144] Although initially suspicious of a British intelligence officer and relative of Sir Reginald Wingate, Zionist leaders were gradually won over by Wingate's frequent visits to Jewish holy places and *kibbutzim*, his learning Hebrew, his enthusiasm for Jewish culture and, not least, by Lorna Wingate becoming an even more vehement Zionist than her husband.[145] However, the decisive factor in Wingate's cultivation of the Zionist leadership was his friendship with Weizmann, whom he first met at a reception at Government House in Jerusalem. Weizmann's position was by now one more of authority than actual power; the relationship between the Zionists and the British was now cooling, and the ascendancy of Ben-Gurion and the Jewish Agency meant that the relative power of the Zionist Presidency, Weizmann's office, was declining.[146] However, it was Weizmann who gained Wingate access to Ben-Gurion, most of the leaders of the Zionist Congress and the *Haganah*, connections which were to prove essential as Wingate set about his stated aim of creating Jewish military units.

In April 1938, still acting officially as an SSO, Wingate made an unannounced visit to the fortified settlement of Hanita (or Hanuta) with a letter of introduction from the Jewish Agency. It was the creation of Hanita, as part of the 'establishing facts' policy, a month before, which decided MacMichael on banning further settlement building without permission, Hanita being under continuous nightly attack, and the strain on police resources deciding MacMichael on the path he took.[147] JSP tactics in defending settlements from nighttime attacks were, for the period 1936-38, as desultory as those of the British; according to the official digest:

> The normal procedure in the almost nightly 'attacks' on Jewish colonies was somewhat as follows. The Arabs would take up positions behind suitable cover after dark from which they could fire at longish range. The first round would be the signal for the Supernumeraries to man their defence posts and open heavy rifle fire in the direction of the enemy, accompanied as a rule by Verey lights. For a short time a fire fight would go on during which targets would seldom be visible to either side and neither would move from their prepared cover. Eventually the Arabs, fearing the arrival of reinforcements and feeling that honour had been satisfied, would withdraw in the dark and return to their homes for the night's rest... Action of this type may sound very unenterprising,

but on the other hand it is difficult to see what else the Supernumeraries could have done with their small numbers and lack of tactical training.[148]

This was as much as they were allowed to do, officially. While the digest praised the determination of the JSP, it opined also that their poor training could make them a liability, their indiscriminate shooting making them a menace to British troops operating in the area, and their lack of formal organisation (seen as a virtue by many Jewish leaders) made coordination with them difficult.[149] The suggested solution echoed the Jabotinsky line on this issue: '[T]o organize and officer the Supernumeraries on the pattern of the regular police, and again, if possible, to place the whole police system under the commander of the military forces.'[150]

Wingate put this into practice, albeit unofficially, at Hanita. After giving a crash course in the relevant skills, he led several unauthorised patrols with Hanita's garrison of forty JSP, one of them crossing the border into Lebanon to survey a suspected terrorist safe house.[151] During this patrol, *Haganah*'s Zvi Brenner recalled, Wingate announced his aim of seeing the previous *Haganah* doctrine, static defence of settlements, replaced by one of pre-emptive action against the terrorists, 'near [their] villages' even if it meant crossing the border into Lebanon; he must still have been unaware of what the *Haganah* was planning at this time.[152] Mosley supplied a colourful account of this action, describing a raid on an unnamed Arab village in which five terrorists were killed and four captured. Wingate then allegedly tortured one of the prisoners to get him to disclose where the gang had hidden its weapons; when this failed, he ordered a Jewish policeman to kill him, to terrify the others into talking, this order being obeyed without question. Dayan and Brenner were also supposedly present when this happened, but Mosley, who interviewed both in the early 1950s, does not record an exact location or date, or even whether Wingate's interrogation techniques worked.[153] This story is not corroborated in any other source – Wingate's later biographer, Christopher Sykes, had the patrol pass uneventfully, its only significance stemming from the incursion into Lebanon – and, placed in the context of British policy in Palestine, takes upon a different significance to that attributed by Mosley and Sykes.[154] However, it is clear and unambiguous that Wingate had used Jewish police in an 'offensive' capacity in an Arab area, contravening British government policy. Shortly after, Wingate organised and commanded the defence of Hanita during a series of *Mujahedeen* attacks, after which the Jews finally trusted him fully.[155]

Wingate had concluded already that 'moving ambushes' of British troops and JSP, operating from Hanita and other Jewish settlements in northern Galilee, could combine with the Tegart Line to seal the frontier, but this model was eventually applied further south and in a situation of immense strategic importance to the British Empire. The point of interest here was the Iraq Petroleum Company's (IPC) pipeline, referred to in the American press as 'the carotid artery of the British Empire'. This was more than just hyperbole: opened after a decade of international wrangling in 1936, the pipeline carried oil the 600 miles from the oilfields around Kirkuk in Iraq to the major terminal at Haifa to the tune of four million tons a year, providing 5 per cent of the UK's domestic needs as well as fuelling a significant portion of the Royal Navy, including the entire Mediterranean Fleet; the pipeline was also supplying France's burgeoning oil industry, the French being partners in the IPC.[156] It was hardly surprising, then, that the pipeline became a major target for the rebels, *Fedaji* sabotaging it almost nightly from the beginning of the rebellion in 1936; no explosives were required, the best technique being to light a fire underneath the pipeline, retreat to a safe distance, puncture the pipeline with a rifle shot, then enjoy the fireworks.[157] The British tried to avert this by patrolling the pipeline with armoured cars and lorry-borne infantry, supplemented by machine-gun posts with searchlights, with JSP covering the final twenty miles on the coastal plain. The British found themselves in a situation analogous to that facing the Turks on the railway, described by Lawrence in his writings: it was impossible to cover the entire length of the pipeline and their patrols were of particularly limited use in the hilly area along the border with Syria, across which most of the well-trained volunteers from Iraq and Syria were infiltrating: the British Army concluded that attacks could be reduced, but not stopped altogether and that, 'In any case, cunning will be the essence of success, which can only be obtained by surprise, and to gain that troops must be prepared to go on and on night after night without any visible results if they are to collect their bag in the end.'[158]

Attacks escalated during phase three of the rebellion, the pipeline being breached in several places per night. Haining, nevertheless, took some convincing that Wingate's proposal would solve this. On 21 May, Wingate lunched with Weizmann and his wife, Vera, in Jerusalem and told them:

> ...[T]hat he had been thoroughly quizzed by Haining. He had come back from Hanita expecting to be reprimanded because of his long absence; but Haining merely asked what he had been doing there. He said he had been (illegally) "training the supernumeraries: the human material is excellent; they could easily defend themselves, and the sooner the better. Haining knew that Wavell had given tacit approval of some of Wingate's 'illegal' activities, and cross-examined him closely.[159]

It was probably on the strength of this 'cross-examination', Evetts' reputation and the severe overstretch of his more conventional forces that Haining became, temporarily, another Wingate backer. In May 1938, with MacMichael's sanction, Haining authorised Evetts and Wingate to train Jewish Supernumeraries to patrol the pipeline and for night time 'ambush work' in 16th Brigade's area.[160] A month later, an Army Order was issued allowing JSP throughout Palestine to patrol and ambush outside their settlements.[161]

The Evolution of the SNS

Wingate produced a written appreciation of 'the possibilities of night movements by armed forces of the Crown with the object of putting an end to terrorism in Northern

Palestine', on 5 June 1938. He began with his objective, 'To set up a system and undetected movement [sic] of troops and police by night, across country and into villages, surprising gangs, restoring confidence to peasants, and gaining government control of rural areas.'[162] He then stated why British forces had not achieved this, exposing his stance on a number of issues and suggesting a strong Evetts influence:

> It has been admitted by the civil authority that, on the approach of darkness, the virtual control of the country passes to the gangsters. In the dark they are free to visit villages without the smallest risk of any action being taken against them. They are free to move without danger anywhere... Neither police nor troops move by night as a general rule. When they do move it is usually by car and on the main roads. When ambushed in so doing, as is to be expected, the practice has been to return fire, a useless proceeding by night, and, after an exchange of shots, to allow the gangs to withdraw unpursued. Surprise has always been inflicted by the gangs, not by our forces, and such will continue to be the case so long as present methods are followed.[163]

Wingate's comments on the results of this are interesting, given allegations made against him by Mosley and Segev: 'The result of all this is that the gangs, who enjoy a warm bed as much as anyone, make a practice of visiting villages by night. *Here they oppress and terrorise the peasants in [a] manner which the Government could not rival even were its objective to do so.*' [Italics mine][164] His solution blended 'village occupation', Evetts' recommended night tactics and the guerrillas' own methods:

> There is only one way to deal with the situation; to persuade the gangs that, in their predatory raids, there is every chance of their running into a government gang which is determined to destroy them, not by an exchange of shots at a distance, but by bodily assault with bayonet and bomb... What is needed, therefore, is to produce in the minds of the rebels the conviction that the armed forces are able to move at night as freely and dispersedly [sic] as themselves, without their being able to obtain, as heretofore, previous knowledge of such movement, that whenever they enter a village to prey it is more than likely that they will be surprised there; that, even when they move across country by the most isolated tracks, they are liable suddenly to be attacked – not by a distant exchange of shots, from which little is to be feared, but by bodily encounter for which they are totally unfitted.[165]

Wingate echoed Callwell and Evetts in arguing that guerrillas were 'unfitted' for this kind of combat due to fear of cold steel:

> The rebels have shown that, while they are able to face attacks when occupying covered and previously prepared positions, they are quite unable to face any kind of charge or surprise onslaught. This is their character, and experience will not change it. In person they are feeble and their whole theory of war is to

cut and run. Like all ignorant and primitive people they are especially liable to panic.[166]

Lieutenant Rex King-Clark of the Manchester Regiment, who was to command a Night Squad and temporarily take over command of the whole organisation when Wingate was wounded at Dabburiya, went into greater detail:

> There were two main points that we learned very quickly on these shows: one was that it is practically impossible to hit anyone with rifle fire at night; and conversely that one is not likely to be hit. We, on several occasions, exchanged shots at point blank range without damage to either side: and secondly, the Arab, as long as he can previously prepare his position and line of retirement, can present a modicum of resistance, but that if completely surprised he is as lost as a child and runs around with his rifle and bandolier clasped firmly in his hand, and a bewildered look on his face, without making any real effort to escape or putting up any show of resistance... This particularly applies... to the armed villager, and, also, though to a much lesser extent, to what might be termed, the regular bandit.[167]

Observations by two very different officers touching on an original and common theme in Wingate's military thought: effective warfare should be dialectical, human-centred and designed to direct British strength in command, training and 'national character' against enemy weaknesses in these same areas, turning superiority in training, aggression and initiative into tactical advantages. Here, British troops and Jewish policemen were better educated and armed, and had the advantages of systematic training and coordinated command – '[T]hey know more about war than the gangs': consequently, it should be possible for purpose-trained 'government gangs' to defeat many times their number of disorganised and poorly-led insurgents.[168]

Wingate followed by recounting his early intelligence-gathering patrols, and lessons learned. The two most important were that, firstly, his 'government gangs' should be supported by an intelligence network capable of identifying bottlenecks in rebel routes of movement and supply, critical vulnerabilities upon which patrols could be concentrated, and that, secondly, the 'government gangs' should pay frequent visits to Arab villages, 'both arms and gangsters would be found there at times, and the Bedu would rapidly cease both to fear and to afford asylum to the gangs'.[169] Given that villagers would almost certainly detect and report the government gangs' presence to headmen, subtlety was pointless; far better to establish a strong presence, the better to impose British will upon the Arab population:

> [I]t is best to pay a visit to a village on the way home, waking up the Mukhtar [headman] and assembling a few villagers. It can be pointed out to them that terror by night will in future be exercised, where necessary, by [the] Government, whose forces are close to hand and able to visit any area at a moment's notice; that, consequently, failure to notify the presence of a gang will be regarded as

evidence of complicity, since the excuse of terrorism will no longer be valid... It is my belief that, once the Arabs believe the truth of such statements, it will not be long before cooperation is forthcoming.[170]

The counter-terrorist effort should centre upon 'ambush squads' consisting of ten men, an NCO and an officer, based not in an Arab village, as other British units were, but a Jewish settlement, the one base where they could be assured of safety between operations and from which information would not be leaked.[171] Several squads would be formed into a 'Night Movement Group', under the command of a single officer overseeing all training and recruitment, coordinating action with 16th Brigade, collating and disseminating intelligence, and operations.[172] Command responsibility should be devolved downwards due to the wide dispersal of sub-units, as Wingate realised in drawing up tasks for the Group commander. However, his aim was to 'coordinate all night movements from one centre which is in touch with all Government Intelligence Centres.'[173] Wingate was aware that counter-insurgent operations, more perhaps than any other type, are driven by intelligence. Details of his intelligence system, unfortunately, have not survived, but he made allusions in reports to using Arab guides and informers. Wingate, predictably, deemed these unreliable: indeed, he felt most intelligence reports were unreliable, and that more accurate predictions of insurgent activities might be had if he could learn the overall *intent* of the insurgent leadership in his area rather than details of the movements of individual gangs.[174]

Wingate established his headquarters and training centre at Ein Harod, in northeastern Palestine, near the border with Transjordan and covering the pipeline, in May; other detachments were stationed in Hanita and Ayelet Hashahar.[175] Evetts assigned to him thirty-six British soldiers from 16th Brigade under Lieutenant H.E.N. Bredin of the Royal Ulster Rifles, who was appointed second in command, Lieutenant Rex King-Clark of the 1st Manchesters and Second Lieutenant Michael Grove of the 2nd Royal West Kents. The remainder of Wingate's force consisted of eighty Jewish Supernumeraries, twenty-four of them *Haganah* members also, and the *Haganah* viewed this first unit as one of its own – *Plugot Ha'esh*, the unit of fire.[176] Officially, they were JSP under military command, and were referred to as 'SNS Police' in official correspondence.[177] They were, therefore, simultaneously members of the British security forces and the *Haganah*. There is little doubt that Wingate was aware of this and approved of it, so the Hebrew press's claims of a 'covenant' between Wingate and the *Yishuv* was probably only a mild exaggeration.

Yigal Eyal, the Israeli historian, argues that Wingate's arrival was a major boost to *Haganah* morale at a difficult time, and his influence was still being felt, via his trainees at Ein Harod, ten years later, in the War of Independence.[178] Wingate aimed at teaching tactical drills to ensure a rapid, consistent and reliable response when a terrorist gang was encountered by night.[179] This was instilled initially by unit drill, combined with individual training in weapons handling and fieldcraft from British corporals and sergeants. Wingate's objective, evidently, was to train the Supernumeraries as British infantrymen, with drill and guard mounting competitions and practice for falling out for orders being a regular part of life at Ein Harod.[180] Wingate's squad organisation reflected his faith in 'bayonet and bomb', each squad being divided into two five-man sections, trained to march in single file, led by a scout – often Wingate himself – some forty yards ahead, followed by two 'bombers' carrying ready grenades. Upon 'bumping' a gang, torch signals from the scout would tell the sections whether to adopt 'battle' (spearhead) or ambush formation.[181] A training memorandum Wingate produced in August 1938 indicates what happened next: a signal for 'ambush' formation would initiate a set sequence of events, beginning with the squad leader sending the bombers 100 yards up the track in the direction the gang was going; when the gang was level with the sections:

> Both squads run one behind the other alongside the enemy and each man chooses and bayonets one of the enemy. The leader fires one shot, and the two bombers throw their bombs forward on the track into the head of the enemy party, thus inducing further panic, and throwing the gang back on [their] attackers.[182]

Contrasting with previous British and Jewish reliance on sometimes indiscriminate area fire, there was to be strict fire discipline, 'When in doubt, don't fire. The initial order to fire will always be given by the squad leader.'[183] Much of the six-day Ein Harod training programme was given over to battle drills, bayonet and grenade training, and night exercises, with intensive 'dry' practice in daytime; however, as Jewish volunteers had other duties in the *kibbutz*, just five hours per day could be given to military training, something which Wingate may have failed to consider in assigning tasks subsequently.[184] King-Clark, who seems not to have known of the *Haganah*, described the Jewish volunteers as 'mostly tradesmen and professional men from Tel Aviv and Haifa', plus a few volunteers from the *Diaspora*, including at least one American, and repeated, throughout his diary, the opinion that their presence was not only politically risky, but their individualism, civilian habits, and lack of physical fitness were undermining the Squads' effectiveness; however, he did note that there were a few 'tough types', including a former sergeant from the Imperial German Army, who took to training quickly.[185] There were also cultural problems: British soldiers were under King's Regulations, but the Jews, as irregulars and mainly *kibbutzniks*, held numerous meetings and committees to investigate grievances; the absence of any formal disciplinary mechanisms meant that Wingate often resorted to punching or slapping erring Supernumeraries, a practice illegal (but still common) in the British Army.[186] However, even King-Clark conceded that the Supernumeraries' motivation was high, Wingate's success with them stemming from the strength of his personality and his ardent Zionism: 'An odd gentleman, but one of great determination and the courage of his convictions, no matter how much they may change from time to time'[187] Bredin recorded that while his British soldiers regarded Wingate as 'more or less round the bend' they also admired him for 'his courage, his energy, his undoubted brains and the fact that no obstacle ever deterred him', while 'he was regarded as related to the Almighty by the Jews, whose cause he so deeply supported.'[188] Allon – who did not serve with the Night Squads, but saw action with Sadeh and FOSH – recalled that Wingate 'regarded himself, in practice, as a member of the *Haganah*, and that was how we all saw him – as the comrade and, as we called him, "the Friend" *[Hayedid]*' and that Wingate and the *Haganah* viewed the SNS as another means of securing training from the British army.[189] Ya'akov Dori, the future chief of staff of the IDF, was a squadsman, and recalled Wingate opening a training course with:

> We are establishing here the foundation for the army of Zion… Difficult times have come, and all lovers of freedom must unite and prepare themselves to stand in the breach. Your people, whose friend I am, has suffered more than any other. If it fights, it will achieve its independence in its own land.[190]

Wingate not only disagreed with the British government policy of negotiated partition, but also now said so in public, albeit in Hebrew, perhaps so his British colleagues could not understand him.[191] Moreover, the *Haganah's* strategic agenda was different from the British: to them, the Night Squad role was to secure territory around Jewish settlements in Galilee – 'establishing facts' with military force.

The Night Squads go into action

A comprehensive system for night ambush work was devised with 16th Brigade's Headquarters. All ambush operations were to be directed by the Intelligence Cell at Nazareth, which allocated ambush areas to police and Army units; no ambushing could take place outside these areas, except by the Night Squads, unless cleared by the Intelligence Cell.[192] Wingate divided the pipeline into sections and assigned a Night Squad patrol to each: if they encountered a gang, a patrol was to let off a Verey light (a type of flare) to alert the other Squads so they could converge 'on the sound of the guns' or cut its line of retreat: at other times, he would position a Squad in static ambush while the others swept the pipeline.[193]

The Squads went into action on 3 June 1938, when a patrol, led by Wingate himself, scattered a group of *Fedayeen* on the pipeline, wounding two. On 11 June, two patrols surprised and chased *Fedayeen* into the village of Danna, and in the ensuing fight, two *Fedayeen* were killed, three wounded and six captured, an encouraging beginning.[194] On 14-15 June, Wingate produced a training memorandum, 'Principles Governing the Employment of Special Night Squads', in which he refined his ideas based upon the experience of these first patrols. He opened by reporting that the inhabitants of the area were now respecting curfews, and that the pipeline had not been damaged for a week, 'When four weeks have passed punctureless it will be time to claim that this result is due to the new method.'[195]

Once the area around the pipeline was pacified, the Night Squads should expand:

> [T]he guarding of this section of the line should be handed over to the supernumerary squads which have been trained by and have cooperated with the [Royal Ulster Rifles] squad. Should… subsequent measures be taken by

the Jama'iya [insurgent high command] in DAMASCUS for the renewal of the sabotage and the terrorism in this area, early news of their intentions should be obtained by Intelligence Centres, and, in the event of a strong rebel gang being sent into the area, one British Special Night Squad can be dispatched there to deal with it, with the help of the supernumeraries already operating there. Meanwhile, other SNS's [sic] will have begun to operate in other areas. Should they prove equally effective in combating terrorism the rebel HQ will have more than it can cope with. The general policy will be, therefore, gradually to open up all areas by night, making every use of the facilities afforded by police and supernumeraries...[196]

Wingate now saw the Squads as the kernel of a counterterrorist organisation covering the whole of Palestine, incorporating army, police and paramilitaries, with Jewish Supernumeraries at its core:

Jewish supernumeraries, especially those drawn from colonies are excellent material for our purpose... A British Night Squad, reinforced by two supernumerary squads, becomes three British Night Squads controlled by a British Officer. All squads are highly mobile, know the theatre of operations thoroughly, and contain members with a fluent knowledge of all three official languages.[197]

Wingate then resumed an old theme from the Sudan: the use of deception and superior mobility to unbalance the enemy and disrupt his decision making. He made no attempt to conceal his view that British officials and 'friendly' Arabs were leaking information to the insurgents, and believed this could be turned to the counter-insurgent forces' advantage:

It should be assumed that any move communicated to any Arab... will be passed on to those concerned. In practice this circumstance can be used by us to ensure the passage of information we wish to be passed... It should be assumed that any move previously communicated to several British officials, will, in one way or another become known to the rebels. The remedy is to tell no one the details, and the minimum of persons the general idea.[198]

Surprise moves were important not only for security, but also the sudden, unpredictable arrival of patrols in Arab areas would create a sense of Night Squad ubiquity: '[C]apital should be made of the fact that we have entered an area without a soul knowing, and that we are there to represent the force of the law.'[199] Surprise resulted from misinformation – as in Sudan – masking patrols behind police or army activity, or by having squadsmen leave a *kibbutz* individually by daylight, then rendezvous and arm themselves after dark.[200]

However, shortly after this, *Fedayeen* responded by shifting towards large numbers of simultaneous sabotage attacks by small parties or single saboteurs, which the Jews called 'pellets', and were harder to pin down and stop. Wingate's response was twofold.

Firstly, he acquired some machine-guns from 16th Brigade, and switched to combining patrols with small, static ambushes, a technique which killed enough would-be *Fedayeen* for attacks on the pipeline to cease altogether.[201] Secondly, and more controversially, he set out to dominate the area around the pipeline via pre-emptive raids, using Jewish fighters in majority Arab areas in an apparent contravention of official policy. On the night of 11/12 June 1938, Wingate personally led a raid, consisting of three squads, on the village of Jurdieh, on the Palestine-Lebanon border; not only was he unequivocal that his aim was to 'destroy' a gang reported to sleep there, but he took the raiding force through Lebanon to hit it from the rear; two insurgents were killed, and Sykes reported that the Arab headman at Jurdieh then asked his Jewish opposite number at Hanita for a truce.[202] The Night Squads switched increasingly to this kind of activity from July, Wingate arguing that the sudden, unpredictable arrival of army and police patrols in Arab areas would create a sense of Night Squad ubiquity: [C]apital should be made of the fact that we have entered an area without a soul knowing, and that we are there to represent the force of the law.'[203] These 'visits' were, he claimed, producing the desired mindset in the local Arab populace:

> These mysterious appearances and disappearances have already proved to have a powerful effect on the minds of peasants and gangsters on the pipeline. They have resulted in curfew being kept in villages and Bedu encampments where there are no roads.[204]

King-Clark disagreed with this policy from the beginning, recording in his diary: 'I don't imagine the Arabs are going to enjoy having a bunch of Jews wandering through their villages at night, as I feel certain the latter will not let slip any opportunity of inflicting damage on persons or property that may arise.'[205] He was also rather less than flattering in his description of the Squads' early operations, which he recalled as:

> [F]orced marches to the scenes of many fires… with bursting lungs and aching legs over ground which invariably seems to include a field of waist-high and very sharp thorns, followed up with what we hoped would be a lightning raid on the nearest and most likely village – which always seemed to be at the top of the highest hill in the vicinity – where we put the Mukhtar in the picture and told him what fine fellows we were and how uncomfortable it would be for him if he allowed such nonsense as the burning of crops to continue.[206]

All this seems understated, presuming one accepts Segev's allegation that these 'visits' were actually brutal, sometimes murderous, reprisal attacks. Segev's main sources are the memoirs of one of Wingate's Jewish squadsmen, Tzion Cohen, and the testimony of two others, Chaim Levakow and one identified only as 'Schlomo', and he also extracts *Haganah* reports, one by Allon.[207] Segev began by quoting Cohen:

> We would get close to a village where the oil pipeline had been sabotaged. We'd wait there until dawn and then enter the village, rounding up all the men and

forcing them to stand with their faces to the wall and their hands behind their backs. Wingate and his Englishmen would inflict the punishment because he did not wish to fan the Arab's hatred for us.' Cohen was referring to whip lashings on the villagers' bare backs... First, Wingate would stand on a rock and give the villagers a scolding in broken Arabic. As time went on, Tzion Cohen wrote, the punishments became more severe. Sometimes Wingate would make the villagers smear mud and oil on their faces. On occasion he would shoot and kill them.[208]

According to Ben-Gurion, many Jews were unhappy about developments in Galilee: some *Haganah* officers objected to Wingate's methods because 'an offensive against the terrorists might disturb the neighbourly relations between Jewish settlements and Arab villages' and on another occasion, representatives of Galilee settlements were reprimanded by the Jewish Agency after complaining to them about Wingate.[209] However, on 17 June 1938, following complaints from Arab headmen, the local District Commissioner told Wingate that 'indiscriminate searches' of Arab villages by Jewish police must cease.[210] Whether these complaints arose from fear of Wingate or of *Mujahedeen* reprisals for having Jews in their village is unclear. A discussion of Segev's sources will follow, but there is similar and more reliable, if less shocking, testimony from others. Brenner, who otherwise idolised Wingate, recounted that Wingate forced suspects to swallow oil-soaked sand as part of an interrogation; King-Clark alluded to an incident on 28 June 1938, when Corporal Fred Howbrook of the 1st Manchesters drew his revolver to threaten a man whom he believed had a concealed weapon; a scuffle ensued, and Howbrook accidentally shot another man.[211] There seems to have been general concern over the 16th Brigade's conduct of operations from senior British commanders. In November 1938 – shortly after Wingate's departure from Galilee – Major General Richard O'Connor, commanding 6th Infantry Division in southern Palestine, wrote to his wife:

> There is definitely a certain degree of Black & Tan methods about the Police... I have issued stringent orders against harshness & unnecessary violence on the part of our own soldiers & I am sure they will be obeyed apart from the odd few, who there will always be. *Jack Evetts has always (between ourselves) encouraged his men to be brutal, as being in the end more humane. I disagree with him over this* [Italics mine].[212]

In December 1938, Haining wrote to O'Connor and Major General Bernard Montgomery, warning:

> Unnecessary violence, vindictiveness which is un-British; killing in cold blood, are incidents on which there must be no doubt as to our and the Army's attitude; and defections from the standard we must adopt must be thoroughly investigated and, if proved, punished in exemplary manner.[213]

O'Connor's copy had a covering note from Evetts saying the warning was 'mainly for Monty', Evetts' and Wingate's divisional commander.[214]

Wingate's 'ruthlessness' will be discussed below. Suffice to say at this stage, the ban on village searches seems to have prompted a change in operational method. Wingate closed his second paper by resuming the argument that aggressive night-time patrolling should become the basis of British counter-rebel strategy, directed by a specialist headquarters:

> I believe that the night raid carried out by squads armed with bomb and bayonet and seeking opportunity to assault the enemy, and directed from a centre in touch with all information in the hands of Government and able to command the support of the civil authority and police, will succeed in reverting the state of affairs in the rural areas and turn the tables on the gangs.[215]

Wingate's frequent substitution, in this and other passages in this paper, of the word 'patrol' with 'raid' was perhaps subconscious, but it is notable that he was soon becoming more aggressive tactically and operationally. Patrols were escalated, Wingate ordering King-Clark to take another into Lebanon on 22 June.[216] Ambush patrols on the pipeline continued throughout late June, a Royal West Kents Squad ambushing an insurgent gang on 19 June, killing four.[217]

Escalation

Night Squad operations soon extended to pre-emptive attacks on *Mujahedeen* assembly areas involving several patrols acting in combination, exemplified by the action at the village of Dabburiya on 10/11 July. These involved the very methods of envelopment Wingate had scorned a decade earlier, the standard deployment involving Squads being lorried to widely dispersed locations, from which they would then converge upon the objective: this led to a potentially lethal breakdown in command and control at Dabburiya.[218] The first such action took place at Kaukab el Hawa a few days before Dabburiya, and in response to this, and to the success of the Night Squads on the pipeline, *Mujahedeen* raided Nazareth, murdering several Arab 'collaborators'. Wingate's intelligence sources reported this force as regrouping in the area between Ein Mahil and Dabburiya and in his report on the Dabburiya action he stated unambiguously that his aim was, once again, 'to find and destroy' the gang, a major escalation from 'ambush work' near the pipeline.[219] Not only did this contradict the agreed policy of not using Jewish units for offensive operations in Arab or disputed areas, but is unclear whether Wingate had the authority to do it and if so, from whom.

MacMichael sent a report on the employment of Jewish units to the new Colonial Secretary, Malcolm MacDonald, on 2 July, in which he stated that the principles agreed in the March 1937 meeting had 'been consistently followed throughout the disturbances up to the present time. That is to say that although Jewish supernumerary policemen have now been raised to about 5500… they have been employed mainly in the static and passive defence of Jewish settlements, areas and enterprises.'[220] However, different situations necessitated different responses: hence, in some areas,

the JSP were authorised to patrol the areas around their settlements, and they were also employed in protecting railways and workers constructing the Tegart Line.[221]
Most significantly:

> I have also sanctioned the employment of a small column of Jews and British troops operating under the command of a British military officer in Galilee both to afford better protection for the pipeline and also when occasion demands for ambush work in Galilee generally and in particular on the northern frontier which in its present state is very liable to attacks from foreigners from the Lebanon.[222]

MacMichael reiterated that the broad principle of using Jews defensively had been obeyed and that:

> I should like, at the same time, to emphasise that in every case the modifications have been dictated by reasons of utilitarian expediency and not at all by political or psychological considerations. In short, Government have confined the role of armed Jews to one of passive defence as opposed to active aggression... I can conceive of no circumstances in which I could approve the employment of armed Jews whether in small or large bodies as a political gesture...[223]

MacDonald concurred with the continuation of existing policy and stated that he was 'fully prepared to support the use of Jewish supernumerary police for defensive purposes.' However: 'I note that a small column of Jews and British troops is being employed on operations in Galilee, including (on occasion) "ambush work". I assume that "ambush work" can properly be regarded as falling within the category of defensive or protective operations?'[224] Wingate's interpretation of 'defensive' and 'protective' was already deviating from this, and extended eventually to pre-emptive raids – offensive operationally and tactically – using Jewish fighters in majority Arab areas, beginning at Dabburiya, which was also one of the largest of such actions.

The raid on Dabburiya saw Wingate deploy four 'cutoff' patrols in an arc south of the village while he led an assault from the north; the operation fell victim to 'friction', much of it due to the inexperience of Wingate's troops. Wingate was hit three times by fire from his own side, and of the six Night Squad casualties sustained at Dabburiya, four were to friendly fire. Ten insurgents were reported killed, and four bodies were recovered the following morning.[225] For this action, Wingate received the Distinguished Service Order (DSO), a British decoration awarded for exceptional leadership under fire by an officer commanding a company-sized force or larger; given that this would need to be approved by both Evetts and Haining, this indicates perhaps that Wingate's interpretation of 'defensive' and 'protective' and theirs concurred at this time, if not later on, and that the Army had little objection to using Jewish police on such operations. Wingate viewed Dabburiya as further vindication of his ideas:

> We learned... that however unpleasant it may be for the enemy, village fighting by night is both dangerous and difficult. The difficulty of knowing what is

happening is increased. More deliberation and care is called for than is suitable for an encounter in the open. All this is obvious but the personnel concerned have now learned it. Although none of the officers commanding squads had seen the country they were operating in before, no one got lost, late or made a mistake. This... proves that such operations at night by infantry are perfectly practicable.[226]

In fact, mistakes were made, people did get lost, and Dabburiya opens two recurring issues: firstly, whether Wingate sometimes set his troops tasks too ambitious for their level of training; and secondly, a propensity for his account of events to differ drastically from that of everybody else involved. Bredin recalled in a 1969 interview that Wingate 'appeared to regard his soldiers as automatons... He had no truck with those who failed, whether through laziness, ignorance and weakness.'[227] This may have blinded him to his leading a unit consisting largely of part-timers, many with little previous military experience, stiffened by a small number of regulars having to communicate with them via interpreters and themselves deemed by their senior commanders to be weak in night-fighting. Indeed, contradicting the popular view of the Night Squads as a largely Jewish affair, Bredin had his Ulster Riflemen do most of the 'operational work' within his squads, with JSP coming on patrols largely for 'on the job' training, 'their training was what interested Wingate most.'[228] This consisted of a few days of part-time instruction, after which a recruit would be sent on his first patrol, three weeks of this being deemed adequate to produce a squadsman.[229] Yet, the 'hammer and anvil' tactics Wingate used at Dabburiya required high standards of fieldcraft, skill-at-arms and discipline: King-Clark had anticipated previously that the Jewish squadsmens' hasty training and lack of experience, and the confusion of night operations, could lead to a 'friendly fire' incident, and Dabburiya ('a cock-up of the first water') proved him right.[230]

Three things seem to have gone wrong at Dabburiya. Three sections, commanded by Wingate, King-Clark and Grove respectively, were dropped by lorry at different points around the village, the motor-transport section then moving off to a holding position to the south. King-Clark's section soon got lost in the dark and took no part in the fighting, although he heard '45 minutes of sporadic fire' coming from the direction of Dabburiya, contrasting with the epic battle recounted in Wingate's report.[231] Grove's section advanced towards Dabburiya too quickly, engaging in a firefight with the terrorists before the main assault was scheduled and firing a Verey light to alert the rest of the force, but also alerting the rest of the terrorist gang. Wingate was hit when he engaged a group of terrorists on the southern edge of the village, the motor transport section seeing this and, thinking they themselves were under fire, firing on the general area in which Wingate was engaged with their section machine gun.[232] For the first but not the last time, Wingate 'spun' a potentially embarrassing situation, claiming in his report that 'the unexpected appearance from the blue of three successive squads in answer to Lt Grove's [Verey light] must have alarmed the rebels' and possibly changed the course of the battle.[233] Yet it seems that the Dabburiya battle had the desired strategic effect: King-Clark took over command of the Night Squads while Wingate was recuperating from his wounds, and reported that its patrols encountered not one single guerrilla throughout the entire second half of July, nor were there any attacks on the pipeline.[234]

Wingate's Dabburiya report was one of several official documents he produced while recuperating. The report suggests that the escalation to attacking suspected terrorist bases rather than just monitoring them was rooted in a hardening attitude towards the Arab population, and was calculated to intimidate:

> The Mukhtars and villagers... represent themselves as unwilling victims of terrorism. The truth is, as my recent experiences have shown, that in these remote rural areas every fellah is a potential gangster. So long as he thinks he can escape punishment for complicity this state of affairs will continue... [T]he attack on Government and the Jews is regarded with general approval by Moslem peasants who have, hitherto, experienced little difficulty in persuading the Government of their comparitive [sic] innocence of crimes committed in their vicinity, but, in reality, by themselves. I attribute the cessation of sabotage on the pipeline not to any change in this direction, but to the experience that anyone hanging about the line for an unlawful purpose was liable swiftly and silently to vanish away.[235]

From a memorandum on the development of the Night Squads, produced at the same time, Wingate argued that they should expand to over 200 from their existing strength of 90-100, with 150 more Jewish police, enlisted for the duration of hostilities, and more British personnel drawn from 16th Brigade.[236] Another long-term source of friction emerged, Wingate simply expecting the Army to produce whatever resources he demanded, regardless of actual availability: 'I will obtain the necessary transport from Jewish sources. For its use, the Government will pay, on claims presented by me. It will be dirt cheap.'[237] He was dismissive of dissent, particularly those claiming the employment of Jewish police on offensive operations in an Arab area would be counter-productive:

> Personally I think that the alleged trouble caused by their use as Supernumeraries is a pure myth, finding its origin in the hostile imagination of various Arab functionaries. There would not appear to be the slightest foundation in fact for the view that a single additional shot has been fired which can be attributed to the use of supernumeraries. Quite the reverse is the fact. Were it not for the success attending the operations of Jewish supernumeraries there is evidence that many more determined attacks would have been made upon colonies. If the Arab 'indignation' at the use by Government of loyal supernumeraries to prevent sabotage on the pipeline takes the form of a cessation of this sabotage, it would seem we want more of it...[238]

Wingate closed this passage by defending the new, pre-emptive strategy: '[S]abotage ceased purely owing to the offensive, not the defensive measures I have taken. So long as I confined myself to the line sabotage increased...'[239] Wingate, therefore, identified his operations unambiguously as 'offensive' in official correspondence and was open about the role of Jewish supernumeraries in them. Moreover, from Dabburiya onwards, Wingate prioritised such pre-emptive actions, involving the entire force acting in concert.[240] Allon recalled that some of these actions involved cooperation with Sadeh and FOSH; although Allon did not specify which, this is consistent with Wingate's and the Jewish Agency's viewing the Night Squads as part of the *Haganah* and the kernel of a Jewish army.[241] Concurrently, Wingate pressed Evetts and the *Haganah* to increase both the size and the firepower of the Squads; this was refused, but King-Clark noted that the basis for Wingate's new doctrine was a surreptitious increase in the number of Jewish volunteers at Ein Harod, so that Jewish soldiers began to outnumber British substantially. Moreover, Wingate apparently had official approval if not outright backing. In his official dispatch to London of 24 August 1938, Haining – despite any private misgivings he may have had – wrote:

> I cannot speak too highly... of *the Special Night Squads that have been organized by both brigades for offensive Night work*. These Night Squads have done particularly valuable work in southern GALILEE in protecting the I.P.C. pipeline. In this area they have been organized and trained by Captain O.C. WINGATE, Royal Artillery, from my Staff, who has shown great resource, enterprise and courage in leading and controlling their activities. *These Squads have been supplemented by Jewish supernumeraries who have done excellent work in combination with the British personnel*. The story of the inception and gradual development of this form of activity, and its successful results, provide a great tribute to the initiative and ingenuity of all concerned. The constant presence of the Night Squads on and about the pipeline is now a rarity instead of a nightly occurrence. There is no doubt that the innumerable small engagements resulting from ambushes... have caused considerably more casualties among the enemy than is officially known. [Italics mine throughout][242]

Another admirer was Harris, who commented that the best anti-rebel work in Palestine was 'done by "special" night squads (very secret) composed of a selected officer and up to say thirty mixed volunteer soldiers and sworn in local (mostly Jew) toughs'; Harris felt that such a gendarmerie was 'what is really lacking in the internal security provisions locally.'[243] In an official report of September 1938, Evetts argued that all three brigades in 8th Division should form night squads, and stated that he had allowed Wingate to forward to Haining a proposed Night Squad structure for the whole of Palestine.[244]

Moreover, from this time, Jewish participation in counter-terrorism expanded, in reaction to overstretch among British units and the collapse of the Arab police. Needless to say this has been largely overlooked in previous works on Wingate, possibly because it does not suit the myth-makers. 14th Brigade, south of 16th Brigade's operational area, organised night squads of its own, although what role their Jewish supernumeraries performed, if any, is unclear. Another combined

British-JSP night squad was raised in southern Palestine to protect the Palestine Electric Corporation's line from Zichron Ya'akov to Rosh Ha'ayin, another favourite *Fedayeen* target.[245] From July, JSP mobile patrols (*Manim* in Hebrew) were organised to protect sensitive areas; by spring 1939 there were sixty-two 8-10 man patrols, and the *Manim* had exclusive responsibility for covering the Haifa-Lydda railway: each *Manim* company had a Jewish second-in-command nominated by the Jewish Agency, therefore, by the *Haganah*.[246] On 11 September 1938, MacMichael granted Haining authority to attach 200 JSP to army units on six-month contracts:

> They... would be payed [sic] clothed and armed by the Police Department but they would be attached permanently to British military units and would to all intents be part of those units. Their duties would be essentially protective namely to provide escorts and detachments in cases where the use of troops would be uneconomical...[247]

The Night Squads by now formed a more thoroughly trained and experienced force, as demonstrated by a dawn raid on an insurgent-held village near Afula in early September. Wingate had, post-Dabburiya, devised new tactical drills developing Evetts' technique of drawing a gang into the open via tempting them into engaging an apparently 'soft' target; this was aimed specifically at guerrillas occupying villages and was therefore explicitly pro-active and offensive. Wingate trained his squadsmen to gradually encircle a village, concentrating on setting ambushes on likely exits: once the village was surrounded, they should signal their presence with noise and Verey lights, so inducing the guerrillas to try and break out, whereupon they would be ambushed by 'bayonet and bomb' along their escape routes.[248] At Afula, Wingate placed a cordon of sixty men around the village during the night and, at dawn, sent a truck with six armed squadsmen hidden in the back into the village, under the guise of a Jewish settlement truck which had lost its way. Bredin recalled:

> It worked like a dream. Men came running out and started firing. The drivers of the truck leapt out, staggered to the side of the road as though they were cold meat. This brought the eager Arabs – 40 or 50 of them – further into the open... When the Arabs were in full sight, our men closed in. One or two of the Arabs tried to gallop off but were shot down. I and [a] few men chased a small group who got through our net. They were going fast towards Mount Gilboa. To overtake them, all but one of us ditched our weapons and, as we ran, we passed the remaining rifle to one another like a baton in a relay race.[249]

Haining praised a later Night Squad raid in his November dispatch, again not concealing its offensive aim: 'Perhaps the most dramatic [action] of all was the Night action at KAFR LIDD... where five special Night Squads surrounded a gang resting in the village, killing fourteen and capturing two, together with some important documents.'[250] As of the summer and autumn of 1938, the Night Squads, far from the aberration that some of Wingate's biographers try to present, were an integral and valued part of Britain's counterinsurgent strategy in Palestine, and carrying out a growingly offensive role.

Indeed, it was apparently with official approval that the Night Squads graduated to the next and most controversial stage – reprisal attacks. Given the reactive, intelligence-driven nature of these operations, they were often executed rapidly and on Wingate's own initiative, and there are indications that participants sometimes let rage triumph over discipline. The first such action resulted when Chaim Schturman, a veteran Zionist, head of the Ein Harod settlement and a friend of Wingate's, was killed by a mine in mid-September. There are conflicting versions of what happened next. One is that Wingate tracked down and destroyed the *Fedayeen* gang which laid the mine in an ambush in the open countryside.[251] The other is that, within hours, Wingate raided the nearby Arab village of Beit Shean (or Beisan), issuing orders to round up all suspected rebels and shoot those trying to escape. Brenner recalled:

> Without any plan of action or any preparation, with Wingate at our head, we entered the Arab part of Beit Shean, which swarmed with gang members, and began to beat and trample anyone in our path. Wingate himself went out of control, entering stores and destroying whatever was in them...[252]

At least two were killed, but Sykes claimed that accounts of this incident were later exaggerated by the insurgents for propaganda purposes; Brenner recalled Wingate suffering pangs of guilt after the Beat Shean incident, assembling the Night Squads and giving a lecture against collective punishment – British Army policy at the time – and being angered greatly when the pro-rebel headman of Tantura was shot dead while trying to escape on a later operation.[253]

The next large operation, in which all previous elements drew together, was launched in reaction to a major terrorist atrocity at Tiberias on 2 October 1938. A large *Mujahedeen* gang, many apparently high on hashish, entered Tiberias on the Dead Sea coast and murdered nineteen Jews, eleven of them children in a nursery who had their throats slit before being set alight: the death toll may have been higher had the raiders not given themselves over to looting. The attack was a political disaster for the British, as the battalion garrisoning Tiberias, the 1st South Staffords, did not intervene, some of its soldiers being trapped in their barracks by Arab machine-gunners, while others in the town hid until the shooting stopped (some, purportedly, under tables in a favourite restaurant).[254] Wingate quickly redeployed two squads covering another village and ambushed the gang on its way out of Tiberias, killing at least forty; the Night Squads were the only British unit to engage the Tiberias gang, and Wingate moved outside of 16th Brigade's operational area, without orders or authority, to do so. On 3 October, the Night Squads caught the remainder of the gang between Dabburiya and Mount Tabor, and in a combined attack with the RAF, killed another fourteen.[255] Fortuitously, the new GOC Middle East, General Sir Edmund Ironside, was touring Palestine, and rushed to Tiberias upon hearing of the attack, coming across the aftermath of Wingate's ambush. Ironside noted Wingate's name as one to remember, and subsequently became another patron.[256]

After Wingate

By October 1938, Wingate was showing signs of mental and physical exhaustion, and shortly after the Tiberias incident, returned to Britain on leave. In November 1938, the rebellion entered *Phase Four*, the Army resuming large-scale offensive operations against the insurgents while the British government sought to enforce a political solution. Following the Munich conference, Britain (prematurely) ceased viewing Germany and Italy as threats to her interests in the Middle East, while attempts to resolve the revolt peacefully broke down over disagreements over the Balfour Declaration and the Mandate and the British Government's refusal to negotiate with terrorists.[257] The release of units held back for home defence allowed the British a more aggressive strategy than in the previous ten months, encouraged by the desperate state the guerrillas had reached by this time. Terrorism turned the rural Arab population against them from a combination of weariness at constant village searches, curfews and other restrictions and also the large criminal element among the guerrillas using the rebellion as cover for drug and weapon smuggling and protection rackets extorting primarily from the very Arab peasants they claimed to be 'liberating.'[258] By the end of 1938, a new factor had emerged – Arab vigilante gangs, attacking the insurgents in revenge for previous atrocities; the first of these 'peace gangs' was formed at Jenin by Fakhri Abdul Hadi, who had led guerrillas against the British in 1936, an indicator of how quickly the rebellion was imploding.[259]

The other major factor was the arrival in Northern Palestine of the British Army's most capable and ruthless senior commander, Major General Bernard Montgomery, assuming command of 8th Division, including 16th Brigade, in December 1938. Montgomery's favoured pattern of operations could have been lifted straight from Callwell or Simson: the British were 'definitely at war' and any return to civilian control could only follow the complete destruction of the rebels in battle.[260] There was a resumption of cordon and sweep operations by mobile columns, with the specific aim of killing insurgents, and greater use than before of night-time raids on villages suspected of harbouring guerrillas, now involving all units, not just the Night Squads. Montgomery singled out 16th Brigade for particular praise – 'Jack Evetts require[s] no urging in this respect! During the ten days ending today we have killed a hundred in my divisional areas…'[261] – this at a time when O'Connor, Monty's counterpart in southern Palestine, was expressing disquiet about Evetts' methods. On 1 January 1939, Montgomery reported that the rebel gangs were breaking down into small groups, their activities limited to sniping or sabotage.[262]

That the Night Squads were 'suppressed' immediately after Wingate's departure from Palestine is another myth. The reality is that they were active in Montgomery's operations well into 1939: in May 1939, 16th Brigade reported that Night Squad activity meant that gangs were no longer operating from villages, and were therefore cut off from their main sanctuaries and sources of supply: however, locating the gangs was now becoming more difficult, and more night ambush work was the solution, 'A few highly trained night squads and ambush patrols can have greater moral and material effect than columns.'[263] Some of this evidently involved the 'peace gangs', a 'special platoon' of the 2nd Leicesters cooperating with 'pro-government' Arabs from autumn 1939.[264] Contrary to much of the literature, not only did the Night Squads survive Wingate's departure from Palestine, but use of the method expanded. As the idea of using a 'third force' preceded Wingate's arrival, so it continued after his departure.

Whatever the benefits of the method, involving Jews in applying it was now a major issue, and it was now that Wingate became the political embarrassment his biographers depict. He arrived in London just as the Royal Commission set up by the British government the year before under the chairmanship of Sir John Woodhead, aimed at producing a plan for the partition of Palestine agreeable to both communities, published its report.[265] Woodhead recommended a truncated Jewish state, minus Galilee and the Negev, with Jerusalem to remain under the Mandate, and a ban on any further Jewish immigration. The report was endorsed by MacDonald when introduced to Parliament in November 1938. Despite the Woodhead Report now, effectively, being government policy, Wingate aimed to get it rejected, boldness indeed from a serving Army captain. His main tool was an alternative partition plan, devised by himself, Weizmann, and Ben-Gurion, in which the Jews would surrender Galilee and Haifa in return for taking full possession of the rest of Palestine from Tel Aviv down to Aqaba. Wingate discussed this with Lord Lloyd, the former High Commissioner in Egypt and President of the British Council, with whom he lunched with Weizmann and Ben-Gurion on 28 October 1938.[266] Lloyd agreed to submit the plan – a Jewish state completely absorbing Transjordan and differing radically from the Woodhead proposals – to 'some of his Arab friends', and to MacDonald, minus Wingate's calls for a Jewish army.[267] Wingate obtained a more sympathetic hearing from the Conservative MP, Zionist, anti-appeaser and former minister, Leo Amery, who became a lifelong supporter. Amery's diary entry of 4 November 1938 gives an interesting first-hand account of Wingate's attitudes at the time:

> He gave me a pitiful story of the feebleness, timidity and actual cowardice of the Palestine administration in the face of Arab terrorism. Even Haining, who on the whole has backed him, is afraid for political reasons to police the Palestine-Trans-Jordan frontier with anything except the [Transjordan] Frontier Force which is Arab and makes no real attempt to prevent the smuggling of arms.[268]

The most prominent contacts Wingate made in this period were Basil Liddell Hart and Winston Churchill. Liddell Hart was acquainted with Weizmann, Ben-Gurion and Amery, and was perhaps aware of Wingate and the Night Squads already. Wingate presented Liddell Hart with copies of a number of his training papers and reports – now held in the Liddell Hart Centre for Military Archives at King's College, London – and on 11 November 1938, Liddell Hart produced a letter of introduction to Churchill, in which he described Wingate, ironically, as having a 'Lawrence-like role' in Palestine, but – almost certainly parroting Wingate's own views – claimed Wingate was 'hampered by the hesitation of politicals out there to give permission for the expansion of the special force to an adequate role'; he included copies of Wingate's papers 'likely to interest your military mind.'[269] Wingate seems to have first met Churchill not through this letter, but at a party in London on 30 November, providing at first hand his opinion of the current situation in Palestine and the operational effectiveness of the Night Squads.[270] Burchett, for once, may not have been entirely inaccurate in seeing a link between this meeting and Churchill arguing, during the debate on the Woodhead Report, that he had it on 'high military authority' that the Jews could handle the revolt themselves if allowed to raise their own armed forces.[271] Wingate subsequently obtained a private meeting with MacDonald; although a record of their conversation has not survived, one might presume that the Colonial Secretary might not have been impressed to discover that the 'British military officer' from Galilee had graduated from small-scale 'ambush work' to trying to alter government policy steered by himself.[272]

This is probably why the Army's high command turned on Wingate. Not only had Wingate, a serving British Army captain, led Jewish units in offensive operations in a majority Arab area, against policy agreed between the Army, the High Commissioner and the Colonial Office, but he had also provided documentary evidence of this to Liddell Hart, Amery and Churchill, three of the most garrulous and indiscreet individuals in British public life, in addition to approaching the Secretary of State and members of both Houses of Parliament in a highly unsubtle attempt to alter British Government policy. It is probably because of this, not because of any innate hostility to Wingate's military ideas, that the attitude of Wingate's military superiors, particularly Haining – who sanctioned the creation of the Night Squads, praised Wingate in official communications, approved his DSO and apparently turned a blind eye to the discrepancies between his activities and agreed policy – changed. In December, Wingate was ordered back to Jerusalem and reassigned to his old job at GHQ; he was not to lead the Night Squads or any other Jewish unit again, and was subsequently banned from entering Palestine whether on duty or on leave.[273] Wingate was to compound this with a truly major piece of boat-rocking, arising from his annual Confidential Report for 1938, authored jointly by his immediate superior, Wing Commander Alan Ritchie, head of military intelligence in Palestine, and by Haining. Both praised Wingate's imagination and energy, but both commented, in uncompromising terms, that Wingate's attachment to the Jewish cause was affecting his judgement and his performance as an officer.[274] Wingate responded by exercising the right of any officer to appeal to the King over an adverse personal report, and although he was persuaded to drop the matter before it got to Buckingham Palace this was not likely to improve opinions of him among his superiors.[275] Wingate was more successful in his reaction to the 8th Division Intelligence Conference report of 23 January 1939 stating its opposition to 'the dressing up of Jews as British soldiers; in particular it is considered undesirable to have a proportion of Jews in SNS detachments; these should be entirely British' because 'if it is desired to conciliate the Arab, we should not provoke him by using Jews in offensive action against him'.[276] This was a restatement of agreed policy, whatever the abrasive language, but Wingate's response was to send a lengthy written complaint to Montgomery, who not only supported his view, but promised to recommend Jewish squadsmen for decorations.[277]

All this took place against the background of the publication, in May 1939, of the MacDonald White Paper, which took the recommendations of the Woodhead Report a stage further: there would be no Jewish state, Jewish immigration was to cease after five years, and a majority Arab state was to be created after ten years. The White Paper's publication was followed by a 24-hour general strike by Jewish workers on 18 May 1939 and violent demonstrations in Jerusalem and Tel Aviv, during which a British policeman was shot dead by a rooftop marksman. From July to September 'armed Jews both in parties and as individuals' carried out sabotage attacks on both urban and rural areas and 'bodies of armed Jews entered Arab villages and demolished Arab houses in retaliation for outrages.'[278] In his last dispatch as GOC, of July 1939, Haining commented that the White Paper had 'damped the flames' of the Arab rebellion, but was turning the Jews against the British, as demonstrated by Jewish rioting and an increase in bombings by the *Irgun*, ostensibly followers of Jabotinsky although he disowned them when they began attacking British troops and facilities.[279]

The close but unofficial relationship between the British Army and the *Haganah*, on which the Night Squads had hinged, ended as the British began treating *Haganah* and *Irgun* as they had previously treated Arab terrorists. In his first dispatch of August 1939, Haining's successor, Lieutenant General Sir Evelyn Barker, reported that forty-three Jews had been arrested for 'illegal drilling', another thirty-eight had been tried and sentenced to lengthy prison terms, and that, in his view, many Jews were clearly preparing for 'armed intervention.[280] This, and Haining's shifting attitude to arming the Jews, suggests an attitude among many in the British political-military establishment that the Jews should be supported for as long as this served British interests in the region, or at least did not threaten them, which allowed Jews and British to work together for mutual benefit against a common threat. However, should the Jews become a threat to British interests, they should be dealt with as 'severely' as the Arabs before them. It was at this late stage that Wingate's views and those of the rest of the Army can be identified as 'parting company.'

How effective were the Night Squads?

Wingate's methods worked. Evidence for this includes the reduction of attacks on the pipeline, the impact of the Jurdieh and Dabburiya raids and the dislocation of the gangs from their village bases, reported not only by Wingate, but also by HQ 16th Brigade a year later.[281] Indeed, the Night Squads may have been *too* successful, being possibly a factor in the impetus of the terrorist offensive shifting southwards to Judea in autumn 1938, when few other British units were engaged in offensive operations in Galilee.[282] Their operations can be viewed as furthering a tradition in British 'small wars' practice beginning with units such as the Gurkha Scouts of the Northwest Frontier and which was to continue after 1945, as the use of specialist forces and 'government gangs' has become standard counter-insurgent practice in several armies, not least the British. Units formed by Wingate's *protégé*, Michael Calvert in Malaya in 1950–51, Frank Kitson's 'counter-gangs' in Kenya in the 1950s, and the Omani *Firquats* of the 1960s and 70s had much in common with the Night

Squads, mixing British troops with local irregulars, operating from bases inside insurgent territory and using the insurgents' own operational and tactical methods against them; in the late 1940s Fergusson formed two small special units within the Palestine Police, mainly from veterans of various British Special Forces in the Second World War (the most infamous being Major Roy Farran, formerly of Stirling's SAS) with the aim of ambushing and assassinating Jewish insurgents. The British Army has institutionalised many of these practices via 22 SAS, re-founded by Calvert in Malaya, whose soldiers often had roles analogous to the British troops in the Night Squads.[283] It would be extravagant to attribute all this to Wingate, but he can be seen as furthering a 'tradition' in the British Army's approach to counter-insurgency.

The atrocity issue

According to Segev, and refuting most other published accounts, Wingate followed his destruction of the Tiberias gang with a bloody reprisal attack on the village of Hitin, in which ten Arabs were allegedly shot in cold blood.[283] Allon's account of this operation is cited by Segev, and states that Wingate was not present and that three villagers were shot explicitly 'while trying to escape', one of them after firing on the patrol.[285]

Allusions to certain official British pacification methods in Palestine have been made already. However, other, quasi-legal and surreptitious methods were discussed in both private correspondence and official publications. As mentioned already, O'Connor was uneasy about allegations of what was going on in 16th Brigade's operational area, and in December 1938, Haining felt strongly enough about claims in the German press that the British had murdered eleven Arabs at Irtah and Beith Haninah, and were trying to starve the Arabs into submission, to issue an official rebuttal.[286] There was no official British policy of intimidation or reprisal in Palestine, but compelling evidence is available that poor discipline and slack leadership led to several British units committing apparent 'war crimes' in Palestine during Haining's time as GOC. The Royal Ulster Rifles, Bredin's regiment, gained a particularly black reputation: their commanding officer was open about his use of mock executions and deliberate vandalism to intimidate the local Arabs in a conversation with Simonds during a visit the latter made to his area of operations; in September 1938, Ulster Rifles, accompanied by elements of the 11th Hussars, destroyed the village of al Bassa in reprisal for some of their number being blown up by a roadside bomb, killing at least twenty civilians in the attack on the village and then allegedly murdering more by locking them inside a bus before blowing it up.[287] Another regiment with questions to answer was the Black Watch, which in May 1939 carried out an aggressive search of the village of Halhul, during which they confined a number of men in an enclosure with little water and no food for nearly two weeks, fourteen men dying as a result; following the murder of two Black Watch soldiers near the Pool of Siloam, Wavell, the GOC and the regiment's Honorary Colonel, allegedly authorised the 'search' of a nearby Arab suburb, Simonds recalling that 'a lot of Arabs afterwards, were very sorry that it happened.'[288] Much use was also made of 'Oozle Minesweepers', captured insurgents forced to run in front of British convoys on mined roads (a semi-official practice approved by Haining) while some units actually tied them to the front of lorries.[289] When, in November 1938, A.F. Perrett, the Deputy Inspector General of Police on the Northwest Frontier, wrote to his old acquaintance, O'Connor, suggesting the Army in Palestine should form a 'hostage corps' composed of the male relatives of known hostiles, to be placed in the front cars of convoys to deter ambush or pushed in front of police parties into houses where guerrillas were hiding, Haining responded that this was already in effect in Palestine. Simonds recalled in his memoirs that hostages were placed in the leading cars on the Lydda-Jerusalem railway to deter minelayers, two cars being blown up with hostages inside them. Simonds called this 'what might well be termed a British atrocity.'[290]

'Severity' was therefore applied by the British Army in Palestine, and there are reliable accounts of the robust handling of terrorist suspects by the Night Squads. However, while certainly consistent with Wingate's cryptic comments about 'government terror' and his stated opinions on cowing Arabs into behaving themselves, Segev's accounts of Hitin and other encounters can be questioned. He gives no dates for the incidents he describes, nor is any attempt made to corroborate them with other published sources or British official papers. Segev gives the Jewish death toll in Tiberias as fifteen, whereas the figure given in every other account is nineteen, as Segev, indeed, records elsewhere; there is no record of any other atrocity there.[291] In Segev's account, Wingate speaks in 'broken Arabic' and later needs an interpreter, yet had qualified as an Arabic interpreter himself, requalifying in 1936, was used by GHQ Jerusalem as an examiner in Arabic, commanded Arabic-speaking troops for five years in Sudan, and was familiar enough with Palestinian Arabic to translate newspapers and to run an effective intelligence network in Galilee.[292] In the otherwise highly negative personal report from 1939 which prompted Wingate's attempted complaint to the King, Wingate's superior officer, Wing Commander Alan Ritchie, praised his ability as a linguist in both Arabic and Hebrew.[293] Wingate's own attitude is telling, he being at pains to stress that his Squads were better behaved than many other units. When, in 1940, he believed that Haining, then Deputy CIGS, was thwarting another project, he gave over part of a meeting with Ironside, then CIGS, to discussing what he knew about the al Bassa incident, with the implied threat that he might go public if frustrated any further, and pointed out that 'the smallest irregularity on the part of the Jewish-British force under [my] command would have met with instant punishment'.[294] This does not suggest any skeletons lurking in the closet. Moreover, another Israeli historian, Michael Oren, has inspected Segev's sources and discovered some irregularities – for instance, Wingate was not present at the alleged flogging incident at Danna, actually being on leave in London at the time, and Segev has apparently edited his quotation from Tzion Cohen to imply that he was; in actuality, like most of the Jewish squadsmen, Cohen hero-worshipped Wingate and said so in his memoirs.[295] Overall, while there are clearly some verifiable incidents of immoral and illegal treatment of captured insurgents from Night Squad veterans, the balance of testimony indicates that the operations of the Squads were relatively restrained, particularly when compared with certain British actions in Ireland, India and other parts of Palestine, or some of the Jewish militias in the 1930s and later.

Why the controversy?

A strong argument can be made that the current controversy about Wingate owes much to post-1982 Lebanon invasion and post-*Intifada* attitudes to Israel and Zionism, both inside Israel and in the wider world. Your author has experienced a little of this personally: a paper I gave on Wingate and the Night Squads to a Saudi-sponsored conference in London on the history of modern Palestine some years ago, at which speakers from the Palestine Liberation Organisation were also present, ended up being quoted on a pro-PLO website with passages being either paraphrased or placed out of context to make it seem that I was describing a Jewish death squad, and, indeed, that the whole British Army in Palestine had behaved like the Nazis in Eastern Europe or the Soviets in Afghanistan.[296]

Why do this? To begin with, the Night Squads developed against the background of an ethno-religious conflict for control of disputed territory in which the holding of ground at all costs and the attrition of the opposition by battle or massacre were viewed as acceptable strategies by the participants if not by third parties.[297] Such conflicts have become common since 1989, and many counterinsurgent forces since the 1990s have applied an inappropriate response deriving from the entirely different, and growingly irrelevant paradigm of Marxist-Leninist 'revolutionary war': Wingate, Tegart, Haining, Evetts and, before them, Callwell and Simson, seem prescient indeed, given their recommended aim of destroying the insurgency militarily.[298] Moreover, Jabotinsky's 'Iron Wall' philosophy was rooted in acceptance of the inevitability of this kind of conflict, and it may be that Wingate's main contribution to Israeli history is as one of several demonstrating the practicability of the 'Iron Wall' and providing a military doctrine by which it could be put into practice.

To compound the controversy, on several levels, the 'Iron Wall' has worked: as the British-Israeli historian Avi Shlaim put it, 'The Arabs – first the Egyptians, the Palestinians, and then the Jordanians – have recognized Israel's invincibility and been compelled to negotiate with Israel...'[299] However, Shlaim argued also that while Jabotinsky clearly saw the Iron Wall as a means to an end – Arab recognition of the Jewish state's right to exist – most of the Israeli political elite have come to see it as an end in itself, 'a permanent way of life', compromising Israeli security in making them reject the kind of conciliation which may lead to normal relations with the Arab world.[300] Wingate's dismissal of all Arabs as potential terrorists echoes the most uncompromising post-1948 Zionist politicians, Ariel Sharon and Benjamin Netanyahu, and may be an indirect reason for certain post-Intifada Israeli authors' attacks on him.[301]

Wingate's influence on Israeli history is more clear-cut at the military level. The Lexicon of the Israel Defence Force (IDF) states, 'The teachings of Orde Charles Wingate, his character and leadership were a cornerstone for many of the *Haganah's* commanders, and his influence can be seen in the Israel Defence Force's [IDF] combat doctrine.'[302] Wingate's influence on Israeli military policy was confirmed by the founders of the IDF and the State of Israel: David Ben-Gurion, Israel's first Prime Minister, stated that had Wingate lived, he would have been the natural choice to lead the IDF during the 1948 War of Independence; to Moshe Dayan, 'He was a military genius and a wonderful man'; in 1976, Ariel Sharon told Brian Bond that Wingate was his boyhood hero and he 'read avidly' about his exploits in Abyssinia and Burma; when asked about the comparative influence of Wingate and Liddell Hart over Israeli military doctrine, Yitzhak Rabin stated that Wingate's was greater, as did Sharon's mentor, Major General Avraham Yoffe; Yigal Allon listed Wingate at the top of his list of those who had exerted most influence, ahead of Liddell Hart and Sadeh.[303] The Israel Defence Forces have developed a plethora of special operations and counter-insurgency units engaged in retaliatory and pre-emptive operations: this tradition originated via men trained by Wingate or Sadeh, who counted himself as one of Wingate's pupils, writing that 'For some time... we did the same things as Wingate, but on a smaller scale and with less skill. We followed parallel paths until he came to us, and in him we found our leader.'[304] It is perhaps no surprise that in 1939, Ben-Gurion finally authorised the *Haganah* to carry out reprisal operations, ordering the creation of Special Operations units to execute them – some of these are clearly the attacks alluded to by Haining and Barker in their dispatches.[305] Israel's subsequent counter-terrorist strategy has been offensive and based on pre-emption or retaliation, just as Wingate recommended, and has been effective, prompting a number of shifts in Palestinian military strategy, but has also been controversial, given frequent overreactions and the tendency, since the late 1960s, to substitute special forces action with airstrikes or offensives by large formations.[306] It is therefore likely that Israeli allegations against Wingate arise from disquiet about his perceived influence on Israeli external policy and the strategy the IDF has used to follow it.

Friction between Wingate and his British peers in Palestine arose from his involvement in the Mandate's politics. The Wingate of the biographies was truculently Zionist almost upon arrival, many authors claiming this guaranteed the enmity of his colleagues and superiors, who, except Wavell, only backed him under duress. However, viewing Wingate's actions within their historical and institutional context reveals a complex, evolving relationship, in which Wingate initially had the unforced support and protection of British senior commanders, but lost it gradually due to his becoming a political liability. This liability status extended beyond that of a decorated serving officer publicly opposing government policy: that Wingate had permission from Haining to carry out offensive operations involving Jewish police, in a disputed region, is a matter of official record; so is the policy agreed between the War Office, the Colonial Office, the GOC and the High Commissioner, that Jewish police or militia would *not* be used for offensive operations in majority Arab areas. There is a clear contradiction between Government and Army policy here. When and if this became known, as likely when Wingate contacted Lloyd, MacDonald, Amery, Liddell Hart or Churchill, it had the potential to cause an almighty public scandal endangering Britain's status as the Mandatory power, and inflaming Arab opinion across the entire Middle East.

It is here that a key point of departure between Wingate and the rest of the Army emerges. While many British officers advocated arming the Jews, and praised them as soldiers, at no point, anywhere in official correspondence and reports in the public domain, is this linked to fulfilling Zionist political objectives. The Army's aim throughout was the defeat of insurrection against British authority through military means, in which political niceties seem to have been forgotten or disregarded. Moreover, not for the last time, the British Army was caught between two uncompromising groups of nationalists, each regarding any attempt at even-handedness as betrayal. Throughout 1936-39, for instance, the British Government faced repeated accusations from Zionist lobbies in Britain and the USA of pro-Arab bias and not doing enough against the insurgents.[307] This was almost certainly intended to pressure the Colonial Office in directions it would rather not go, and seems not to have reflected the Army's apparently sincere attempts at even-handedness; for instance, Haining's decision to reform the Palestine Police was affected, in part, by the 'Tendency to "pro-Arab" bias on the part of [the] British superior cadre *instead of being wholly impartial.*' [Italics mine][308] Simson, an army officer with experience of Palestine, saw the partiality of civilian officials towards one side or the other as another contributing factor to the violence there since the beginning of the Mandate.[309] The Army also seems to have been prepared to give the Jews the benefit of the doubt, attributing most of the post-1938 trouble to recently-arrived young sophisticates, Haining, for instance, expressing to MacDonald, in August 1939, a belief that recent Jewish immigrants, 'brought up in the tradition of Russian Nihilism' were responsible for much of the Jewish violence.[310] Ben-Gurion commented that the British Army 'did not always support the pro-Arab leanings of the Administration and knew the difference between the Arab gangs and the Hagana [sic].'[311] Moreover, others joined Wingate in his suspicion of the 'politicals' in the Colonial Office. For instance, in January 1939, O'Connor wrote to Edward Keith-Roach, District Commissioner for Jerusalem, castigating him for his over-familiarity with the Mufti: 'The Husseinis have openly declared war on the British regime; they instigate assassination, arson and every sort of disloyalty; whilst I find on all sides, the inclination to act at their dictation and to find excuses for their conduct.'[312] Simonds shared O'Connor's low opinion of Keith-Roach, as did several British and American journalists based in Palestine, all seeing him as the Mufti's 'useful idiot.'[313]

It could be concluded, therefore, that the Army's attitude in Palestine was pragmatic, prioritising restoring order over political imperatives, and apparent impartiality between the two communities, demonstrated by their willingness to use both Jews and law-abiding Arabs as military assets while taking a tough line against terrorists of both ethnicities. In taking the part of one of those communities while demonising the other, Wingate departed from this. This belief was communicated to Liddell Hart and Amery, and possibly to Burchett and Mosley, all of whom apparently accepted Wingate's view unquestioningly (and Burchett's own agenda must not be forgotten), as have subsequent biographers. Where Wingate did part company with prevailing military opinion, it was in intensity, rather than direction, and his personality and politics made him more of a 'maverick', at this stage, than his military ideas, which conformed to established British practice in counter insurgency and British strategy in Palestine. Yet even his politics did not damage his career prospects, as the next chapter will demonstrate.

Chapter Five

Wingate in Ethiopia, 1940–41

> This brilliant action... as a feat of arms carried out by a minute regular force supporting irregulars in very difficult country against an enemy greatly superior in numbers and armament can have few parallels.
>
> *Lieutenant General Sir Harry Wetherall's Dispatch on operations in western Ethiopia, 1941*[1]

> Wingate took me round various offices at Headquarters. As he shambled from one to another, in his creased, ill-fitting uniform and out-of-date Wolseley helmet, carrying an alarm clock instead of wearing a watch, and a fly-whisk instead of a cane, I could sense the irritation and resentment he left in his wake. His behaviour certainly exasperated [General Sir William] Platt, who anyway had little sympathy with irregular operations. I once heard Platt remark... 'The curse of this war is Lawrence in the last'.
>
> *Sir Wilfred Thesiger*[2]

Yet more myths

Wingate's operations in Italian-occupied Ethiopia in 1940–41 have also contributed significantly to the apocrypha about him, the most persistent story being that Wingate 'restored' the Emperor of Ethiopia, Haile Selassie, to his rightful throne by *coup de main*, under the noses of the British Government and Army, who planned to turn Ethiopia into a British protectorate. This is taken for granted in Ethiopia, but has also entered the literature about Wingate, predictably via Burchett and Mosley, but also by David Rooney, who, in a paper given to the British Commission for Military History in 1997, stated explicitly that:

> At the end of the campaign in June 1941, to the chagrin of Platt's two divisions advancing from the north, and Cunningham's three divisions coming up from their base in northern Kenya, Wingate stole the limelight and personally escorted the Emperor Haile Selassie into his capital, Addis Ababa.[3]

Rooney also saw in Wingate's Gideon Force the direct ancestor of the Chindits:

> [Wingate's] acute observation both of his own forces and the enemy enabled him to build up a body of ideas which came to fruition in plans for the Chindits. To keep in touch with his columns Wingate established effective wireless communication, and this was the key to all future Chindit operations.[4]

Luigi Rossetto also presented Wingate's ideas as completely original, a new form of warfare, based on Liddell Hart's 'indirect approach'.[5]

Contemporary documents and testimony – including Wingate's own – suggest these views require some revision. Raising purpose-designed units to operate in enemy-occupied territory in cooperation with local partisans had been the remit of the Military Intelligence (Research) (MI(R)) branch of the War Office at least since 1939, and Wingate's Gojjam operation was one of several initiated in 1940 not by Wingate, but by MI(R)'s Middle Eastern sub-branch, G(R). MI(R) formed an integral part of British strategy, post-Dunkirk, wherein the perceived impossibility of defeating German regular forces in battle, at least in the short term, led the British toward a Fabian strategy based on blockade, long-range aerial bombing and subversion by bodies such as MI(R) and, later, Special Operations Executive (SOE). Wingate's operations in Ethiopia should therefore be placed in the context of this strategy and his ideas, presented before, during and after the Gojjam campaign. Wingate actually inherited an existing operation applying MI(R)'s recommended operational procedures faithfully, and produced afterwards a set of operational procedures of his own derived partially from theirs and shaped by his own experiences in Palestine and Ethiopia. Perhaps the biggest difference was that Wingate insisted, increasingly, on concentration of force and resources, rather than the dispersal and economy of effort that was the hallmark of other MI(R) operations, and his moving away from subversion and partisan warfare – about which he seems never to have been enthusiastic – towards use of purpose-designed regular forces to menace enemy lines of communication, local irregulars being tolerated provided they didn't get in the way.[6] This evolved into the model presented in Wingate's post-Ethiopia papers, which introduce another key theme of his military thought: 'attacking the enemy's plan' – disrupting their preparation for their main effort via establishing a constant, nagging threat to points of critical vulnerability, distracting their attention, forcing them to disperse their forces, and creating a situation friendly forces could exploit.[7] Wingate's Ethiopia operations therefore develop old themes and introduce new ones.

British strategy, 1940–41, and the development of special and raiding forces

Chiefs of staff meetings throughout May and June 1940, facing the imminent expulsion of British ground forces from France, accepted that the best they could do afterwards was to keep the war going until something happened to change the situation, and dwelt regularly on economic warfare, bombing and the 'spread of revolt' as the main means of doing this. Indeed, by 25 May, with the British Expeditionary Force pocketed around Dunkirk, these had become 'the only way' to maintain hostilities.[8] On 7 June, the Director of Military Operations, Major General Sir John Kennedy, speaking from a brief prepared by MI(R), proposed to the chiefs of staff that:

> We are certainly not going to win the war by offensives in mass and the only way of success is by undermining Germany internally and by action in the occupied

territories. German aggression has in fact presented us with an opportunity never before equaled in history for bringing down a great aggressive power by irregular operations, propaganda and subversion enlarging into rebel activities... Seen in this light, the war may be regarded as an inter-connected series of wars of independence... It must be recognised as a principle that not only are these activities part of the grand strategy of the war, [but] probably the only hope of winning the war...[9]

Kennedy was one of many in Britain at the time who presumed that covert operations were integral to Axis strategy. There was some support for this viewpoint: Germany directed the Austrian Nazi Party, and pro-Nazis among the *Volksdeutsche* of the Sudetenland and Silesia, to steer the crises of 1938–39, while in 1940, detachments of the *Brandenburg* special operations units of the *Abwehr*, German military intelligence, often wearing civilian clothing or Dutch and Belgian uniforms, carried out deep reconnaissance and seized bridges ahead of the advancing Panzer columns, perhaps providing the inspiration for widespread rumours of 'Fifth Columns' of traitors operating in Allied countries.[10] MI(R) made much of reports that Germany was organising a worldwide network of 'Fifth Columns' based on German emigrant communities, receiving some moral support in this claim from British Ambassadors in Bulgaria and Romania opining that, in the event of a German drive in the Balkans, both countries would collapse rapidly in the face of airborne invasions supported by Fifth Columns.[11] It was taken for granted in official circles that sabotage and subversion by traitors would feature prominently in any German invasion of England, and Ironside, now Commander-in-Chief, Home Forces, ordered the creation of 'Ironside Units' to counter this threat, with Wingate, in June 1940, contacting Ironside suggesting he could form a Night Squad-type unit to deal with 'Fifth Column' activity in England.[12]

The story of what Ironside called Wingate's 'posse' is to come, but more important in the long term was the strategy Britain adopted from summer 1940 through to early 1942, which made extensive use of special units and organisations to wage 'unconventional' warfare in Axis-occupied territory, perhaps the major driving force behind this being the elevation of the great military romantic, Winston Churchill, to the post of Prime Minister and Minister of Defence, and unofficial strategist in chief. Throughout his life, Churchill remained wedded to the idea that boldness and aggression could compensate for inferior numbers, and, strong believer in national characteristics that he was, that the British in particular excelled in these things. However, Churchill can also be seen as pragmatic: such forces were one of the few means of Britain maintaining hostilities post-Dunkirk. In June 1940, he ordered that offensive operations should be carried out against the coast of occupied Europe, and the task of commanding these raiding operations – the objective being 'to mystify the enemy and cause him to disperse his forces' – was assigned to Lieutenant General A.G.B. Bourne of the Royal Marines, with Evetts attached to his staff as Director, Raiding Operations.[13] Unfortunately, assets for such 'harassing' operations were minimal, consisting of the six Independent Companies formed by MI(R) and MI(R)'s

Training Centre at Inverailort (see below). Four more Independent Companies were in training for 'minor [amphibious] raids' by the end of July, but it was recognised by the War Cabinet that the lack of equipment, particularly landing craft, would limit them to such small-scale raids for the foreseeable future.[14] Bourne was also promised elements from Britain's fledgling airborne forces, Churchill, having observed the impact of German *Fallschirmjägern* in the Low Countries, ordering the creation of a 'Parachute Corps' of 5,000 men in response.[15] Contemporary documents, and early British parachute operations, indicate that the Parachute Corps was envisioned initially as a raiding force, destroying vital objectives and drawing off large Axis formations or carrying out minor harassing operations including sabotage, intelligence gathering or cooperation with resistance movements, all roles Wingate would assign to his LRP forces in Ethiopia and Burma.[16] At Churchill's urging, specialist equipment for raiding and amphibious operations were developed rapidly – the first Landing Craft Tank was being tested by October 1940 – and by the end of 1940, a new command, Combined Operations Command, under Admiral Sir Roger Keyes – who had equal status with the chiefs of staff and therefore direct access to the Prime Minister – was overseeing the development of amphibious and raiding operations.[17] In March 1942, Keyes was succeeded as Director, Combined Operations by Commodore Lord Louis Mountbatten, who was to be another Wingate patron.

These developments were accelerated by the strategy set at chiefs of staff meetings from August to November 1940, which was based on the assumption that defeating the *Wehrmacht* directly, in main-force battle, was not currently possible, but that Germany's rapid expansion left her overstretched and open to attacks on her oil and heavy industry, disrupting which would create 'unemployment, critical shortages... and general economic disorganisation.'[18] Consequently, Britain should tighten her economic blockade on Europe, combine it with an RAF bomber offensive against German industry and use diplomacy to keep potential German allies neutral or perhaps induce them to take a more benevolent stance towards the Allies, particular attention being directed to Turkey and the Balkan states at this time.[19] Moreover, every effort should be made to encourage resistance in Axis-occupied territory.[20] This was fenced around with caveats, the most important of which was expressed in a chiefs of staff meeting in August 1940:

> Subversive operations must not be an end in themselves. They should conform with military operations... It will be important to ensure that subversive movements should not be allowed to break out spontaneously in areas that individually become ripe for revolt. No appreciable results can be expected in the early future and we should organise these activities on a large scale so that they are timed to mature in relation to regular operations undertaken as part of our general policy.[21]

Action should consist of:

98   Orde Wingate

   a) Sabotage of key plants, commodities and communications, to supplement… the blockade and air attack.
   b) Containing and extending Axis forces.
   c) Preparing for a general rising against the Axis, to coincide with the final Allied offensive.[22]

This hinged on 'Adequate preparations to supply the necessary material and physical assistance and support of the revolts… A carefully prepared scheme of propaganda… [and] A clear policy as to the economic and political future of Europe'.[23] The task of supplying 'the necessary material and physical support of the revolts' fell on MI(R), a previously small and obscure branch of the War Office.

MI(R), G(R) and covert operations in 1939–40

From 1939 through to its absorption into SOE in 1940, MI(R) played the leading part in devising British policy towards 'Para-Military Activities', which it encapsulated as:

[A]ll the new features of war involved in the modern German conception of war as total and continuous. It therefore comprises activities both in peace and war which may be summarised as follows:-

a) <u>In Peace</u>
Organisation of the civil populace for war… Propaganda… as an attack on psychology… Political and intelligence activities in other countries, including the infiltration of personnel and creation of potentially treasonable organisations.

b) <u>In War</u>
The above activities, coupled with overt acts of violence against the enemy in the form of sabotage, etc., other than those carried on by the regular forces of the State, operating regularly – together with irregular operations of regular forces.[24]

In September 1939, three separate organisations were tasked with this: Section D of the Secret Intelligence Service, which oversaw sabotage, subversion and misinformation via individual agents, Electra House, the Foreign Office department handling propaganda, and MI(R) at the War Office. MI(R) had developed from GS(R), the research section of the Directorate of Military Operations and Intelligence of the War Office, formed in 1938 with a bland remit: 'Research into problems of tactics and organisation under the direction of the DCIGS [Deputy Chief of the Imperial General Staff]. Liaison with other branches of the War Office and with Commands in order to collect new ideas on these subjects.'[25] Section D and GS(R) presented a joint paper to the Chiefs of Staff in March 1939 arguing that the German seizure of Czechoslovakia and designs on the Balkans had opened up the possibility of 'an alternative method of defence… to organised armed resistance… based on the experience we have had in India, Irak [sic], Ireland and Russia, i.e. the development of a combination of guerrilla and IRA tactics.[26] MI(R) was tasked the following month with putting this into action, instructed by the CIGS, General Lord Gort, to study guerrilla methods with a view to producing a manual for guerrilla warfare 'incorporating detailed tactical and technical instructions, applying to each of several countries' including assessing their vulnerability to such activity.[27] Lieutenant Colonel J.C.F. Holland, head of GS(R) since 1938, co-author of the April 1939 paper, and an enthusiast for guerrilla warfare since fighting the IRA in the 1920s, presented his report in June.[28] This was based on a reading list including *Seven Pillars of Wisdom*, Edgar Snow's *Red Star Over China*, General von Lettow-Vorbeck's memoirs of his irregular campaigns in East Africa during the First World War, studies of the *Francs-Tireurs* in the Franco-Prussian War of 1870-71 and the Arab rebellion in Palestine.[29] Holland stated that:

> [I]f guerrilla warfare is coordinated and also related to main operations, it should, in favourable circumstances, cause such a diversion of enemy strength as eventually to present decisive opportunities to the main forces of his opponent. It is therefore an auxiliary method of war of which we have not yet sufficiently exploited the possibilities.[30]

Holland considered guerrilla activity to be the only viable means of supporting Britain's Allies in central Europe and had already established Missions at British Embassies in eastern and central Europe to gather information on disaffected and potentially subversive people and organisations and the suitability of each country for guerrilla operations and had recommended the creation of teams of guerrilla and sabotage specialists to support them.[31] After this, MI(R)'s role expanded to:

a) Research and preparation of projects for irregular operations as a contribution to normally conducted operations.
b) Technical research and production of devices for such projects.
c) Operation of such projects when they are not the function of any [other] organisation or HQ.
d) Collection of special information when necessary.
e) Recording individuals with special qualifications and their training.[32]

By June 1940, MI(R) had established a training centre at Inverailort, and the Independent Companies (for 'irregular operations by regular forces') mentioned already, after the Allied expulsion from Norway underwent retraining and reorganisation for seaborne raiding operations and became the kernel of the Army Commandos.[33] It was also not only 'recording personnel with special qualifications' but recruiting and training them as well. Holland deemed officers from the regular Army to be unsuitable for covert activity, preferring instead to commission likely candidates from the ranks, the Territorial Army or straight from civilian life, nominating 200 candidates for Officer Cadet Training Units (OCTUs) by April 1940 and securing others by a special 'politico-military' course at the University of

Cambridge.[34] Through these methods and others, Holland recruited Michael Calvert, Peter Fleming, brother of Ian, who would later supervise deception operations in Southeast Asia, the Stirling brothers, David and Bill, David Niven, who returned immediately from Hollywood and volunteered for service on the outbreak of war, and Simon Fraser, the Earl of Lovat, who became Chief Instructor at Inverailort and was to lead Commandos at Dieppe and Normandy.[35] A detachment, G(R), was formed on the Staff of GHQ Middle East in Cairo, its staff including Captain Douglas Dodds-Parker and the explorers Wilfred Thesiger and Laurens van der Post, and in October 1940, instructors from Inverailort were sent to form similar schools in Australia and Burma, the Burma school, with Calvert as its chief instructor, still being in place when Wingate arrived in 1942 and Calvert and some of his instructional staff going on to command Chindit columns.[36]

MI(R)'s best known project of this period involved Calvert and Fleming organising volunteers to form the kernel of a resistance movement in southern England following a German invasion.[37] It also had observers with the British Expeditionary Forces in Norway and France, studying German equipment and tactics, and by summer 1940 was planning support for the Polish and Norwegian resistance, advising the Yugoslav General Staff, planning missions to neutral, but pro-Axis Spain, Hungary and Bulgaria, and devising plans to support Finland against a renewal of Soviet aggression via underground networks in Sweden.[38] MI(R) had also produced a series of pamphlets by Lieutenant Colonel Colin Gubbins, an old friend of Holland's and fellow veteran of the Irish 'troubles', assigned to MI(R) at Holland's request.[39]

MI(R) accepted that to meet British strategic ends, guerrilla activity needed to be fostered pro-actively and perhaps initially even against the wishes of the majority of the target population.[40] An undated, unattributed MI(R) appreciation argued that:

> A successful revolt depends upon adequate planning and organisation and these take time to build up. Unless they arise spontaneously from within the countries concerned… the organisation will have to be fostered from outside. This should not in the end prove impossible of achievement; the Irish revolt was largely fostered from the USA… It was with this end in view that the Bureau Project now in hand by MIR [sic] was initiated.[41]

Yet, Dodds-Parker recalled, the initial approach was to 'keep your powder dry', resisters being encouraged to stay low, build up supplies and networks, and only emerge to fight once a British invasion was imminent; they could, in the meantime, carry out small-scale sabotage, but damage should, as far as possible, be made to look accidental.[42] Consequently, Gubbins' key pamphlet, *The Art of Guerrilla Warfare*, was emphatically *not* a manual for 'revolutionary warfare', being based throughout on the scenario of resistance against occupying forces in cooperation with regular forces of external Allies. Gubbins' summary of the aims of guerrilla activity, from *The Art of Guerrilla Warfare*, outlined that:

The object of guerrilla warfare is to harass the enemy in every way possible within all the territory he holds to such an extent that he is eventually incapable either of embarking on a war, or of continuing one that way already have commenced... This object is achieved by compelling the enemy to disperse his forces in order to guard his flanks, his communications, his supply detachments, etc., against the attacks of guerrillas, and thus so to weaken his main armies that the conduct of a campaign becomes impossible... The whole art of guerrilla warfare lies in striking the enemy where he least expects it, and yet where he is most vulnerable: this will produce the greatest effect in inducing, and even compelling, him to use up large numbers of troops in guarding against such blows.[43]

Modern armies, 'entirely dependent as they are on the regular delivery of supplies, munitions, petrol, etc', and therefore vulnerable to guerrilla attacks on their lines of communication and supply, would disperse to counter them, making themselves vulnerable to offensives by regular forces.[44] The process should begin with acts of sabotage or 'terrorism' by individuals or small groups, escalating via 'The action of larger groups working as a band under a nominated leader, and employing military tactics, weapons, etc., to assist in the achievement of their object, which is usually of a destructive nature' to 'the culminating stage of guerrilla warfare... large formations of guerrillas, well-armed and well-trained, which are able to take a direct part in the fighting by attacks on suitable hostile formations and objects in direct conjunction with the operations of the regular troops.'[45]

A concept Gubbins may have derived from Lawrence, and which played an important part in Wingate's thinking from 1941, was superior relative mobility in the operational environment concerned, which, combined with superior intelligence, would allow the setting of a tempo with which a more formally organised and commanded enemy could not cope. From the *Art of Guerrilla Warfare*:

It is mobility, in information and in morale that the guerrillas can secure the advantage, and those factors are the means by which the enemy's superior armament and numbers can best be combated. The superior mobility, however, is not absolute, but relative – i.e. to the type of country in which the activities are staged, to the detailed knowledge of that country by the guerrillas, etc. In absolute mobility, the enemy must always have the advantage – i.e. the use of railway systems, the possession of large numbers of motors, lorries, armoured cars, tanks, etc...By the judicious selection of ground, however, and by moves in darkness to secure surprise, the guerrillas can enjoy relatively superior mobility *for the period necessary for each operation*. The enemy will usually be in a country where the population is largely hostile, so that the people will actively co-operate in providing information for the guerrillas and withholding it from the enemy. The proper encouragement of this natural situation... will ensure that the guerrillas are kept *au fait* with the enemy's movements and *intentions*, whereas their own are hidden from him. [Emphasis Gubbins'][46]

Above all, Gubbins argued, guerrilla warfare hinged upon leadership: 'The central authority must, and perforce will be, some man of prestige or weight who has been a leading personality in the territory in time of peace… Leaders of local partisan bands will be selected from those of standing or mark in the locality who possess the necessary attributes of personality.'[47] However, British regular officers should be attached, 'either to serve directly as commanders, more particularly in the higher spheres, or as specially qualified staff officers or assistants to guerrilla commanders.'[48] The larger the movement, 'the greater the need for a leaven of regular officers to carry out the basic work of simple staff duties, and to effect liaison with the regular forces', an arrangement becoming more formal as the movement progressed:

> In cases where the guerrillas are a nation in arms, or part thereof, fighting for their freedom in alliance with or assisted and instigated by a third power which is willing and anxious to render all assistance to them, it will usually be advisable for that third power to be represented by a mission at the headquarters of the guerrilla movement. The duties of such a mission would be to provide expert advice, to ensure liaison, to arrange the supply of arms, ammunition, money, etc., and to provide leaders and assistants to leaders, if such were found to be necessary.[49]

The Mission would, in most cases, evolve into a 'guerrilla GHQ', its remit including identifying likely partisan leaders, providing them with weapons, ammunition, explosives and wirelesses, liaison with outside regular forces and devising an overall plan of campaign. At later stages, it would provide technical experts and trained staff officers to coordinate the guerrilla bands and provide them with a degree of regular organisation; Gubbins implied, but never stated, that another function was to ensure that 'powder was kept dry' until guerrilla action could be directed to British strategic ends.[50]

MI(R) also contemplated the use of specially organised fighting units to operate behind enemy lines either alone or in cooperation with partisans. This is pertinent to Wingate in identifying a set of military procedures that previous Wingate literature has either ignored or missed: specifically, the use of specialist light infantry, supplied by airdrop and using close air support in lieu of artillery, to establish a permanent presence in the enemy rear, was discussed by MI(R) almost three years before Wingate raised such units in Burma. On 7 June 1940, MI(R) finished its 'Appreciation of the Capabilities and Composition of a small force operating behind the enemy lines in the offensive': like many MI(R) documents, it is unattributed, but its subject, and date, suggest authorship by Holland, Gubbins or Geoffrey Lias, who produced a similar paper in July. Whoever its originator, the aim of this force was to 'disrupt enemy L of C, destroy dumps and disorganise HQ', its methods being 'to travel fast…avoid organised opposition as much as practicable, except at the objective [and] to attack the weak points in the enemy's organisation, make the sites untenable as long as possible and then, in most cases, depart.'[51] Moreover:

> [I]t would appear essential that this force should act in conjunction with an attack by the main regular formations. In such circumstances, there would be

fewer men to spare for sentries, fewer troops available for pursuit so that the effect of an interruption of L of C might be more effectual, if not decisive. To act before such an offensive might serve to wear down the enemy and to keep more of his forces on L of C but would make surprise less attainable.[52]

The force must travel light, its supplies carried by mules, camels or coolies, to maximise mobility, and any heavy equipment required would be flown in or airdropped.[53] The main fire support should come from the air: 'After a short aerial bombardment and before the enemy had time to emerge from their shelters, the operating force should drive home their attack. This calls for careful organisation and a high standard of co-operation and combined training, as well as good communications' – all things Wingate would be arguing for two years later.[54] The force could penetrate enemy held territory 'in less civilised and less populated countries by raids through sparsely held territory' and also in such cases '[a]ct as leaven to a popular rising. Show the flag and appear in as many places as possible to give rise to rumours of extensive military support.'[55] Lias' paper recommended an overall organisation for behind-the-lines warfare, to prevent premature uprisings and coordinate partisan activity with British strategy. This organisation would place agents and missions in enemy-occupied territory to demonstrate British commitment to the common cause, organise bands of ex-soldiers and coordinate with London; it would be supported by special airborne units dropped into hostile territory to combine with the guerrillas and supplied and supported mainly by air.[56] Therefore, many ideas Wingate put into practice in 1941-44 were on paper before the end of 1940, and given that Wingate's Gojjam campaign was specifically a G(R) operation, and Wingate called for an expanded G(R) organisation in Burma upon arrival in 1942, it is difficult not to see a connection. However, confirming any direct link would be difficult: Wingate was not mentioned in any MI(R) documents, except for situation reports from G(R), and, we reiterate, Wingate never credited any source but himself for his ideas.

G(R) remained independent after MI(R)'s absorption into SOE in the summer of 1940: given the greater opportunity for cooperation with regular operations in the Middle East, both Holland and Wavell, now Commander in Chief, Middle East, felt that G(R)'s activities should be controlled by Wavell's Headquarters, with SOE maintaining a 'watching brief' and supplying some of its funding.[57] Its personnel remained staff officers at GHQ Middle East, and indeed had been busy in that theatre, establishing an office in Khartoum under Lieutenant Colonel Terence Airey to oversee operations in Italian East Africa, sending Missions to Somaliland – where an Operational Centre (see below) and a large body of local partisans were active throughout April and May 1941 – West Africa and the Belgian Congo, and was recruiting Arabic speakers for Missions to the Middle East.[58] However, from June 1940, its main task was escalating revolt in Italian East Africa, and this is where Wingate became involved. It was just as well for him that he did, as he was finding military life after Palestine onerous indeed.

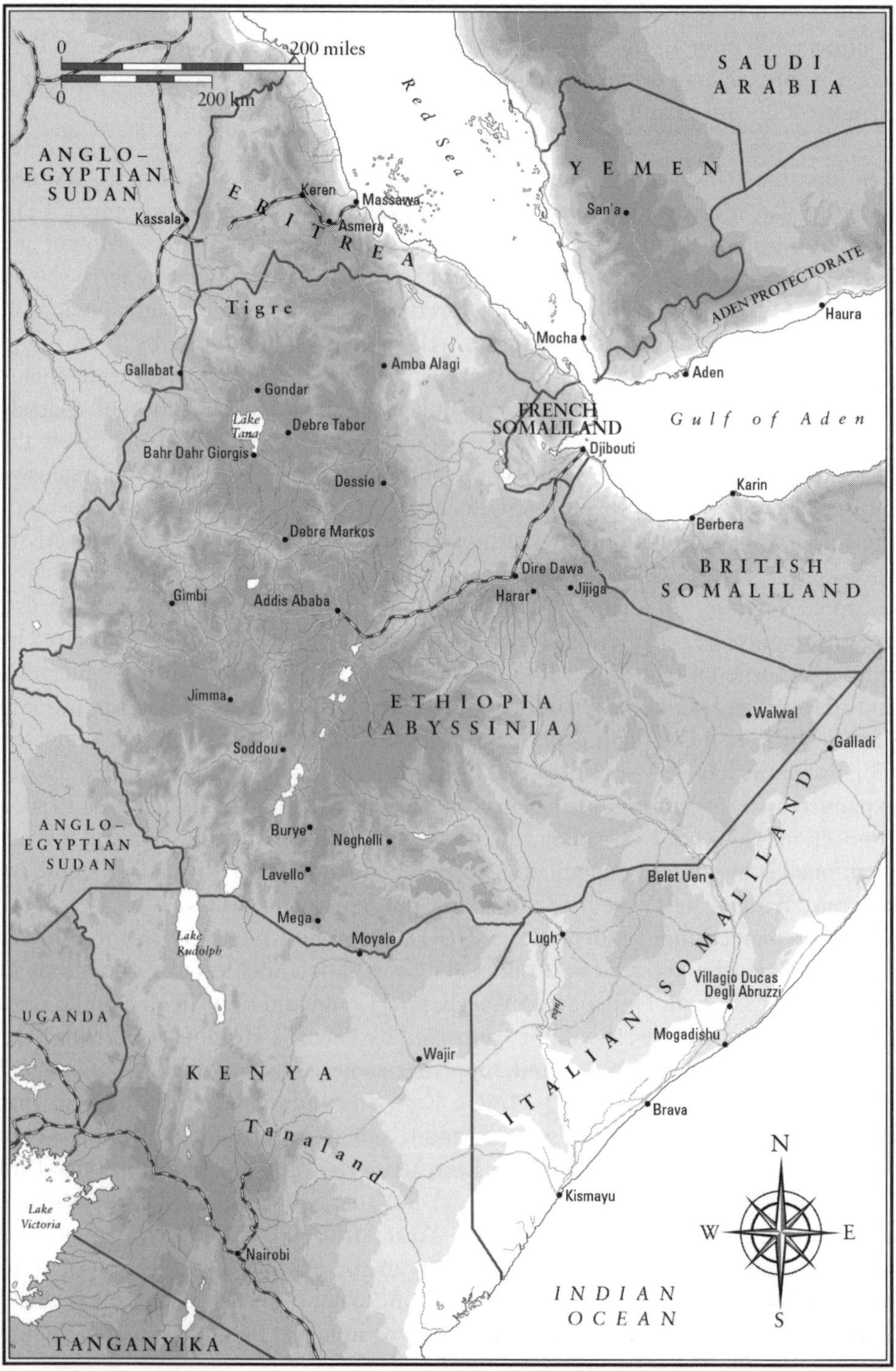
0
200 miles
0
200 km
Red Sea
SAUDI ARABIA
YEMEN
San'a
ADEN PROTECTORATE
Haura
Mocha
Aden
ANGLO-EGYPTIAN SUDAN
ERITREA
Keren
Massawa
Asmera
Kassala
Tigre
Gallabat
Amba Alagi
Gondar
Lake Tana
Debre Tabor
Bahr Dahr Giorgis
FRENCH SOMALILAND
Djibouti
Gulf of Aden
Dessie
Karin
Berbera
Debre Markos
Dire Dawa
Harar
Jijiga
BRITISH SOMALILAND
Gimbi
Addis Ababa
Jimma
ETHIOPIA (ABYSSINIA)
Walwal
Galladi
Soddou
ANGLO-EGYPTIAN SUDAN
Burye
Neghelli
Lavello
Belet Uen
Mega
Moyale
Lake Rudolph
Lugh
Villagio Ducas Degli Abruzzi
ITALIAN SOMALILAND
Juba
Mogadishu
UGANDA
Wajir
KENYA
Brava
Tanaland
Kismayu
Lake Victoria
Nairobi
N
W
E
S
INDIAN OCEAN
TANGANYIKA

Wingate and the Phony War

Wingate spent the twelve months between his departure from Palestine and assignment to Ethiopia as Brigade Major of 56th Light Anti-Aircraft Brigade, Territorial Army, based on the coast of southern England. This was no backwater: from the mid-1930s, an assumption underlying much British defence policy was that any war with Germany would open with the *Luftwaffe* attempting a 'knock-out blow' via a massive bombing offensive against British cities, and consequently, in early 1938, in the build-up to the Munich crisis, the Committee of Imperial Defence recommended that the Air Defence of Great Britain (ADGB) should take priority over all other military requirements, including the possible dispatch of a field force to the Continent.[59] However, in February 1939 the Cabinet agreed to the creation of a British Expeditionary Force (BEF), for deployment to the Continent, and by June 1939, ADGB had equal priority with the BEF. ADGB centred upon a rapid buildup of RAF Fighter Command, begun already in 1937, and the creation of auxiliary forces, particularly anti-aircraft artillery units for home defence, from 1933 the responsibility of Royal Artillery units of the Territorial Army (TA).[60] The new Anti-Aircraft Command consisted of twelve Anti-Aircraft Divisions, not 'divisions' as the rest of the Army understood the term, but geographical commands, each charged with defending a region of the UK from air attack. Within each division there were two Heavy and one Light Anti-Aircraft Brigades, each consisting of four regiments, plus three independent Light Batteries, deployed to cover vital areas (VAs) within their region.[61]

56th Light Anti-Aircraft Brigade formed part of 6th Anti-Aircraft Division, covering Kent and Essex – Brigade HQ was at Sidcup, Kent – and formed part of the first line of defence against air attacks on London from the Netherlands.[62] At the outbreak of war, the War Office halted all enlistment into the TA except for units of Anti-Aircraft Command, deemed to be under-strength, and so the majority of the flood of TA volunteers at the outbreak of war in September 1939 found themselves in anti-aircraft regiments.[63] As was traditional in the TA, training was decentralised and carried out within units, wherever they were sited, on whatever type of equipment the unit held – in 56th Brigade's case, the 40mm Bofors Gun, supplemented by machine-guns fitted to special anti-aircraft mounts.[64] It also remained part-time despite the war, soldiers and non-regular officers living at home and continuing their civilian jobs when off duty.[65] Training was complicated further by Light Anti-Aircraft Brigades not operating as concentrated formations: rather, batteries were attached to the division's Heavy Anti-Aircraft Brigades, themselves deployed around likely targets for air attack, Anti-Aircraft Command ordering, in late 1939, that all guns must be sited within 400 yards of vital areas.[66]

Wingate had to address these issues in his capacity as Brigade Major, an important staff role overseeing training, intelligence and the organisation of operations. He clearly found existing arrangements deeply unsatisfactory, common themes of his papers of the period 1939-40 being that training should be centralised at least to divisional level, that not enough resources were being allocated even to support the existing arrangements and – a familiar concern throughout his career – that existing army 'doctrine' was utterly misguided and should be rethought radically. He argued in a memorandum of 7 November 1939 that there should be a divisional-level training centre for anti-aircraft gunnery, a matter continued in a Headquarters Paper written the same month, discussing problems arising from the rapid expansion of anti-aircraft units in the previous eight weeks, in particular the 'evil' of raising troops to man one specific type of equipment, and then training them piecemeal on battery sites: 'It would seem a matter of common sense that training should be provided on a central, i.e. efficient and economical, basis, and not piece-meal – i.e. overseen by Brigade Commanders.'[67] Failure to do so had, in Wingate's view, resulted in thirty LAA troops out of the forty-one deployed in 6th Division's area being inadequately trained.[68] Existing arrangements were justified on the grounds that centralising AA training would require withdrawing equipment and personnel from front-line units at a time when a *Luftwaffe* offensive seemed imminent, but Wingate felt that the withdrawal of no more than four or five per cent of all guns and ammunition would be necessary.[69] He wanted to see a Light AA 'Training Establishment' in each division, based on the coast to allow maximum use of live fire; this would be supplemented by a central School of Light Anti-Aircraft Artillery, to train LAA units for overseas service and as a general reserve. A Major General, Light Anti-Aircraft Defences, would oversee all this and command all LAA in ADGB instead of the Heavy Divisions, Wingate believing, for reasons to be discussed below, that LAA Brigades should fight concentrated.[70]

As to 'doctrine' for this organisation, Wingate opposed the officially endorsed approach, based upon artillery theory, which involved trying to destroy all attacking aircraft by barraging likely routes to target areas. This was flawed, Wingate argued, because it risked opening fire under unfavourable conditions. Far better, he argued, to concentrate all guns in the immediate vicinity of likely targets, accept that the bomber would, indeed, get through, but reduce the cost-effectiveness of each raid by extracting a far heavier toll than the extant method. The aim of Anti-Aircraft Command should be to defeat the enemy air force through an attritional campaign, rather than defend targets. The most likely form of attack, he felt, would be by low-flying aircraft 'using the contours of the ground'; the best counter to this was large numbers of small-calibre guns, rather than small numbers of heavier ones, which would merely induce the enemy to attack at high altitude, beyond the reach of LAA.[71] Two things were required: firstly, increase the number of LAA troops in 6th Division, from forty-one to seventy-eight; secondly, mass these troops where they would produce the 'maximum casualty producing effect' upon incoming bombers:

> [A] bomber should be looked upon as a very expensive and vulnerable heavy gun with a limited amount of rounds. These rounds or bombs are no more dangerous than shells, and few of them dropped around an average [Vital Area] are likely to cause very serious damage. In such cases as the oil depot at Purfleet etc it is, of course, obvious that the enemy can destroy the bulk of the oil. It only remains to punish him for doing so as heavily as possible.[72]

Wingate noted of this proposal that 'it was not adopted.'[73] Aside from centralisation of training at brigade level, none were, and looking at the overall development of ADGB, with which any staff officer should have been familiar, Wingate's logic seems hard to follow. A School of Anti-Aircraft Defences existed pre-war at Biggin Hill – in the middle of 6th Division's area – and in September 1939, moved to Menorbier in South Wales, with practice camps there and in Somerset.[74] In October 1939, AA Command ordered the withdrawal of all Adjutants, Assistant Adjutants and Administration Officers of the regular army from its TA units, and all but one Permanent Staff Instructor (PSI) from each battery, to staff training establishments.[75] By December, there were Anti-Aircraft Training Regiments, overseeing recruit and specialist training, in Aldershot, Southern and Western Commands – but not in Eastern Command, 6th Division's area.[76] Wingate demanded an increase in the number of batteries of LAA, and the withdrawal of guns from frontline units for training, but the latter was unlikely to receive a sympathetic hearing from the GOC AA Command, General Sir Frederick Pile, then battling the War Office to prevent guns being reallocated from ADGB to the British Expeditionary Force in France; it had been proposed to form seventy-eight new Bofors batteries in February 1939, but as of December, just five per cent of the number of LAA guns required had been deployed, with an allocation, in the London area, of 3,000 rounds per gun, enough for 25-35 minutes' continuous firing with a Bofors.[77] Wingate's proposed Light AA training organisation was therefore superfluous, and was rendered doubly unfeasible by the logistical state of AA Command, as was his proposed rearrangement of Light AA Defences, which may have been sound in theory. As a staff officer, with a training remit, he must have been aware of this, yet, as at other times, Wingate's version of events differed from that of most others, and faced with objections or, worse, being ignored, he saw conspiracy and argued *ad hominem*. One of Wingate's other papers of this period, aimed 'To abate the intolerable nuisance of the telephone in ADGB', is redolent with eccentricity, particularly in its suggestion that headquarters telephones be fitted with a device allowing just one incoming call per hour, in order to spare Adjutants and Brigade Majors the distraction of constant calls.[78] It is difficult to tell whether this paper was intended to be taken seriously – Wingate's friends and subordinates remembered a sly, subtle sense of humour – yet, even if this is a piece of satire, it is pungently worded satire, and that Wingate chose to write upon such trivialities suggests that his suspicion of his superiors was accompanied by growing boredom.[79]

This may explain why Wingate still pursued his political interests. Victor Cazalet, a Conservative MP and leading British Zionist, was a battery commander in 56th Brigade; in the late 1930s, Cazalet had been an active supporter of the 'Redemption of Galilee' movement and now invited Wingate to the fortnightly meetings of his Zionist Committee at the Dorchester Hotel.[80] Wingate was also a frequent guest at Cazalet's country house at Tonbridge, along with Leo Amery. Like Churchill, Amery – who, although Church of England, was of Jewish descent – was until mid-1940 in the political 'wilderness', as a consequence of his outspoken opposition to the appeasement policies of the Chamberlain government, but after 1940 would rise to become Secretary of State for India, member of the War Cabinet and a major benefactor for Wingate. Cazalet's Committee produced proposals for Weizmann to present to the British government, one involving bringing 200 Palestinian Jews to Britain for military training, the origin of which Sykes saw in a memorandum from Wingate to Ironside.[81] Another plan, supported by MI(R), was to recruit Jewish refugees from Europe as saboteurs to operate inside Germany.[82]

The most significant development of this period, however, was the enlistment of Ironside's support for a Jewish Army under British command and the likelihood this would be put into practice, given that Ironside was Chief of the Imperial General Staff. In November, Weizmann and Ben-Gurion arranged to meet Ironside to protest at the imprisonment of forty-three young Jewish men in Palestine for 'illegal drilling'. Ironside told Weizmann that he thought the arrests 'foolish and barbaric', and he ordered the GOC Palestine to reduce the 5-10 year sentences meted out to the forty-three to six months. He also told Weizmann he was certain a Jewish army would be established, although probably not while Leslie Hore-Belisha was War Minister, as 'he was in a difficult position because he was a Jew, and therefore did not want to help.'[83] When, a few days later, the idea of a Jewish Brigade was raised with Wingate, it produced the response that a brigade was not enough: '[O]nly a division included all arms of the forces, and was capable of acting on its own. He insisted we should propose a Jewish division. As a start, he said, five hundred Jewish officers should be trained for this purpose in Britain.'[84] Ben-Gurion told him that he could not afford to have 15,000 young Jewish men – enough for a division – to be taken out of Palestine, but Wingate insisted that by the time the plan was adopted:

[T]he War would have spread to the East. He believed that before the winter was out Germany would turn southwards – and then they would need us. It was agreed that we should propose a division for which recruitment would be in Palestine and abroad, to be used both inside Palestine and outside. Next morning I met Orde alone. He warned us not to rely overmuch on 'friends' in Palestine – they should not be subjected to the test of a conflict of loyalties. He reiterated his belief that the war would spread to the East. Hitler would attack Rumania [sic] and Yugoslavia; Italy would undoubtedly join on Hitler's side, and then the Jewish army would be formed.[85]

Weizmann met subsequently with Ironside, who reiterated his support for a Jewish division and also expressed the view, shared with Wingate, that Palestine could become a powerful industrial base capable of supporting Middle East Command should Axis naval action isolate it from the UK.[86] Wingate's strategic agenda still had its supporters in the higher ranks of the Army.

So did his military ideas. May 1940 brought major changes in British supreme command: Ironside moved from CIGS to become Commander in Chief, Home Forces, presenting Wingate with an opportunity to put the experience of Palestine to use in the defence of Britain. There were already extensive rumours of a British 'Fifth Column', centred on Sir Oswald Mosley's British Union of Fascists (BUF) and affiliated organizations.[87] On 1 June 1940, Wingate proposed to Ironside that he could form a Night Squad type organisation in Britain to deal with such traitors; when asked by Ironside to put a detailed plan to his staff, Wingate, typically, predicted that the force could be ready within a *week* of authorisation.[88] Wingate was instructed to report to General Huddlestone, now GOC Northern Ireland, who, according to Wingate's own account, 'was delighted by the proposed force and said it was exactly what was urgently needed to curb activities disloyal elements and encourage loyal elements. The sooner it was available the better.'[89]

By 6 June, Wingate had 150 volunteer soldiers and ten officers from 56th Brigade, with Cazalet as his second in command.[90] However, when Wingate reported to GHQ Home Forces the same day, he found objections. Many personal accounts in Wingate's papers are written in the third person, and are possibly transcriptions of now-lost diary entries made for posterity's sake by Lorna or her mother, Ivy Paterson, or possibly as notes by Christopher Sykes. The account of Wingate's meeting at GHQ reads as follows:

> Wingate... was present at a telephone conversation between General [Sir Bernard] Paget and General [Sir John] Anderson, A/CIGS WO, in the course of which General Anderson appeared to tell General Paget that General Haining [now Deputy CIGS] had strong personal objections to Captain Wingate...[91]

After his meeting with Paget, Wingate attended a conference at the War Office, where:

> No objections were raised except on the grounds that the IRA might be annoyed and thus hostilities precipitated. Wingate replied that General Huddlestone considered that the effect of the employment of the proposed force would be the opposite of that suggested. The impression given to Wingate was that the decision to dispose of the scheme on personal grounds had already been arrived at.[92]

Wingate's account of his subsequent interview with Ironside indicates he now regarded Haining as a personal enemy. This conversation has been alluded to already: Wingate's comments about Haining, and the behaviour of units under his command in Palestine, would have been deeply disconcerting were they made public:

> Wingate... complained of the personal attack on himself as improper. He pointed out that apparently it was suggested that he was proposing to use Black and Tan methods whereas, as General Ironside knew, the methods employed by Forces under Wingate's command in Palestine had been the exact opposite of these, and that a high standard of soldierly conduct and compassion to foes had been the rule. This had been necessary, even if not otherwise desirable, in view of the numerous enemies he had had in Palestine as a friend of the Jews. He reminded General Ironside of certain atrocities committed by other Government Forces in Palestine under General Haining's command...and

pointed out that the smallest irregularity on the part of the Jewish-British Force under his command would have met with instant punishment.

General Ironside said that he supposed General Haining was nervous that movement in Northern Ireland might start something and he thought Wingate more likely to do this than anyone else. He did not suppose the objection was fully personal.[93]

Threatening a senior officer with blackmail would normally be cause for dismissal, but fortunately for Wingate, Haining seems to have had even fewer friends in high places, and was, indeed, earning the contempt of at least one figure of growing power. Seven months after Wingate's meeting with Ironside, General Sir Alan Brooke, Dill's successor as GOC Home Forces, described Haining as 'quite useless as Vice Chief of Staff. He understands nothing about military matters and messes everything up' and was muddling War Office business which Brooke then had to sort out. When the new CIGS, Field Marshal Sir John Dill, visited Washington in February 1941, Brooke commented '[M]eanwhile Bob Haining officiates for him! A poor substitute and one who may well make some mistakes and will want watching.'[94] In the light of such comments, Haining's departure for the Middle East, as Intendant General, later in 1941, could be viewed as a demotion. Moreover, Ironside told Wingate that, objections notwithstanding, he intended to employ his force, telling him to report to General Sir Ronald Adam, GOC Northern Command, 'Should Adam like the idea it could be tried out there'.[95] Wingate had a constructive meeting with Adam on 9 June, the same day receiving a letter from Ironside:

> It has been decided to employ your posse in the Southern portion of the Northern Command. General Adam will take you on with enthusiasm and I am sure you will get a chance. As far as I can see, there has been a rumour of 5th Column in Lincolnshire for some time, but no actual discovery. This is a very likely place in which to land.[96]

When Wingate conferred with Adam's staff, he was asked to produce the unit. Upon returning to GHQ Home Forces to expedite its assembly, he discovered he had to submit details of the establishment to the War Office for approval. Having done so, he learned that the War Office 'might or might not approve after an indefinite period for consideration.'[97] There the matter rested until the threat of German invasion receded in August, and Wingate's comments on the staff, on this occasion, seem justified:

> If WO had been helpful it could have had all <u>essential</u> details by [3 June]. Wingate was available for conference during the entire period, and, had the reaction to the suggestion been positive and not negative the whole establishment could have been made out… within a few hours… It is not thus that nations win wars. The fault is not where the WO will put it – on GHQHF.[98]

Rumours of a large, pro-Nazi Fifth Column, of course, turned out to be exactly that, and were already dying down after the BUF was proscribed and Sir Oswald Mosley and many of its members interned in May 1940.[99] The few agents the Germans landed in the UK were quickly intercepted by MI5, and Nazi 'subversive' activities against the UK were limited to the rather pathetic efforts of a tiny group who never left Axis territory, most notoriously Leo Amery's son, John, and William Joyce, AKA 'Lord Haw-Haw', both hanged for treason after the war. This episode is important, however, in illustrating that far from being a pariah, senior commanders were prepared to listen to at least some of Wingate's suggestions for dealing with this threat and look for work which fitted his talents.

On 10 June, Italy declared war on Britain and France. At a meeting of the Middle East Cabinet Committee in July, Amery, now Secretary of State for India, suggested that the ideal man to lead partisan forces in the Italian possessions in Africa was 'a certain Captain OC Wingate... a much more virile and solidly based Lawrence, but with much the same sort of power of inspiring others.'[100] Wavell, now Commander-in-Chief, Middle East, had already contacted London requesting Wingate for such duties.[101] Wingate was thinking along these lines already, but attached to his political agenda. On 15 July, Weizmann met with Haining, who promised to telegraph Wavell authorising him to recruit Jewish soldiers and NCOs in Palestine; this was followed by a plan approved by the Secretary of State for War, Anthony Eden, to raise a Jewish force of 10,000, 3-4,000 from Palestine, the remainder refugees from Europe.[102] Wingate responded with a plan to assemble this force in the Tibesti Mountains, from which it would strike north into Italian Libya.[103] When Wingate met with the new CIGS, Dill, on 17 July, he was told unequivocally that he was going to the Middle East.[104] Upon reporting to the War Office a day later for further details, he was ordered to report to GHQ Middle East in Cairo and was also expressly prohibited from entering Palestine or Transjordan at any time, be it on duty or on leave.[105] This was on Wavell's orders and probably linked with the situation in Palestine, which had been deteriorating rapidly since the White Paper, with bank robberies and ambushes of government vehicles by the *Irgun* recurring throughout summer and autumn 1940.[106] Given the politically risky nature of Wingate's previous activities there, his presence in Palestine may have been viewed as unduly provocative for *both* communities, which is almost certainly why he was directed to East Africa via routes other than Palestine.

G(R) and resistance in Ethiopia

Previous writers claim almost universally that the British 'establishment' opposed the incitement of resistance in Ethiopia, and that the whole idea would have died without Wingate. Burchett proposed that 'Cairo and Khartoum were thick with missions of various kinds, most of them backed by glorified camp followers who were looking for concessions and special areas to exploit as soon as [Ethiopia] was occupied.'[107] Haile Selassie was ignored by these 'international sharks... racketeers and stock market strategists' until Wingate arrived and told him to appeal directly to 'the people of England, America and China', after which Churchill 'settled the hash of the speculators' while Wingate flew the Emperor into Ethiopia as a *fait accompli*, the revolt arising thereafter.[108] Mosley had Wingate adopt the cause of the Emperor as a personal crusade, hand-pick a team of fellow believers – including Dodds-Parker and Airey, both actually serving with G(R) months before Wingate arrived, and neither that enthusiastic about the Ethiopian resistance – and use Wavell's and Churchill's authority to remove those in his way.[109] Sykes was aware of SOE – although he could not reveal this, as its existence was classified until the 1960s – but he did mention the 'department of the General Headquarters known as G(R)', and discussed its role in Ethiopia obliquely.[110] Both Sykes and Royle emphasised the lack of enthusiasm for Haile Selassie among the British high command, and portrayed the Gojjam campaign almost as a 'three man band', between Wingate, Colonel Daniel Sandford, who will feature prominently below, and the Emperor.[111] Even Anthony Mockler's *Haile Selassie's War*, which discussed the activities of the various G(R) Missions in detail, implied that Wingate devised the plan for the Gojjam operation entirely from scratch.[112] Likewise, David Shirreff, in his otherwise superb history of the Gojjam revolt, did not mention G(R) at all – Dodds-Parker, for instance, was merely a 'staff captain at GHQ' – and presented the thesis that the entire operation was originated by Sandford, the hero of his book.[113] Conversely, Professor M.R.D. Foot presented the operation as an SOE project, even though G(R) was still *de facto* a separate organisation, under the command of GHQ Middle East.[114]

Little of this is supported by contemporary documents. Ethiopian resistance to the Italians was chronic from 1936, and from 1937 had logistical support from the French *Deuxième Bureau* and, from 1938, training from anti-fascist Italian veterans of the International Brigades, courtesy of the Comintern.[115] Nor were the British idle: Electra House accumulated 10,000 rifles and a large treasure chest in Sudan from 1938, and around the same time, Dodds-Parker, then a District Commissioner in Sudan, issued several hundred rifles to his friend, the Ethiopian aristocrat, Ras Mesfin Sileshi, on condition he did not use them until Italy declared war on Britain.[116] In late 1938, Captain Richard Whalley of the SDF corresponded with the Foreign Office on the possibility of a 'scallywag show' in Ethiopia, requesting 'H.S. ESQ' be sent to East Africa with 'a prearranged plan with HMG for cooperation during, and after, event', allowing Whalley to recruit Ethiopian refugees in Kenya, forming them into a guerrilla unit with which 'I shall try to annihilate the Italian company in vicinity Lake Rudolf… capture all arms for use further into the country, to arm tribesmen, &c, for the drive of Italians on to SDF.' A concurrent offensive, under the joint command of the British explorer and friend of the Emperor, Wilfred Thesiger, and the Ethiopian Crown Prince, would threaten Addis Ababa. If Whalley could have 4,000 rifles, 200,000 rounds of ammunition, 10,000 Maria Theresa dollars (currency across most of Northeast Africa and Arabia) and enough wirelesses to coordinate his guerrillas, 'it would go down to history [sic] as one of the greatest routs ever…'[117] That guerrillas could pin down Italian effort sufficiently to prevent their army in Italian East Africa being a threat to Sudan or Kenya was to be a common argument in the months ahead, Major Mallaby of the War Office commenting to ED Cavendish-

Bentinck of the Foreign Office (the future chairman of the Joint Intelligence Committee) on 27 April 1939 that this might be the only feasible way to hold Sudan, given the small size of its garrison.[118]

Yet, when MI(R) inherited this project in mid-1939, it found little enthusiasm from British authorities in Khartoum, who had reported already that the Italians had pacified southern and eastern Ethiopia, the only serious resistance remaining in the west, the heartland of Ethiopia's traditional ruling ethnic group, the Amhara. Supporting these 'bitter enders' was viewed in Khartoum as not worth the effort and likely to provoke an Italian invasion of Sudan.[119] However, this did not preclude contingency planning, and G(R) produced a list of likely operatives for Ethiopia, the most significant being Colonel Daniel Sandford and Lieutenant Colonel Hugh Boustead.[120] Sandford, a retired British officer, had explored in Ethiopia since 1907, farmed there since 1921 and, from January 1935, acted as an advisor to Haile Selassie, becoming a close confidant. Sandford escaped from Ethiopia during the invasion of 1935 and from his home in Guildford he corresponded and visited regularly with the Emperor, in exile in Bath, over the next three years.[121] In September 1939 he was working in Wavell's intelligence cell in Cairo, from where he was sent to Platt by Wavell 'to retain at your discretion for work in connection with the ABYSSINIAN project.'[122] Another former Army officer – he had been a junior officer in the Royal Navy when war broke out in 1914, then absconded and joined the South African Army as a private soldier - Hugh Boustead spent many years in the Sudan Political Service before joining the SDF in 1939. In October 1940 he was named specifically in the first MI(R) proposal to penetrate western Ethiopia, a plan to take two squadrons of the Sudan Horse up the Nile Valley; however, G(R) then designated him as Commanding Officer (CO) of the Frontier Battalion of the SDF, raised specifically to garrison G(R) bases on the frontier and inside western Ethiopia, in which capacity he served under Wingate.[123]

Ironside and Wavell's Chief of Staff, Major General Arthur Smith, produced a policy for the 'conquest of Abyssinia' in September 1939; this incorporated 'Native risings encouraged by Guerrilla tactics by British columns and by Propaganda', in which Sandford evidently had much input.[124] These 'native risings', it was emphasised, should not go off at 'half-cock', part of the caution of the Sudan authorities being attributed to fear that a 'half-cock' operation was exactly what was ensuing.[125] To prevent this, it was recommended that a 'Guerrilla Commandant' should be appointed to GHQ Khartoum to oversee a G(R) staff including 'several guerrilla leaders', to ensure the rebellion was prepared and timed properly.[126] As to operations, Ironside suggested that 'small camel columns should be formed and should live on the country', and in southern Ethiopia, 'small self-contained columns mainly for harassing purposes on the lines of East Africa Campaign of last war.'[127] Wavell felt 'that there has been a tendency in the past to look on an offensive in Abyssinia too much on the "regular operations scale". He feels – with the CIGS – that operations should be conducted more on the lines of those undertaken by Lawrence of Arabia.'[128] These would substitute for an invasion of Italian East Africa, freeing regular forces for the Mediterranean.[129]

Sandford, under Wavell's orders, contacted resistance leaders inside Ethiopia from October 1939 onwards, and also pressured the authorities to allow Haile Selassie to come to Sudan as soon as possible.[130] Dodds-Parker, recruited into G(R) from the Grenadier Guards in 1940, reconnoitred the Sudan-Ethiopia border, assessing the chances of rebellion in border regions, while GHQ Middle East ordered the assembly of arsenals near the border and the recruitment of British and Ethiopian volunteers for several G(R) Missions which, once Italy declared war, would enter Ethiopia to distribute arms, coordinate the rebellion and provide the resistance with technical support, as prescribed in Gubbins' pamphlets.[131] Consequently, when Italy declared war, on 10 June 1940, Wavell could issue operational instructions to G(R) that very day. The intent was to 'spread the revolt over the whole of ITALIAN EAST AFRICA and so harass the ITALIANS as to make them expend their resources on internal security.'[132] This would be supported logistically and directed, via the G(R) Missions, by the overall British commander in the region concerned – General Sir William Platt, GOC Sudan, in the case of Gojjam – who would also send 'Technical Advisors' to assist resistance leaders.[133] A secret appendix to the Operational Order went into detail: Missions were to enter Ethiopia, thereby:

a) Giving technical advice to the ABYSSINIAN Rebel Leaders
b) Co-ordination of the activities of the various Rebel Leaders
c) Acting as a channel for communications between C in C Middle East and the Rebel Leaders for political and administrative purposes.[134]

Also conforming with Gubbins' prescriptions, each Mission controlled several Report and Advisory Centres (later redesignated Operational Centres), moving forward of the main Mission to:

a) In an advisory capacity…form a link between the Mission HQ and outlying Rebel Leaders.
b) [P]rovide a link in the supply organisation between the bases and the Rebel bands.
c) As representing the Mission to advise the local Rebel Leader.[135]

The Head of the Mission was designated explicitly to steer rebel operations in central Ethiopia through controlling their supplies: 'To do so, he must have the necessary prestige, and this can be most easily acquired if the Rebels learn to regard him as the authority through whom they apply for the assistance they require.'[136] Sandford was to command Mission 101, the largest, tasked with penetrating the Gojjam plateau, the heartland of the Amhara elite, and then believed to be the main centre of resistance. On 21 June 1940, Platt issued operational instructions: Sandford was to 'coordinate the actions of the Abyssinians under my [Platt's] general direction'; Mission 101 was to be established inside Ethiopia by 1 August 1940, and should direct the rebels to prevent the Italians deploying troops away from northwest Ethiopia.[137]

This was boosted when Haile Selassie, dispatched on Churchill's orders, arrived in Khartoum on 27 June 1940. Mission 101 entered Ethiopia on 12 August 1940, Sandford deciding already that central and eastern Gojjam should be Mission 101's main area of operations because it was the rebel area most accessible from Sudan. It was also the best location to spread the revolt in the directions required by Platt, its central position in western Ethiopia granting access to the main roads heading north and south from Addis Ababa, the capital and main administrative centre. By mid-September Sandford had established a base at Sakala, in northern Gojjam, and persuaded rival Ethiopian chiefs to begin attacks against the Italians with gifts of arms and money; Boustead's Frontier Battalion had established supply dumps on the frontier and was escorting supply convoys to the Mission. Sandford also informed Platt that the locals were enquiring when Haile Selassie would return, in his view essential if the resistance was to be escalated.[138] He was encouraged by what he saw as the keen response to a proclamation from the Emperor spread by Mission 101 and dropped as leaflets all over Ethiopia, and recommended that the Emperor should establish a headquarters on the natural fortress of Mount Belaiya by December 1940.[139]

Unfortunately, the parlous state of GHQ Middle East's logistics led to the resistance taking a low priority. Haile Selassie saw this as arising from hostility from the 'establishment' in Cairo and Khartoum, communicating this opinion in several telegrams to Churchill.[140] This was one issue addressed by the Ministerial Conference at Khartoum on 28-31 October 1940, at which the Minister for War, Anthony Eden, General Jan C. Smuts, the South African Prime Minister and member of Churchill's War Cabinet, Wavell, Platt and General Sir Alan Cunningham, the GOC East Africa, formulated policy towards Ethiopia. Wavell argued here that Italian forces in Italian East Africa were cut off and running out of supplies, so the resistance should be sufficient to contain them. Consequently, the border posts at Gallabat and Kassala should be retaken, and then used as entry points for supplies to the resistance.[141] Platt projected he could retake Gallabat by mid-November, and Kassala thereafter, provided he received reinforcements, while Cunningham could begin operations against Kismayu, in southern Italian East Africa, by January 1941.[142] The conference also decided upon policy towards the Emperor: it was agreed that, while there were doubts about his acceptability to the Amhara nobility and other tribal groups, he was still the best available rallying point and should be used as such.[143] The Emperor, therefore, was placed at the heart of the resistance by British government policy and military strategy well before Wingate's arrival in East Africa.

Of equal interest is the meeting between Eden, Wavell, Platt's Chief of Staff, Brigadier Scobie, and Majors Brown and Sugden of G(R) on 29 October, at which the hitherto haphazard arrangements for the resistance were revealed to a clearly furious Eden. It emerged that just 5,073 out of a promised 10,000 rifles had been issued to the resistance, most of these being Zulu War vintage, single-shot Martini-Henrys, rechambered to .303 calibre and intended originally for Local Defence Volunteers (later the Home Guard) in England; just 735 of the more modern Lee-Enfield .303s were available, and Ethiopians arriving on the frontier asking for weapons were being turned away.[144] Two responses were agreed upon: the recruitment of 'free' Ethiopian battalions from refugee camps in Kenya and Sudan, which had begun already, should be escalated, and, as Haile Selassie had requested British officers to train and command them, it was agreed that this should be 'examined'; moreover, as the battalions' principal role would be as the Emperor's bodyguard once he entered Ethiopia, they should be trained and equipped as regular infantry, not guerrillas.[145] Secondly:

> Another request was for an officer representing the British Army to whom, in Colonel Sandford's absence, the Emperor could address military questions. It seemed evident… that what was needed was a senior staff officer to do for the revolt here what Colonel Sandford was doing the other side of the frontier. At present there was no coordination. General Wavell said he would appoint an officer for this purpose.[146]

Conforming with the Operational Order of 10 June, G(R) Technical Advisors would be attached to the resistance, which now, at Haile Selassie's insistence, would be designated officially as 'patriots', and the creation of the Report and Advisory Centres would be accelerated.[147] As to the 'senior staff officer' to liaise between the revolt and the Emperor, Amery and Wavell were firm that this should be Orde Wingate. In August 1940, Amery had written to Lord Lloyd proposing Wingate should lead 'whatever Jewish force is raised in Palestine', but when Lloyd rejected this, Amery suggested him for Ethiopia.[148] The same month, Amery wrote to Haining, the Deputy CIGS, suggesting Wingate could be used in either the Middle East or Ethiopia, making the telling observation that Wingate was '[n]ot altogether easy to fit into any ordinary disciplined organisation but very much the man for a small show on his own.'[149] Interestingly, in the light of former differences with Wingate, Haining replied saying that, in response to Amery's suggestion, he had cabled Wavell offering him Wingate as 'suitable for leading irregulars or rebels in Abyssinia.'[150] Wavell had apparently contacted London already to request Wingate 'to fan into flame the embers of revolt that had smouldered in parts of the Abyssinian highlands ever since the Italian occupation', as he put it after the war, although Wingate's initial remit was less ambitious.[151] Wingate arrived in Khartoum in early November, his official role delineated in a letter from Platt to the Emperor of 10 November. He was appointed General Staff Officer 2 (GSO2) on Platt's staff, as a major, with the duty of promoting the rebellion; 'He will maintain close touch with Your Imperial Majesty on all military matters connected with the rebellion, and will represent my Headquarters in such matters.'[152] Circumstances point to Wavell summoning Wingate to administer 'shock therapy' to what he perceived as a flagging operation, unlikely to endear either man to its planners. Dodds-Parker was attached to Wingate as his General Staff Officer 3; a detailed description of the duties of this job might not be strictly relevant to any historical study, as Dodds-Parker's main role in reality seems to have been pacifying the numerous senior officers Wingate insulted over the following months, and he attributed his survival in the post largely to being the only man in Khartoum that

Wingate trusted and the only man in G(R) that Platt trusted.[153] Whatever his talent for finding enemies, far from being a lone voice, driving an operation no one else wanted, Wingate was expected to do what he did by senior commanders in the theatre.

Wingate takes charge

In his official report on the Gojjam operation, Wingate made his first use of the term 'doctrine'. This resembled Lawrence's 'idea that produces friendliness' in the local population, although Wingate might not have liked having this pointed out: 'The first essential for a successful campaign behind the enemy's lines is a clear and definite war aim for the patriots to pursue. It is... important that it be preached by men of integrity and personality; otherwise it will not be believed.'[154] It is apparent from statements in Wingate's papers from 1940 onwards that his 'doctrine' was intended to be more than just this: it was the political message to be conveyed by military action, shaping organisation and strategy.[155] The 'doctrine' for Ethiopia was:

> 52 nations let you down in 1935. That act of aggression led to this war. It will be the first to be revenged. We are not, as your exploiters the Italians say, merely another imperialism. We offer you freedom and an equal place among the nations. But what sort of place will this be if you have had no share in your liberation? Fight then under your Emperor against odds. We are bringing you trained troops to help you. All of you who have taken service with the enemy will be admitted to the Emperor's service with equal rank and emoluments.[156]

Consequently, Wingate noted, 'it is vital to our cause that we should make it plain to the world that we were being generous as well as just to Ethiopia. For early evacuation of Ethiopia to be practicable it was necessary to support the Emperor's authority and provide him from the first with an army' as G(R) were trying to do with the Ethiopian battalions.[157] Developing his ideas at approximately the same time as Mao Zedong and a generation before Che Guevara, Wingate evidently viewed the political context of guerrilla warfare as its main shaping factor. In this case, his presumption was that Britain and the League of Nations had done nothing to punish the Italian invasion of Ethiopia in 1935–36, and that the aim of operations now was to correct this error. He seems to have formulated this view after meeting with Haile Selassie shortly after arriving in Khartoum on 6 November 1940. According to Wingate's *Report*, the Emperor was in low spirits, telling him that little had been done to make the rebellion 'practical politics' and that he feared he was just a pawn. Wingate's response was apparently that the liberation of Ethiopia was 'an indispensable part of the British war aims' and that it was essential that Ethiopians play the leading part in this. The Emperor should take as his motto a proverb found in Gese: 'If I am not for myself, who will be for me?'[158]

Wilfred Thesiger, at that time a subaltern in the SDF, was ordered to report to Wingate shortly afterwards. His record of their first meeting provides some indication of Wingate's ambitions at this stage:

118   Orde Wingate

[H]e immediately launched into his plans to invade Gojjam, destroy the Italian forces stationed there, reach Addis Ababa before the South African Army from Kenya could do so, and restore Haile Selassie to his throne... It was obvious as he talked that Wingate never doubted he would be given command of the forthcoming campaign in Gojjam, even though Colonel Sandford... and Colonel Boustead... were a rank senior to him.[159]

Wingate was dismissive of what had been done so far:

[T]he material aids [Mission 101] brought... were negligible. They were not, and at that time could not have been, supported by our aircraft, and future developments clearly show that, while the effect of their presence on the Italians was mildly encouraging, that on Ethiopians who adhered to the Italian government was nil. To sum up, the Mission... was too inconsiderable and unsupported to raise more than a query in the minds of the population... [T]he Mission should be of a character and scope to command the respect of the people with whom it has to deal and should... be given a call on air support, which is by far the most convincing... way of indicating to the population concerned the bona fides of our enterprise.[160]

More damningly, from his *Appreciation*:

[I]t should be settled beforehand, as precisely as possible, what tasks the Mission is to carry out, and the head of the Mission should, from the first, be placed in touch with the Commander of the force which is later to operate behind the enemy's lines... There was no effectual collaboration between the SUDAN and Col. SANDFORD, nor did there appear to exist any feasible plan of campaign that was likely to produce tangible results in the time available.[161]

Note the presumption that the Mission Head and the commander of the fighting force inserted behind enemy lines would be different people, not implicit in Gubbins' writings or, indeed, in G(R)'s planning and preparation for Gojjam.

By October 1940, G(R)'s efforts centred on Mission 101's supply base at Faguta and an outstation, Mission 101 North, under Major Arthur Bentinck, in the Lake Tana region, north of Gojjam. Whalley was supporting patriots in southwest Ethiopia from the Boma plateau in southern Sudan, and other Missions were forming.[162] Having raised the Emperor's morale, Wingate flew to Faguta to confer with Sandford on 20 November, ostensibly to improve cooperation between GHQ Khartoum and Mission 101.[163] Wingate noted that this visit 'served its main purpose which was to convince me that my plan was workable', yet the records of this meeting provide the earliest evidence for the different approaches to the rebellion advocated by these two officers.[164] Sandford was pleased that regular supply convoys would now be coming his way, and by the impending arrival of the G(R) Operational Centres which Wingate would train, and offered advice on their organisation.[165] However, consistent with his arguments for more centralised command and control, Wingate wanted logistical support to be the sole responsibility of the Operational Centres, under his command, whereas Sandford preferred the existing arrangement wherein the Mission was responsible for distributing arms and money (echoing Gubbins).[166] Sandford had decided already that British 'Advisory and Store Centres' should be established in Gojjam, with dry-weather roads being built back to Sudan, along which supplies for the patriots should arrive, along with Haile Selassie and his bodyguard, at the earliest available opportunity. His aim was to secure Gojjam as the stronghold of a 'Free Ethiopian' Government and a base for guerrilla offensives against the roads running north from Addis Ababa to Eritrea and southwest to the Kenya border.[167] Prospects for this were dwindling. On 8 December, Ras Hailu, the hereditary lord of Gojjam, who had been collaborating with the Italians since 1936, returned to Debra Markos, the capital of Gojjam, wearing an Italian general's uniform, to a tumultuous reception, following this with a triumphant tour of the countryside. Two chiefs defected from the resistance to the Italians, and Ras Hailu promised the Italians he could pacify Gojjam for them provided they made him *Negus*, or king, of Gojjam (as his father had been before him). Concurrently, a large force of cavalry under his son, Lij Mammo, began scouring the countryside for guerrillas.[168]

Wingate's approach now seemed more valid. It is here, not the politics or strategic aim of the rebellion, that Wingate parted company with his peers:

Hitherto we had made the mistake of appealing to the cupidity and self interest of the Ethiopians by offering them money and poor quality war material. These qualities were all on the side of the enemy. Courage, faith and self respect, these were the qualities we could appeal to successfully because they were on our side. We had first to convince the Ethiopian, suspicious as he was of all white men, of our bona fides. This meant he must see us fighting not by his side but in front of him. His contact with our young officers must convince him that...we were not only brave soldiers but devoted to the cause of his liberties.[169]

Wingate proposed that the British should not just send personnel in to distribute arms and money and perform staff work:

[C]ease trying to stimulate the revolt from without, using agents, but...enter amongst the patriots using small columns of the highest fighting quality, with first class equipment, to perform exploits and to teach self sacrifice and devotion by example instead of by Precept. *By doing so we should not only fan the revolt to proportions that really threatened the enemy's main bases, but should also assume its direction and control – a most important factor in any future settlement.* [Italics mine][170]

Wingate was therefore raising the role of the Operational Centres from advice, coordination and administration to that of fighting units intended to spearhead the military phase of the revolt. This was evident from the organisation and training he provided his penetration forces, which were divided into three types: the G(R)

Operational Centres, an independent Ethiopian mortar platoon, drawn from Ras Mesfin's retainers, and two regular battalions, one Ethiopian, the other Boustead's SDF Frontier Battalion. Wingate intended to form ten Operational Centres, each consisting of a British officer (captain, major or SDF *Bimbashi*), five sergeants and 200 Ethiopians divided into ten guerrilla squads, intended not to advise, but to fight: 'By doing exploits [sic] these young officers were to obtain an ascendancy over the patriots in their areas and were to keep in constant touch by wireless with the directing staff. The latter would thus be able to direct the available force into the most profitable channel.'[171] The Ethiopian contingent for the first three Operational Centres was recruited from volunteers from the refugees in Sudan, trained by Wingate himself, while other centres were to be raised by Sandford inside Ethiopia and trained by Mission 101 in Gojjam, and this proved more problematic.[172] Wingate was also promised four Ethiopian refugee battalions, but found the 1st not to his satisfaction and broke it up to form the first three Operational Centres, while 3rd and 4th Battalions never arrived; only 2nd Ethiopian Battalion reached Gojjam.[173] The final element of his force, and the only one near full strength, was the Frontier Battalion, which became Wingate's 'spearhead'.[174]

To Wingate, guerrilla warfare was a matter for professional experts, a view reinforced by his training methods. As in Palestine, Wingate taught tactics through battle drills, instilled via explanation on sand models, demonstration by instructors, and imitation until the squads matched his required standard.[175] The aim was apparently to instill set tactical methods and responses upon guerrilla forces via formal training, a move towards their 'regularisation' and not something mentioned in any MI(R) or G(R) document. As to the strategy these trained guerrillas were supposed to carry out, Wingate echoed *Seven Pillars* again, almost certainly unconsciously, but also some of Gubbins' proposed guerrilla strategy:

> Guerrillas aim at bringing the enemy to a stand-still in the heart of this own occupied territory. It is impossible for any enemy always to present an unbreakable front at all points. Where his troops are living, training, resting, recreating and recovering from the effects of conflict with our regular forces, the enemy is compelled to lay himself open to attack. In normal conditions he counts upon his foe being unable to attack him in his rear areas; he counts upon the local population being either friendly or cowed. Guerrilla warfare, in the first place, is therefore possible only when a large proportion of the civilian population surrounding the enemy's back areas is friendly to the guerrillas. Where this is so, however, unrivalled opportunities exist for ambush and surprise of every description. The essence of guerrilla warfare is...surprise combined with security. Both are obtained by the employment of numerous bodies so small that: (a) the enemy cannot find them to strike at; (b) if one or two are destroyed, it makes no difference to the success of the general campaign.[176]

Wingate's aim, evidently, was to initiate an offensive inside Italian occupied territory, tied to British strategic aims, built around his 'trained guerrillas' supported *by* rather than supportive *of* the patriots. He also revived a common theme: creating a sense of his ubiquity in the mind of the enemy via use of superior mobility, as Lawrence proposed in *Seven Pillars* and Callwell had done in *Small Wars*.

Wingate decided, while visiting Sandford, that Haile Selassie should establish a preliminary headquarters at Mount Belaiya, approximately halfway between the frontier and Gojjam. By December 1940, G(R) had secured enough camels to begin sending convoys to Belaiya to build a supply dump sufficient, Wingate estimated, to support the two regular battalions and the Operational Centres, and the first Operational Centre entered Ethiopia in late December.[177] However, logistics soon fell victim to the environment, Wingate noting that:

> I had hoped that Sandford's Mission would succeed in purchasing some five thousand mules to take over from the camels in the precipitous areas. It proved unable to provide these and the camels had to go wherever we went, with the result that the majority died in the course of the campaign.[178]

In fact, *all* of the 15,000 camels G(R) purchased in late 1940 were dead by June 1941, Wingate reporting that they died through stubbornly refusing to eat the plentiful grazing on the Gojjam plateau, and popular tales have it that the route from the border to Gojjam could be found simply by following the trail of stinking carcasses.[179] Whatever the cause, the mass attrition of the camels, the principal means of transport, inflicted considerable strain upon the campaign in its early stages and the expedition's precarious logistical state was to be another factor causing Wingate's doctrine to evolve in practice.

The mission evolves

The strategic context changed during training, initially as a result of the *debacle* at Gallabat on 6-10 November 1940, where Brigadier William Slim's 10th Indian Brigade's attempt to take a pair of Italian-occupied forts on the Sudan-Ethiopia border was defeated. A well-planned, well-prepared and initially successful attack fell victim to factors beyond Slim's control – principally most of his small tank force breaking down on the rocky terrain and a 'green' British battalion assigned to him shortly before the attack routing after being bombed for the first time.[180] Wavell called a conference in Cairo on 1-2 December 1940 to update British strategy in Africa and the Mediterranean; present were Platt, Cunningham, General H.M. Wilson (GOC Egypt) and Air Marshal Sir Arthur Longmore, with Wingate invited to speak on the progress of the Ethiopian resistance. Wavell informed the conference of *Compass*, to be launched ten days later, and ordered that pressure be stepped up concurrently on Italian East Africa. In the south, pressure would be exerted 'by means of small mobile columns' operating from Kenya, Cunningham being ordered to advance on Kismayu, in Italian Somalia in May or June, after which a penetration should be made into southwest Ethiopia in conjunction with forces operating from Boma in Sudan.[181]

These would presumably consist largely of Whalley's patriots, as Wavell intended the main effort to be via guerrilla activity:

> The ruling idea in my mind... at this conference was that the fomentation of the rebel movement... offered with the resources available the best prospect of making the Italian position impossible and eventually reconquering the country. I did not intend... a large scale invasion... I intended that our main effort should be devoted to furthering and supporting the rebellion by irregular action.[182]

This formed part of Churchill's reaction to the German buildup in Bulgaria, threatening Greece and Yugoslavia: on 31 December 1940, he ordered that Italian forces in Italian East Africa should be destroyed by the end of April 1941, thus releasing British troops for deployment elsewhere, principally to Greece. Wavell reinforced Sudan with 5th Indian Division, straight from India, plus two bomber squadrons, with 4th Indian Division redeploying from the Western Desert during December and January. The end of November 1940 saw the under-strength 1st South African Division, two African Brigades, two fighter squadrons and two bomber squadrons deployed under Cunningham in Kenya.[183] Operations were to begin on 19 January 1941, with Platt's 4th and 5th Indian Divisions striking at Kassala while Cunningham's 1st South African Division and 11th and 12th African Brigades pushed into Italian Somalia with the objective of capturing the capital, Mogadishu.[184] There was no initial intent to drive on into greater Ethiopia, and Platt's stated aim for the Gojjam rebellion was to pin Italian forces which might otherwise be used to reinforce Kassala, conforming to Holland's prescribed role for MI(R).[185] Wingate understood this implicitly and agreed with Platt a bold move to distract the Italians, taking the campaign to its next stage:

> I pointed out to General Platt that at that moment, Xmas 1940, the enemy was prepared for us either to advance in force towards Gojjam, or to make out a major attack on Eritrea. He would rapidly transfer air forces to whichever front he considered the most dangerous. Platt's attack could not begin until the end of January. If the Emperor entered a few days in advance this would divert the enemy's attention and lead to the preliminary transfer of enemy aircraft. The plan was approved. The necessary covering operations were carried out; and, on 20th January 1941, the Emperor crossed the frontier at the place chosen by me on the River DINDER.[186]

Platt felt the presence of the Emperor would increase Italian interest in the Belaiya-Gojjam area and draw forces away from other fronts; thus his insertion had the aim of supporting Platt's thrust into Eritrea, as Wingate understood.[187] Moreover, under the influence of Sandford's reports, it was still hoped the Emperor's re-entry would bring a mass uprising, although Wingate was already circumspect: 'The patriot forces appear, as I expected, to be able to move at will. They have their being within the guts of the enemy. Such forces, however, must be wisely directed or they tend to get out of control and invite disaster.'[188]

Nevertheless, Wingate's ambition was soon evident. Having established the Emperor at Belaiya, on 6 February Wingate and Sandford flew back to Khartoum for a conference, chaired by Platt, on policy for the campaign, on 12 February 1941. Wingate had written previously to Platt suggesting an expanded G(R) organisation, proposing himself as GSO1 and 'Commander of British and Ethiopian Forces in the Field' with Mission 101 assisting him.[189] This was confirmed at the conference: Wingate, promoted Lieutenant Colonel, would 'direct the patriot operations in the field', while Sandford, now a Brigadier, was appointed the Emperor's personal advisor.[190]

Wingate's operational plan, approved at the conference, was clearly not one for a protracted guerrilla campaign:

> My primary objective was to drive the enemy out of Gojjam. After that I intended to move on and cut the North and South communications between the capital and Dessye [not 'harass', as Platt instructed]. I knew the enemy would attack as long as possible along his Roman roads, and that, if I wanted to fight him, I must do so on these roads. I knew that he would resent the attack of Haile Selassie as an assault on his prestige and that if he were not hard pressed he would resume the offensive... With these facts in mind I made the following plan. I would divide my force into two parts, in the proportion of one to three. The weaker force should contain the Northern Italian Force until reinforced and strong enough to go on and cut the Dessye-Gondar road. The stronger force, under my own immediate command I would direct upon the Nile bridge at SAFARTAK [at the far western edge of Gojjam, on the main road from Addis Ababa into Gojjam] thus cutting the enemy's retreat, and then proceed by a process of night attack plus fifth column penetration to reduce the various garrisons.[191]

The northern thrust, commanded by Wingate's old friend from Palestine, Major Anthony Simonds, summoned to East Africa at Wingate's request, was already moving towards Bahr Dar Giorgis as Wingate and the Emperor entered Ethiopia, and consisted of No.2 Operational Centre and No.3 Patrol Company of the SDF Frontier Battalion; it was designated Beghemder Force, after Beghemder province, northeast of Gojjam, in which it was to operate.[192] The main body, aimed at Safartak, Wingate designated Gideon Force, a title he had wanted to give the Night Squads.

Gideon's tricking of the Midianites into attacking each other in the dark was one of this deeply spiritual soldier's favourite Biblical tales, and it is difficult not to see parallels in the tactics Wingate adopted 'to reduce the various garrisons'. By day, Operational Centres harassed communications around the fortified towns which lined the 'Roman Roads', planting mines and ambushing and sniping smaller convoys, while Boustead's Frontier Battalion 'shot up' the towns themselves with long-ranged mortar and machine-gun fire. By night, they attacked 'secretly, often and from as many directions as possible, to attempt to create in the minds of the garrisons of these localities the same erroneous impression of our strength.'[193] Parties of forty to fifty approached Italian camps under cover of darkness; one element laid mortars and machine-guns on Italian campfires while the other followed a similar attack pattern to the Night Squads, closing within ten yards, then throwing grenades and charging in with the bayonet: having carried the position, they would then set up to ambush any counter-attackers, before withdrawing at first light.[194] The Italians were most helpful, lighting fires night after night, providing excellent beacons for Wingate's raiders; they did not patrol the countryside surrounding their camps nor even set picquets and so were surprised effortlessly. They responded to attacks largely by barraging the surrounding countryside with every gun, mortar and machine-gun available, in all directions and apparently aiming at nothing in particular, wasting vast amounts of ammunition and, in Platt's words, 'waging a war of nerves on [themselves].'[195]

The Sudanese soldiers of the Frontier Battalion proved superbly proficient in these operations. Others were less so. It was Simonds who first drew attention to perhaps the major factor affecting the subsequent evolution of Wingate's plan. The first report Wingate received upon his return to Belaiya on 15 February 1941 was a letter from Simonds at Engiabarra, on the main Italian road behind Dangila. Upon climbing the Gojjam escarpment, Beghemder force had been asked to leave the immediate area by the locals, and Simonds noted:

> There is a very distinct and noticeable apathy in the Gojjam, an attitude that 'why fight & get killed, we have suffered enough for five years, let the British conquer the Italians & then we can take back Ethiopia for ourselves.' This is a very real attitude and you must face up to it.[196]

G(R)'s Mission 107 had already found the Galla and Amhara of southern Ethiopia keener on killing each other than the Italians; Major Arthur Bentinck, commanding Mission 101 North in Beghemder, faced constant complaints from local chiefs about alleged British duplicity towards Ethiopia and refusals to cooperate unless more rifles were forthcoming, and reported despairingly of G(R)-supplied rifles being used for hunting, or bribing potential supporters, or sold on to *Shifta* or even the Italians, and G(R)-supplied ammunition being wasted in constant, incessant celebratory fusillades.[197] In truth, there was no such thing as a 'typical' patriot. The Ethiopians in the Operational Centres and the Mortar Platoon, drawn mainly from Ras Mesfin's retainers, proved keen, disciplined and efficient throughout the operation. Despite the atrocious leadership of their white officers – Wingate was to eventually sack their CO in the field – 2nd Ethiopians also acquitted themselves well and with a high level of bravery: they held their ground against almost the entire Italian garrison in Gojjam as it tried to retreat across the Charaka River on 6 March 1941, despite odds against them of nearly 20:1, while the retainers of the senior noble, Ras Kassa, fighting under Wingate later in the campaign, charged Italian positions with sword and shield.[198] Local guerrillas were a different matter. As irregulars, their performance often depended on their standard of leadership which, to Ethiopians, was linked to

Captain Orde Wingate in Palestine in 1938 (left) and Brigadier Orde Wingate in India, 1943 (right). Just five years separate these photographs, but so does some arduous campaigning in Ethiopia and Burma.

Brigadier Michael Calvert, a great fighting soldier and leader, and Wingate's most loyal subordinate, but perhaps not the most reliable of witnesses.

Field Marshal Earl Wavell (centre) with Brigadier Bernard Fergusson (second right, with Wingate visible at far right). Wavell was Wingate's great benefactor, while Fergusson, of all his subordinates, was closest to being Wingate's intellectual equal.

Field Marshal Lord Slim, seen here on the right as GOC Fourteenth Army, listening to Major General Douglas Gracey, gave his qualified support to the second Chindit operation and became Wingate's severest and most influential critic after the war.

General Sir Reginald Wingate was Orde Wingate's second cousin. As Kitchener's chief of intelligence and Governor of the Sudan and Egypt, he had been a figure of immense importance in the British Empire of the early twentieth century and was to exert some considerable influence over Orde's early career.

T.E. Lawrence was another distant relative, although Wingate went to great pains to stress the distance. The two men may have been alike in appearance and temperament, but their ideas on guerrilla warfare were poles apart.

Fawzi al Quwuqji, who was to command Arab insurgents over three decades. Rather than the irregular 'guerrillas' of popular myth, in 1936–38 he relied upon a hardcore of full-time fighters with regular army experience and training.

The operations of Wingate's Special Night Squads in Palestine fit not only into British strategy for dealing with the insurgency, but also into the 'Iron Wall' concept of Vladimir Jabotinsky, seen here as an officer in the British Army's Jewish Legion of the First World War.

Moshe Dayan, Yitzhak Sadeh and Yigal Allon. Sadeh's FOSH, a special unit within the *Haganah*, was beginning to adopt an aggressive and pre-emptive approach to dealing with Arab guerrillas before Wingate's arrival in Palestine, yet he, Dayan and Allon counted themselves among Wingate's disciples.

The Night Squads were drawn from volunteers from the Jewish Settlement Police, almost all of them also *Haganah* members. Wingate was fully aware of *Haganah* involvement, and encouraged it.

The Emperor Haile Selassie of Ethiopia with Brigadier Daniel Sandford on his right and Colonel Orde Wingate to his left, inspecting a map during the successful operation against the Italians in the Gojjam region of Western Ethiopia. Sandford, an ardent servant of the Emperor, wanted to see a mass popular uprising in his support, whilst Wingate wanted something altogether more controlled and tied to British strategic objectives in the region.

Above: Wingate leading the Emperor back into Addis Ababa, 5 May 1941, an event which has led to some persistent myths growing up about Wingate's Ethiopian campaign.

Left: Unlike the British Army, the Japanese had training and tactics ideal for jungle warfare, which proved devastatingly effective in Malaya and Burma in 1942. Slim and Wingate had different views on how to puncture the myth of the 'Super-Jap'.

Wingate's first Chindit operation, Operation *Longcloth*, was carried out with a mixture of British, Gurkha and Burmese troops, none of them 'Special Forces' by any definition of the term.

A combination of supply by airdrop and mule transport granted the Chindits a level of mobility other units lacked in the mountainous jungles of northwest Burma.

Another key factor was the use of large, mule-portable wireless sets with a purpose-designed communications net to coordinate the activities of columns dispersed over a wide area of northern Burma.

The addition of the USAAF No.1 to his Chindit Forces took Wingate to a new level of ambition. Now the Chindits could carry out major operations deep in the Japanese rear with the aim of capturing major objectives and destroying large Japanese formations, with the main killing instrument being air power, exemplified by this Air Commando B-25 Mitchell.

Admiral Lord Louis Mountbatten with Chiang Kai-shek and Madame Chiang. Mountbatten, the Supreme Allied Commander in Southeast Asia, was another powerful backer of Wingate and the Chindits, but this did not prevent him from being linked by some with the 'anti-Wingate conspiracy' after the war. Having to accommodate the chronically difficult Chiang was a factor in setting the agenda for the second Chindit operation.

One of the very last photographs taken of Wingate, and a much-reprinted one at that. He is shown here in the 'Broadway' Stronghold, 100 miles behind Japanese lines, during Operation *Thursday* with Colonel John Alison second from left with M1 Garand carbine and Calvert third from left. The officer with glasses and slouch hat standing behind Wingate is his aide de camp, Captain George Borrow, a veteran of both Chindit operations who was to die with Wingate in the air crash of 25 March 1944.

Far from the 'maverick' of popular myth, Wingate's operations were an integral part of British strategy in all the theatres in which he served, and were rooted in established British Army practice. He also has much to say to military practitioners of the twenty-first century.

rank: the retainers of senior Amhara nobles were full-time warriors and were often brave and aggressive; those lower down the social scale – the type most prevalent in Gojjam – were often little more than local *Shifta* on the lookout for loot, more of a menace to their own side and the local civilian population than they were to the Italians.[199] Dodds-Parker recalled that the first consignment of rifles Sandford took into Gojjam was doled out to all comers 'and that was the last thing anyone ever saw of them'.[200] Wingate himself commented repeatedly on the lack of aggression of many local tribesmen, and their unwillingness to venture outside their own territory, let alone carry out pursuits, while Simonds reported that a war band of some 1,000 local tribesmen, ostensibly cooperating with Beghemder Force under his command, had refused to press home a night attack against a far smaller Italian force, allowing the Italians to escape.[201] The most serious incident came in the latter stages of the Gojjam operation, when Bellai Zeleka, a prominent guerrilla leader trusted previously by the British, was bribed successfully by Ras Hailu to allow a large Italian force to retreat through his territory unmolested.[202]

It was with these concerns in mind that Wingate issued a standing order on 9 February, restricting the issue of weapons to Ethiopian tribesmen. Each Operational Centre carried 230 Springfield Rifles – a gift from the US government – eleven machine-guns and large amounts of grenades and explosives; Wingate ordered that:

> All this war material belongs to the Operational Centre and will on no account be issued to any patriot who is not going to become part of the Operational Centre and operate directly and permanently under its command... Issue of Springfield rifles to local feudal patriots is prohibited until further orders. The policy is to issue the feudal retainers with French rifles, or other inferior equipment. If possible issues to feudal retainers should be avoided altogether.[203]

This contradicted MI(R)/G(R) set procedures and Sandford's interpretation of why the Mission was in Ethiopia. Wariness about patriot support – escalating rapidly into vitriolic contempt about their motivation and effectiveness – seems to have been the major factor shifting Wingate from the idea of a general guerrilla campaign to one of a small number of units operating under regular command and control. As early as 7 February, he had sent a communication to G(R) Khartoum based on his own observations and Simonds' reports:

> Reference issue arms and ammunition (.) SANDFORDs proposed issues run counter to [Platt's] approved scheme and in my judgement [sic] lead to a situation out of our control (.) Small number patriots reaching BELAYA are not recruits for us to train Emperors bodyguard as agreed but emissaries local chiefs to whom they return (.) Their arming should take second place if we do it at all (.)... SIMONDS reports left at BELAYA confirm...uncoordinated patriot activity.[204]

A day later he confided in Boustead:

> I am worried about… these numerous chits authorising feudal patriots to draw arms. As you can see for yourself at BELAYA arms given to feudal patriots are arms thrown away in nine cases out of ten – and we haven't arms to throw away… *Further, do not forget that the campaign will be fought by the armed forces. These are the Operational Centres, the Ethiopian Battalion and the forces under your own command. The supply and maintenance of these is your first consideration. Forgive me if this is already perfectly clear to you, but as these views are not entirely shared by certain other people, you may have been given a one-sided picture.* [Italics mine][205]

Those 'certain other people' clearly included Sandford, whose actions throughout the campaign indicated that he saw its objective as a mass guerrilla uprising in western-central Ethiopia, beginning with issuing arms to the locals as far and wide as possible. By March 1941, he was probably alone in this hope.

Problems of troop quality were compounded by poor command and control. How David Rooney can argue that Wingate established 'effective wireless communication' with his guerrilla columns is baffling, particularly when Wingate himself commented, after the campaign:

> [T]he whole art consisted in the ready manipulation of separated columns to a common end from a common centre. This manipulation was made almost impossible at times by the appallingly low standard of the signals provided… A thoroughly incapable officer was put in charge… The operators were lazy, ill-trained and sometimes cowardly. The best were Ethiopians, who had trained themselves. But the real fault was not that of the little men on the spot, but that of the Staff Officers who would not appreciate that if it is important to provide good signals for a regular unit in a regular operation, it is vital for operations of small columns within areas occupied by the enemy.[206]

Wingate's correspondence files indicate that he had neither the sets nor the personnel he had requested, Colonel George Green, of Wavell's Staff, telling him in December 1940:

> [I]t is quite out of the question to provide you at once with either operators or sets. As you will appreciate, communications in the Western Desert are stretched to their utmost… Both operators & sets to satisfy your immediate requirements would have to come from units now in action, & that is clearly impossible.[207]

The evidence of Wingate's correspondence files is that, rather than 'effective wireless communication', operational orders, reports and requests for supplies were handwritten, usually in pencil, with varying levels of legibility, on pages torn out of exercise books or – Simonds' preference – Italian official stationery, and carried by runner, although typewriters seem to have been available to Wingate and Sandford.[208] Messages are jumbled chronologically, suggesting they were written and sent when convenient, not when required, and the timing of arrival and response depended upon distance from HQ, with repercussions for the smooth flow of information and reactions to it. Moreover, the 'incoming' file is filled with complaints, from Sandford, Boustead, Major Edward Boyle, commanding 2nd Ethiopians, and even Simonds, about difficulties in contacting Wingate and the frequent lack of information and direction coming from him. Wingate's 'headquarters' consisted of himself and his personal secretary, Avram Akavia, a former Night Squadsman from Palestine summoned to East Africa at Wingate's request, and indeed, Wingate commented to Sandford in March that 'I... am suffering acutely from lack of clerical and official staff. I have only one clerk to type my orders... and do everything else that a commander in the field requires from a normally copious staff.'[209] This was compounded by the poor state of communications necessitating Wingate's constantly moving around to observe how the situation was developing among his units for himself (and sometimes taking it upon himself to lead patrols or even night raids in person), the principal reason for complaints about not being able to find him. This may have been less of a problem had the forces under Wingate's command been of more even quality, and working to a common effective operational and tactical doctrine, which would have meant they could be relied on to continue the mission even when cut off from above, but, Frontier Battalion and Operational Centres apart, this is precisely what Wingate did not have.

By March, Mission 101 had a permanent line of communication back to Sudan, with Royal Engineer units constructing a motorable track, allowing stores to be lorried to Matakal, on the western edge of Gojjam, from where they would be carried forward to Burye by camel convoy, and a South African Air Force flight of three Ju-52s began regular shuttle flights from Sudan to Burye on 17 March.[210] Consequently, Wingate's 'Master-Plan' now resembled less a guerrilla campaign than an offensive by an unusually organised and under-strength regular brigade, a situation emphasised by its fixed line of communications, regularising of its training, organisation, logistics and staff arrangements and by the need to keep certain units concentrated under Wingate's direct command. Indeed, as the campaign progressed a resemblance to the 'small wars' model of all-arms, self-contained columns, supported by local irregulars, driving in behind the enemy, becomes apparent, Wingate's tactical approach increasingly resembling that of British forces concurrently engaging the Italians in North Africa, albeit with no tanks and a few mortars in lieu of artillery. The biggest engagement of the campaign has been alluded to already: on 6 March, when the Italian garrison of the fortified town of Burye – 6,000 men, with armoured cars and close air support – retreating towards Debra Markos, the largest town in central Gojjam, following incessant guerrilla attacks on its lines of communication by the Operational Centres, took Gideon Force's 2nd Ethiopian Battalion by surprise at the Charaka River. In the subsequent battle, the Italians stormed defensive positions arranged hastily by 2nd Ethiopians and eventually broke through, effectively destroying the battalion, although taking 650 casualties themselves.[211] In his official reports and private correspondence on this action, Wingate dishonestly portrayed this as an attempted 'decisive battle' – he had 'turned' the Italians out of a strong defensive position and was now trying to destroy them on the march by using his force's superior mobility to establish blocking and ambush positions onto which they were 'driven' (almost as Callwell recommended and O'Connor's XIII Corps had done with larger Italian forces in North Africa); had he air support, the Italians would have been annihilated.[212] He gave further impression, therefore, that his aim was swift victory through mobile, but 'conventional' warfare rather than the gradual wearing-down of a guerrilla campaign. Where local irregulars were involved, it was in support of regular forces; note Wingate's stated tactical aim in the following passage:

> The modus operandi of the small regular forces is to ambush and cut communications and deliver night attacks, etc. on isolated positions. At the same time, by their presence they stimulate neighbouring patriot activity. After a few days in a given locality a large but temporary patriot force collects and cooperates with the regular nucleus. The enemy, perpetually harassed, eventually decides on flight, when an opportunity occurs for causing his complete disintegration through air action.[213]

In pursuit of this new aim, Boustead was made CO of Gideon Force, with Wingate promoted to Commander of British and Ethiopian forces in Gojjam.[214] By early March, news reached Gideon Force of the defeat of the main Italian force in Ethiopia, at Keren, and Wingate banked upon this producing three things: firstly, the greater air support upon which his mobile operations would hinge; secondly, the final collapse of Italian morale, arising from fear that the British would now pour reinforcements into Gojjam; thirdly, a boost in Haile Selassie's authority leading to an escalation of patriot activity, now it was clearer who was going to win.[215] These cohered into a modified version of his 'Master-Plan':

> The patriot forces... which the Emperor's authority and prestige can raise, are not such as to enable them to deliver successful assaults on the enemy's fortified positions; they are such as to be able to forbid the enemy's movement and to pursue his forces once he leaves [them]. Our... object, therefore, after re-equipping and reinforcing the regular nucleus, will be to produce on the spot a large patriot force under the direct command of His Majesty the Emperor in person.[216]

Wingate therefore had some use for the patriots. The first and most obvious was as a guerrilla force harassing Italian communications and small forces on the move while leaving 'high intensity' conventional fighting against larger forces and defended positions to the regular troops of Gideon Force. The second was playing a part in the increasing use of bluff, propaganda and psychological attack, marking Wingate's subsequent operations in Ethiopia. On several occasions, beginning at the key Italian fortified town of Debra Markos on 30 March, Wingate offered terms to Italian commanders with the implication that they had a brief opportunity to surrender to British-commanded regular forces, who would abide by the Geneva Convention, and if refusing this, they would be left to the patriots, who might not.[217] Even the erudite Dodds-Parker took it for granted that the patriots would castrate any white man, British or Italian, falling into their hands, and Wingate took this fearsome reputation and turned it into a weapon, another example of his making tactical use of 'national characteristics'.[218] This produced one of the best-known episodes of Wingate's career – and the one of which he seems to have been most proud – his inducing the surrender of an 14,000-man Italian force to an Ethiopian one less than a third of its size at Addis Derra in May, after the liberation of Addis Ababa. He employed the same 'scare tactics' he had planned for Debra Markos, his initial message, of 19 May, reading:

1. Since our last encounter at Debra Markos I have been engaged on the difficult task of organising your ex-Colonial troops into guerrilla brigades. One of these, led by Ras Kassa [Haile Selassie's cousin and the most skilful of the patriot leaders, whose sons had been murdered by the Italians after surrendering under a false amnesty] I have brought with me from Addis Ababa. Two more are on the way...
2. In addition to these guerrilla forces, a patriot contingent two thousand strong has just reached me...
3. As you are no doubt aware, the Duke of Aosta and his army have surrendered to-day to the British Forces at Amba Alagi [this was true].
4. I have been ordered to withdraw all British personnel from your neighbourhood during the rainy period, leaving the conduct of the operations against you to the very considerable guerrilla forces under Ras Kassa... who are now assembling around you... I linger here for perhaps twenty-four hours more only in the hope that you will decide not to sacrifice needlessly the lives of so many brave men... If you refuse this last offer, control passes out of my hands...[219]

This was a bluff; Ras Kassa's forces were almost out of ammunition and starting to go home, and the largest force of 'patriots' in the area were local Muslims, armed by the Italians but who had changed sides upon hearing of the surrender of Keren. Yet the Italian commander at Addis Derra, *Colonello* Saverio Maraventano, confirmed in his memoirs that Wingate's scare tactics were the key factor in his eventual surrender, on 23 March: 14,000 Italians had been induced into capitulation by 5,000 patriots and 150 British.[220] Again, Wingate's methods indicated a strong belief that 'national characteristics' could be meshed to produce a desired military outcome, in this case, from 'soft, panicky Italians' facing 'merciless Ethiopian savages' (who in actuality treated captured Italians chivalrously almost without fail). Reports of the time show that this was not an isolated ruse – as it has been presented in Wingate's biographies – but common practice by the British throughout the latter stages of the operation. Boustead made similar threats to leave the garrison of Debra Tabor to the charity of the patriots on 19-20 May, although he and Simonds were withdrawn before it could tell; on 22 May, Thesiger induced the garrison of Agibar fort to surrender with a similar threat.[221] Indeed, it may be that Wingate and Boustead arrived at the technique jointly, inspired possibly by a communiqué Wavell proposed to send the Italian Viceroy, the Duke of Aosta after the British liberated Addis Ababa, telling him that unless the Italians capitulated immediately, Wavell would be unable to protect Italian nationals except in areas already under British occupation.[222] Wingate was again showing he was not above lifting ideas from others and then claiming them as his own.

The impact on Wingate's ideas

Wingate submitted his 'Appreciation of the Ethiopian Campaign' to GHQ Cairo on 18 June and produced 'The Ethiopian Campaign, August 1940 to June 1941' after his return to London in November 1941. Both illustrate Wingate's tendency to write strategic manifestos rather than straightforward reports, the core of both being Wingate's new theory of Long-Range Penetration – his first use of the term – distilled from 'lessons learned' from Gojjam. The 'Appreciation' has an angry and sometimes irrational tone, being written while Wingate was suffering the effects of cerebral malaria and in the build-up to his suicide attempt. He opened by disparaging his famous relative: 'It became increasingly clear that the type of operation usually associated with the name of Lawrence, is wasteful and ineffectual. In fact, psychologically, it is wrong, and deprives us of much of the best support available'.[223] The 'Wrong Method' had been demonstrated in Ethiopia (by implication, by Sandford):

> On entering the area, the commander gets in touch with the local patriot leader, and after an exhortation, suggests that the leader can do something to help out some operation. The patriot at once replies that he desires nothing better but has no arms... The commander asks how much he wants [and]... promises a fraction which he hands over and waits for results. These are nil... or, possibly, bogus reports of activities this type of commander believes to be true.
>
> The patriot argues thus: 'This person evidently needs my... help; so much that he is willing to part with arms he must know I have only the most rudimentary idea of how to use. Ergo, he has no one to fight for him, and so is prepared to give me this substantial bribe. Therefore, he is in a weak position, and may well be beaten. If that happens I shall be in the soup. That is an argument for not fighting, but no argument for not taking what he offers... I think on the whole, that the best and kindest way will be to accept the help with gratitude; to hold it in trust in case some day I can use it safely against the common enemy, and, meanwhile, to get to learn how to use it by settling once and for all that dispute over the water with the Smiths.'[224]

The 'Right' method entailed a commander entering enemy territory with 'a small but highly efficient column with modern equipment and armament, but none to give away' and asking for nothing more than information:

The patriot goes away thinking – 'This is curious. The force is very small, but no doubt much larger ones are at hand, or he wouldn't be so confident... I'd better watch this.'

The... commander carries out a successful night attack. Next day comes the patriot saying – 'Why didn't you tell me you intended to attack? I could have been of great help to you.'

'Oh well you have no arms, and you're not a soldier. And after all why should you get killed? That is our job... you have no arms or ammunition, and I have none to spare.'

'It is true that I have very little ammunition, but what I have I want to use in support of my flag.'

'Very well, come along with me... [I] can probably find some useful work for your followers. But I shall judge you by results, and if you make a mess of it, I shan't be able to use you again.'

Result – the patriot rushes to the fray with keenness and devotion. He regards the commander as his leader. It is a privilege to help him.[225]

This 'corps d'elite' would be more effective than 'peddlers of war material and cash' because resistance depended upon appealing 'to the better nature, not the worse... We can hope that the rare occasional brave man will be stirred to come to us and risk his life to help our cause... All the rest – the rush of the tribesmen, the peasants with billhooks, is hugaboo.'[226]

So much for Wingate as advocate of 'people's war': history bears him out here, as historically insurgencies have hinged on a trained, activist minority – for instance, the infiltration into Palestine of 'volunteers' from the wider Arab world who did most of the actual fighting in the rebellion, while to cite just one more recent example, the Provisional IRA's strength has been put at a maximum of 1,200 active members, and some estimates had them as low as *fifty*, in a Northern Irish Catholic population of 600–750,000.[227] This has been recognised by some distinguished practitioners: based in his experience with the French Army in Indochina and Algeria, David Galula noted that 'In any situation, whatever the cause, there will be an active minority for the cause, a neutral majority, and an active minority against the cause.'[228] Decades before, Lawrence proposed that 'Rebellions can be made by 2% active in a striking force, and 98% passive sympathetic'.[229] Indeed, the leading British post-war expert on counterinsurgency, General Sir Frank Kitson, contended that involving large sections of the populace risked problems arising from indiscipline and competing agendas, something Wingate discovered the hard way in Ethiopia just as the Arab rebels had in Palestine three years before.[230] Wingate seems to have been perceptive in his 'regularisation' of the Ethiopia operation, and his subsequent arguments that effective guerrilla operations hinged on a trained, professional 'hard core'. Some more recent practitioners might concur, having organised their activities around just such a full-time 'hard core' very different in action from the keen amateurs of myth and theory: a striking passage in David Kilcullen's *Accidental Guerrilla* describes the ambush of a US Special Forces team in Afghanistan in May 2006, the Taliban carefully setting out a firing line and blocking positions, and hitting the Americans with a timed fire plan coordinating machine-guns, mortars and snipers; the impression is of well-trained, well-disciplined and, indeed, *professional* force like the one Wingate envisaged; a similar impression is had from Tim Pat Coogan's description of the Provisional IRA carrying out fire and manoeuvre exercises in the hills around Dublin in the 1970s.[231] Beyond the battlefield level, the coordinated series of attacks on important targets in Afghanistan and Pakistan in late April 2012 by the Taliban and/or Haqqani Network, planned and trained for eight weeks beforehand, indicates a fair understanding of coordinating operations over a wide geographical area to achieve maximum strategic effect.[232] Wingate's emphasis on the need for outside support is telling also, as this hard-core must have sufficient firepower to defeat regular forces on the battlefield, and no subject stimulates as much 'hugaboo' as insurgent logistics. Chairman Mao presented the rather twee image of peasant guerrillas arming themselves with hunting rifles, spears and farming implements, supplemented over time with weapons taken from defeated foes or manufactured in backwoods workshops; Che Guevara detailed how desperate guerrillas might initially use shotguns and hunting rifles, in time turning some of those shotguns into incendiary mortars, and suggested that the grateful peasantry might be taxed in kind for food and raw materials.[233] All this jars somewhat with the massed artillery and anti-aircraft guns with which Vo Nguyen Giap invested Dien Bien Phu in 1954, the Taliban's Russian-made mortars, sniper rifles and DSHK heavy machine-guns, or Hezbollah barraging Israeli villages with Katyusha multi-barrel rocket-launchers. That sort of firepower has to be procured and paid for, and while some parts of the globe combine huge, unregulated small arms markets with ease of smuggling – most notably Afghanistan and adjacent regions of Pakistan, and parts of Africa and Latin America – and the lax ethics of certain arms dealers may be exploitable, there are more efficacious methods of securing it. Overlapping insurgency is the very phenomenon Wingate was describing without actually using the term *proxy war*, wherein outside powers utilise local actors to wage war against an enemy, or take control of a territory, in lieu of overt commitment of regular forces. In the tradition of MI(R) and SOE, some countries have dedicated entire 'Fourth Forces' to this role, the most prominent including the Central Intelligence Agency (CIA) Special Operations Division, the Iranian Revolutionary Guard's al Quds Force and the covert operations branches of Pakistani Inter-Services Intelligence (ISI); al Qaeda represented a relatively new phenomenon, a non-state actor waging proxy attacks against Western targets using local groups.[234] Proxy warfare usually underpins the supporting power's global or regional strategy. In the 1970s, the Soviets were supporting directly the Vietnamese National Liberation Front, the Popular Front for the Liberation of Palestine and insurgencies in South Africa and Rhodesia, and via their proxies, Cuba, Libya, South Yemen and the Palestine Liberation Organisation, were arming and training insurgents and would-be insurgents in Venezuela, Guatemala, Uruguay, Nicaragua, El Salvador, Peru, Northern Ireland, Italy, West Germany, Angola, Mozambique and Oman.[235] The most successful and influential insurgency in the modern era (so far) was the Afghan resistance to the Soviet occupation of the 1980s; it is likely that this would have collapsed mid-decade had the CIA and ISI not taken matters in hand, seeing an opportunity to inflict a similar 'death by a thousand cuts' to that the Americans had suffered in Vietnam, supplying the *Mujahedeen* with large numbers of US and British made weaponry, withdrawing numbers of them to Pakistan and Europe for training, and ISI attaching advisors to resistance leaders.[236] More recently, the Iranian Revolutionary Guard Corps has used its proxy, Hezbollah, to create a mini state within southern Lebanon which executes open warfare against Israel, and hit Jewish interests in Latin America and US facilities in Saudi Arabia. Iran also inserted agents into majority Shi'ite areas of southern Iraq, following the abortive uprising of 1991, recruiting locals who became the kernel of the Shi'ite insurgency which expelled British forces from Basra in 2003–09. Following the 2011 'Arab Spring', the IRGC has inserted teams of Iranian advisors, commanded by a Guard Corps Brigadier General, into Syria to train and command pro-government militias in that country's civil war, and from 2013 these were joined by fighting units of 'volunteers' recruited from Iraqi Shi'ite veterans of that country's insurgency against the US-led occupation, trained in Iran and commanded by IRGC officers, a modern analogue to Gideon Force's Operational Centres; in 2013 similar teams of Iranian-trained 'volunteers' were reported as supporting the Shi'ite al Houthi rebels in Yemen.[237]

At the battlefield level, support from the 'occasional brave man' from the local community was still essential because of the pattern of operations Wingate saw developing since 1939 – deepening the battle by deploying fighting forces in the enemy's rear areas, along his lines of supply and retreat.[239] Wingate introduced Long Range Penetration with a rough definition (several others would be offered over the next two years):

> The German, so far, has not had to attempt long range penetration (as distinct from sabotage) because he had always had the advantage of numbers and weight of armament, and so is usually conducting an offensive. But an army whose main forces are compelled…to adopt a defensive role cannot in the nature of things conduct short range penetration (i.e. penetration that links up at once with a general forward rush, which has, in fact, a tactical, as opposed to a strategical employment. Such penetration is carried out by mass descents of parachute troops, by small armoured thrusts with accompanying air contingents, and other means of close penetration.) Long range penetration can, however, be more effectual man for man, and weapon for weapon, than close penetration… [W]e are not discussing sabotage here, but something far more effectual: actual war and rebellion on the enemy's L. of C. [lines of communication] and in his back areas.[239]

This should be the role of specialist units, 'given the best armament available for [the] purpose' and 'under the command of the commander in chief of the whole theatre of operations.'[240] Operations should be targeted carefully:

> The force should be given an objective such that the gaining of it will vitally effect [sic] the campaign in question. It is a common error to think that something has been achieved when forces have been assembled in desolate areas

far from points vital to the enemy. Something is achieved only when the enemy's communications have been effectively broken and his armed forces in the rear areas destroyed. This is done only by hard fighting.[241]

To succeed in this 'hard fighting', the force should have dedicated air support, with air staff at its headquarters, which should also include a propaganda officer.[242] Planning should be guided by 'doctrine': 'The force must operate with a definite propaganda... or creed of war... based on truth, and not lies. Lies are for the enemy. The truth is for our friends.'[243] Wingate was recognising the importance of a clear-cut cause for insurgent guerrillas perhaps more than any other type of combatant: insurgency can be described as 'armed populism', the insurgents claiming to be fighting for the rights of 'the common people' against unfair and arbitrary rule by corrupt, self-serving elites or foreign invaders; the hopes and dreams of 'the common people' will be met once the elites are unseated and the insurgents are in power.[244] Wingate seems to have recognised this in drawing up his 'doctrine' for Ethiopia, although he became growingly cynical about it as the operation developed, and his subsequent writings indicate a growing appreciation of another truism of guerrilla insurgency – once fighting breaks out, more pragmatic criteria assert themselves, the population rallying not behind the most worthy cause, but the side they think is going to win the military struggle and thereby guarantee their security.[245]

Wingate wrote his second missive, 'The Ethiopian Campaign', after his return to London and his cure from cerebral malaria. This was shorter and more objective, with more emphasis on narrative and 'lessons learned.' The Gojjam operation now centred upon the patriot uprising: 'In Ethiopia the local population not only made possible the advance of the British armies, but a separate patriot campaign played a decisive part in the defeat of the enemy's plan and the conquest of Italian East Africa.'[246] This represented Wingate's first mention of the Sun Tzu-like concept of 'defeating the enemy's plan', using manoeuvre and diversion to force him to dissipate his forces, prevent him concentrating for battle and distract him from his main effort.[247] Wingate concluded the 'Ethiopian Campaign' by proposing that British strategy should centre upon penetration operations:

> It is a mistake to imagine that operations of the kind described are possible only in a country like Abyssinia. They are possible wherever there is a patriot population... The scale of the success, and the magnitude of the odds, even making every allowance for the nationality of the enemy, justifies the belief that campaigns in other countries where there are patriots, even when occupied by Germans, will prove practicable... Let us select a force in the manner described, let us train it, let us arm and equip it suitably, let our military command regard it with favour, let aircraft be allotted for its support; and you will have a force many times as strong and efficient as the force with which I gained these successes. I may say in passing that the type of fighting I refer to has nothing to do with the operations of Commandos. I am talking of forces which live and fight in the heart of the enemy's territory.[248]

Suitable theatres included Spain, Morocco and Algeria and, as Japan had entered the war in December 1941, 'In the Far East there must already be several areas where such a force could operate with great detriment to the enemy.'[249] Moreover, penetration operations should spearhead the liberation of Europe:

> All modern war in inhabited areas is war of penetration. The military problems correspond to those of revolt... If we are to control the first stages of liberation in Europe in order to avoid general anarchy, we had better start assembling forces of the type I have described. Their ultimate aim will be to form that coordinating and controlling element which alone will allow us to bring hostilities quickly and finally to a close.[250]

That 'controlling element' was vital in order to prevent unintended consequences. In Afghanistan in the 1980s, the CIA confined itself entirely to being a peddler of weaponry and (mainly Saudi) money, via ISI.[251] Consequently, those 'doing exploits' in Afghanistan were ISI and the Arab volunteers of Osama bin Laden, the 'doctrine' was Sunni Muslim unity against Godless outsiders, and the outcome was not a dispute over the water with the Smiths but with the USA, the al Sauds and the Pakistani government over the future of the Islamic world.[252] Likewise, Wingate would likely have warned against the CIA's attempt, in autumn 2001, to buy another army in Afghanistan, and would have felt vindicated by the Northern Alliance's conspicuous lack of aggression, allayed only by a combination of even bigger bribes and by US Special Forces deploying among them and summoning close air support.[253] He might have been more satisfied with Operation *Iraqi Freedom*, eighteen months later, which saw US Special Forces deployed to areas held by the Kurdish *Peshmerga* earlier in the operation, in greater numbers, with a common 'doctrine' – toppling Saddam Hussein – and with the airpower of a US Navy carrier group, B-52 and B-1 heavy bombers, and AC-130 gunships on call from the beginning.[254]

Others drew lessons from the Gojjam operation. Dodds-Parker related that the use of aircraft for resupply – albeit limited – guided him in organising the first covert supply flights into Yugoslavia in 1942.[255] The Operational Centres had performed satisfactorily in Ethiopia, both as fighting units and *foci* for resistance, and were to be used by SOE as Operational Groups and 'Jedburgh' teams in Europe and Asia in 1944–45.[256] However, the most obvious difference between SOE's activities and those proposed by Wingate was scale. The Jedburghs were military personnel who operated in uniform, but were far from the substantial fighting units Wingate envisaged, consisting as they did of two Allied officers and a wireless operator; moreover, their role was to distribute arms and coordinate the activities of resistance elements with Allied offensives.[257] They therefore resembled Gubbins' model for such units rather than Wingate's.

The following chapters examine how these ideas – Wingate's and G(R)'s – evolved when confronted with a radically different scenario, albeit one which Wingate anticipated: facing the Japanese in the jungles of Southeast Asia. They also detail the reception they received from Wingate's peers in that theatre. It was these operations which took Wingate to the pinnacle of his career, and, indirectly, to his death.

Chapter Six

Wingate in Burma (1) – The Origins of the Chindits, 1942–43

Only in one direction did there seem any prospect of action in the near future. It lay in the person of a broad-shouldered, uncouth, almost simian officer who used to drift gloomily into the office for two or three days at a time, audibly dream dreams, and drift out again... In our frenzy of planning, we used to look on this visitor as one of those to be bowed out, as soon as it was possible to put a term to his ramblings; but as we became aware that he took no notice of us anyway, but that without our patronage he had the ear of the highest, we paid more attention to his schemes. Soon we had fallen under the spell of his almost hypnotic talk...

Brigadier Bernard Fergusson[1]

Wavell used Wingate... as in irritant to stir up his junior generals. He did this by extolling his original ideas on war and battle in a self-confident and masterly manner. [When Wingate first met Slim] Slim pointed out that he had just taken over, he was not impressed by the units under his command who had not been taught how to fight orthodox warfare let alone guerrilla warfare and that he had no troops at all to spare for what he considered useless and unnecessary diversions.

Brigadier Michael Calvert[2]

Wingate in Burma

Wingate was summoned to India in March 1942 by his old benefactor, Wavell, now a Field Marshal and Commander in Chief, American, British, Dutch and Australian Command (ABDACOM), with overall responsibility for all Allied operations in Burma and Southeast Asia. So began the best-known period of Wingate's career, culminating in Operations *Longcloth* and *Thursday*, the Chindit operations of 1943 and 1944. These operations followed three distinct patterns. The first, devised in 1942, prior to the British retreat from Burma, was never put into practice, and involved a straightforward adaptation to East Asian conditions of the Ethiopian model, a guerrilla campaign involving indigenous 'patriot' irregulars organised by a revived G(R), with a small hard core of purpose-trained regular troops. Wingate's second model resembled that presented in his *Appreciation* of the Gojjam campaign – 'deepening the battle' through columns of purpose-trained regular light infantry, supplied by airdrop, attacking or threatening vital logistical targets deep behind Japanese lines with the intent of disrupting their planning process and forcing them to divert forces away from the main battle. Operation *Longcloth* was an experiment on the practicability of this model. The third model added an air-land element, columns now being inserted behind enemy lines by glider and operating from defended temporary airstrips or 'Strongholds', from which they were supplied and reinforced, and with dedicated battlefield air support. The aim here was the more ambitious one of steering Japanese forces into 'killing zones' around the Strongholds, where they could be destroyed in detail, mainly from the air.

The growing scale of Wingate's forces in Southeast Asia is notable. Wingate's initial model of operations involved a force similar in size and organisation to the one he commanded in Ethiopia – four columns created from two battalions, supporting a number of G(R) Operational Centres, and consisting of probably no more than a couple of hundred men. By 1943 and Operation *Longcloth*, this had become a brigade, consisting of eight columns, and when *Thursday* was launched a year later, it was with a force equivalent in manpower to two British Infantry divisions, supported by a specialist unit of the United States Army Air Force (USAAF) comprising fighters, bombers and a large transport element. At the time of his death in March 1944, Wingate was proposing a continent-wide offensive involving the equivalent of an Army Group. Alongside the impact of all this upon a theatre pressured horrendously by logistical overstretch went the ongoing issue of Wingate's interpersonal style, most significantly Kirby's allegation that *Thursday* went ahead under pressure from London and Washington, against the advice of those on the ground in Asia. Yet here, as in Palestine and Ethiopia, Wingate presented an identifiable form of warfare tailored to his interpretation of the cultural strengths and weaknesses of his opponent and intended to fulfill his interpretation of Allied strategy. Other British commanders in Southeast Asia did likewise. Whatever the proposed solution, the problem was the same – how to beat a Japanese Army which terrified its opponents.

Warfare in Southeast Asia, 1940–41

Wingate arrived in India to find an atmosphere conducive to his kind of operation. G(R) and SOE were active already in the region, and there were other specialist units and formations planning to operate against Japanese rear areas.[3] From early 1941, the anticipated scenario in Asia was a Japanese attempt to weaken the resistance of China, which they had invaded in 1937, by cutting the Burma Road, China's main supply route from Southeast Asia, which ran across Burma – British Imperial territory – from Assam in India with another branch south to Rangoon, Burma's capital and main port.[4] From 1940, the Japanese pressured the British diplomatically to close the road. The British viewed this as indication that the Japanese might use force against the road, and in November, Major General L.E. Dennys was appointed Military Attaché to the Chinese Government in Chungking, but was also designated, secretly, as head of Mission 204, a G(R) Mission under the orders of Far Eastern Command (and which had survived the rest of G(R)'s absorption into SOE).[5] Air Chief Marshal Sir Robert Brooke-Popham, Commander-in-Chief, Far East, wrote to the War Office in April 1941 arguing that, as a contingency, a corps of Chinese guerrillas should be created, consisting of fifteen companies commanded by officers from the Indian Army, with specialist British personnel attached for demolitions work, a guerrilla school being created in Burma to train them.[6] Brooke-Popham requested a Royal Engineers officer as chief instructor for this guerrilla school and Major Michael Calvert was relocated from Australia, where he had been chief instructor at a similar school created by MI(R) for the Australian Army.[7] Mission 204 was given the remit, 'By providing the cadre for a Chinese Guerrilla Corps d'Elite [sic], to contain the maximum number of Japanese forces in China and relieve pressure on British forces elsewhere.'[8] Guerrilla forces were therefore to be diversionary, defensive and act as substitute for action by main armies, as with earlier operations in East Africa.

This was also apparent in the strategy developed over the following months, Brooke-Popham writing to London in August to argue that, while Britain should avoid direct confrontation with Japan, this did not preclude Dennys suggesting to the Chinese that they should prepare demolition of key sites in southern China, nor the infiltration into areas adjoining Burma of 'personnel trained in demolition work', nor the opening of arms smuggling routes across the Himalayas.[9] The War Office communicated to Wavell, the new Commander in Chief, India, in September 1941 that, given Britain's strategic situation, were the Japanese to attack the Burma Road, the only practicable response would be 'infiltration of [a] limited number of British personnel into China to assist guerrilla operations and demolition work.'[10] The Chinese government should not be informed, and such action could not be attributed to the British government, but to 'volunteers' perhaps akin to the International Brigades of the Spanish Civil War or the American Air Volunteer Group, the 'Flying Tigers', commanded by General Claire Chennault, fighting the Japanese already over China.[11] The main component of Mission 204, Calvert's guerrilla school at Maymyo in Burma, was therefore given the cover name of 'Bush Warfare School', and his trainees were organised into cadres called 'Commandos.'[12] To conceal its intent further, Mission 204 came under GHQ India, which controlled its budget, although operational command was delegated onto Dennys.[13] It was anticipated the Mission would operate in Southeast China, around Canton and Hong Kong, and in east-central China around Hankow, and it was proposed to create another guerrilla school, at Liyang.[14]

Other covert warfare organisations were active in this region. SOE established its Oriental Mission in Singapore in May 1941, to organise guerrillas in China, Malaya and the Dutch East Indies; in July, they set up No.101 Special Training School near Singapore to train civilian and military personnel to form 'stay behind parties' in the event of a Japanese invasion; another Mission was set up in India, on Amery's initiative, in August, and reported directly to the Viceroy.[15] Sir Frank Nelson, head of SO2, the department of SOE which had taken over most of the roles of MI(R), soon suggested that Mission 204 should be 'amalgamated' with SOE, producing a 'line to take' from the War Office: Mission 204 trained British officers to lead Chinese guerrillas after the beginning of war with Japan; SOE operated in civilian dress and could be active before hostilities broke out.[16]

Who was responsible for which kind of operation became a side-issue when hostilities finally erupted in December 1941. GHQ India proposed in mid-December that if the Japanese continued their offensive into Malaya, and reinforced it by road and rail links running through their puppet-ally, Thailand, the British should form defended bases at all points leading from Burma into Thailand from which 'small mobile guerrilla columns' could operate inside Thailand, against airfields and railways. Behind this, a field force of at least two divisions should be prepared for an offensive into northern Thailand in April 1942, concurrent with a Chinese offensive from Yunnan; the columns should begin training 'at once', implying a new and separate organisation from Mission 204.[17] While never acted upon, this proposal is interesting, given GHQ India's alleged hostility to Wingate's not dissimilar proposals.

The Japanese struck first in Burma, however, and it was soon apparent that the British faced an opponent far more able than themselves. Singapore fell in February 1942, and the Japanese 15th Army took Rangoon in March. Allied forces then held a line between Prome and Toungoo in southern Burma until the Japanese launched a second offensive around their left flank, from Thailand. In April the Japanese drove on Mandalay, the biggest city in northern Burma, and the Indian border and by mid-May the Allies had lost the whole of Burma, excepting an enclave around Fort Hertz in the northeast. Anglo-Indian forces suffered 14,000 casualties during their 900-mile retreat, the longest in history. With the gradual cutting of China's other supply routes in 1939–41, the Burma Road became so important to the Chinese that the Chinese President and Generalissimo, Chiang Kai-shek, offered his best troops, two German-trained 'Armies' (the equivalent of British or American divisions) under Stilwell, for the defence of Burma, these retreating into India alongside the British. Securing Burma, the Japanese reckoned, would not only complete the isolation of China, but would provide their 'Greater East Asian Co-Prosperity Sphere' with a natural western frontier and a major source of oil and rice. From 1942 to mid-1943, the Japanese were content to remain on the defensive in Burma, even shifting troops and combat aircraft away from Burma to the Pacific; as late as October 1942, Japanese strength in Burma was estimated as just four divisions. The British were of a like mind; from the official report of Earl Mountbatten, Supreme Commander Southeast Asia 1943–45:

> [I]t had been held that the disease-ridden jungle-covered mountain ranges formed an impenetrable barrier, and that an offensive campaign across them was a military impossibility. Even if an enemy succeeded in penetrating on foot with mule transport, it was thought, he could not hope to maintain himself – and indeed it was this fact that really arrested the Japanese advance on the boundaries of India in 1942 – but by the same token the opinion was widely held that a successful Allied offensive overland would also be almost impossible.[18]

Consequently, the only major operations in Burma between the 1942 retreat and the Allied offensives of spring 1944 were Wingate's first Chindit operation and XV Corps' ill-fated offensive in the Arakan region of southern Burma of September 1942–May 1943, both limited in scope and intent.

Geography was the key factor here. The theatre was huge: Slim compared commanding operations along the 700-mile India–Burma frontier from his headquarters in Comilla to controlling a campaign in the Alps from London, with no roads and railways between them, while Stilwell compared his regular flights from the Chinese wartime capital at Chungking to GHQ India at New Delhi to flying from New York to Denver.[19] Burma had no land communications with India, and is cut by several mountain ranges running north-south, from the Himalayas to the sea, with major rivers running between them; these rivers were the major lines of transport and communication in Burma, and the few major roads also ran north-to-south. According to Mountbatten:

> Any invasion from India would have to take place over mountain ranges, in places more than 9,000 feet high, covered by an almost impenetrable jungle through parts of which... it was impossible, even without enemy opposition, to advance more than two to two and a half miles in twenty-four hours.[20]

To this was added the monsoon. From mid-May to late October, heat and humidity rise sharply and Southeast Asia is frequently covered by opaque clouds up to an altitude of 30,000 feet; these can produce storms dropping over seven inches of rain in 24 hours, accompanied by gales capable of tearing an aircraft apart in flight. Burma's geography and meteorology resulted in operations there resembling those of a bygone age. Firstly, as in Europe before the development of metalled roads, there was a clearly defined 'campaigning season', coinciding with the dry season of November–April, when Burma enjoys relatively fresh, dry weather. Secondly, for the first time since the American Civil War, more soldiers were lost to disease than to enemy action; Western standards of hygiene are impossible in any jungle, and jungles worldwide are infested with leeches, typhus mites, venomous invertebrates, the amoebae which cause dysentery and the greatest killer of all, malarial mosquitoes. Consequently, it is unsurprising that throughout 1943, the ratio of Allied soldiers in Southeast Asia admitted to hospital for disease to those for combat wounds was 120:1; even with improvements in tropical medicine, the ratio was still 20:1 in 1944 and 6:1 by the end of the war.[21]

The Imperial Japanese Army had trained for these conditions; the British had not. The Japanese had also been careful to prepare the political battlefield. The anti-British Burmese nationalist movement became a willing tool of Japanese Military Intelligence, swallowing whole the myth of the 'Greater East Asian Co-Prosperity Sphere', and there is also extensive – but largely circumstantial – evidence for Japanese penetration of the Indian National Congress. Subhas Chandra Bose and the Indian National Army aside, there was the coincidence of the emergence of Mahatma Gandhi's 'Quit India' movement with the retreat from Burma, Gandhi's call for any Japanese invasion to be met with passive rather than active resistance, and the large and bloody Congress-agitated uprising in northeastern India, which continued into 1943 and included apparently carefully planned sabotage of communications into Burma just as the crisis there was reaching its peak, and which Wavell took for granted as the work of 'enemy agents'.[22] SOE admitted Japanese subversion in Burma caused them some difficulty, and it was to have considerable bearing on penetration operations in Burma in 1942-43, including Wingate's.[23] The extensive resources the Japanese invested in cultivating Burmese nationalists paid off: as if to confirm the efficacy of both Holland's and Wingate's ideas, Burmese agents spread the propaganda of the Co-Prosperity Sphere and the invasion was accompanied by extensive arson and sabotage in British-occupied towns, Slim admitting that saboteurs got 'short shrift' when caught; more direct was Stilwell, heading the US Mission to Chiang's HQ in Chungking, and Chiang's *de facto* chief of staff and commander of Chinese forces committed to Burma, who approved a standing order that Burmese saboteurs could be summarily shot.[24] Of even greater use to the Japanese was the 'screen' of Fifth Columnists preceding their advancing army and guiding them to and around British positions, some interesting support for Wingate's argument that the best use for local partisans was to improve the mobility of regular forces.[25] Fifth Columnist infiltration also crippled the special units of the Burma Frontier Force (BFF), raised in 1941 to delay and harass any Japanese advance into Burma from Thailand. These irregular units each consisted of around 500 Burmese under British officers with local knowledge, each unit organised into two mounted troops and three infantry companies.[26] While providing a useful screening role in the British retreat from Burma, like many other local forces it was hastily assembled, poorly equipped and eventually fell apart through desertions.[27] The untrustworthiness of many Burmese also forestalled SOE's plans to create 'stay behind' parties in Burma.[28]

Penetration tactics in rough country were an integral part of Japanese warfare. Captured Japanese Combat Instructions, translated and circulated among British commanders for intelligence purposes, indicated a doctrine which was sophisticated, yet also of its time, in being rooted in ethnic and cultural assumptions about the superiority of Japanese over Westerners, the principal objective of Japanese battlefield doctrine being to 'smash and disrupt the enemy's command organisation', it being presumed that the cowardly *Gaijin* would panic without direction from above. This would be compounded by cutting their supplies by concentrating effort against airfields, supply dumps and lines of communication.[29] Japanese commanders issued simple, broad orders, usually detailing a single objective, and subordinates were expected to 'demonstrate initiative' in pursuing this (although often failing egregiously to do so in practice). Tactically, emphasis was on noisy frontal distraction attacks by small 'jitter parties', allowing larger forces to use cover or darkness to infiltrate weak spots in the enemy front line or go round a flank to deliver the main attack behind him, against their supplies and communications.[30]

The defence of Burma in 1942 was assigned to the Burma Army, under General Sir Harold Alexander, its main combat formation being I Burma Corps or 'Burcorps', commanded by Lieutenant General Sir Ronald Hutton until succeeded by Slim in March 1942. Two divisions made up I Burma Corps, both formed only shortly before and consisting largely of recent recruits without combat experience. 17th Indian Division had been organised, trained and equipped for desert warfare in the Middle East, was entirely motorised, and, incapable of operating far from roads except in open country, was crippled following the action on the Sittang River on 22–23 February 1942, when two of its brigades were forced to abandon most of their vehicles and heavy equipment after the divisional commander, Major General Sir John Smythe, ordered the one remaining bridge blown; one anonymous report noted that its combat performance seemed to *improve* after losing its vehicles.[31] 1st Burma Division was raised hastily after the outbreak of war, equipped with captured Italian heavy weaponry, and manned largely by Burmese, with all the problems that brought. These units relied upon orthodox lines of supply and communication, and regular supply convoys. In the 1942 campaign, the few roads along which convoys could move were usually clogged with refugees, a situation appreciated by the Japanese, aggravating it with deliberate terror of the civilian population and also taking the opportunity to infiltrate British lines disguised as fleeing Burmese, one East Asian looking much the same as any other to a British squaddie. Reliance on mechanical transport for supply tied British forces to narrow fronts centred upon roads and motorable tracks, leading to, as Slim put it, British strategy in 1942 being based upon 'a rather nebulous idea of retaining territory' leading to the dispersal of Anglo-Indian forces over wide areas and usually with no mutual support.[32]

Consequently, the jungle was left to the Japanese, whose tactics seemed purpose-designed for such conditions. The Imperial Japanese Army was a predominantly light infantry force, trained to live off the land, or by plunder, and to use enemy supplies, including weapons and ammunition: that Japanese units could operate temporarily independent of any communications against a foe who could not survive without them created perfect conditions for Japanese tactics, as described in the 1943 British doctrine for jungle warfare:

> The Japanese always tried to advance on as broad a front as possible, making use of all available communications as to routes of approach. On gaining contact, their methods were to fix a front and attack by encirclement... Encirclement was usually made in the form of simultaneous attacks in depth, one coming in on a smaller arc than the other. The shallower attack would normally come in at a depth of about 1,000 yards and would probably be initiated by the commander of the leading battalion, while the deeper attack would come in at a distance up to five miles, and would probably be initiated by the regimental commander.[33]

'Hooking' forces moved in concentrated columns without scouts or picquets, relying on the jungle for cover and local Burmese for guidance and intelligence, to establish fortified blocks across main supply routes 5-6 miles behind the front line, in areas difficult for artillery or tanks. Some of these blocks were very large, it taking a two-day battle to remove one established at Prome during the 1942 campaign.[34] *Notes from Theatres of War* emphasised the shock effect upon British-Indian units, presuming they were facing no more than a large patrol in front, suddenly finding a Japanese battalion or regiment dug in astride their lines of supply and retreat.[35] The 'hook and block' was complimented by the Imperial Japanese Army Air Force (IJAAF) enjoying almost complete air supremacy throughout early 1942: the British were therefore not only denied air reconnaissance, but the IJAAF also attacked supply convoys with impunity and acted as 'flying artillery' for 'hooking' attacks by ground troops. It is hardly surprising that Slim noted British commanders acquiring 'a road block mentality which often developed into an inferiority complex'.[36]

This complex spread far and wide. At Wingate's arrival, the British Indian Army was suffering from major morale problems, the most obvious manifestations referred to by contemporaries as 'Green Hell' or 'Super-Jap' syndrome. The jungle was an alien environment not only to British soldiers, but also to most Indians: there is strong contemporary testimony that the combination of darkness, poor visibility, unfamiliar noises and the apparent ubiquity of the Japanese had deleterious psychological effects, one anonymous report referring to the jungle 'Having a marked effect on [the] nerves of young troops.'[37] In another example of ethnic stereotyping, the view spread that the Japanese soldier, toughened by an arduous oriental upbringing and the Samurai ethic, was fully 'at home' in the jungle, and his superior fieldcraft, ability to keep going 'on a handful of rice a day' and maniacal devotion to his Emperor meant he would always have a decisive advantage over his pampered, city-bred white opponents.[38] The author 'Aquila' was more balanced than most, but tells much of attitudes in 1942–44 – note the effortless racialism, unsurprising given that many Allied propaganda cartoons of the time portrayed the Japanese as monkeys, sometimes complete with tails:

> It soon became clear that the country was so difficult that small parties of Japanese with their greater mobility could only too easily threaten our unwieldy land lines of communication, and that European troops requiring a cumbersome commissariat organization behind them were at a great disadvantage... What was needed was some way of alleviating this deadlock whereby better troops were being defeated and out-manoeuvred by the Japanese, who took to the conditions in Burma as apes to the jungle.[39]

To many, this seemed hopeless. On two separate occasions in April 1942, General Sir Harold Alexander and his Chief of Staff, Brigadier T.J.W. Winterton, admitted to Stilwell that British soldiers were 'simply afraid of the Japs' – and Stilwell, who seems to have hated the English far more than he did the Japanese, made frequent amused references to 'windy Limeys' in his diaries.[40] Prior to transferring to Wingate's command from Wavell's staff, Bernard Fergusson was told by a colleague: 'You'll be mad to go into the jungle with Tarzan [Wingate was nicknamed after Edgar Rice Burroughs' jungle-lord, then featuring in a popular series of films starring Johnny Weissmuller]... The fellow's a crackpot. In any case, the British cannot compete with the Japanese in the jungle. It's suicide to think you can crawl through their lines. They'll hunt you down every time.'[41] It was probably with such attitudes in mind that Fergusson made numerous sardonic references to the 'Green Hell' in his published work.[42] Another who never subscribed was William Slim, who viewed the Japanese as just another opponent, with weaknesses that could be exploited. Slim noted the 'Super-Jap' being more a bogeyman for troops manning the lines of communication in India than for those actually facing him in the jungle, although this was a problem in itself, infecting new drafts under training in India and leading to a high incidence of desertions among new British units moving up to the front. Far greater factors in depressing morale, in Slim's view, were the low priority given the Burma theatre in terms of supplies and reinforcements – Burma being prioritised third after Europe and the Pacific throughout the war – and the general lack of attention from home, this period seeing the beginning of the use of the term 'Forgotten Army'.[43]

This malaise gave cause for concern at the highest levels. The *Official History* recounted that Churchill had firm – and predictable – ideas on what remedial action to take:

> He demanded that new commanders should be found, that troops whose morale had been lowered should be severely disciplined and that, if regular Indian Army troops were incapable of fighting the Japanese in the jungle, commando formations should be developed.[44]

Churchill determined on retaking Burma as part of Britain's long-term strategy for defeating Japan, but there were differences with the Americans on to how to proceed. Appreciations by the War Cabinet and Combined (British and American) Chiefs of Staff, made in 1942, concluded that Japan would not invade India, and that Japanese strategy would henceforth be entirely defensive, aimed at inducing war-weariness among the Allies.[45] In response, Churchill demanded Japan 'should be engaged all over her Empire, to maximise the overstretch on her already inefficient resources.'[46] This would involve invading Burma, a strategic objective for both Allies, but for different reasons. In January 1942, Churchill wrote to Wavell that 'China bulks as large in the minds of many [Americans] as Great Britain' and that the US Chiefs of Staff considered the Burma Road 'indispensable for world victory.'[47] The Americans saw clearing the Burma Road as a means to an end – breaking the blockade of China quickly so that Chinese forces could be strengthened, the better to pin Japanese forces away from the Pacific, and to secure China as a base for a US Army Air Force (USAAF) bomber offensive against the Japanese home islands.[48] This strategy was favoured by Chiang – predictably – and by Chennault, from March 1943, Commanding General of the US Fourteenth Air Force, based in China, and possibly the only westerner Chiang trusted, principally because unlike Stilwell, he always told Chiang what he wanted to hear.[49] Washington therefore pressed for the earliest possible reopening of the Burma Road, which would necessitate an Allied offensive into northern Burma.[50] In the interim, they established what was, at the time, the largest airlift in history, the air-bridge from India over the 'Hump' of the Himalayas to Chungking, the Chief of Staff of the USAAF, General H.H. Arnold, making this a strategic priority from early 1942.[51] The British, especially the old Imperialist, Churchill, had no sympathy with the venal and almost compulsively treacherous Chiang, the War Cabinet concluding in 1943 that opening the Burma Road would help China 'on psychological rather than practical grounds.'[52] The British objective was to regain their imperial possessions in Burma, Malaya and Singapore.[53] Throughout 1942 and into 1943, Churchill pressed Wavell to carry out a seaborne invasion of southern Burma, aimed at retaking Rangoon, then driving north to clear the Burma Road so securing the rest of Burma, and he and Mountbatten argued consistently for sea landings in southern Burma, Malaya, Singapore and the Andamans until the diversion of resources for Operation *Overlord* finally rendered this impossible.[54] Indeed, when South East Asian Command (SEAC) was established in 1943, some wags commented the letters actually stood for 'Save England's Asian Colonies'.

Wingate presumed, from his arrival in India to his death two years later, that British efforts would centre on land offensives from India through northern Burma to Thailand and beyond, and also seemed keen on obtaining the goodwill of the Chinese through demonstrating British resolve to defeat the Japanese on the Asian mainland. Consequently, his operational thought was more consistent with *American* strategic aims than British, and he was to obtain rather more consistent cooperation from the Americans than from GHQ India or 14th Army. However, strategy is limited to what can be delivered on the battlefield, and before either of these strategies could be enacted, some means of defeating the Japanese Army in the jungles of Burma would need to be devised.

British thought on jungle warfare

Callwell had outlined the demands of jungle warfare as early as 1906. Dense foliage, and the absence of roads, made normal communications or logistics impossible, so operations should consist of the methodical advance of small infantry columns with local scouts and guides, their supplies being carried with them by bearers or animals. There should be as much devolution of command authority as possible, the main tactical units being the platoon or section. The jungle offered tactical opportunities for those willing to use 'guerrilla' methods – infiltration, flanking and turning, ambush and surprise raids, and small fortified positions, if sighted correctly, could hold up far larger forces; the risk of outflanking and infiltration necessitated all-round defence, centred on these fortified bases.[55]

The first post-Burma retreat British 'doctrine' for jungle warfare was summarised in *Military Training Pamphlet Number 52 – Forest, Bush and Jungle Warfare Against a Modern Enemy*, published in August 1942 and representing prevailing British thought on jungle warfare as of the first Chindit operation and Arakan offensive. *MTP52* drew upon the British experience in Malaya and Burma in 1942 (where there were so many 'successes' the more innocent reader might think the British had won), but there were also almost as many examples derived from the Wehrmacht fighting in pine forest in Poland and Russia and in the Ardennes in 1940, perhaps not the best analogies.[56] *MTP52* prioritised maintaining mobility in heavy forest, which it saw as essential to maintaining the initiative; this hinged upon training troops to travel light, on choosing the right porterage – it was conceded that commanders might have to reduce their motor transport, if not dispense with it altogether – and by allowing junior commanders to exercise initiative.[57] Poor visibility made control of sub-units difficult, leading to a need to attack 'within well-defined courses', and *MTP52*'s core objective, the control of roads. Given what had happened recently in Burma their faith in maintaining the road network seems optimistic to say the least:

> All control must centre on the road or main communication, which is generally the only tactical feature of any importance. To gain control of the road is of major importance in winning a battle. Provided that the road is held in depth, that the maximum numbers are held as a mobile striking force for counter-attack and that the means of control exist to alter the defensive organization quickly for the purpose of countering encirclement no amount of enveloping tactics or infiltration can be decisive.[58]

Extensive use should be made of fighting patrols to gather information on the enemy through raids and probes, while wearing down his resolve.[59] Offensives should consist of large fighting patrols advancing along 'main axes of communication', battle beginning when these contacted the enemy.[60] Once battle was joined, the aim should be 'the elimination of the enemy's control, the centre of which will almost invariably be on the main axis or road, as a preliminary to the annihilation of his forces' to be achieved by encircling, infiltration or direct assault down 'the main axis'.[61] It was presumed that other arms' participation would be essential, artillery laying a 'rolling barrage' down the main axis while British tanks or armoured cars drove down it to burst through enemy blocks, as they had failed to do repeatedly in 1942.[62]

As to defensive tactics, jungle conditions made surprise attacks, infiltration and outflanking almost inevitable, therefore, defences 'must be both mobile and aggressive.'[63] Defence should be in depth, and consist of fortified positions organised for all-round defence, containing enough supplies to be self-sufficient 'for several days'.[64] Each such position would be a pivot for a 'mobile striking element', a large fighting patrol sweeping the surrounding jungle, providing early warning of any attack, and ambushing any incoming enemy on the lines of the 'floater platoon' described by Skeen.[65] This was synthesised eventually with the system of 'boxes' first used by General Sir Claude Auchinleck in North Africa in 1941. Each 'box' was a fortified position set up for all-round defence, held by a brigade with extensive supplies, its tactical role being as a block of artillery and anti-tank firepower: if attacked, the 'box' was to halt the enemy with massed artillery, while a reserve of tanks and motorised infantry counter-attacked his flanks and rear.[66] The model of the 'box' and *MTP52* would be developed to East Asian conditions both by Lieutenant-General Geoffrey Scoones, commanding IV Corps at Imphal-Kohima, and by Wingate, there being a notable resemblance between the 'boxes', *MTP52*'s defended positions and the 'Strongholds' used on Operation *Thursday*. In Burma, all British units were trained to form a box whenever they halted, and where possible, heavy weapons were deployed in a box of their own supporting other boxes in the area; the area around each box would be patrolled aggressively in order to deny the Japanese intelligence on the layout of the box.[67] Forces deployed in boxes could stand fast, supplied by air, and pin Japanese forces in place, allowing them to be trapped and destroyed between the box and by counterattacking reserve forces, the tactical model Slim was to apply at Imphal-Kohima.[68]

Another section of *MTP52* inviting comparison between Wingate's methods and others' is that on the use of 'Local Volunteers and Guerrilla Forces'. This conformed largely to the model advanced by MI(R) and G(R), pre-Ethiopia. Specialist officers and NCOs should be attached to existing resistance movements, with members of the local settler population – farmers, planters, forest officers – or Colonial Office officials advising them, in order to provide the resistance with organisation and liaison with regular forces. However, irregulars were unreliable; they tended to fight in their own time and to their own agenda and so the best use for them was as a diversion, harassing the enemy's rear areas and forcing him to redeploy troops away from the front.[69] Wingate would probably have concurred, and restated his belief that the offensive against the enemy rear was the task of regulars.

Wingate's first operational model – G(R) and Gideon Force Revisited

Wingate arrived in India because Amery, his old benefactor, had suggested to the Chief of the Imperial General Staff, Field Marshal Sir Alan Brooke, that he might prove useful in the Far East and Wavell, his other old benefactor, agreed enthusiastically.[70] Upon arrival, Wingate found himself an unattached major, acting lieutenant colonel, with a loose brief from Wavell to see what he could do to organise operations behind Japanese lines to create 'breathing space' allowing other forces to reorganise in Burma.[71] Guerrilla action was once again being used as a substitute for conventional operations, and again because it was one of the few viable options available. And again, Wingate prioritised imposing a degree of coordination upon the existing Army units, Mission 204 and the BFF before molding them to his own model of 'penetration warfare'.[72]

Dennys was killed in an air crash before Wingate could meet him.[73] Consequently, Wingate's first contact with Mission 204 came when he visited the Bush Warfare School on 22 March 1942, where, despite the presence there of a number of old G(R) hands who knew Wingate from Ethiopia and universally distrusted him, he and Calvert impressed each other greatly and began both a productive professional partnership and a close friendship.[74] Wingate also met with Lieutenant General T.J. Hutton, commanding I Burma Corps and the senior British operational commander in Burma, and three days after visiting Maymyo, produced his first document, 'Notes on Penetration Warfare, Burma Command, 25/3/42'. Wingate's aim was, from the beginning, to execute the kind of operations in depth he advocated in his reports on Ethiopia, and therefore did *not* take inspiration from the Japanese, although there were similarities: he was clearly impressed by Japanese tactics and cited previous Japanese actions in support of his own proposals. By this time, Mission 204 had been converted into a fighting unit of three squads, made up of Calvert's instructors and trainees, attached to 17 Division of I Burma Corps for raiding and sabotage operations, which it performed constantly and well throughout the retreat.[75] Wingate began his 'Notes' by arguing that assigning the Mission 204 squads to divisional-level command, and constraining the depth of penetration attacks to just behind the front line, wasted a precious asset:

> Owing to the failure of the Chinese to implement General Dennys' Mission, the Contingents have been placed at the disposal of the nearest formation Commanders. These Commanders are admittedly ignorant of the technique of employing such troops, and it is evident that they will become mere raiding parties, implemented for the occasion with what regular troops are required and can be spared.
>
> Such is not war of penetration, and no considerable results can be expected from such employment...[76]

Wingate then presented a new description of Long Range Penetration. As in his Ethiopian 'Appreciation', it consisted of combining specially trained regular columns and local partisan forces to attack targets far enough behind enemy lines to have 'strategic' effect. LRP's part in 'strategy' hinged on technological advance:

> Modern war is war of penetration in all its phases. This may be of two types – tactical or strategical. Penetration is tactical where armed forces carrying it out are directly supported by the operations of the main armies. It is strategical where no such support is possible, e.g. where the penetration group is living and operating 100 miles or more in front of its own armies.
>
> Of the two types, long range penetration pays by far the larger dividend on the forces employed. These forces... are able, wherever a friendly population exists, to live and move under the enemy's ribs, and thus to deliver fatal blows to his Military organisation by attacking vital objectives, which he is unable to defend. In the past, such warfare has been impossible owing to the fact that the control over such columns, indispensable both for their safety and their effectual use, was not possible until the age of easily portable wireless sets. Further, the supply of certain indispensable materials... was impossible until the appearance of communication aircraft.[77]

The 'Notes' indicated that Wingate's views on local guerrillas had not changed: they could be effective against occupiers wary of losses, restrained in their use of force and constrained by a morality which forbade reprisals against the civilian populace – as might be the case with US and Allied forces in Iraq and Afghanistan after 2001. However, if facing a ruthless opponent, prepared to kill prisoners or destroy property in reprisal for guerrilla action, insurgent forces' emotional ties to the populace constrained their freedom of action: the Japanese and the Germans were just such opponents, as had been the British in Palestine, and the Soviets were to prove in Afghanistan in the 1980s.[78] Wingate's answer was to insert columns of regular troops to protect guerrilla forces, to divert enemy attention from them, and to stimulate further revolt by example:

When opposing ruthless enemies, such as Japanese or Germans, it is wrong to place any reliance upon the efforts of the individual patriot, however devoted. Brutal and widespread retaliation instantly follows any attempt to injure the enemy's war machine, and, no matter how carefully the sabotage organisation may have been trained for the event, in practice they will find it impossible to operate against a resolute and ruthless enemy... All concerned, Military and civilian, should disabuse their minds of the fallacy that there are going to be any guerrilla operations in Burma except those that can be carried out under the aegis, and in the neighbourhood of regular columns. Guerrillas are born and not made. Essentially a guerrilla soldier is a man who prefers death on his own terms to life on the enemy's. Such were the Rifi in Morocco, and the majority of them were killed; such were the Caucasian Moslem insurgents against the Soviet troops... they were mainly exterminated; such were the Ethiopian guerrillas, who continued to fight for 5 years after the Italian occupation; they were steadily being exterminated when we intervened... Mere dislike of the enemy does not produce guerrillas. Burning hatred based on religion or other ideal [sic] will do so. It is clear, however, that in Burma we need not expect to find guerrilla operations, actively carried on by groups favourable to ourselves or hostile to the enemy, without considerable encouragement on our part. Such encouragement will be provided by the creation of long range penetration groups, who...will both take advantage of and sustain the resistance of local patriots.[79]

Direction by such columns could also aid coordination with regular forces in theatre, as Gubbins stated in *The Art of Guerrilla Warfare* and Wingate in his 'Appreciation', and both documents agreed it would ensure political coordination, particularly that guerrillas would not pursue their own interests to the detriment of Allied objectives.[80] It was for similar political reasons that Wingate rejected a proposal being presented at the time that Pathan levies could be used as penetration troops, presumably on similar lines to the French *Goumiers*.[81] In rejecting their possible employment in Burma, Wingate revealed again his belief in the usefulness of terror in insurgency – note also the double standards evident in this passage:

The employment of such levies on work which requires the highest military qualities that a soldier can possess is folly, and will have disastrous consequences. It is an erroneous idea, very prevalent in British circles in this country, that toughness is a military quality much to be desired for [the] defeat of the enemy. The more savage and brutal the human being, the better the soldier, seems to be the argument. Those who have seen actual fighting are aware that the soldier must behave with the strictest rectitude, not only towards his own side, but also towards the enemy. The qualities that are of value in war are intelligence and courage. Savagery in fighting is a drawback in any body of troops however skilled, and the tendency to loot and rapine common to uncivilised levies, when operating among alien populations, can do nothing by dis-service to the side they serve. It is recommended that any such commandos be employed purely as local raiding troops in areas occupied by a population hostile to us.[82]

As to organisation and direction, Wingate recommended forming a G(R) cell at the headquarters of whatever formation under which the LRPG group would operate.[83] This should consist of officers with 'at least some comprehension and previous experience of the special problems they will be expected to solve', ideally a combination of Calvert's instructors and officers of Mission 204 rotated through his school: 'The object should be to use the instructional side of war of penetration as a means of affording change of occupation to officers on operational duty and also to ensure that all instructors have recent experience of the application of the principles they are teaching.'[84] The cell would oversee an LRP group controlled directly by the corps commander, who would also provide the troops, and attacking objectives 'the gaining of which will decisively influence the enemy's operations.[85]

The 'Notes' formed the basis of a series of lectures Wingate delivered to senior British and Chinese officers over the next few days, but events soon overtook him. On 29 May, a 300-strong penetration force of G(R), BFF and Royal Marines, under Lieutenant Colonel Musgrave of Mission 204, operating on 17th Indian Division's right flank on the west bank of the Irrawaddy, was surprised and destroyed by a larger Japanese force at the village of Padaung. This was precipitated by a combination of Japanese 'hooks' (which Wingate described as 'short-range penetration') infiltration of the village by hostile Burmese and disguised Japanese soldiers, and the abysmal performance of the BFF, many of whom threw away their weapons and ran off before the Japanese were even encountered.[86] The Padaung disaster opened I Burma Corps' whole western flank, and in the following three days, the Japanese penetrated the front of the Corps in several places, meaning Corps HQ were unwilling to spare troops or staff facilities to implement Wingate's proposed LRP organisation. Wingate noted that 'There is little doubt that the Corps Commander [now Slim] was fully justified in taking this view.'[87] Calvert, who arranged their first meeting, recalled they almost immediately had differences over methods, his account not only encapsulating the two commanders' attitude towards each other, but Calvert's view of them also:

Wavell used Wingate... as an irritant to stir up his junior generals. He did this by extolling his original ideas on war and battle in a self-confident and masterly manner. On this occasion Slim pointed out that he had just taken over, he was not impressed by the units under his command who had not been taught how to fight orthodox warfare let alone guerrilla warfare, and he had no troops at all to spare for what he considered useless and unnecessary diversions. Slim talked very much from the pre-war Staff College text book. He had been confronted with an appalling task for which he would need every one of his rapidly diminishing number of soldiers. He could certainly not afford to let the last of them volunteer for an attractive sounding but possibly futile diversion.[88]

Upon returning to Maymyo on 2 April, Wingate wrote an 'Appreciation of chances of forming Long Range Penetration Groups in Burma', a series of proposals updated and adapted from the 'Notes', for the situation developing on Burcorps' front. Wingate noted the destruction of the Musgrave force and the performance of BFF troops, and also emphasised the similarity of Japanese methods to his own:

> [T]he Japanese have successfully done what we hoped to do. They have penetrated the Western Hills (using the sympathies of the local inhabitants), with columns of irregular and lightly armed troops who have been allotted the vital role of cutting the communications of our main force... Whether the enemy intends to use this penetration on a large scale, or only on the limited scale we have witnessed, is uncertain. It is, however, certain that he stands to gain very greatly by pushing this penetration northwards as fast, and is great numbers, as possible. The areas he is now entering... are old rebel areas, where he will find enthusiastic support.[89]

Wingate's view of why the Musgrave force failed marked his becoming more specific about the objective of LRP – to disrupt the enemy's decision-making process through threatening points of critical vulnerability in his command and logistical infrastructure, and through this impose his will upon the enemy. He began by again castigating what he saw as British commanders' inability to appreciate the value of such depth operations:

> Lt Col Musgrave's force was not used as a force of penetration, but simply as a corps of observation, with the function of observing and delaying the enemy... There was in fact no penetration on our side of any kind, either short range or long range... Lt Col Musgrave's operation was merely a delaying action.
>
> Small forces cannot <u>prevent</u> large forces from carrying out their plan. They can, if properly used... compel the larger force to alter its plan by creating an important diversion, i.e. by positive and not negative action. Forces which have the role of penetration should never, therefore be told to prevent the enemy from carrying out some operation, but should be given the task of surprising and destroying some important enemy installation or force, which will have the effect of changing the enemy's plan. They will... thus prevent the enemy from doing what he intended to do, but the means for doing so are purely offensive and not defensive.[90]

Wingate appreciated that the situation prevented the immediate creation of penetration forces, but argued that not having a G(R) cell at I Burma Corps' HQ would result in existing G(R) assets being squandered like Musgrave's. Such a cell would be responsible for penetration operations, recruitment and training, liaison with SOE, police and civil administration, obtaining currency, and propaganda. As to units, Wingate recommended the breakup of four infantry battalions – two British and two Indian – to be melded with existing G(R) elements to form two groups of four columns each, something which, it can be surmised, would have not had Slim's willing cooperation. Most significantly, Wingate mentioned for the first time resupply by air, demanding 'Communication aircraft, sufficient to deliver 20 tons a week over a carry of not less than 300 miles', and 'R.A.F. Officers of Bomber and Fighter experience allotted to columns and Group H.Q.' as well as wireless sets with a range 'not less than 300 miles.'[91]

Two factors resulted in this concept being supplanted. Firstly was the collapse of the Allied front in Burma and the subsequent retreat. Secondly was the hostility of most Burmese to the British Empire, forestalling any hope of raising a large patriot resistance for Wingate's columns to support. General Sir Harold Alexander, GOC Burma during the retreat, estimated that the population of Burma was ten per cent pro-British, ten per cent pro-Japanese, and eighty per cent likely to fall behind whoever was winning, and in 1942, that was not the British.[92] The groundwork laid by the Japanese in subverting the Burmese population paid off, and in the light of the collaboration of many Burmese with the Japanese, as late as 1944, Fergusson, commanding 16th Infantry Brigade during Operation *Thursday*, was telling soldiers in his brigade headquarters not to trust them.[93] However, the largely Christian tribes of the northwest Burmese mountains, the Chins, Kachins and Karens, remained strongly pro-British, and were soon resisting the Japanese fiercely, allowing free passage for any Allied penetration force through the thickly wooded hills they inhabited. Indeed, there was to be considerable competition for the hill tribes' affections among various British special and covert forces: earliest of these was the Burma Levies, founded in the Chin and Kachin Hills at the behest of the Governor of Burma, Reginald Dorman-Smith (Eric Dorman-Smith's brother) in December 1941 by Lieutenant Colonel H.N.C. Stevenson, a former Frontier Service official with many years' experience of the region and who supported the Kachins' aspirations to independence with the same zeal with which Wingate supported the Jews. Stevenson's 2,000 Karen guerrillas were soon receiving SOE resources and training, and were acting in concert with the SOE-led North Kachin Levy (NKL), a force some 600 strong, which provided intelligence on Japanese movements in the area.[94] These forces' activities may have delayed the Japanese advance into the Shan States of northern Burma for two days, and they also protected the flanks of retreating British forces and guided stragglers and civilians to safety. Once Burma was overrun, they were ordered to hide their weapons and await the return of the British.[95]

Wingate responded to the retreat by producing a new model of LRP operations with more in common with that presented at the end of his Ethiopia 'Appreciation', and, in several ways, a reaction to Japanese actions. Others had different views on how to beat the 'Super-Jap' at his own game.

Same enemy, different ideas

Allied commanders detected two key vulnerabilities in the Japanese Army. Firstly, despite the temporary independence of some units from regular lines of supply during their 1942 offensives, at theatre level, the Imperial Japanese Army needed lines of supply and reinforcement as much as any other. The Japanese attitude to logistics was as careless and haphazard as that of their German allies: several times in 1942, Japanese operations in Burma and elsewhere had to be built around limitations of supply, and offensives might have been halted were they not able to use captured Allied supplies and vehicles, and during the battle for New Guinea, Japanese troops were ordered to capture supplies post-haste in order for future offensives to be possible.[96] Actual systems of supply were pre-modern: prior to his Japanese 15th Army launching the Imphal-Kohima offensive in 1944, Lieutenant General Mutaguchi Renya's request for fifty road-building companies and sixty mule companies was denied by Southeastern Army Headquarters in Rangoon, and he was reduced to using bullock carts, locally requisitioned cattle and a few motor vehicles to carry his supplies, diverting material away from other fronts in Burma to accumulate the stocks needed.[97] Slim appreciated this early: shortly after taking over XV Corps in May 1942, he consulted a Chinese general who had participated in the Chinese defeat of the Japanese at Changsa, the only land victory against them at that time. Thanks to their 'very small administrative margin of safety', the trick, Slim perceived, was to 'lock' the Japanese in battle for the nine days for which they usually had supplies available, prevent them capturing one's own supplies, and counter-attack when they ran out, a model Slim applied at Imphal-Kohima in 1944.[98]

It was the other perceived Japanese weakness that interested Wingate, and from it he developed a different conception of how to beat them. From jottings in his notebooks, public statements and training pamphlets written subsequent to *Longcloth*, it is evident that Wingate was less awed by *Bushido* than many at the time or since:

> The Japanese is as unpredictable as the village pye dog. One moment he will cringe and fawn on the stranger, and at the next he will snap or bolt. This is his natural make up, but his military doctrine and carefully fostered belief in his own national superiority has introduced a predictable quality to his tactics and conduct on the battlefield when things are going well. By exploiting these we can shake his faith in his invincibility and superiority and allow his natural character to come into play.[99]

Others noticed this. As early as 1937, Stilwell and other Americans observing the war in China noted the repetitiveness and predictability of Japanese tactics and the lack of initiative of even senior Japanese commanders.[100] Even 'hook' attacks followed set drills: in *Defeat into Victory*, Slim cited the Japanese divisional commander who squandered an opportunity to destroy the remains of 17th Indian Division by over-rigid adherence to orders; told to bypass Rangoon and attack it from the west, he established a strong roadblock to cover his flank, on the main road leading north out of Rangoon, trapping British forces there; despite the scale of British attacks against the block indicating the gravity of the situation, once the remainder of the Japanese division had passed, the block was withdrawn, allowing 17th Division to escape.[101] Australian forces in New Guinea reported Japanese troops apparently blindly following orders, and if confronted with an unexpected situation, there would be a noticeable pause in the fighting as they worked it out, during which they could be hit very effectively with a counterattack.[102]

A consensus was emerging among some officers, therefore, that, far from 'jungle supermen', the Japanese Army had flaws which Allied commanders could exploit. The disagreement was on how. Slim tended, increasingly, towards tying the Japanese into battles in which superior British firepower could be brought to bear, inducing the Japanese to squander men and resources. Wingate felt that perceived weaknesses in mindset and command philosophy could be exploited through movement and infiltration.

Wingate's second model – Long Range Penetration, supported by air

Wingate took a dialectical approach to beating the enemy, building his operational theory around how the weaknesses of the Japanese soldier and his commanders – their lack of initiative and confusion at the unexpected – could be exploited via the strengths of their British counterparts. In an article on *Longcloth* written for the Army Bureau of Current Affairs in late 1943, Wingate argued the best means of bringing 'Japanese national character' into play was by attacking the decision-making process of Japanese commanders, freezing them into indecision and denying command to the soldiers, who, lacking personal initiative, needed it more than Westerners:

> [T]he Japanese mind is slow but methodical. He is a reasoned, if humourless, student of war in all its phases. He has carefully thought out the answer to all ordinary problems. He has principles which he applies, not over-imaginatively, and he hates a leap in the dark to such an extent that he will do anything rather than take it… On the other hand, when he feels he knows the intention…of his enemy he will fight with the greatest courage and determination to the last round and drop of his blood.
>
> The answer is evidently never to let him know the intentions or strength of his enemy but always to present him with a situation which he does not thoroughly understand… Our own methods, as opposed to those of the Japanese, were always to present him with a new situation which he could not analyse…[103]

Wingate reasoned that under such circumstances the salient characteristics of the British soldier, 'firstly, intelligence in action, i.e., originality in individual fighting, and, lastly, on the morale side, great self-reliance and power to give of his best when the audience is smallest', could become tactical advantages.[104] British military effort should be directed in a specific way, summarised in Wingate's training notes for *Longcloth*:

> To use a prize-fighting parallel, in the forward areas the enemy's fists are to be found, and to strike at these is not of great value. In the back areas are his unprotected kidneys, his midriff, his throat and other vulnerable points. The targets… may be regarded, therefore, as the more vital and tender portions

of the enemy's anatomy. In the nature of things, even when he realises the threat that [we] constitute to his tenderer parts, the enemy cannot provide the necessary protection... except by dropping his fists, i.e., withdrawing troops from the frontal attack against his main adversary.[105]

The main tool would be Long Range Penetration: 'This is strategical as opposed to tactical penetration. It influences not only the enemy's forward troops but his whole military machine, and his main plan.'[106] Others advocated penetrating the Japanese front line to attack it from behind, but Wingate felt it 'a fatal error' for LRP units to engage Japanese front-line troops.[107] Instead, they should penetrate 2-300 miles behind Japanese lines, to establish bases from which attacks on lines of communication could be launched.[108] From a late 1942 paper on projected LRP operations:

> The effect of these attacks will be the allotment of enemy troops to the pursuit and destruction of Columns. Immediately therefore, after the attack on a major objective, the force will split into single Columns each with a suitable role in the L of C Area. Columns will employ the methods taught during training to lead the enemy punitive Columns on a wild goose chase. The diversion they will create in this manner should compel the withdrawal from forward operational areas of very considerable enemy forces for the defence of L of C installations, and pursuit of Columns.[109]

These attacks would not be guerrilla raids, but assaults by regular troops on targets of strategic importance, which might involve engaging large formations. However, guerrilla methods – dispersal, concealment, superior fieldcraft – would be used to infiltrate defended areas, avoiding combat until necessary: 'Colns [sic] achieve their results by skilful concentration at the right time and in the right place, when they will deliver the maximum blow against the enemy. The essence of LRP is concentration, the method of dispersal is only a means to achieve ultimate concentration.'[110] Moreover, Wingate advocated an aggressive approach to dealing with Japanese formations at odds with that which might have been taken by a guerrilla force. A passage from his late 1943 training pamphlet echoed the Australian recommendation:

> The offensive almost always pays against the Japanese. An L.R.P. column must avoid action if it is likely to cause delay in reaching the objective, but if the Japanese block your progress attack them and force them onto the defensive so that they are compelled to conform to you. Overdoing the defensive and evasive aspect of L.R.P. is likely to result in losing more lives from drowning, starvation or even thirst than would be the case if the column attacked and gained the boats, food or water it required. Once you have decided to attack use bold hard hitting tactics. He is slow in the uptake so take advantage of this and hit him before he can plan.[111]

However, killing Japanese troops and destroying supplies was less important than diverting Japanese forces from their main effort: 'The withdrawal of enemy forces from forward areas to protect their long and vulnerable lines of communication from incessant spasmodic attacks by Columns, should compel the enemy to alter materially his plan of operations, and should thus assist the achievement of our own objective.'[112]

LRP forces would require technological help to maintain them so deep inside hostile territory, and it was in logistics and communications that Wingate began to depart from prevailing British Army practice. *MTP52* still envisaged the British relying on 'orthodox' lines of communication, supplies being accumulated in the operational area at lorry heads and then carried forward by animals or porters, hence the emphasis on controlling roads. Wingate's forces would be resupplied entirely from the air, columns carrying supplies with them by mule, bullock or horse, thereby freeing them from the scarce road network to manoeuvre cross-country.[113] Air support was central to LRP, along with another important innovation of the inter-war years, the portable wireless; according to Wingate:

> [LRP] is made possible by two factors comparatively new to war... These factors are firstly, the power of wireless to direct and control small or large bodies of men in the heart of enemy territory, and, secondly, the power of aircraft to maintain such troops with essential supplies; to make physical contact with them where this is necessary; and finally, and most important, to employ them to make its own blow against the widely scattered and invisible enemy effectual.[114]

Holland and others in MI(R) had discussed resupply of penetration forces by air as early as 1940, as covered already, and Calvert authored a pamphlet on this subject while with MI(R).[115] *MTP52* had commented that air transportation 'was not practicable in thick jungle', but parachutes or gliders could be landed in clearings, an assumption shared by Wingate until the latter stages of *Longcloth*.[116] This may have been based on experience gleaned during the 1942 retreat from Burma, where the British had begun using aircraft to resupply front-line units via airdrop, and from June 1942, when their ground lines of supply were cut by the monsoon, a number of outlying detachments relied entirely on air resupply and reinforcement.[117] More ambitious use of air supply was made in New Guinea, scene of the first major land victory over the Japanese: Australian troops, retreating across the Owen Stanley Mountains, had been supplied partially by air, while during the Allied counteroffensive of October 1942–January 1943, the 2/126th US Infantry Regiment had been supplied exclusively from the air.[118] Recognising the necessity for such a capability, in late 1942, India Command began to raise air supply units from the Royal Indian Army Service Corps (RIASC), the first being ready in time to support *Longcloth*, and Slim at XV Corps was, by 1943, considering the use of air supply to sustain an entire division in the field.[119] Allied forces took other steps to reduce reliance upon road-bound logistics. Australian forces in New Guinea used mules from 1942, and the period following the retreat from Burma saw 17th and 39th Indian Divisions begin conversion to 'Indian Light Divisions', consisting of just two brigades rather than the usual three, with only a light scale of jeeps and four-wheel drive lorries, relying mainly upon six

Mule Companies of the RIASC for logistical transport and with their engineers and artillery operating entirely on an animal-pack basis.[120]

Air supply and light formations based upon animal transport would therefore have featured in the British effort in Burma without Wingate. However, Wingate was suggesting what Holland and others had been advocating in 1940, that specialist penetration units, resupplied solely by airdrop, carrying supplies on pack animals and with close air support replacing artillery and tanks, could penetrate into the enemy rear, wage war on their lines of communication, and evade retribution through carefully timed dispersal and superior mobility. Such columns could also be a vital auxiliary to Allied air offensives: '[F]orces of this nature are better placed than any other ground forces to assist the air arm to direct its strategic offensive, supply it with detailed air intelligence, and exploit on the spot the opportunities created by its attacks.'[121] Consequently, there could be an integrated air-land offensive against Japanese rear areas:

> Columns should not be ordered to exploit strategic bombing unless this is in accordance with the general plan of operations of the force. The Columns are the means by which such exploitation is rendered possible, not that by which it is carried out. Provided the force has gained the upper hand over the enemy, such exploitation will be carried out by the Guerrilla organisation, which will grow as the Force succeeds in imposing its will on the enemy…i.e. R.A.F. co-operation must be aimed to help the Force win the battle against the enemy L of C organisation.[122]

Wingate also argued that 'It is most desirable that co-operating aircraft should be kept on the job, and not be changed with every action' – for part of the Allied air effort to be dedicated to supporting LRP operations.[123] Wingate's view of air operations echoed the developing Allied doctrine for tactical airpower, then being shaped in the Middle East by Air Marshals Arthur Coningham, Arthur Tedder and Harry Broadhurst. Most influential was Coningham, commander of the Northwest African Tactical Air Force from February 1943, who demanded that the first priority of a theatre air commander should be to guarantee air superiority via the destruction of enemy aircraft, after which Allied airpower should be massed against enemy reserves and supply columns, close support of the army on the battlefield coming below this on the list.[124] One of Coningham's keenest disciples was Lieutenant Colonel Philip Cochran, who served as a fighter pilot with the USAAF in North Africa before jointly commanding No.1 Air Commando on Operation *Thursday*.[125] It is unclear whether Wingate was familiar with these developments. However, it is apparent from his papers that Wingate agreed that the best use of airpower was destroying enemy communications and reserves: however, he differed from Coningham in two ways. Firstly, in adding a ground element to the offensive against enemy communications; secondly, in insisting that LRP forces should have organic air support. Coningham was firm that air operations should be controlled at Army or Air Force level, all missions requiring approval from the Air Force Commander, who would cooperate with the Army Commander without being subordinate to him, and would have sole responsibility for setting airpower priorities in the theatre of operations.[126] Wingate was to demand that air elements supporting LRP should be under the LRP commander, presumably an Army officer.

Indeed, Wingate was unequivocal that, to have maximum strategic effect, LRP operations should be directed by a single, specialist commander working at theatre level. From his 1943 LRP pamphlet comes the argument that columns, coordinated by radio, could operate to a 'Master Plan', using superior mobility to concentrate against points of critical vulnerability and, having dealt with them, could disperse into smaller, faster, more elusive elements before moving on:

> Brigades operate independently of each other, but under the centralised control by wireless of the L.R.P. force Commander. Similarly columns normally penetrate enemy held territory independently on a wide front but controlled by the Brigade Commander by means of wireless. Two or more columns having individually affected penetration may be concentrated for a particular operation... Having achieved the object they will again separate, thereby retaining their advantages of mobility and elusiveness and preventing the enemy from concentrating superior force and pinning them down.[127]

This would produce the strategic impact Wingate sought:

> L.R.P. forces by deploying Brigades from different directions many hundred miles apart, and by dispersing the columns of each Brigade over a wide area, force the enemy to guard every vital point in the whole of his rear areas so he will be weak everywhere and strong nowhere.[128]

In a training pamphlet written after *Longcloth*, Wingate suggested a philosophy of command and control which, although centralised, was also mission driven, tolerant of initiative, and aware of the dispersed nature of the operations it was to direct:

> The Column's axis of advance conforms to the plain laid down by Brigade. The actual route is the Column Commander's responsibility... The Brigade plan will be designed to ensure that the Japanese appreciation is wrong, and the action of columns must not only conform to this plan but must... always be unpredictable.[129]

Column commanders would not only have considerable devolved authority, but were expected to show initiative at all times:

> The Column Commander must be engaged on a continuous appreciation of the situation, constantly reviewing the everchanging [sic] factors and modifying his plans to suit them. He must, however, retain the initiative and not surrender this to the enemy... This implies being unpredictable, offensively minded, and

mobile...Depending on the progress of the battle, the Column Commander will commit additional platoons into action or in pursuit, and will decide that the opposition is too strong and evasive action must be taken.[130]

Such can be discerned in Wingate's propensity in operational orders to state his intent in terms of desired effect upon the Japanese ('16 Bde will forbid the enemy possession of the areas INDAW, NABA and BANMAUK, by the use of road blocks and Strongholds...')[131] and under 'Method', frequently offering a range of suggestions or options which subordinates might adopt or ignore as they saw fit. Wingate also took an elastic approach to operations once troops were committed, and expected likewise from his brigade and column commanders; prior to *Longcloth* he wrote:

Leave at all times... wide scope for the Commander for adjusting the role to changing conditions, and exploiting any success gained... The force can be switched from one set of objectives to another without endangering its security or rendering it useless, provided the necessary latitude as to date and method is left to the Commander on the spot.[132]

Such free-form, results-driven operations hinged upon accurate intelligence and efficient communications. For *Longcloth*, Wingate obtained four tons of maps of northern Burma and carpeted the floor of his operations room with a one inch to one mile scale map of Burma, with other maps and aerial photographs papering the walls, and carried out five days of map briefings to his column commanders, insisting they develop an intimate familiarity with the geography of the area of operations.[133] Both Chindit operations were preceded by frequent, extensive overflights of the area of operations with column and brigade commanders on board, and by short-ranged officers' patrols into Japanese territory, so giving commanders familiarity with the geography of the region, allowing them to move across it effectively without direction from above.[134] A column's main source of tactical intelligence was constant patrolling of the surrounding area. Wingate was fortunate in having attached to him from the start 2nd Battalion, Burma Rifles, a unit recruited from the hill tribes of Northern Burma and officered by a combination of hill tribesmen promoted from the ranks, local British settlers holding wartime commissions and British Army regulars. Their designated role was as a scouting force, carrying out reconnaissance patrols up to thirty miles ahead of their designated column, at which they excelled, and liaising with the local population, not only gathering information, but recruiting reliable local guides; on *Thursday* they were supplemented by large numbers of locally recruited guerrillas.[135]

The other branch of the information system was communications. Each column carried one wireless for communication with Brigade Headquarters and another for talking to the Air Base, all signals being in Morse code and enciphered. IV Corps, Wingate's parent formation on both operations, assisted with a 24-hour radio watch for all sets and by broadcasting regular intelligence summaries, opening the possibility of commanders converging 'on the sound of the guns' even without communications from their immediate superior headquarters.[136] For *Longcloth*, all messages to and between columns were routed through brigade headquarters, leading to frequent communications logjams which rather upset Wingate's original intent. Based on a suggestion of Fergusson's, for *Thursday*, each brigade had a rear headquarters back in India, listening in to all radio traffic within the brigade, and in the case of columns being on the move, and the wirelesses – non-portable and carried by mules – being out of action, once they re-established communications, they could update on the situation.[137]

LRP and other Allied penetration forces in Asia, 1942–43

LRP forces needed to be melded with extant Allied strategy, raising two issues: how Wingate's proposed organisation would cooperate with the other special and penetration units being assembled in India, and how far they might have departed from the role and status of such forces elsewhere in the British Army at this stage in the war.

Lieutenant Colonel Stevenson's Burma Levies have been mentioned already. SOE planted agents and stay-behind parties among the hill tribes during the retreat, but did not begin operations in earnest until 1943.[138] Two new forces were also present. The first of these was the American covert operations organisation, the Office of Strategic Services (OSS).[139] OSS agents were operating in Burma by 1943, controlled by Stilwell in Chungking, and their activities were not only uncoordinated with, but also sometimes compromised those of British special forces with Stilwell's tacit encouragement, and relations with the British were aggravated by a noticeable cocksureness and 'cowboy' mentality, again probably encouraged by Stilwell.[140] The second was 'V' Force, raised by Wavell from the Assam Rifles, a police unit comprised of Gurkhas under British officers, trained by SOE to act as 'hard core' to a 10,000-strong guerrilla force recruited from hill tribes on both sides of the Burma-Assam border and intended to harass Japanese communications when they invaded India – a remit not entirely dissimilar to that of G(R)'s Operational Centres in Ethiopia before Wingate took charge of them.[141] When the invasion did not happen, 'V' Force switched to covert intelligence gathering and liaison with the local population, operating through a combination of small, irregular tribal units and individual agents.[142]

That Wingate's LRP units should be separate from these 'guerrilla' forces was accepted early. Rough lines of demarcation were set at a meeting chaired by the Director of Military Operations, Burma, Major General Osburne, on 24 April 1942, at which Wingate, Stevenson and Colin Mackenzie, head of SOE's Oriental Mission, discussed 'guerrilla operations in Burma.' Osburne opened by encapsulating policy for guerrillas vis a vis LRP units – 'Former mosquitoes, latter regular dets. – Both working in co-operation for common cause' – the 'common cause' being a common plan, made by the commander-in-chief, combining the actions of regular units, LRP and guerrillas.[143] Wingate then explained the role of LRP at this stage: 'Colns of all arms varying in strength and composition in accordance with each particular situation... say, inf. coy, section of mountain artillery, Sapper and Miner detachment, signal detachment, intelligence and guerrilla personnel', each column carrying supplies for three weeks, the remainder delivered by air.[144] Targets would be airfields, headquarters, depots and railheads, the objective 'creation of insecurity in rear areas of L.of C.'[145] Stevenson and Wingate agreed that cooperation between LRP and guerrillas would be essential, and therefore, arming and directing the hill tribes should be a priority.[146] Osburne would recommend to the Commander in Chief, Burma (Alexander) that an LRP Brigade be formed, suggesting a force based on two battalions supplied by India Command; an LRP training centre should be formed in India, with Mission 204 co-located with it. Wingate, with characteristic over-optimism, estimated he could train this Long Range Penetration Group (LRPG) in eight weeks, after which it could be deployed to support operations against Akyab or Moulmein, in southern Burma.[147] However, Mackenzie argued that northern Burma provided greater opportunities for cooperation with guerrillas, and it was agreed that Stevenson and SOE should maintain guerrilla activity there until the LRP Group was ready for operations.[148] Subsequently, in June 1942, Wingate was appointed acting Brigadier and received authority from the War Office to form his LRPG, to which Mission 204's reinforcements would be directed, effectively marking the end of G(R) as an independent entity.[149] Despite this early cordiality, Brigadier D.R. Guinness, the Deputy Head of SOE's Oriental Mission, recorded that Wingate 'disliked and suspected' SOE – and many other senior British military officers felt likewise.[150]

Wingate was perhaps fortunate to still have Wavell's patronage, as the institutional mindset forming the background to his operations in Ethiopia and, indirectly, to LRP, was mutating. As early as January 1942, official misgivings were expressed about the perceived over-use of Jock Columns by Eighth Army in North Africa, to the effect that they could not press home attacks or hold ground and were instilling a 'tip and run' mentality in many officers.[151] When Montgomery arrived to command Eighth Army in August 1942, he decreed that 'The policy of fighting the enemy in brigade groups, Jock columns, and with divisions split up into bits and pieces all over the desert was to cease. In future divisions would fight *as* divisions [emphasis Montgomery's]'[152] At Alamein in October, the objective was to secure breaches in the Axis front line via a methodical battle of destruction, Eighth Army fighting strictly to Montgomery's 'Master Plan', the basic fighting formation being the division and control of artillery being centralised at Corps level.[153] Moreover, from mid-1942, as GHQ Far East continued to allow Special Forces commanders to settle a division of labour between themselves, GHQ Middle East created a new branch, G Staff Raiding, to coordinate the actions of the expanding crop of Special Forces in its region both with each other and with the main armies. This was necessary due to the sheer number of such units then deployed in the Mediterranean. By the end of 1942, David Stirling was presiding not only over the SAS, now at battalion strength, but a French SAS Squadron, the Greek Sacred Squadron, the Folbot Section of the Royal Marines and the Middle East Commando, a total strength of over 1,000.[154] The LRDG had expanded to two squadrons, commanded by Lieutenant Colonel

Prendergast after Bagnold was appointed an Advisor at GHQ Middle East. From 1943, it also included No.1 Long Range Demolition Group, which preferred to be known as Popski's Private Army, after its commander, Major Vladimir 'Popski' Peniakoff, a Belgian of Russian parentage.[155] Alongside these regular units were extensive guerrilla and resistance movements in southeastern Europe organised by SOE.

As to roles, the LRDG retained primarily a reconnaissance unit, Hackett, and the official historian of the desert war, Major General ISO Playfair, paying tribute to its Road Watch patrols, which kept a detailed census of all Axis military traffic along the main coastal road from April-November 1942, providing some prior warning of major Axis operations, while Montgomery himself referred to its finding a route through the 'sand sea' to the south of the Mareth line, in December 1942, allowing the New Zealand Division to outflank this position in the battles of the following March.[156] Prior to March 1942, the LRDG had the additional task of scouting for the SAS and conveying it to its objectives, the latter's prime objective being the destruction of Axis aircraft on the ground. The SAS destroyed 126 Axis aircraft in twenty airfield attacks between December 1941 and March 1942, including thirty-seven in one raid on Christmas Day 1941.[157] In summer 1942, the SAS became independent of the LRDG upon acquiring its own armed jeeps, and by July, had hit every Axis airfield within 300 miles of the front line.[158] During the Alamein battles, the SAS destroyed thirty German aircraft on raids near Sidi Haneish, but after this, Stirling was redirected to Rommel's communications, including ports, ending this period with a catastrophically unsuccessful raid on Benghazi.[159]

An un-codified British Army 'doctrine' for penetration forces was, therefore, emerging by late 1942. The theatre commander was to direct them against enemy rear areas in support of the main battle, evident in the deployment of the various British Special Forces in North Africa in 1942 and the proposed roles for their counterparts in Burma. However, differences were also apparent: it is clear from contemporary sources that in Europe and the Middle East, special forces were expected to produce 'empirical' results of direct use to the main armies – information gathered, aircraft destroyed or supplies interdicted, for example.[160] In the Far East, the aim remained more esoteric, and as it was in 1940 – to divert and overstretch enemy forces and disrupt their planning and preparation. An illustration of this difference comes from Hackett's recalling the LRDG's complaint to G Staff Raiding that SAS raids were disrupting their activities through the large numbers of Germans sweeping rear areas after an SAS attack, forcing the LRDG to vacate those areas – yet a heavy enemy response, leading to forces being redeployed from the front, was Wingate's very objective.[161] Another difference was also emerging – scale. Whereas the North African forces, V-Force, SOE and the others operated in small units, or covertly, Wingate proposed to insert a brigade-sized force, with some logistic elements and air support, into hostile territory for an extended period. And this is what he did in the spring of 1943.

Chapter Seven

Wingate in Burma (2) – Operation *Longcloth* and its Consequences

We were a well-balanced fighting force, 20,000 or more men, all potential Jap-killers and no hangers-on, going to the hub of the situation in order that we might cut some of the spokes. Then with pressure on the rim, the whole structure might break down.

Brigadier Michael Calvert[1]

I found Wingate stimulating when he talked strategy or grand tactics, but strangely naïve when it came to the business of actually fighting the Japanese. He had never experienced a real fight against them, still less a battle. The Japanese, unlike the Italians, were not to be frightened into a withdrawal by threats to their rear; they had first to be battered and destroyed in hard fighting.

Field Marshal Lord Slim[2]

The Chindits

Wingate was firm that his LRP Groups were not 'special forces', and was sceptical about units which were:

I have seen a great deal of volunteers, and volunteer units in this war, and I am convinced that the volunteer proposal is wrong from the Imperial point of view... To sum [up] briefly the existing unit with its known establishment 'Espirit de Cor' [sic] and known proportions of specialists, trained personnel, etc., can be quickly and readily adapted to this type of operation. Once learned the lessons are never forgotten. The volunteer unit takes four times as long to adopt anything... I consider that any healthy Englishman will make a successful Guerrilla, if he puts his mind to it, puts his back to it, and is given [the] right training.[3]

This is just as well, as – contradicting the accusations of Slim, Kirby and others – Wingate's first LRP Group hardly constituted a leeching of quality manpower from the front line in India. Wingate was assigned three infantry battalions, formed into 77th Indian Infantry Brigade, a cover name, as it contained no Indian troops, although its Gurkhas were technically part of the Indian Army. Ex-G(R) staff aside, the Brigade was made up, apparently, of what GHQ India could spare. 13th Battalion, King's Liverpool Regiment, were a mixture of conscripts and wartime volunteers mainly in their thirties, none of whom had seen combat, and who had spent the first three years of the war on garrison duties in Britain and India; 3/2nd Gurkha Rifles were another wartime unit, which had just completed basic training (Fergusson recalling 'the average age of the Gurkha... looked to be about 15 years old') and most of whose British officers were themselves but recently trained, few speaking Gurkhali, and only the Commanding Officer and Gurkha Major having any previous operational experience.[4] Highly fortunate, then, that Wingate also had the one remaining battalion of the Burma Rifles, who proved themselves invaluable time and again on both Chindit operations. Alongside the infantry battalions was 142 Company, made up of the remains of Mission 204, supplemented by volunteers from the Royal Engineers and other infantry units, which was to provide a squad of 'fighting saboteurs' for each column. Each column would also have attached to it an RAF Section consisting of a pilot-trained officer and signalers, tasked with coordinating supply drops and close air support.[5] 77th Brigade was organised into a fighting, rather than a raiding force. The Brigade was divided into eight columns, four British and four Gurkha, each commanded by a major and intended to operate independently, each consisting of a headquarters, an infantry company, a reconnaissance platoon from the Burma Rifles, a support section, with two three-inch mortars and two Vickers machine-guns, an animal transport section, with eighty mules or bullocks, an air liaison section, with an RAF officer (Flight Lieutenant Robert Thompson with No.3 Column on *Longcloth*) and wireless operators, a Commando platoon from 142 Company, a medical team and a Royal Signals detachment; on *Thursday* the Commando Platoons of some columns were up-gunned into assault pioneers, equipped with flamethrowers, a favourite weapon of Wingate's.[6] There were, therefore, radical differences in scale, personnel and organisation between 77th Brigade and units such as the SAS or LRDG. Wingate stressed that 'an important point to grasp is that the troops that carried out this enterprise were in no respect chosen for their fitness for this or any other type of warfare, but were simply the men who normally get drafted into the infantry during a great war.'[7] This was not quite true, as the ferocious training programme to which these 'ordinary' soldiers were subject prior to *Longcloth* soon began to demonstrate. Training began in July 1942, taking place entirely in the field, at Saugor in central India, chosen because of its resemblance to northern Burma. Wingate emphasised 'toughening' his soldiers to the jungle, the aim of the two to three day cross-country marches (full equipment, across rough country in the heat of an Indian summer, soldiers' meals limited to what they were carrying, at least one river crossing) upon which the early training programme centred, being apparently as much to weed out 'the sick, lame and lazy' as it was to improve the fitness and field skills of the survivors (British Special Forces use not dissimilar methods of selection into the twenty-first century).[8] During the course of this 13th King's shed 200 men for medical reasons and what Wingate, with a rare euphemism, called a 'marked lack of enthusiasm'; these were replaced by younger men from other regiments, including a new commanding officer, Lieutenant Colonel S.A. Cooke of the Lincolnshire Regiment, and Wingate estimated that 77th Brigade eventually comprised the pick of forty different regiments and corps; Fergusson's No.5 Column, ostensibly based on 13th King's, ended up with officers from thirteen units, including eleven infantry regiments.[9] 3/2

Gurkhas suffered in equal measure, 'weeding out' reducing its number from 750 to 550, and a large draft arrived in November 1942, just a few weeks before the end of the training period, embarking on *Longcloth* trained only partially for the mission.[10] Problems were compounded by Wingate and Calvert being the only two personnel in the Brigade with any guerrilla experience – it seems that numerous Mission 204 personnel refused to serve with Wingate – and so they had to carry out much of the instruction personally, slowing the training process further.[11]

Once the unsuitable were gone, and he was satisfied with the conditioning of the remainder, Wingate set about turning them into an effective LRP force. This began with the officers, whom he trained largely himself, setting them complex tactical exercises on sandpit models, or, alternatively, double-timing them around the exercise area (many recalled the pace he set as closer to sprinting) from stand to stand, at each stand setting them tactical problems based on the ground before them, before cross-examining them mercilessly on their proposed solutions. Wingate's aim was not only to instill his doctrine for action, but also to develop tactical instinct.[12] They would then graduate to field exercises. These began with extended map briefings, wherein Wingate would describe a particular operational situation, have other officers or soldiers play the part of locals with further knowledge to be extracted by careful questioning, after which the officers under training would have to plot the estimated locations of enemy forces, the routes of marches, the locations of supply drops and road blocks, all having to conform with Wingate's overall plan. They would then go out with their troops and do it for 'real'.[13]

As with all military training, soldiers' training began with individual skills, and then worked upwards. Individual training involved intensive reinforcement of infantry skills – marksmanship, physical fitness and fieldcraft and tactical movement in the jungle – alongside those required for dispersed operations behind enemy lines. The most obvious of these is that everyone, from private soldiers upwards, was taught cross-country navigation without maps, by memory or using the sun and stars, and in picking the best going by sight; all were also taught basic sabotage and demolition skills by Calvert and his team.[14] Once individuals were trained to Wingate's satisfaction, section and platoon exercises began. Little detail of these survives, but it seems once again that Wingate made extensive use of one-day exercises aimed at teaching not only tactics and fieldcraft, but also instilling standard procedures for setting up defended camps at night, river crossings and, most importantly, for receiving supply drops, a particularly complex and dangerous business, given a drop's potential to indicate a column's presence to the Japanese.[15] In addition, he produced set drilled procedures for assaults on villages and ambushes and attacks in the jungle.[16]

It was also during training that the LRPGs acquired the name by which they would be better known. 77th Brigade adopted a badge depicting a *Chinthe* or *Chinthey*, another example of Wingate's using titles and symbols of spiritual significance, as the *Chinthey* is the guardian of the Pagodas and the only creature in Buddhist mythology allowed to use force. Indeed, the badge was to have major propaganda impact inside Burma, Wingate becoming 'Lord Protector of the Pagodas' to the Burmese. Yet Wingate, to his eternal annoyance, mispronounced *Chinthey* as 'Chindit' during several speeches and press interviews, this term being seized upon after *Longcloth* by the press, after which it became the commonly accepted title for the LRPGS.[17] However, more serious matters were emerging.

Wingate and the Indian Army

Fergusson recalled that, even as 77th Brigade assembled: 'Nobody seriously believed in [Wingate] except General Wavell, and everybody regarded him as a bit of a nuisance. In GHQ his brigade was irritably known as "the Chief's [Wavell's] private army," and himself as "Tarzan" or "Robin Hood."'[18] Nowhere, apparently, were these feelings more apparent than with the Staff Duties and Training Section of GHQ India. The Staff Duties and Training Section of any headquarters in the British Army were responsible for training and organisation, this involving the devising, publishing and dissemination of training programmes and the establishment of schools and other training establishments: this might entail analysing 'war problems' and forming solutions, usually in the form of new technology or new types of unit.[19] Wingate's LRP Groups were just such a new type of unit, raised to deal with a 'war problem', and the Director of Staff Duties at GHQ India, Major General S. Woodburn Kirby, was responsible for policy in this field across India Command, where Wingate's force was to assemble. Consequently, although Wingate had been authorised by the War Office and Wavell to form his LRP Groups, negotiation and discussion with the SD Department, to turn his theoretical concepts into units and formal training programmes, was necessary.

'Negotiation and discussion' were rarely on Wingate's agenda. The SD India Department first became aware of Wingate in May or June 1942, when Wingate commandeered one of its senior officers' secretaries to type an operational proposal which was then passed over Kirby's head to Wavell.[20] At the opening conference between Wingate and the SD Department, Kirby, aware of Wavell's interest and Wingate's reputation, took the chair himself, to be treated by Wingate, Lieutenant Colonel A.R. Nevill, an officer on Kirby's staff recalled, 'in front of his own staff and the other staff representatives present, as if he were the inefficient manager of a rather unsatisfactory multiple store', Wingate presenting a shopping-list of equipment demands, to be met immediately, regardless of availability. This culminated in a surreal discussion concerning miniature compasses, as hidden inside collar studs for use by SOE, which Wingate wanted converted into fly buttons.[21]

Their subsequent relationship was reflected in a report Kirby produced, presumably following this meeting, and Wingate's response. Kirby's report has not survived, but its content can be construed from what Wingate had to say about it. Kirby had apparently accepted LRP in principle, but had contended its application would be more difficult than in Ethiopia, due to the hostility of the Burmese, and, given the situation in India at the time, that Wingate might do better to form special units of volunteers, to a strength of around 1,300, rather than demand existing units to a strength of 3,000. Wingate replied with a detailed four-page rebuttal in which he reiterated that he was not trying to form Special Forces and in his view, such forces had demonstrably failed, although he seems to have selected his supporting examples carefully. The BFF special units and Commando units in Ethiopia and Crete failed 'due partly to lack of esprit de corps, partly to mishandling, partly to bad leadership' and, more contentiously, 'Elsewhere other Commandos failed to prove themselves of value for precisely the same reason', this in May 1942, after Stirling's mass destruction of Axis aircraft in North Africa and the Commandos' greatest success hitherto, at St Nazaire in March. Wingate contrasted this 'failure' with the success of Gideon Force, the 'one successful example of penetration by ourselves in this war'. Wingate concluded by acknowledging that Kirby had accepted his overall concept and commented 'I suggest he might find my experience in this type of warfare a help to him in drawing up plans'; a force of 3,000, formed from existing units, would have the esprit de corps he valued so highly, would train quicker – he estimated he could be ready in six weeks – and would produce a higher proportion of fighting troops.[22]

There is, therefore, some contemporary testimony and circumstantial evidence supporting the view that Kirby's later assessment of Wingate arose from personal animosity. This went on. Calvert, visiting New Delhi in early August, wrote to Wingate at Saugor warning him of the mood at GHQ India: senior staff officers were 'spreading canards' expressing the view that Wingate's LRP scheme was impracticable and that he was unfit to command: 'One general said that 10% of your ideas were brilliant but the other 90% were dangerous and sometimes absurd.' Calvert ascribed this to 'jealousy, listening to gossip and guilt owing to their own unpreparedness.' Calvert tried to see Alexander, still GOC Burma, to report a perceived lack of cooperation from GHQ India, but was told he was too junior to meet him directly; when he said he would send a report to Wingate to show Wavell, he was warned by a staff officer that 'us regulars must stick together.'[23] In a subsequent letter, Calvert begged Wingate for a 'case' to put before Wavell, having learned that GHQ India were planning a visit to 77th Brigade, following a 'panic telegram' from Central Command concerning the number of sick from 13th King's which had been copied to forty-three different offices, including the DSD (Kirby) and Director of Military Intelligence (DMI), both openly hostile already.[24]

Wingate's response set the tone for what was to come. He began by assuring Calvert that he had seen this coming, and what followed demonstrates amply his unshakeable self-belief:

It is because I am what I am, objectionable though that appears to my critics, that I win battles. It is ludicrous that, in a war where defeat after defeat is suffered... an officer with my fighting record should be discredited and ruled out of the field by tittle tattle and personal accusations made covertly... [T]he truth is that there is not one of my critics who will dare to dispute the facts with me. The methods they use are those more fit for secret police than for British officers... Common sense tells us, after a series of disasters, to listen to the man who has more successes to his credit. On my subject, I'll listen to Mihailovitch's [sic – Colonel Drazha Mihailovic, commander of the Royalist *Chetnik* guerrillas in Yugoslavia] comments with deep respect but not to those whose information is limited to a few vicarious brushes with the Japanese.[25]

Wingate found enemies lower down in the Indian Army. Brigadier Shelford Bidwell had some post-war correspondence with former Chindits who implied that the Gurkhas, 'those arrogant soldiers', found some of Wingate's proposed tasks, particularly muleteering, *infra dignitatum*.[26] Overall, the 3/2nd, certain of its officers in particular, did not perform well on *Longcloth*, culminating in three extremely rare incidents of Gurkhas panicking under fire, Wingate reporting two of these with characteristic bluntness in his Official Report on the operation: more seriously, during *Longcloth*, he sacked two Gurkha officers as column commanders in the field, naming one of them in his report as 'lethargic', the other as 'unfit to command men.'[27] In his Report, Wingate blamed the poor performance of the Gurkhas on the 'slow wits' of the soldiers and the inexperience of the officers leading to their not absorbing training at the necessary pace, yet John Masters, an officer of 2/4th Gurkhas, who, like Fergusson and Dodds-Parker, admired some aspects of Wingate while deploring others, criticised Wingate for training Gurkhas via 'mass suggestion', rather than the patient, paternal methods preferred in most Indian, African and Arab units of the British Imperial Army.[28] However, there is another side to the argument. The 3/2nd had just two officers with any combat experience and just two who could speak a reasonable standard of Gurkhali, to command a battalion full of hastily trained teenaged boys; indeed, the GHQ India historian agreed with Wingate that the Gurkhas were 'not quick witted', not good at animal handling, and absorbed new tasks more slowly than British or Indian troops.[29] Add to this a general lack of enthusiasm about the mission among the officers, which may have trickled downwards irrespective of language barriers. Calvert's report on his mainly Gurkha No.3 Column on *Longcloth* contains numerous anecdotes of callow, undisciplined and occasionally panicky behaviour from his Gurkhas. Physically fearless and always leading from the front, Calvert was perhaps the ideal Gurkha commander, but even he had to 'grip' them under fire more than once; echoing Wingate's sackings of the column commanders, he demoted several NCOs and at one point considered reducing several Gurkha officers to the ranks 'as we had some good havildars [Gurkha sergeants] who were better'; morale and discipline in No.3 Column were close to collapse by the end of *Longcloth*.[30] The performance of some Gurkha troops on this operation may therefore have owed as much to regimental *hubris* as to any flaws in Wingate's methods. However, this is not to deny that many in 77th Brigade found Wingate hard to take. Lieutenant Philip Stibbe, a platoon commander in 13th Kings, recalled:

> Some of [Wingate's] orders were... unorthodox in the extreme... Saluting was to be cut down to the minimum. Everything was to be done at the double. Everyone must eat at least one raw onion per day. Only shorts were to be worn when it was raining. Swearing must stop. Thursday was to be Sunday... No officer was to go sick and a man must be either sick or fit; if he was sick he was to do nothing; if he was fit he was to do everything. Orders were to be obeyed at once.[31]

With raw onion-eating, Wingate led by example, reporting in official correspondence that he ate up to six per day, a practice begun in Palestine; Mr F.J. Hill, who served as a muleteer on *Longcloth*, has confirmed an oft-repeated 'Wingate story', being one of a group of Chindits who had raw turtle's eggs forced upon them by the Force Commander in person.[32] Once, Wingate fired over the heads of a group of officers caught without weapons; on another, he expected officers to jump out of a lorry he was driving at high speed.[33] Such behaviour, combined with Wingate's appearance – he resumed the beard, solar topee and scruffy uniform from Ethiopia and temporarily banned all shaving in the Brigade to save time – likely contributed to the comments made at GHQ India to Fergusson and Calvert and the attitude of the Gurkha officers. Wingate's idiosyncrasies are pertinent: firstly, the amateur dietician may have had some impact on 77th Brigade's effectiveness on *Longcloth*, to be discussed below; secondly is the issue of special forces commanders needing to be tactful and politic, to avoid suspicion of creating 'private armies', outside chains of command, and not antagonise superiors and colleagues. Wingate, of course, was for much of the time the opposite of tactful and politic, and apparently took great delight in antagonising a certain type of officer.

Operation *Longcloth* and its impact

Longcloth was planned initially as an attack on Japanese communications along the line of the Irrawaddy River and beyond in support of a combined British-Chinese offensive into northern Burma. When this was cancelled, due to logistical problems and characteristically uncooperative behaviour from Chiang, Wingate persuaded Wavell that it should proceed anyway as an experiment testing his methods and possibly to forestall any possible obstruction from GHQ India.[34] Consequently, Wingate's plan was open-ended: 77th Brigade would cross the River Chindwin, the main barrier between India and Japanese-occupied Burma, to attack the road and railway running from Mandalay to Myitkyina; having done this, he would then decide on whether to continue attacks on the railway or cross the River Irrawaddy to attack the railway between Shwebo and Myitkyina – the main Japanese airfield menacing the 'Hump' air bridge – before withdrawing into India or pushing on into China.[35]

Longcloth went ahead from February to May 1943, 77th Brigade penetrating to the Irrawaddy and beyond, destroying several bridges and blowing the Mandalay-Myitkyina railway, the main Japanese supply route to their forces in the north, in more than seventy places.[36] The Chindits learnt valuable lessons. Perhaps most important was that well-trained and acclimatised British troops had little to fear from the jungle, and that there were more types of bush than the simple 'primary/ secondary jungle' given in official training publications, each providing its own tactical costs and benefits. Provided noise and camouflage drills – which Wingate enforced rigidly – were respected, a large force could become virtually invisible to air and even ground forces unless at very close range, a notable feature of *Longcloth* being the large number of successful ambushes of Japanese forces. Also noticeable was the growing lack of aggression of the Japanese, who seemed satisfied, in many cases, to confine themselves to shelling positions they thought were held by Chindit forces with mortars and artillery, from a distance.[37] There was a consensus, even among Wingate's critics, that one of the benefits of *Longcloth* was the irreparable puncturing of the 'Super-Jap' myth.[38]

Wingate's faith in technology was also vindicated: he was in regular wireless communication with 77th Brigade's parent formation, IV Corps, in Assam, until late

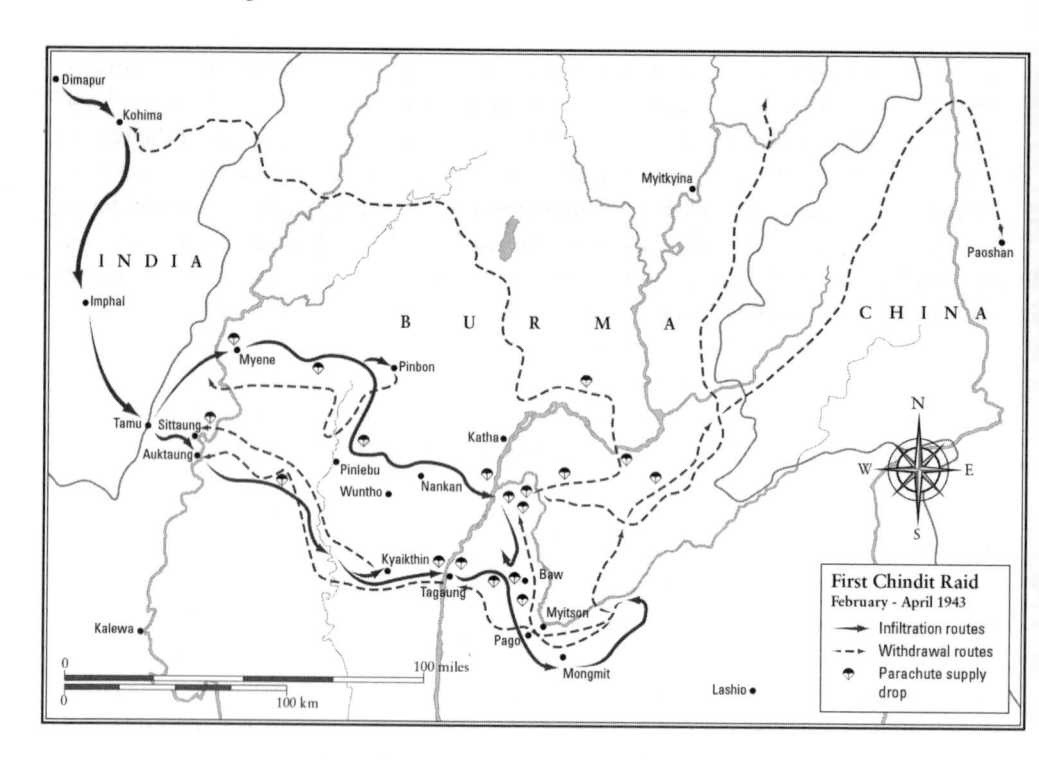

March, by which time he was over 170 miles behind Japanese lines, and was also able to coordinate airdrops – at one point, sixteen sorties delivered 70,000 pounds of supplies over a 48-hour period. It was also discovered that, contrary to previous training documents, supply drops could be made in thick jungle, meaning that it was no longer necessary to concentrate upon clearings or other obvious dropping zones.[39] *Longcloth* demonstrated that a brigade-sized formation could penetrate nearly 200 miles behind enemy lines to attack deep communications, supplied entirely by air, provided it had adequate air support.

Wingate kept his word on devolving authority. Because of the trust he held in them, Wingate tended to select Calvert, commanding No.3 Column, and Fergusson, No.5 Column, as his 'spearheads', assigning them the most important tasks and granting them more latitude and flexibility than certain others. There were noticeable differences between the three on operations and tactics: Calvert's aim was, from the beginning, to 'kill Japs' in their 'safe' areas in as large a number as possible, mining and booby-trapping the route around him and constantly begging Wingate's permission to send out fighting patrols and ambush parties, which he often led personally. Wingate and Fergusson, conversely, aimed to divert Japanese strength as far back as possible, Fergusson in particular being keen to infiltrate through the jungle to the railway avoiding any serious contact with the Japanese or any activity likely to draw attention, yet also ensuring to visit as many villages as possible to procure supplies and 'show the flag' in what emerged as a staunchly pro-British area.[40] From 6 March, it was these two commanders who led the attack on the railway, Calvert cutting the line in seventy places and destroying two bridges while the screen of ambushes he threw around the railway repulsed a fierce Japanese counterattack at Nankan, while

Fergusson destroyed a bridge, dynamited a gorge and destroyed a Japanese platoon in a surprise encounter at the village of Kyaikthin.[41]

The operation was not an unvarnished success, however. Having attacked the railway, Wingate decided to proceed across the Irrawaddy, where he hoped to contain the Japanese for the remainder of the period before the monsoon by raiding the Shwebo-Myitkyina railway, seize the airfield at Indaw as a base for reinforcement and resupply, and detach a Mission under Captain D.C. Herring of the Burma Rifles to escalate resistance in the Kachin Hills of northeast Burma.[42] Yet he had lost the element of surprise which he always valued so highly; the Japanese were closing in on 77th Brigade, he had given them a line on which to concentrate, and had concentrated the brigade into a triangle between the Irrawaddy and Shweli rivers, mainly open country well served by roads and devoid of overhead cover. The area also had little water, a particular worry for Calvert, who enforced strict water discipline on No.3 Column and recorded that his North Africa veterans compared the heat with the Western Desert.[43] Moreover, Fergusson reported, Wingate's decision to use large, infrequent supply drops meant that troops had to go for extended periods on short or even no rations, and any attempt to forage was drawing Japanese attention; many of No.5 Column were showing signs of both severe hunger and heat exhaustion.[44]

IV Corps ordered Wingate to withdraw on 24 March, as he was now over 170 miles inside hostile territory, and his supply aircraft were unable to carry out sufficient sorties to resupply the Brigade effectively at that range.[45] Wingate therefore decided to break the Brigade up into small parties which infiltrated through the surrounding Japanese and returned to India.[46]

77th Brigade began the operation in February with 3,000 men, and by the beginning of June just over 2,000 had returned to India. Of the missing, 120 were soldiers of the Burma Rifles who stayed behind voluntarily to organise resistance; 430 had been taken prisoner, and 450 were dead.[47] Moreover, many of those who returned to India were suffering from malaria, malnutrition, or, in many cases, both, and would be unfit for further soldiering without an extensive period of hospitalisation.[48] Fergusson was unequivocal about the causes of this – the short rations upon which Wingate kept the Brigade throughout the operation, evidently believing they could keep going on nuts and Shakapura biscuits, as he did himself, supplemented by what they could forage: in post-war correspondence with Slim he recounted having to abandon starving soldiers by the trackside, completely unable to help them, and that he had threatened to resign if Wingate did not correct this before any further operations.[49] Another potential resignation issue had been Wingate's alleged 'abandonment' of hill tribes who had helped the Chindits to the retribution of the Japanese.[50] Wingate, therefore, had his critics within his own forces.

Longcloth's Impact

Fergusson agreed that operationally, *Longcloth* had achieved little in the short-term, but disagreed with Slim on the operation's long-term impact: '[W]e amassed experience on which a future has already begun to build.'[51] Calvert, typically, was more bullish:

This operation can be compared, for its success and failures, with the Dieppe operation in that it paved the way both technically and in the hearts of men for the final offensive and the overthrow of the enemy. Its greatest achievement was the final proof that airpower in the form of air supply could… give back to the ground forces mobility and freedom of manoeuvre without being tactically tied to ground communications. As with seapower, the influence of airpower could mean that an army was free to strike anywhere as long as it had superiority in the air and a sufficient air merchant fleet to bring the goods direct to the fighting man.[52]

Longcloth demonstrated – albeit ambiguously – the possibility of company to brigade-sized formations, penetrating hostile territory, being supplied entirely by air, provided they had adequate air support, which *Longcloth* had not. Such had been forecast by Holland and others at MI(R) in 1940, and, indeed, *Longcloth* could be cited as fulfillment of Holland's projections as much as Wingate's.

Moreover, *Longcloth* had a profound impact on strategy in Southeast Asia. Wingate argued that LRP's aim was forcing the enemy to alter his plans at the 'strategic' level, and from this point of view, *Longcloth* succeeded beyond even Wingate's and Wavell's intentions. Pondering factors likely to affect any Allied attempt to retake Burma, Slim felt it would be of enormous advantage for the Japanese to attack first, on ground of British choosing, enabling the British to destroy 'three or four' Japanese divisions quickly and easily; 'The thought of how to do this constantly nagged at my mind, but my generalship was not enough to find a way to provoke such a battle.'[53] Wingate stumbled upon it for him. Contrary to the impression given in Mountbatten's Official Report, the Japanese were not planning to stand on the defensive in Burma. Prior to *Longcloth*, Japanese 18th Division's commander, Mutaguchi, had planned a limited offensive, up the Hukawng Valley in northern Burma to capture Tinsukia, cutting the railway upon which Stilwell's Chinese forces, assembling at Ledo, relied for supply and reinforcement.[54] *Longcloth* demonstrated to Mutaguchi that it might be possible to go straight across the Chindwin and the hills on the Burma-India frontier in either direction; the Tinsukia plan was scrapped, and, upon being promoted to command of Japanese 15th Army, Mutaguchi determined to launch a pre-emptive attack across the Chindwin to seize Imphal, Kohima and Dimapur and forestall any British offensive across the Chindwin.[55] This led to the battles for Imphal and Kohima, Slim's finest hour, the most decisive battles of the Burma campaign, and which provide much of the operational context for Operation *Thursday*.

Longcloth's impact upon Allied strategy was equally significant. In early May, in response to a communiqué about *Longcloth* circulated by HQ IV Corps, large numbers of British pressmen arrived at Imphal to interview Chindits as they emerged from Burma, Auchinleck lifting a previous press ban on the operation.[56] By 21 May, most newspapers in India were carrying the story, and several journalists from London newspapers interviewed Wingate, Fergusson and other Chindit commanders. On 7 July, the story of *Longcloth* broke in the British national press and, as Sykes put it, 'The men who wanted to prevent further Wingate ventures had to recognise that their opponent was a national hero.'[57] Why, given the realities of the operation, was this so? To begin with, there was one British soldier willing to challenge the 'Super-Jap' in his own element. Mountbatten, in his official Report, outlined the contribution *Longcloth* made to this: 'Brigadier Wingate's operations had made it abundantly clear that our troops, when properly trained in the technique of jungle warfare, were superior to those of the enemy.'[58] Slim agreed upon the significance of *Longcloth* for Allied morale: 'For this reason alone, Wingate's raid was worth all the hardship and sacrifice his men endured, and by every means in our power we exploited its propaganda value to the full.'[59]

At the political level, *Longcloth* strengthened British claims to be playing its part in the war against Japan, of growing importance in dealing with the Americans. The Allied strategic agenda for 1943 was set at the *Trident* conference in Washington, in May 1943. *Trident* saw the already considerable acrimony between the British and Stilwell come out in the open. Stilwell, believing the Chinese were on the point of collapse and suffering incessant nagging from Chiang and his cronies, pressed for an overland offensive into northern Burma, to reopen the Burma Road, before the end of the year: he was backed in this by his old friend General George C Marshall, Chief of Staff of the US Army.[60] Chiang, under Chennault's influence and with support from Roosevelt, advocated building up American airpower in China, Chennault claiming that with 150 fighters and eighty bombers, he could sink 500,000 tons of Japanese shipping in six months, severing their sea communications with the outside world from the air so effectively ending the Pacific war on his own.[61] Churchill and Brooke opposed this, based on reports from Wavell that no offensive into northern Burma would be possible before at least November 1943, due to the need to build all-weather roads and railways into Assam, adjacent to Burma. The British stance was that reopening the Burma Road could only be expedited by retaking Rangoon, by sea – Operation *Anakim* – and then pushing northwards, requiring assembly of forces for an amphibious landing in southern Burma, not for a land offensive in the north.[62] A compromise was reached by which there would be a buildup of US airpower in India, air supply to China would be escalated to the 10,000 tons per month Chennault estimated would be necessary for his air offensive, there would be limited seaborne operations against Arakan, in southern Burma, and overland offensives from Assam and Yunnan aimed at tying down Japanese forces which might be deployed elsewhere and with the long-term aim of reopening the Burma Road.[63] It was also decided that a new Allied theatre-level command, Southeast Asia Command (SEAC), should be created to oversee these, and that Admiral Lord Louis Mountbatten would become its Supreme Commander.[64]

Churchill was disappointed by GHQ India's reaction to these proposals. Wavell reported that morale in India was still low, that the rapid expansion of the Indian Army in 1942–43 meant that further training was necessary before any offensives could be contemplated and that communications in Assam and upper Burma were so undeveloped that only those areas of Burma with all-weather roads – almost none – could be re-taken.[65] On 7 July, news reached Churchill of *Longcloth*, and he communicated with Brooke and the other British chiefs of staff comparing GHQ India unfavourably with Wingate ('[A] man of genius and audacity... The Clive of Burma') and suggesting that Wingate, still only an acting brigadier, should take charge of all offensive operations against Burma.⁶⁶ Brooke, who admired Wingate but recognised his limitations, headed off this outburst of Churchillian enthusiasm, dissuading Churchill from putting Wingate in charge in Burma at a private meeting on 25 July 1943. However, they agreed on the value of LRP operations, and next day, Churchill minuted the Chiefs of Staff ordering 'Maximum pressure [in Burma] by operations similar to those conducted by General [sic] Wingate, wherever contact can be made on land with the Japanese.'⁶⁷ Churchill's admiration was strengthened further by Wingate's official report of the operation, and Wingate was summoned to London to meet with Brooke and make the necessary measures for an expansion of LRP forces. Upon returning to London, Wingate was invited to Downing Street by Churchill, who proposed that Wingate should accompany him to the next inter-Allied conference, *Quadrant*, in Quebec in August, arranging also that Lorna should accompany them. Churchill wanted to show the Americans that the British shared their resolve to inflict rapid, decisive defeat on the Axis on the European and Asian mainland, taking along also Wing Commander Guy Gibson VC, commander of the 'Dam Busters' raid (who seems to have taken a major dislike to both Wingates).⁶⁸

Operation *Thursday* was a direct result of decisions made at *Quadrant*, based upon Wingate's presence there. Wingate, invited by Churchill initially for cosmetic purposes, met with Roosevelt and the Combined Chiefs of Staff and presented a memorandum and outline plan on how northern Burma might be reoccupied during the dry season of 1944; this marked a departure from prevailing British opinion, although the retaking of Northern Burma was one of the key objectives set by *Trident*.⁶⁹ Wingate proposed a force of 19,000 British, 7,500 Gurkhas or Africans, 6,000 mules and ponies and 100 jeeps, supported by 12–20 Dakotas.⁷⁰ These would form three LRP Groups (Brigades), one to be inserted into northeast Burma from China to attack communications from Mandalay to Bhamo, one to attack the Shwebo-Myitkyina railway and one to operate in central Burma against communications from Kalemyo to Kalewa. The intention remained the same as before:

> The purpose of [these] operations was to create a state of confusion in enemy-held territory by disrupting his communications and rear installations, which would lead to progressive weakening and misdirection of his main forces, and to indicate suitable targets for the tactical air forces which would enable the strategic air offensive to be driven home. Such operations would inevitably produce favourable opportunities for an offensive by the main Allied forces...⁷¹

The aim was to enable a major offensive in north Burma, British forces advancing on Pinlebu and Indaw from Assam, with Stilwell's Chinese moving along the Hukawng Valley to take Myitkyina and reopen the Burma Road.⁷² *Longcloth* had demonstrated that LRP Groups could not operate for more than twelve weeks without replacement, and so three further Groups would be required: these could also support a further offensive from northern into southern Burma in 1944-45. Wingate also predicted that 'Since the only effective answer to penetration was counter-penetration', the Japanese would respond with an attack on IV Corps' communications in Assam: consequently, two further Groups should be created to strike back at the communications of Japanese forces carrying out this counter-offensive.[73] He also proposed the creation of a LRP Headquarters of corps level – a lieutenant general's command – with two 'wings' of four LRP Groups each; veterans of *Longcloth* would form the nucleus of this force: what was required above all was to create in India 'a machine for turning out LRP groups at a steady and increasing rate.'[74]

The Chiefs of Staff ordered that Wingate be allocated 70th Infantry Division, causing enormous bitterness at GHQ India, as it was the only fully trained and equipped British division in the theatre. He also received a brigade of 81st West African Division, and the creation of a force headquarters was authorised by the Chiefs of Staff, with the option to attach the whole of 82nd West African Division at a later date.[75] The Chiefs proclaimed confidence in Wingate's ideas: 'We fully support the general conception of these Long Range Penetration Groups and feel they will be most useful in the war against Japan.'[76] These ideas formed a key part of British proposals made at Quebec, where the British Chiefs of Staff outlined their proposal to raise six LRP Groups, and argued that Wingate's proposed operation had the potential to reopen the Burma Road – a major departure from their original intent to avoid northern Burma altogether.

In subsequent meetings with Roosevelt and the American Chiefs of Staff – Generals Marshall and H.H. ('Hap') Arnold for the Army and USAAF respectively and Admiral Ernest King for the US Navy – Wingate described *Longcloth* and outlined his proposals for a future expansion of LRP.[77] Marshall and Arnold were to have a major indirect influence upon the subsequent development of Wingate's ideas.

Quadrant decided as follows:

- There should be a British Supreme Allied Commander, South East Asia, with an American Deputy, presiding over a combined staff and Naval, Air and Army Commanders-in-Chief. Mountbatten was appointed Supreme Allied Commander, with Stilwell as Deputy. British-Indian ground forces allocated to operations in Burma were formed into 11th Army Group, under the Army Commander in Chief in India, General Sir George Giffard; 11th Army Group comprised the new Fourteenth Army, under Slim, which would face the Japanese at the front, and Eastern Command, a training and administrative formation under Auchinleck's direct command as GOC India.[78]
- China was to be kept in the war, and the striking power of Allied air forces in China to be built up, through expanding the air route from Assam to China across the 'Hump'.[79]
- '[O]ur main effort' should be ground operations aimed at reopening land communications to China.[80]

Mountbatten's first task was to report on the feasibility of amphibious operations against northern Sumatra, southern Burma and the Kra Isthmus of Thailand and, most significantly for this thesis, 'To carry out operations for the capture of upper

Burma in order to improve the air route and establish overland communications with China. Target date, mid-February 1944', dependent upon the state of communications in Assam.[81] By implication, this would involve at least eight LRP Brigades operating in northern Burma with major Allied ground offensives from Assam and Yunnan exploiting the situation created thereby, leading to the clearing of Burma, north of the 24th Parallel, and the reopening of the Burma Road. This was emphatically Wingate's interpretation of *Quadrant*: in subsequent correspondence he cited *Quadrant* repeatedly – even after developments elsewhere caused its objectives to be modified – in support of demands that the role of LRP, and resources allocated, be preserved and escalated.

Whatever GHQ India's misgivings, LRP operations went ahead in northern Burma in 1944, and on a greater scale even than predicted by Wingate at *Quadrant*. They also reflected American war aims in the theatre and were therefore enabled by extensive material support from the Americans, particularly General Arnold, who, at Mountbatten's request, created and assigned a specialist unit of the USAAF, No.1 Air Commando, under Colonels John Alison and Philip Cochran, to provide dedicated air support for future Chindit operations.[82] Further indication of the investment the Americans put into Wingate was the scale of equipment they supplied his expanded LRP organisation: Lee Enfield rifles and Sten guns were replaced by American M1 Garands and Thompson submachine guns, communications were enhanced by American 'walkie-talkie' hand-held radios and, perhaps most fondly remembered by former Chindits, Wingate's favoured diet of dried fruit and Shakapura biscuits, supplemented by turtle eggs, was replaced by American K-Rations.[83] They also committed a brigade-sized American Army unit, Brigadier General Frank Merrill's 5307th Provisional Infantry Regiment, codenamed *Galahad* but known more widely under its newspaper propaganda nickname, 'Merrill's Marauders'. *Galahad* consisted of 3,000 volunteers, including many Pacific veterans, and was intended to form the basis for three American LRP Groups organised and trained identically to Wingate's; it formed in the USA in September 1943 and arrived in India in late October to begin training in Wingate's methods; accordingly, it had 700 mules allocated and USAAF pilots attached to coordinate air resupply and act as forward air controllers.[84] Interestingly, Wingate never accepted *Galahad* as an LRP unit, because it had not trained under his direct supervision, had not made use of his training literature and was only under his command for one exercise.[85] *Galahad* was to be used by Stilwell as a short-range penetration force, performing 'hooks' around Japanese forces in his advance down the Hukawng Valley in February-June 1944 before acting as conventional infantry in the final battles around Myitkyina, the main objective of the offensive.[86]

Indications of London's support for Wingate included the breakup of 70th Division and the lobbying for other British, Commonwealth and Allied forces to be assigned to his operations. In September 1943, the Vice Chief of the Imperial General Staff, General Sir Archibald Nye, suggested that an Australian brigade should be reorganised and retrained as an LRP Group – whether it would be deployed to Burma is unclear – while in early 1944, Chiang assigned 200 Chinese troops to go to Silchar

Wingate in Burma (2) – Operation *Longcloth* and its Consequences   177

to undergo LRP training, an arrangement aborted by Wingate's death.[87] Wingate had previously announced he would resist attempts to set up LRP Groups with 'untrained, untested... troops from China' but was more enthusiastic about another proposal, agreed between Churchill, Brooke and Mountbatten at Quebec, that three Commandos, under Lord Lovat, should be assigned to SEAC as an amphibious LRP Group under his training and command.[88] Churchill's support was key throughout this period, and such was Churchill's enthusiasm for Wingate that when the latter was struck with typhoid upon his return to India in October 1943, Churchill ordered daily reports on his health from the GOC India, Auchinleck, something, it might be surmised, that he might not have required for most other major generals.[89] Such high-level backing explains why Wingate was able to bypass both GHQs India and Fourteenth Army with the frequency and alacrity which he did over the following months and probably also explains the bitter resentment this caused.

The political context for Wingate's ideas had, however, evolved by March 1944, and the launch of *Thursday*. Upon arriving in India in October 1943, Mountbatten flew to Chungking to confer with Chiang, who agreed that two Chinese Armies would participate in the *Quadrant* operations, one operating from Ledo in northern India under Stilwell, the other from Yunnan; however, he made his support contingent upon an amphibious operation, supported by an Allied battle fleet, occurring concurrently somewhere in Southeast Asia – as usual, his reasoning was opaque, but this demand was to have consequences.[90] In November 1943, Chiang reiterated this demand at *Sextant*, the conference of Allied leaders and the Combined Chiefs of Staff in Cairo: Mountbatten was promised a battle fleet and sufficient sealift for three divisions, and in late November, Chiang agreed that all Chinese forces in India should be assigned to SEAC.[91] Yet in December, the combined Chiefs of Staff ordered that all SEAC's amphibious assets return to Europe, pending Operation *Overlord*.[92] Chiang, accusing the Americans and British of 'breach of faith', cancelled the Yunnan offensive.[93]

The only operations left available to SEAC were rather less ambitious than those decided at *Trident* and *Quadrant*:

- Maintaining supplies across the 'Hump' at 10,000 tons per month, the priority being supporting Chennault's US 14th Air Force in its offensive against Japanese shipping in the China Sea.[94]
- An overland offensive in Arakan, by the British 15th Corps of Fourteenth Army.[95]
- An offensive from Ledo by Stilwell's Chinese Army, with the intention of clearing the Burma Road as far as Myitkyina. Stilwell's Chinese American Taskforce (CAT), known also as Ledo Force and consisting of two American-trained Chinese divisions, began its advance in December 1943, with several thousand troops from the US Army Corps of Engineers constructing a new road (the 'Stilwell Road') and a pipeline behind it. The lack of aggression of senior Chinese commanders (Chiang cronies one and all) was notable: by the end of the month, Mountbatten was complaining in official communications about the slowness of the CAT's advance and its 'bad tactics' against the Japanese; by February 1944, it was trying to

advance through the dense 'creeper country' of the Hukawng Valley against strong resistance from the elite Japanese 18th Infantry Division, slowing it further.[96]
- Operation *Tarzan*, the dropping of the recently formed Indian Parachute Brigade on the vital Japanese airfield and supply centre of Indaw, with 26th Indian Infantry Division then being flown in to exploit.[97] This, and the Yunnan and CAT offensives were intended to be mutually supportive, and the slowness of the CAT advance led General Sir George Giffard, the Commander in Chief 11th Army Group and SEAC's overall ground force commander, to decide, by the beginning of December, 'that the operation as planned is no longer feasible' although operational instructions were still issued.[98]
- An advance across the Chindwin from Assam by IV Corps, to pin Japanese forces that might otherwise face Stilwell.[99]
- Operations in the Japanese rear by Wingate's LRP Groups, intended to ease Stilwell's advance down the Hukawng Valley and create a situation that the IV Corps offensive from Assam could exploit.[100] December 1943 saw Mountbatten send Wingate to Chungking to persuade Chiang – unsuccessfully – to renew the Yunnan offensive, which would now consist of a limited Chinese advance to exploit action by 77th Brigade, which would be inserted by air into northeast Burma around Bhamo, planning proceeding on this presumption into 1944.[101]

Throughout late 1943 and early 1944, LRP assets in India were built up to six brigade-sized groups – fewer than the eight mandated at *Quadrant* and considerably fewer than the possible sixteen that would have resulted from the various proposals for Allied and Commando LRP Groups. These six brigades were formed into a double-strength division, given the cover name of 3rd Indian Infantry Division, but referred to officially as Special Force (the Division was overwhelmingly British, Gurkha and West African, with only a few small contingents from the Royal Indian Engineers and Service Corps). Special Force consisted of 14th, 16th, 23rd, 77th, 111th and 23rd West African Brigades, supported by the Air Commando, with Wingate, now promoted major general, in command. Major General W.G. Symes, the former GOC 70th Infantry Division, was appointed Deputy Commander, and Derek Tulloch was Brigadier, General Staff. For operational and logistical purposes, Special Force formed part of Fourteenth Army and was under Slim's orders for *Thursday*.

Therefore, the political and military-strategic context for Wingate's ideas, as of late 1943, was shaped partially by him. It centred, increasingly, upon an overland offensive in northern Burma to either reopen the land route to China or, more realistically, pre-empt and spoil Japanese moves against India. This was the scenario upon which Wingate had predicated his future LRP operations, as presented at Quebec. Moreover, the Combined Chiefs of Staff authorised a massive expansion of LRP forces, including American, Commonwealth and Chinese troops, to participate in these operations. Therefore, far from being an 'outcast', Wingate was now closer than ever to creating what he viewed as a new form of warfare, or, at least, a new type of unit. Among those expressing reservations about an overland offensive were Giffard and Slim: a review of their alternative plans and operational models provides a good illustration of differences between Wingate's ideas and those of other senior Army commanders in Southeast Asia in 1943-44.

Giffard, Slim and 'Tactical Overmatch'

In a review of projected operations, from December 1943, Giffard expressed his pessimism about the ability of LRP brigades in northern Burma to draw off sufficient Japanese forces to speed Stilwell's advance, and argued that logistical problems would slow the advance of IV Corps to the point where the Japanese could redeploy to meet any threat posed. He was also dismissive of a proposal to reinforce the CAT Force with British or Indian troops, pointing out that GHQ India could spare just one division and that moving even this would require a major logistical effort involving the redirection of at least two air transport squadrons from elsewhere.[102] He proposed an alternative plan involving an advance by IV Corps from the Kabaw Valley to capture and drive through a road to Kalewa, a town on the River Chindwin, combined with continuous operations by LRP Groups in northern Burma, aimed at creating a firmer base for Allied offensives in 1944-45 while inflicting maximum casualties upon the Japanese.[103] What is interesting about this plan is that Giffard seems to have envisaged a major alternative role for the Chindits, possibly even seeing them as a surrogate for the CAT advance.

Slim was more ambivalent, both about an offensive into northern Burma and the role of LRP. Indeed, given the importance of *Defeat into Victory* in shaping postwar perceptions of Wingate, and their respective roles in 1944, as commander of the main Allied army facing the Japanese and originator and commander of the major offensive effort in northern Burma for that year, it is pertinent to compare and contrast Slim's and Wingate's proposals for defeating the Japanese.

The published versions of *Defeat into Victory* and the *Official History* played down the acrimony between Slim and Wingate considerably. Writing to Giffard in April 1956, Slim commented of *Defeat into Victory* that he had been 'a little too kind' to Wingate, and in April 1959, told Kirby, in reference to the *Official History*, that he was being 'too generous' to the Chindits in assessing their contribution to the Imphal battles – and, as discussed already, neither of these works is charitable to Wingate or the Chindits in their final form.[104] He was even more pungent in a letter to Bernard Fergusson (who agreed broadly with his assessment): 'Personally I doubt if [Wingate] was a genius except for short intervals, even though he had what most people consider a qualification for the role in that he crossed the border line of lunacy... more than once.'[105] In a private note on Sykes' biography of Wingate, Slim expressed a belief that Wingate was lying when he claimed that he had a direct right of appeal to Churchill, and even if he had, it was 'subversive' of his command of Fourteenth Army; the impact of *Longcloth*, moreover, had been blown out of all proportion as 'propaganda'.[106] In earlier correspondence, he dismissed Wingate's argument that LRP could be the main offensive arm in Burma as 'a nonsense' and played down Wingate's role in the development of air supply, commenting (accurately) that the model of air supply applied by Fourteenth Army in the 'Admin Box' battle in Arakan in February 1944 was actually that applied subsequently, not that used on the Chindit operations.[107]

The vitriol was not all shot in one direction. In a 1970 interview, following Slim's death, Fergusson recounted that by 1944, Wingate's opinion of Slim had hardened: he had 'no confidence' in Slim, spread 'anti-Slim propaganda' among the officers of Special Force in the buildup to *Thursday* and even referred to his Army commander as a 'stupid ass' in front of subordinate officers.[108] This probably explains the approach to Wingate taken in their published works not only by Slim, but by Kirby, who leaned almost exclusively upon Slim's version of events, as did others later. It might, therefore, be easy to see the differences between Wingate and Slim as arising simply from a clash of egos rather than ideas, but, while this was undoubtedly a factor, even a cursory survey of Slim's approach to defeating the Japanese shows there were profound intellectual differences as well.

Slim's priority throughout 1943–45 was to defeat the Japanese Army in Southeast Asia as cost-effectively as possible. Units making up Fourteenth Army had known nothing but defeat for nearly two years, and whatever the impact of *Longcloth* on morale in England, their confidence was low. Consequently, 1943 saw Slim and Auchinleck instigate a programme of major reorganisation and training emphasising jungle tactics, survival skills and aggressive patrolling, culminating in a succession of large-scale raids into occupied Burma in late 1943 and early 1944. The intention of this was not only to harden the British Indian Army to jungle warfare, but also to kill off the 'Super-Jap' myth for good.[109] Slim and Lieutenant General Geoffrey Scoones, commanding IV Corps, intended to do this via applying such overwhelming numbers and firepower against them that the Japanese simply would not stand a chance. This began even before *Quadrant* and the creation of Fourteenth Army: on 10 July 1943, a company of the Lincolnshire Regiment – approximately 100 men – attacked a Japanese machine-gun post – probably fewer than ten; on 17 August, a company of 1/10 Gurkha Rifles, supported by artillery, attacked another Japanese machine gun post.[110] As the summer progressed, the raids escalated into major spoiling attacks summarised by Slim as 'attack[ing] Japanese company positions with brigades fully supported by artillery and aircraft, platoon positions by battalions.'[111] The aim was to build confidence: '[W]e could not at this stage risk even small failures. We had very few, and the individual superiority build up by successful patrolling grew into a feeling of superiority…We were then ready to undertake larger operations.'[112] Slim was also unequivocal that tanks should be used 'in the maximum numbers available', even in jungle warfare, on the basis that 'The more you use, the fewer you lose', this becoming an unofficial motto for the whole of Fourteenth Army.[113] This principle had been applied throughout Slim's career: for instance, finding his route into Vichy-controlled Lebanon blocked by a small Vichy French force at Deir-ez-Zor in 1941, Slim, as GOC 10th Indian Division, hit them with an entire brigade plus an outflanking column moving in from behind; during the second Arakan operation of February 1944, Slim deliberately built up his numerical superiority in ground forces to five-to-one over the Japanese because, he claimed, once again, Fourteenth Army could not afford any more defeats.[114] Logistics were also rectified. Partially at Mountbatten's behest, resupply by air was practiced by all units in the hope of reducing reliance on roads and the size of logistical echelons of combat units, with General Arnold creating specialist USAAF Combat Cargo Groups to complement this.[115] Not only were LRP units trained and organised to carry out offensive operations supplied purely by air, but so were two brigades of 81st West African Division, one assigned to Wingate, the other serving with its parent formation in the Kaladan Valley, covering the flank of XV Corps' offensive in Arakan in January–February 1944.[116] At one point during the Imphal-Kohima battles of February–June 1944, eight divisions were supplied purely by air, and six were moved largely by air also.[117] Slim practiced air-based logistics on a scale that even Wingate had not envisaged.

Slim argued consistently that the war in Burma could be resolved only by the destruction of the Japanese armies in battle, entailing the concentration of the utmost force against their main fighting formations.[118] His stated aim in building up the five-to-one advantage in the second Arakan operation was to 'smash' the Japanese offensive and so build British confidence.[119] Likewise, at Imphal, his aim was to 'smash' the attacking Japanese armies.[120] This shaped his concept for how the battle should be fought. Appreciating the Japanese skill in short-range penetration and that in a country as vast as Burma, static lines of defence could always be cut, Slim and Scoones adapted the 'box' concept to Southeast Asia. 'Boxes' would be established along Japanese lines of advance, giving them no option but to attack or leave their own lines of communication open to counter attack by mobile forces operating from the 'boxes' or from neighbouring areas. Upon taking command of Fourteenth Army, Slim ordered that all forward units, upon finding their lines of communication threatened or cut, should stand fast and dig in for all-round defence, whereupon they would be supplied exclusively by air, and ordered his logistical staff to intensify training in air supply accordingly.[121] As it became apparent that the Japanese were about to launch an offensive into Assam via the Imphal plain, the defensive plan adopted by Slim and Scoones – IV Corps held the main front in that area – put these orders into practice:

> The plan for what we knew would be the decisive battle was first for Imphal plain to be put into a state of defence. This entailed the concentration of the scattered administrative units and headquarters into fortified areas, each of which would be capable of all-round defence... The two all-weather airfields at Imphal and Palel, vital to the defence both for supporting air squadrons and for air supply, became the main strong-points or 'keeps' in the defence scheme. The garrisons of these fortified areas and keeps were to be found mainly by the administrative troops themselves, so that the fighting units and formations would be free to manoeuvre in an offensive role.[122]

The four Indian divisions in IV Corps would carry out a fighting withdrawal from the edge of the Imphal plain while these strong-points were built behind them. Two of these divisions would then combine with the Indian Parachute Brigade and an independent tank brigade to form a mobile striking force, which would be reinforced by two or three more divisions arriving by rail and air from other fronts.[123]

The objective was to crumble the advancing Japanese formations through defensive firepower before counterattacking: 'The Japanese would…be allowed to advance to the edge of the Imphal plain, and, when committed in assaults on our prepared positions, would be counter-attacked and destroyed by our mobile striking forces, strong in artillery, armour and aircraft.'[124]

The difference between Slim's concept of operations and Wingate's was summed up eloquently by the American official historians of the Second World War in Asia, Romanus and Sutherland: Slim wanted to draw the Japanese forward onto ground of his choosing in order to destroy them, Wingate to force them back by a threat to their rear.[125] Wingate's Strongholds bore some resemblance to 'boxes', as will be discussed, but were to be used offensively, to divert enemy strength away from the main advance through threatening their lines of communication. However, as will be shown, Wingate came to view his Strongholds as analogous to Slim's boxes, aiming to draw the Japanese into battles of destruction. Slim's assumption was that the Allies, at least initially, would be on the strategic defensive, enunciating in 1942 that:

> The surest way of quick success in Burma is not to hammer our way with small forces through jungle when the Japanese has every advantage, but to make him occupy as much area as possible, string himself out until he is weak, and then, when we have got him stretched, come at him from sea and air. By luring him northwards…we get a better chance to get in behind his forward troops.[126]

It would be necessary to lure the Japanese forward in order to bring Slim's intentions to fruition. This was not incompatible with Wingate's ideas – he had, after all, predicted a Japanese offensive into Assam at Quebec – and he was to view the Imphal offensive as an opportunity to turn *Thursday* from a supportive to a decisive operation. However, a major difference soon emerged as to *where* the decisive blow against the Japanese should be struck, by IV Corps in Assam or by Special Force in northern Burma. Slim's view was that the Chindits were 'strategic cavalry', but, unfortunately, he did not present his views on what the role of cavalry in general should be.[127] However, it is apparent from *Defeat into Victory* and his postwar correspondence that he was supportive, with qualifications, of Wingate's original concept, a lightly equipped force harrying Japanese communications in support of a general offensive.[128] Another illustration of Slim's view of penetration forces were his complaints to Mountbatten in June and September 1944 to the effect that, for all the different penetration forces then operating inside Burma – SOE, OSS, the Secret Intelligence Service, Army Intelligence Corps, Royal Marines and others – he was receiving little useful intelligence on Japanese forces there.[129]

However, from late 1943, Wingate's view was that air supply and support meant that LRP Groups were now capable of striking decisive blows against Japanese main forces with Allied main forces advancing to occupy territory cleared thereby. His Chindits would, therefore, be the main 'strike arm', with the rest of the Army in support.

Chapter Eight

Wingate in India – go ye to the Stronghold

Turn ye to the stronghold, ye prisoners of hope; even today I declare that I will render double unto thee.

Zechariah, 9:12, King James Version

Longcloth was the most straightforward of all Wingate's operations, involving as it did a relatively small, homogeneous force, carrying out a plan and operation less complex even than in Ethiopia. Conversely, for *Thursday*, he had a force almost ten times the size of 77th Brigade, consisting of multiple elements, each directed at several objectives spread across a large area of northern Burma, these being changed, cancelled or – most awkwardly for the historian – amended subtly before and during the operation, and in which some were more successful than others, with varying implications for the rest of the operation, which were sometimes not felt immediately. It also centred on a new concept: the use of aerial mobility to place LRP forces near key points in the Japanese infrastructure where they could establish permanent fortified bases from which they could threaten Japanese communications, so forcing the Japanese to divert troops away from the main front. Moreover, a key aim of any LRP operation would now be to draw said diverted Japanese troops into battles around those fortified bases where they could be killed in large numbers by the LRP Group's own firepower and organic close air support. The key factor in this evolution was the generous supply of equipment and supplies by the Americans, beginning with the Air Commando.

The Air Commando

It was the attachment of No.1 Air Commando that seems to have begun the process by which the operational model for *Longcloth* evolved into that of *Thursday*. The Air Commando's air assets consisted initially of:

- 13 C-47 (Dakota) Transports
- 12 Norseman C-64 Light Transports
- 150 Waco (Hadrian) Gliders
- 100 L-1 and L-5 Light Aircraft
- 6 YR-4 Helicopters – the first helicopters to be deployed on any military operation
- 30 P-47 (Thunderbolt) Fighters.[1]

By the commencement of *Thursday*, the Air Commando was supplemented by a squadron of 15 B-25 Mitchell medium bombers and its Thunderbolts were replaced by P-51 Mustangs. The Mustang's 2,000-mile range had already allowed it to escort USAAF bombers from Britain to Berlin, changing the course of the air war in Europe, and it now bestowed similar depth, in theory, to LRP operations.[2] The Commando's air-ground potential was enhanced, prior to *Thursday*, by the attachment of a US Army combat engineering company with air-transportable bulldozers, tractors and other digging and construction equipment.[3] Moreover, four Dakota squadrons of the RAF and two of the USAAF supported Special Force at various times.[4]

According to its joint commanding officer, Colonel John Alison, the Air Commando's missions were:

A) To increase substantially by gliders and light transport, potential capacity of the R.A.F. and 10th U.S. Air Force to maintain L.R.P.G.s by air
B) To increase actual mobility of columns themselves by providing air lifts over difficult terrain where no tactical advantage in surface penetration.[5]

Once its gliders and transports inserted Special Force behind Japanese lines, the Air Commando's primary role would be battlefield close air support, supplemented by casualty evacuation, and, from late 1943, it trained and exercised intensively with Special Force with particular emphasis upon these roles.[6] There was also practice of glider landings and supply drops, and it is interesting to note that Alison saw his mission as improving the mobility of the Chindits, just as Wingate was moving towards the more positional approach of the Stronghold.

The Stronghold and its consequences

The attachment of the Air Commando meant that having to infiltrate the Japanese front line, and follow this with a long and arduous march to Japanese areas of critical vulnerability, might now be avoided. The Air Commando's gliders might now land advance parties of engineers deep in occupied Burma, there to construct airstrips on which transport aircraft could fly in LRP forces. The idea seems to have grown from a short-lived plan to insert 77th Brigade at Paoshan, in northern Burma, by air; Wingate had planned for the rest of Special Force to infiltrate into northern Burma on foot, as on *Longcloth*, but in January 1944, it was discovered that the Japanese were covering all the crossings of the Chindwin, in order, the British believed, to prevent this very thing.[7] Mountbatten then ordered Wingate, Slim and Major General G.E. Stratemeyer, commander of Eastern Air Command, responsible for all air operations over Burma, to devise a plan for the aerial insertion of a large LRP force. Troop Carrier Command, SEAC, and the Air Commando had sufficient aircraft to lift two LRP brigades into northern Burma in early March 1944 and another two later in the month, meaning that just two brigades would have to march in.[8] Consequently, *Thursday* became an airborne operation aimed at establishing air-supplied Strongholds from which Chindit columns could attack Japanese communications.

Holland and others at MI(R) theorised about such operations nearly four years before, and Gideon Force had been part-supplied by air. OSS had established several permanent airstrips for supply, reinforcement and casualty evacuation in Japanese-occupied Burma by the end of 1943.[9] However, as with air supply in general, Wingate parted from previous practice in intent and scale, arguing that the Chindits might now be capable of establishing a permanent presence in the Japanese rear, deepening the main battle, with close air support from Air Commandos providing the main offensive punch and divisional sized forces being flown in to exploit.[10] According to Tulloch, such operations would hinge upon five conditions:

1. An operational area in which LRP…formations could move swiftly and undetected in the dry season.
2. Air superiority over the Japanese but not at his stage amounting to complete air supremacy (…Monsoon conditions…would immediately preclude regular supply by night)
3. An enemy whose supply lines were known…and which were so sited as to be vulnerable to a degree, since the country across which they ran did not permit deviation from the main supply routes.
4. Reliable and accurate support by bomber and fighter aircraft available which would replace the artillery support accorded to normal formations. (This could *only* be relied on during the dry season)
5. Last, but not least, an assured supply line virtually impregnable during the dry season….The vital common factor was '*in the dry season*'. In monsoon conditions Long Range Penetration Forces lost their mobility and their fire power, while regular supplies could not be maintained. [Italics Tulloch's].[11]

The monsoon was the next most important factor behind the dispositions of the Japanese, and to allow operations to continue during the monsoon, Wingate intended to create safe harbours behind enemy lines from which smaller-scale raiding operations could continue during the rains; during his discussions with Mountbatten in London in summer 1943, Wingate proposed to create Dakota-capable airstrips in the jungle around Indaw, an area he had surveyed during *Longcloth*.[12] The attachment of gliders and transport aircraft now meant that this could now be done on a far larger scale and far more aggressively, and the basis of future LRP operations would now be the 'defended airport' – Wingate's initial terminology – or *Stronghold*. Whatever the name, Wingate had a role for the Strongholds beyond that of a 'base': they were to lie at the heart of an entire new template for defeating the Japanese. This becomes apparent from Wingate's much-quoted and reproduced memorandum on Strongholds, which began by outlining their tactical and logistical functions:

The Stronghold is an asylum for L.R.P.G. wounded.

The Stronghold is magazine of stores.

The Stronghold is a defended airstrip.

The Stronghold is an administrative centre for loyal inhabitants.

The Stronghold is an orbit round which Columns of the Brigade circulate. It is suitably placed with reference to the main objective of the Brigade.

The Stronghold is a base for light planes operating with Columns on the main objective.[13]

Each Stronghold would be established by two columns of an LRP brigade, either marching in or landed by the Air Commando's gliders, securing a suitable area of flat, cleared ground. Engineers would then fly in and prepare an airstrip, upon which the rest of the brigade would fly in and the position would be fortified with the addition of artillery, anti-aircraft guns, and at least one line infantry battalion as garrison troops. Once completed, each Stronghold would consist of a fortified area, incorporating earthworks and minefields, large enough to hold a battalion or two columns, two troops of artillery, and a rest area for up to 200 personnel. An adjacent airstrip would be cleared, with taxiways into the Stronghold itself; while the strip should be Dakota-capable, it would be used primarily by light aircraft to deliver small amounts of supplies and evacuate wounded, Wingate suggesting that ten such aircraft should be dedicated to each Stronghold. The bulk of supplies would still be delivered by air-drop in or around the Stronghold.[14] Wingate recommended that Strongholds should be as inaccessible as possible to Japanese forces, being built in the centre of approximately thirty square miles of broken country, not well served by roads or trails and only passable to pack animals, but with friendly villages in the area.[15]

This was because Wingate had another purpose for the Stronghold more ambitious than a simple raiding base – carrying the 'box' deployment into the enemy rear as on offensive rather than defensive measure. The objective now would not only be to divert Japanese forces away from the front, but to lure said forces into situations where they could be destroyed in detail:

The Stronghold is designed to fulfill a definite function in the employment of L.R.P.G.s; a function which has hitherto been neglected. In all our recent contacts with the Japanese it has been apparent that any dug-in defended position sited in remote areas where it is almost impossible to assemble a concentration of artillery and extremely difficult to make accurate reconnaissance without heavy losses is capable of a most obstinate and prolonged defence against greatly superior force... From this I draw the inference, firstly, that it is foolish to direct attacks against defended enemy positions if by any means he can be met in the open, and, secondly, we should induce him to attack us in our defended positions. It is obvious that columns of L.R.P. have an unrivalled chance of meeting him in the open and that, therefore, they should even more rarely need to attack him in his positions. In fact, it may truly be said that they should do so only when the position concerned has already been isolated by the action of Columns for a considerable time, or there is other reason to suppose that the position will put up a weak resistance. We wish, therefore, firstly to encounter the enemy in the open and preferably in ambushes laid by us, and secondly to induce him to attack us only in our defended Strongholds.[16]

Wingate understood that LRP attacks upon Japanese lines of supply would result in the Japanese trying to locate and destroy the columns' own source of supply. In another echo of 'small wars' practice, each Stronghold, therefore, would have at least two 'floater columns', patrolling the surrounding countryside out to a few thousand yards with the intention of detecting and slowing down any approaching Japanese force.[17] These would drive off any Japanese reconnaissance patrols, hopefully provoking the Japanese to commit a larger force, of around regimental strength. This probably would not have the benefit of tanks or artillery support, as the country in which the Stronghold was located meant that only ordnance which could be man or mule-packed could be brought in, and any attempt to build roads would provide a prime target for attack by floater columns.[18] Upon this force approaching, the Stronghold commander should reinforce his floater columns:

> In this way, the enemy is met under ideal conditions; making an approach whose route can be forseen [sic] through country with which we are more familiar than he, and compelled to move slowly to cover his road construction. Under these conditions, two Columns should find little difficulty in cutting up a regiment.[19]

Should the Japanese reach the Stronghold, they would have to attack its fortifications under attack from behind by floater columns.[20] However, the main 'killing instrument' would be airpower, delivered upon Japanese forces concentrated for attack upon the Strongholds by the Air Commando's Mitchells and Mustangs, the latter as effective as fighter-bombers and ground strafers as they were as fighters. Special Force also had a squadron of RAF Vengeance dive bombers train with it, although this was reassigned elsewhere by *Thursday*, despite Wingate's protestations.[21] USAAF pilots had trained in battlefield close air support, 'on call' from the ground, since 1941; their aircraft carried HF radios allowing direct communication with ground troops, unlike the VHF radios used by the RAF, meaning that the Air Commando's Thunderbolts and Mustangs could provide faster and more flexible response than the RAF, with the Mitchells being held back for pre-set attacks on area targets such as supply dumps or large troop formations.[22] During *Thursday*, Wingate ordered that priority in the use of the Mitchells should be given to bombing the heavy Japanese concentrations around the 'Broadway' Stronghold and the 'White City' block established by Calvert's 77th Brigade astride the main Japanese lines of communication, with the secondary role of breaking up Japanese formations assembling for counter-attacks, evidence that Wingate was seeking to use these positions to lure the Japanese into destructive battle.[23] In an operational order for *Thursday*, Wingate referred to '[The] Development of close support aircraft… in close cooperation with columns in order to give the latter the equivalent of artillery and armour support, thus raising the potential of the 3rd Indian Division to that of an abnormally active Army Corps' and that the attachment of the Air Commando was 'unique in conception and should help us to apply revolutionary methods.'[24] In December 1943, Wingate stated to Mountbatten his belief that future warfare would hinge upon close air support of infantry on the ground, and that the Chindits were forerunners of this.[25]

Strongholds, with airpower support, would leave the Japanese with no option but to commit a large force, of divisional size or above, with appropriate air assets in support, all having to be diverted from elsewhere.[26] The Brigade commander might then recall columns from other LRP operations to reinforce the Stronghold or the floater columns, but this should not be at the expense of threatening Japanese lines of communication, so drawing in further Japanese forces to protect them.[27]

There is a detectable resemblance between the Strongholds and the pattern for the defence of the Imphal Plain devised by Slim and Scoones, Wingate also hoping to force the Japanese into 'killing zones', in his case by using the air route to establish fortified positions on or near their most important lines of supply then, once luring them in, destroying them through battlefield airpower and counterattack from the rear by mobile forces. Slim noted caustically: 'Scoones must have been amused to find this appear as a new Wingate method of defence' and it is not unreasonable to see Wingate's tactical inspiration laying in Fourteenth Army's plans for the decisive battle against the Japanese.[28] However, the Stronghold stemmed as much from concepts devised by Wingate before his arrival in Burma as it did from anything devised by IV Corps. Wingate consulted on the feasibility of such operations with the senior British airborne commander, Lieutenant General Sir Frederick Browning, when Browning visited India in September 1943, and with Major General Ernest Down, commanding 44th Indian Airborne Division, all some time before *Thursday* or the Imphal battles. Wingate was always ambivalent about the use of parachute troops. In his report on *Longcloth*, he viewed their possible use with some enthusiasm, believing that they could be used to provide rapid reinforcement of Chindit columns and exploitation of their action; however, any attempt to use them in future LRP operations foundered on the lack of trained parachutists in India and on Down's lack of enthusiasm for Wingate and his ideas.[29] By spring 1944, Wingate had changed his opinion: 'Since this Parachute Brigade has not received the training which it requires, it is in any case of doubtful value. The use of Parachutists in BURMA… is already an obsolete form of warfare.'[30] It might be appended to this that until the SAS perfected the technique of tree-jumping in Malaya in the 1950s, terrain imposed restrictions on where parachutists could and could not be used; using them in the hilly jungle country of northern Burma invited the possibility of losing as many, if not more men to accidents as to enemy action. The alternative would be to drop them in open areas which the Japanese could identify and concentrate upon, as with supply dropping prior to *Longcloth*. However, Tulloch suggested in 1972 that a small number – perhaps just two or three – of airborne pathfinders, dropped to survey a potential Stronghold area 24 hours before the main fly-in, might have prevented many of the accidents incurred during glider landings in *Thursday*.[31]

The Strongholds also supported the model of operations Wingate had been advocating since 1941. One of the aims of *Thursday* was to stir revolt among the Kachins, Lieutenant Colonel D.C. Herring being ordered by Wingate to recruit, train and then command Kachin guerrillas operating deep in Japanese-occupied territory. Consistent with Wingate's Ethiopia reports, and his directives and memoranda of 1942, this was to happen only in areas where Chindit columns could support and protect them, with a Stronghold to be established in Kachin country from where these could operate, something which apparently led do a clash with SOE, who had agents operating in the same area and to a similar mission.[32] Fergusson added a further role to the 'Aberdeen' Stronghold from which his 16th Brigade operated on *Thursday*, a permanent – so he thought at the time – centre of British government and administration, protecting the local tribespeople from the Japanese and distributing food and medical supplies flown in from India.[33] The aim throughout, however, was to use the air route to establish a permanent presence, based on box-like positions, on and around enemy lines of communication, consisting of specialist penetration forces cooperating with local partisans, the type of operation that MI(R) were speculating upon in 1940.

Wingate by the Chindits

Interestingly, some of Wingate's colleagues were expressing their thoughts on his possible 'place' in British strategy and military history in the build-up to *Thursday*. In a memorandum of November 1943, Calvert, the keen military historian, ruminated upon a detected similarity between LRP and the strategy applied by the Duke of Marlborough in the Low Countries in the 1700s. Seventeenth-century warfare, Calvert argued, hinged on fortified supply bases and therefore tended to revolve around sieges; Marlborough had upset this by forcing his enemies to fight him in open battle, after which their bases fell rapidly.[34] Likewise, in North Africa, armoured forces had defeated Axis forces in the open desert, allowing infantry divisions to move up to assault their forts.[35] Calvert also saw the Chindits' role as being to defeat Japanese forces in the field, then contain them in their bases, allowing heavier forces to advance and besiege them.[36] However, this required changes in tactics: columns would infiltrate into Japanese rear areas, whereupon they would concentrate as brigades astride lines of communication, forcing the Japanese to attack them under unfavourable circumstances.[37] Calvert's objective, therefore, was to use LRP to draw the Japanese into battles of destruction in their own rear areas; this came some time before Wingate presented his Stronghold concept and a Calvert influence cannot be discounted, although, as usual, Wingate credited nobody but himself for his ideas, Calvert was too respectful of Wingate to argue, and there is no documentary evidence of any link. Almost at the other end of the scale was Brigadier WDA ('Joe') Lentaigne, who commanded the Chindit 111th Brigade on Operation *Thursday* and who would succeed Wingate in overall command of the operation following his death. According to his brigade major, John Masters, Lentaigne was horrified by the expansion of Special Force to nearly two divisions in strength and Wingate's intent to go after large Japanese formations, a sentiment he repeated to Tulloch, post-*Thursday*.[38] Two brigades, as was planned pre-*Quadrant*, he argued, were sufficient to pin larger numbers of Japanese forces, but this needed to accompany offensives by the main armies both to allow and to exploit this. Although Special Force had six brigades, Lentaigne believed they had insufficient firepower to be able to fight major battles and the only way for it to have this would be to divert air assets away from the main front.[39] Upon learning of the Air Commando, Lentaigne conceded it might ease this problem, but not to the extent that Wingate hoped.[40] Although Lentaigne left no memoirs, from Masters' account it appears that the prevailing view in 111th Brigade was that the Chindits should be a guerrilla and raiding force aiming at battle *avoidance*.[41]

Wingate, therefore, parted company with his colleagues in SEAC in several ways. Most obviously, as of 1943–44, was his advocacy of airborne and air-portable troops carrying the battle into the enemy rear. While this resembled the 'box' defences used in North Africa and by Fourteenth Army in Arakan and at Imphal-Kohima, Wingate intended to use air movement to turn this from a defensive to an offensive method by placing his 'boxes' on or near Japanese lines of communication in such a way that the Japanese would have to counter-attack under unfavourable conditions. Given the scale and intent of his post-*Quadrant* LRP forces, and the way in which Special Force fought the Japanese during *Thursday*, it would be inaccurate to describe Wingate, as of 1944, as a commander of guerrillas or Special Forces.

Chapter Nine

Wingate in Burma (3) – Operation *Thursday*, 1944

To the army officers at Imphal and Delhi who met him about this time, he seemed happy and super-confident, serenely absorbed in his campaign and concerned only with its day-to-day operation.

Leonard Mosley[1]

Thursday as 'decisive operation'

A common theme running through Wingate's correspondence in the build-up to *Thursday* was his objection to another limited operation.[2] There were also complaints about inadequate support from GHQ India and Fourteenth Army for Special Force's training programme, the limited scale of troops Slim was willing to spare to garrison the Strongholds, and the perceived lack of ambition of the proposed exploitation of *Thursday*. Among what follows is an investigation of how Wingate intended *Thursday* to be not only the decisive military operation in the reconquest of northern Burma, but the first of a series of similar operations which would ultimately remove the Japanese from mainland Asia altogether.

This began in December 1943, when Giffard was asked to comment on the feasibility of large-scale LRP operations in northern Burma. In an *aide mémoire* of 28 December, Giffard stated that the prognosis was not good for the operation *Thursday* was supposed to support, Stilwell's advance down the Hukawng Valley. The plan to reinforce Stilwell with a British brigade foundered on the only two brigades available not yet having animal transport. The redirection of these brigades, and animal transport for them, would reduce SEAC's reserves further. As for flying in troops to reinforce the Chindits, either the objective would have to be within a few days' march of the front line, or they would need to secure an all-weather airfield, or the force would have to extricate before the monsoon. The minimum force should be a brigade, anything smaller being liable to being 'mopped up'. This, and supporting aircrew, would have to be retrained; finally, airborne forces might take excessive losses from Japanese air defences. Giffard concluded that 'I do not... consider that this is a feasible operation this spring.'[3] Wingate's response to Giffard, his senior commander, was characteristically pungent: the Chinese would not, in his view, fight alongside Indian troops anyway; a British brigade could have another's mules assigned to it; garrison troops would not require retraining, nor would aircrew, who would simply be ferrying between airfields, and Giffard was opposed in principle to any kind of LRP operation, along with GHQ India and Fourteenth Army.[4]

Wingate's feud with these headquarters continued into January 1944, even as preparations for *Thursday* advanced. In a memorandum – possibly not circulated –

192 Orde Wingate

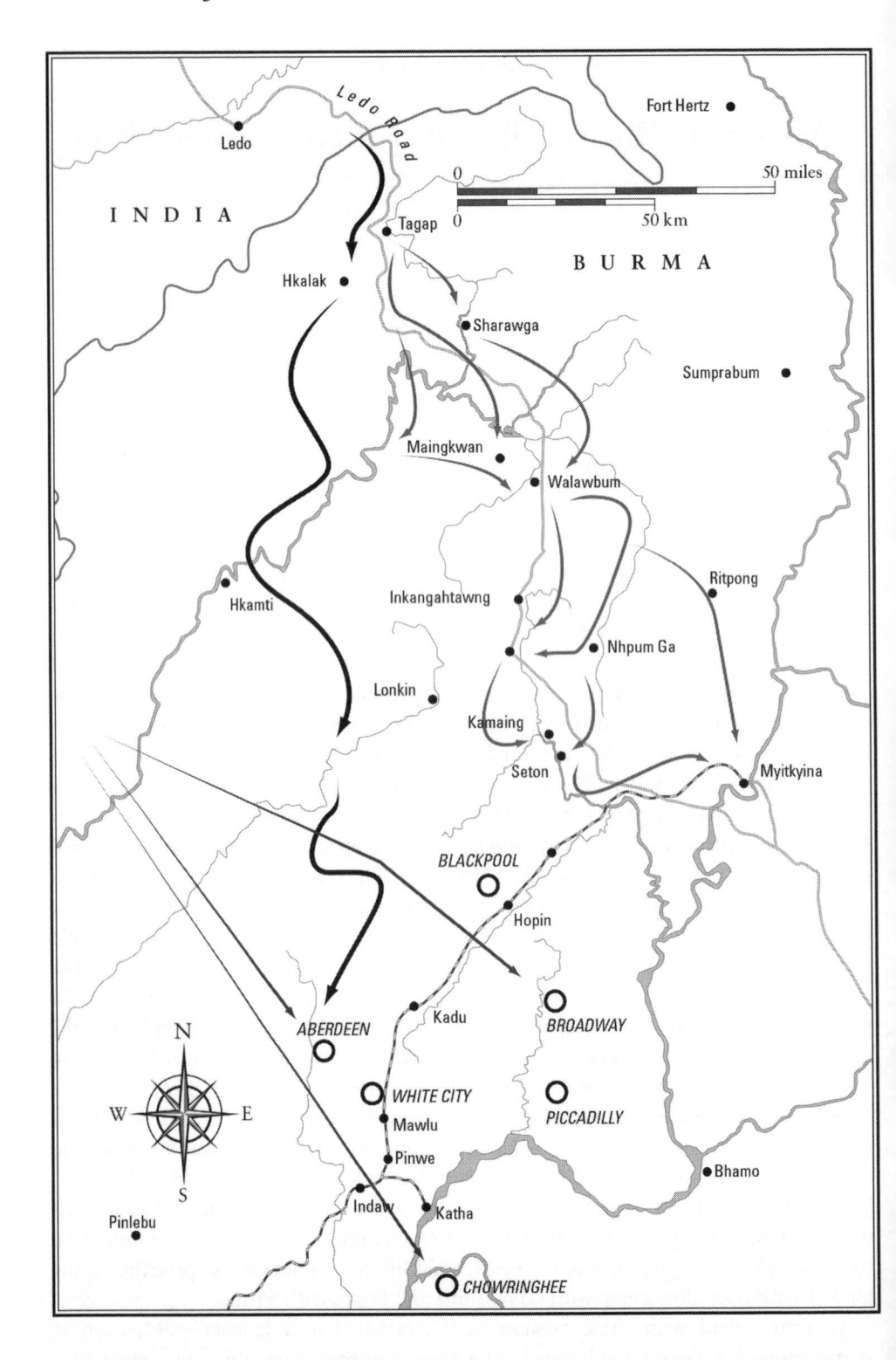

of 9 January 1944, he reviewed the impact of developments since *Quadrant* on the proposals he had made there. He argued that without any large-scale Allied offensive to follow up, the Japanese could concentrate against the Chindit brigades, who would then be left with no option but to break up and retreat as in 1943. He devised the Stronghold concept partially as a precaution against this, but with the absence of a general offensive, their object, to attract Japanese attention away from the front, would be defeated before the operation even began.[5] There were also regular complaints about the non-cooperation of the RAF, too frequent and repetitious to be repeated in detail.[6]

Wingate's mood improved on 11 January 1944, when intelligence was circulated that Mutaguchi's 15th Army was concentrating east of the Chindwin for its Imphal offensive. Wingate's brigade commanders, surveying potential crossings of the Chindwin, had already found them all blocked by Japanese troops.[7] Wingate predicted an offensive similar to that he foretold at Quebec, an attack on IV Corps' lines of supply and retreat, developing into a possible counter-penetration against Stilwell's communications also.[8] In response, he urged upon SEAC an airborne counter-penetration centred on 77th and 111th Brigades establishing fortified blocks along the railway between Mohnyin and Mawlu and destroying railways south of Wuntho – Mutaguchi's main lines of supply – while 16th Brigade seized the airfield and communications node at Indaw and destroyed Japanese supplies and the road and rail network in the surrounding area. The Stilwell offensive would continue, and one brigade of IV Corps would cross the Chindwin to exploit the Chindit landings: 'Such an operation...will defeat the enemy's main effort, and even bring his plan to a disastrous end.'[9] All that was required was for Special Force to be given priority use of 500 gliders and sixty Dakotas.[10]

Wingate, therefore, believed he had found a means by which LRP could defeat the Japanese at theatre level. Tulloch provided further evidence for this with his testimony that Wingate, secretly, devised a 'Plan A' and a 'Plan B' for *Thursday*. 'Plan A' was the original, to support Stilwell's attempt to reopen the Burma Road; 'Plan B' involved doing this *plus* committing two LRP brigades against Japanese 15th Army's rear as it attacked Assam.[11] 'Plan B' would require LRP forces to operate during the monsoon, and Tulloch claimed that Wingate devised the Stronghold concept partially in response to this need.[12] A problem here is that there is little corroboration of a complete and explicit 'Plan B' from any of Wingate's papers, or, apparently, in any other contemporary document, even the 'Stronghold' memorandum, although this did presume the Chindits would seek battle against heavier Japanese forces than hitherto. However, that Wingate might have planned a 'decisive' operation, rather than a supportive one, emerges from his operational orders. In his Operational Order for *Thursday* of January 1944, Slim issued the following instructions to Special Force:

ROLE

Your role is to create a situation which will:-
a) Assist the advance of Combat Tps (LEDO Sector) [Stilwell]
b) afford a favourable opportunity for YOKE force to advance [in the hope of getting Chiang to change his mind] and

c) provide opportunities for exploitation for 4 corps
Of these tasks the most important is to assist in the advance of Combat Tps (LEDO Sector) [Italics mine].[13]

Compare this with Wingate's Operational Order of 2 February 1944, his stated intention being 'to compel the enemy to withdraw from all areas in BURMA north of the 24th Parallel' a similar, but far more ambitious remit to that given him by Slim, although it does echo Tulloch's 'Plan A'.[14] Slim's instructions were to ease Stilwell's path and create a favourable situation for Fourteenth Army, but Wingate was by now seeking to use LRP and Strongholds to inflict a theatre-level defeat upon the Japanese and so fulfill the remit given him by the Combined Chiefs of Staff at Quebec, even though the scenario upon which it was based was almost a year out of date. He would do this by seizing Indaw; Bernard Fergusson, whose task this would be, agreed that Indaw was the vital hinge in the supply infrastructure for Japanese forces throughout Upper Burma:

> It was the last and northernmost centre of communications possessed by the Japanese. Roads radiated from it north, south, east and west; the Myitkyina railway ran through it from south to north, and the subsidiary spur line to Katha... Around and in it was a cluster of important dumps, supporting the whole force opposing General Stilwell in the north, and capable also of supplying the divisions opposing our army on the Chindwin.[15]

Neutralising Indaw would disrupt severely the communications of the Japanese 18th Infantry Division, then slowing Stilwell's advance down the Hukawng Valley, and of the Japanese 31st Infantry Division on the Chindwin and would, it was hoped, compel the Japanese to alter their plans for northern Burma. This perhaps explains Wingate's design for *Thursday*, his language not suggesting a guerrilla operation but something far more ambitious:

> 16th Infantry Brigade, 77th Indian Infantry Brigade and 111th Infantry Brigade will converge upon the focal point of INDAW in such a manner and with such timing as to cut effectually the enemy communications with 31st and 18th Divisions. The governing principle of the operation is concentration at the decisive point. The decisive point for operation "THURSDAY" consists of a circle 40 miles radius whose centre is INDAW within which therefore I intend to concentrate twenty-four columns... Towards the end of the operations it will become a battle of wills. We will stay where we belong at INDAW...[16]

Calvert, now commanding 77th Brigade, was even more explicit, stating his aim in the 'Intention' paragraph of his operational orders for his battalion commanders:

> By the cutting of his L. of C. and by inflicting as much damage as possible on his men and material, to gain such moral and material ascendancy over the Japanese in this area that he will be forced to withdraw his remnants south of parallel 24 [degrees] in defeat and rout.[17]

The Stilwell offensive would continue, and one brigade of IV Corps would cross the Chindwin to exploit the Chindit landings: the result would be decisive: 'Such an operation...will defeat the enemy's main effort, and even bring his plan to a disastrous end.'[18] The Chindit Brigades were tasked as follows:

- 77th Brigade, under Michael Calvert, would be glider-landed and air-ported to Okkyi and Shweli behind Indaw on 6/9 March, there to establish Strongholds codenamed 'Broadway' and 'Piccadilly'. Columns would issue from these to cut communications running north from Indaw to Japanese 18th Division in the Hukawng, to its base at Myitkyina in particular. 'Broadway' was to be held at least until 1 June.
- 111th Brigade, commanded by Lentaigne, would land at these Strongholds on 10/13 March and then proceed north and south of Indaw to its operational area to the northwest. This would be around Kawlin, Lentaigne being instructed to block the railway from Kawlin to Indaw in two places; this would provoke the Japanese into sending troops from Indaw and Pinlebu, and so one column should be sent to ambush their line of approach while the remainder fell back into the forest around Kyaikthin before hitting the railway from another direction, then falling back on 'Broadway' in mid April.
- Independent columns would move east from 'Broadway' into the Kachin Hills with the intention of stirring up the hill tribes and menacing communications between Bhamo and Myitkyina.
- *Thursday* would be opened, however, by 16th Brigade, commanded by Bernard Fergusson, crossing the Chindwin and advancing on foot to the area north-west of Indaw by 10 March. En route it was to attack Lonkin in concert with No.1 Air Commando in order to draw elements of Japanese 18th Division away from Kamaing and so ease Stilwell's move down the Hukawng. Fergusson would then move on Indaw itself, setting up a Stronghold called 'Aberdeen' in the vicinity; 111th Brigade would have drawn off enough of Indaw's garrison to make it easy for Fergusson to hook round Indaw and seize it from the south-east. Its two airfields would then be incorporated into a new Stronghold based on Indaw itself, sitting right alongside the key Japanese supply node in northern Burma and dislocating all Japanese operations depending on it. The monsoon was expected towards the end of these operations, and the three brigades were due to be relieved by others prior to being withdrawn to Stilwell's lines by the time it arrived.

The operation

16th Brigade began its march to the Chindwin in early February 1944 and almost immediately the need to put the brigade across high mountains via a single track in unseasonably foul weather cancelled out any advantages in mobility granted by air supply, Fergusson eventually crossing the Chindwin ten days behind schedule.[19] Wingate then revised his plan: he predicted accurately that 16th and 77th Brigade's arrival would result in the Japanese reinforcing Indaw, and so ordered 111th Brigade to prevent this by establishing road and rail blocks south of Indaw and 16th Brigade, upon arriving in the Indaw area, to establish the 'Aberdeen' Stronghold before assaulting Indaw from the north (not the southeast, as planned before), before the Japanese were established there in too much strength.[20]

The airborne part of *Thursday* began on 5 March 1944. The landings could take place because the Allies had air superiority over northern Burma. Six weeks before *Thursday*, Allied air forces had carried out forty attacks on Japanese airfields and road and rail communications, destroying eighty Japanese aircraft on the ground. Simultaneously with the fly-in, the Air Commando's Mustangs and Mitchells carried out heavy attacks on Japanese airfields, destroying fifty-six aircraft on the ground in the first three days of the operation and fortuitously disrupting Mutaguchi's air assets for the upcoming offensive.[21] Sixty-two of the Air Commando's gliders and transports reached the site of Calvert's designated Stronghold, 'Broadway', on the first night, bringing in 900 men, 100 mules and twenty tons of supplies: 12,000 men, and requisite supplies, had been flown into the Strongholds around Indaw by 13 March.[22] Wingate then changed his mind again. He had intended 111th Brigade to establish a Stronghold called 'Chowringhee' on the Irrawaddy but then, to speed their arrival in Burma, he decided they should be delivered by air via 'Broadway'. However, fear of congestion at 'Broadway' saw the 'Chowringhee' scheme revived, and 111th Brigade began to set up at 'Chowringhee' on 6/7 March – and then Wingate, noting the closeness of the fly-in route to a Japanese airfield and that 'Chowringhee' lay in the dry area beyond the Irrawaddy he was forced to abandon the year before, decided to commit the rest of 111th Brigade via 'Broadway' after all.[23] It is unsurprising that Wingate was remembered with so little affection by 111th Brigade's officers, as not only did his constant chopping and changing result in the brigade being split between two widely separated Strongholds but, worst of all, it prevented it from pinning Japanese reinforcements heading for Indaw, with repercussions for Fergusson's planned attack there.[24]

By 9 March, Calvert was sending out columns from 'Broadway' to cut roads and railways north of Indaw and to strengthen Kachin and Chinese guerrillas beyond the Irrawaddy. 'Broadway' was bombed by the Japanese on 13 and 17 March, the Japanese losing several aircraft to a flight of RAF Spitfires stationed temporarily in the Stronghold. 'Aberdeen' averaged two Japanese air raids per day throughout this period, as well as an average of three attempts to disrupt supply flights.[25] On 15–18 March, Calvert established the 'White City' fortified block on the railway north of Henu – personally leading a Gurkha *kukri* charge to clear the position beforehand, as mentioned already – and so cut Japanese supplies to Myitkyina, Stilwell's principal objective. The Japanese reallocated a regiment, around 6,000 men, of 53rd Division, then entering Burma from Siam, to deal with the block; this force launched a series of attacks on 'White City', beginning with patrol-level probes and leading to a battalion-level attack on the night of 21 March which almost carried the position but was repelled with 64 Japanese killed; attacks continued throughout early April.[26]

Conversely, the Indaw attack was a near-disaster. 16th Brigade was minus two columns, away in the north, 111th Brigade's dispersal by Wingate had prevented them stopping the Japanese reinforcing Indaw, and their activities to the south of Indaw had alerted the Japanese to the possibility of an attack on the town. Consequently, when 16th Brigade attacked Indaw on 22–29 March, they were met by 2,000 Japanese troops dug in and waiting for them; when the assault began, surprise was compromised further by an advance by rear-echelon troops 'wanting a go' following and joining the assault group from 'Aberdeen' without permission. The nature of the country – hilly, and covered in thick jungle with virtually no tracks or paths – made it difficult to impossible for Fergusson to move around and observe the battle and so to coordinate the attacks and react to Japanese moves. After three days of fighting three of his six columns were crippled and this, and fear that 'Aberdeen' was about to be attacked, compelled him to withdraw behind heavy bombing from the Air Commando.[27]

Despite Wingate's actions, Mutaguchi remained focused on his offensive into Assam. Believing the Chindit forces were too weak and distant to have any real effect on this, he initially sent a force of just three battalions plus two companies of walking wounded to defend Indaw and, interestingly, mirrored Wingate by arguing that the landings in his rear made a Japanese offensive a critical necessity.[28] The Japanese commander-in-chief in Burma, General Kawabe, possessed more accurate intelligence, was skeptical about the Imphal offensive and Mutaguchi anyway, and assembled a force of 18,000 men, including a brigade and an independent infantry regiment, plus eventually the whole of 53rd Infantry Division from Malaya, to deal with Special Force. This began to assemble at Indaw in March and was another factor in 16th Brigade's failure to take that objective.[29] Despite the tactical failure at Indaw, Wingate certainly had succeeded in diverting large numbers of Japanese troops and a considerable amount of Kawabe's attention.

The Imphal offensive began in late March 1944, and brought the Japanese onto ground of Slim's choosing, onto IV Corps' boxes and away from Stilwell's advance in the north.[30] Mountbatten commented that 'our hopes were considerably raised by this Japanese offensive [but] the situation was at times to prove extremely dangerous for us.'[31] Now the offensive was developing, Fourteenth Army was reluctant to commit more troops or aircraft to *Thursday*. In particular, it needed every available Dakota to supply IV Corps' 'boxes', and to airlift 5th Infantry Division from Arakan following the defeat of the subsidiary Japanese offensive there.[32] Previous authors have made a great deal of Wingate's desire to fly in two more LRP Brigades to attack Mutaguchi's lines of communication (the 'Plan B' described by Tulloch), and his subsequent request, direct to Churchill, for four more Dakota squadrons to be diverted to India from elsewhere so they could fly in. However, this is usually done either to illustrate differences of opinion and style between Wingate and Slim, as done by Kirby and Slim himself (who did not mention the message to Churchill) or as a sign of Wingate's strategic prescience, as by Tulloch.[33] Contemporary communications and written orders tell a more intricate story, illustrating the real strategic aims of both commanders at this time, and providing some contemporary evidence for Wingate's 'Plan B'. This originated with a conversation Slim had with Tulloch on 8 March, wherein Slim stated that he might need the Chindit 14th and 23rd Brigades, Wingate's designated reserve, to reinforce Imphal, and – yet more evidence for their difficult personal relationship – allegedly told Tulloch not to inform Wingate.[34]

An ensuing meeting saw Slim agree that if the two brigades were inserted into Burma within the first twelve weeks of *Thursday*, before they were due to relieve the first three brigades, then they would operate under Wingate's command; Tulloch also claimed Slim agreed they should be used against the rear of Japanese 15th Army.[35] This now became a priority for Wingate. On 12 March, he sent a memorandum to Mountbatten – which has not, apparently, survived – outlining his 'Plan B', based on inserting the two brigades across 15th Army's communications at Meiktila and Pakokku.[36] On 15 March, Tulloch signalled Wingate, reporting a discussion with Colonel Bert Lyons, the US Army Liaison Officer at HQ Fourteenth Army, concerning Wingate's intent to keep five brigades inside northern Burma throughout the monsoon; this would require a greater scale of air transport than hitherto and, given the need to maintain supplies over the Hump, a request should be made for two or three Dakota squadrons to be diverted from another theatre.[37] On 16 March, Wingate replied, expressing astonishment at the move by air of 5th Infantry Division from Arakan to Assam, and that the aircraft used 'would be better employed on exploiting victory' supporting Special Force inside Burma, rather than reinforcing a static position; the move should not divert Special Force from introducing 14th Brigade into Burma forthwith[38]. On 17 March, Tulloch reported that 'some staff' were urging Slim to attach 14th Brigade to IV Corps, Slim agreeing with Tulloch that this would be a 'gross misuse' of a LRP Brigade. Tulloch felt that 'the more Japs cross the CHINDWIN the better, as if our plans succeed they should never return'; 14th and 23rd Brigades should be inserted into northern Burma, as 'they will be worth ten times as much to 4 Corps placed BEHIND the enemy than they would be placed in front.'[39]

Corroboration for 'Plan B' came from Fergusson, perhaps the most measured and reliable source from within the Chindits themselves:

Wingate told me all this at Aberdeen [16th Brigade's Stronghold] on the 23rd of March, and confided also that the situation might affect his famous Plan. Already, he said, he was being urged to keep his two remaining brigades, the14th and 23rd, under his hand, in case they were needed to help repel the Japanese advance. This he was determined not to do. His was an offensive move, as opposed to the defensive strategy to which we had so long been thirled, and which irked intolerably his fiery spirit. Rightly or wrongly…he foretold that the Japanese effort would overreach itself, and that *pourvu que ça tienne*, the Jap armies would eventually starve. To remove his remaining Brigades out of reach of the High Command, he proposed to commit them both forthwith, before his right to do so had been abrogated.

14 Brigade was to come in first… and they would co-operate with me against Indaw, working south from Aberdeen and then threatening against Indaw from the west. 23 Brigade would follow, but *Wingate had not made up his mind where to send them*. [Italics mine – 23rd Brigade would eventually be used in the Imphal-Kohima battles in a short-range penetration role, as Wingate and Tulloch feared].[40]

On 21 March, Wingate apparently bypassed Slim, sending a signal to Mountbatten for direct communication to Churchill. Wingate saw the Imphal offensive as a major Japanese mistake 'which... can be made [to] prove fatal to them.'[41] All that was required was for Churchill to direct four more squadrons of Dakotas to India for Wingate's use and to give him his 'full backing'; although Wingate made no direct link between *Thursday* and Imphal in this signal, his attitude can be inferred:

> Success of THURSDAY means no more hump and the destruction of four Japanese divisions (.) Get Special Force four transport squadrons now and you have all Burma North of twenty-fourth parallel plus a decisive Japanese defeat (.) But get use these four squadrons and let the truth be told about what has happened and is happening (.) General SLIM gives me his full backing (.)[42]

Mountbatten forwarded the signal to Churchill, but appended his comments: while SEAC could never have too many transport aircraft, he and Giffard were mystified as to why Wingate needed these extra squadrons, and he had asked Air HQ SEAC 'to investigate this question as a matter of urgency'; he also commented upon the 'hysterical' tone of Wingate's communication and told Churchill that Wingate was 'showing signs of strain' – according to Slim.[43] Moreover, Giffard had returned from the front, where he had discussed the situation with Slim: they agreed that the expulsion of the Japanese from west of the Chindwin and then from northern Burma would be a slow process, and they would have to be defeated on the Imphal plain first; however, more transport aircraft would speed the process, and so they supported the request for additional Dakotas – albeit with a different agenda from Wingate's.[44] Slim's attitude was summed up in two communications to Giffard of 22 and 23 March. He opened the first by outlining what he saw as the essentials of jungle warfare, 'well trained, tough infantry and Air Transport'; he felt vindicated by the advance of Stilwell's forces, the February 'Admin Box' battle in Arakan and 'the promising situation of the Special Force behind the enemy lines.'[45] The Japanese 15th Army was not only committed against IV Corps, but under pressure from Stilwell to the north and Wingate from behind; Slim felt that with enough aircraft to fly in reinforcements to Imphal, 'we can, within the next month, smash the enemy forces West of the CHINDWIN [and] be presented with an opportunity whose exploitation might easily lead to a really major victory.'[46] However, more air transport was needed urgently, in order to supply Allied forces without ground communications, but also to allow 'reinforcing formations, e.g. *additional LRP Brigades or other formations can be flown in behind the enemy*. [Italics mine].'[47] Slim was already having to request aircraft be diverted from the 'Hump', and so desired not only four additional RAF Dakota squadrons, but also five USAAF.[48] On 23 March, Slim repeated his argument, reporting that he did not have enough aircraft to support either IV Corps or Special Force, but with sufficient aircraft, he would have the opportunity to win a major victory.[49] This would depend upon 'the employment of all Special Force and elements of 4 Corps East of the CHINDWIN'; consequently, Slim backed Wingate's request for further aircraft.⁵⁰ Churchill replied the same day, to the effect that he did not think that the tone of Wingate's message was 'hysterical', that he intended to broadcast the success of *Thursday* to the British people, and that he was prepared to make direct representation to Roosevelt to get the Dakotas required.⁵¹ Wingate's influence still went high, and Tulloch claimed that as a result of Wingate's signal, five USAAF Dakota squadrons and one RAF were diverted from the Middle East to India, but these figures are closer to those in Slim's request than Wingate's.⁵²

Operational differences between Slim and Wingate were subtler than previous authors have allowed for. Slim, apparently, wished to increase the scale of Special Force's operations behind Japanese 15th Army, but as a means of supporting Stilwell's advance, which, along with *Thursday* and Imphal, Slim saw as one great battle for Assam and northern Burma, to be won via overstretching Japanese strength and then defeating it in extended fighting. Wingate's aim was to win a rapid victory *inside* northern Burma: the Imphal offensive drew Japanese forces forward and away from his area of operation, giving him an opportunity to exploit. In the event, Slim allowed Wingate to fly 14th Brigade into Burma on 21 March, and the fly-in of 14th Brigade and 3rd West African Brigade (the latter designated as Stronghold garrison troops) was completed by 12 April. In an operational instruction issued on 27 March, three days after Wingate's death, 14th Brigade was ordered specifically to cut road and rail communications behind Japanese 31st Division, forming the northern pincer of Mutaguchi's offensive, suggesting that Wingate's intention, at the time of his death, *was* to shift to a counter-penetration aimed at defeating the Japanese offensive.⁵³ This was the only operational order issued by Wingate linked to any 'Plan B', but it is compelling evidence for this plan. However, even more compelling is a series of memoranda Wingate sent to Mountbatten shortly before his death, in which he outlined his vision for LRP, post *Thursday*.

The future of the Chindits, according to Wingate

On 10 February 1944, Wingate wrote to Mountbatten arguing that SEAC should base all future offensive efforts around LRP forces:

> It does not seem to be realised that if Operation 'THURSDAY', which is being carried out by unsupported LRP Brigades, succeeds in driving the Japanese out of Northern BURMA, the superiority of LRP to normal formations in a normal operation…will have been abundantly proved, and there will no longer be any grounds for claiming that normal Divisions have any function in South East Asia. They should instead be broken up into LRP Brigades (Airborne), Assault Brigades, and Airport Garrison Brigades, organized into larger formations corresponding to divisions and corps but with rather different scope and functions…⁵⁴

These forces, Wingate argued, would form a viable alternative to Operation *Culverin*, the proposed amphibious invasion of the Dutch East Indies (which Mountbatten purportedly preferred to an overland offensive in Burma). Were *Culverin* abandoned,

SEAC could launch an overland offensive towards Hanoi and Bangkok, LRP Brigades leap-frogging from Stronghold to Stronghold:

> In the van will be the deeply penetrating columns, a mass of enemy between them and the territory occupied by us. The operations of these columns will progressively force the enemy to withdraw. In territory from which he has withdrawn, normal communications may be built up, and garrisons living in fortifications introduced. At certain distances behind the forward wave of penetration will come defended airports. In the van with the LRP Brigades will be Strongholds with their Garrisons... The capture of BANGKOK and HANOI may well result in the giving of an amphibious role to India Command (Nov. 45) and the LRP thrust would then continue to carry a chain of defended airports across CHINA to the coast where it would meet up with seaborne forces.[55]

Wingate detailed the tactical role of these forces in another paper, of February 1944:

> The process of conquest would probably follow the lines which are to be worked out in Operation 'THURSDAY', i.e. severing of communications, establishing Strongholds in areas inaccessible to wheeled transport, introducing Garrisons into areas evacuated by the enemy, which will become defended airports, and this way gaining control of the whole territory.[56]

Wingate apparently viewed *Thursday* as a test of a new form of warfare in which the objective would be strategic victory via a series of airborne invasions, forcing the Japanese to fall back from occupied territory by threat to their communications or destroying their forces by forcing them to contest control of vital territory on unfavourable terms. What had begun, in early 1942, as a series of proposals for supplementary guerrilla operations, had returned to the vision that Wingate had presented in his post-Ethiopia papers, of LRP being used to bring hostilities to a conclusion.

Thursday – the latter stages

Wingate's fatal air crash came on 24 March, as he was flying back to India in an Air Commando B-25 after a visit to 'Broadway' and 'White City'. Slim appointed Lentaigne, the most senior brigade commander in the field, to replace Wingate; Fergusson might have been better qualified and more experienced in Chindit operations, and he had the trust of Slim and GHQ India, but he and Calvert were probably seen as too junior, too close to Wingate, and unlike Slim and Lentaigne, were not from the Brigade of Gurkhas. This is not to disparage Lentaigne, who shared Calvert's fearlessness and aggressive leadership style, and was liked by his men and junior officers, but as noted already, he was seen as something of a 'plodder' by Calvert and was never enthusiastic about Wingate or his ideas. Among Lentaigne's first actions was to rescind Wingate's order to 14th Brigade, instead sending it south of Indaw to prevent the Japanese reinforcing the town further.[57]

Lentaigne then consulted his brigade commanders on what to do next: Calvert and Fergusson argued strongly against any attempt on Mutaguchi's communications, both calling for increased support for Stilwell by combining an renewed attack on Indaw with a drive northwards, through the Hukawng valley to link up with CAT Force, consistent with Wingate's argument that LRP should support offensive, not defensive operations.[58] On 7 April, directing Special Force against Japanese 15th Army's communications was finally ruled out, and two days later, Slim ordered Lentaigne to concentrate on supporting Stilwell. The principal force facing Stilwell, the veteran Japanese 18th Infantry Division, relied on supplies concentrated at Mogaung, to the north, meaning that the existing deployments of Special Force were not as important as supposed previously, and in order to maintain Special Force throughout the Monsoon, then looming, it would be essential to secure an all-weather airfield. Consequently, Lentaigne decided to abandon 'Broadway', 'Aberdeen' and 'White City' and move north to threaten Mogaung and Myitkyina, a redeployment deemed to be more useful to Stilwell and also allowing Special Force to make use of all-weather airstrips in the Hukawng.[59] The move would culminate in four Chindit brigades attacking Mogaung from the south while a Chinese force attacked from the north.[60]

On 27 March, the Japanese attacked 'Broadway' again, and 'White City' on 6–14 April, culminating in an attack by a reinforced brigade, supported by tanks, artillery and aircraft; during these battles, the support of the Air Commando tipped the balance on several occasions.[61] On 3 April, Mountbatten, against Lentaigne's wishes but in accordance with Wingate's prescribed pattern of operations, ordered 111th Brigade to join 14th Brigade in attacking Mutaguchi's communications in and around Indaw. By 27 April, 14th Brigade had destroyed twenty-one fuel and ammunition dumps, 15,000 gallons of petrol, cut the railway south of Indaw in sixteen places and mined most of the roads and trails in the area; at the end of April, 16th and 14th Brigade finally took Indaw without opposition and wrecked all Japanese installations in the region.[62]

According to Mountbatten, the principal strategic impact of *Thursday* was on the logistics of the Japanese force attacking Imphal and Kohima. Mutaguchi had his troops carry a minimal level of supplies, anticipating the capture of British supplies as the offensive drove forward. In this, he was mistaken: 'When his original plan had broken down, the enemy's attempts to improvise had been frustrated by continuous air offensives against his rear supply-lines… and troop concentrations [some of it by the Air Commando] and by the operations of the LRP Brigades behind his lines'.[63] It would appear, then, that operations against Indaw had some effect on Japanese logistics which might have been greater had the whole of Special Force been committed behind Japanese 15th Army as Wingate had urged.

This was never to be. 16th Brigade was withdrawn to India, flying out of 'Broadway' and 'Aberdeen', which were then abandoned. 'White City' was given up on 9 May, and all artillery and engineering stocks were also flown back to India, while the remaining Chindit brigades were transferred to Stilwell's direct command. Given that Stilwell used (or perhaps more accurately, abused) the Chindits as conventional infantry, having them assault Japanese troops in dug-in positions around Mogaung with minimal firepower support, the study of Wingate's vision should perhaps cease here.

After Wingate – 'All Chindits Now'?

There was almost universal agreement in SEAC that *Thursday* had demonstrated the efficacy of air supply to troops engaged at the front. According to 'Aquila', writing on the Burma campaign in the *RUSI Journal* in 1945, air supply '…has enabled us to achieve great economies in manpower, in motor transport and in the provision of road-making material, and has given our forces a flexibility which has allowed them to overcome all the disadvantages with which we were faced in the initial stages of the Japanese war.'[64] During the Allied offensives into Burma in 1944–45, Fourteenth Army received nine-tenths of its supplies by air: two divisions were able to continue their advance through the Kabaw Valley in August 1944 thanks to air supply, and the outflanking move during Slim's great victory at Meiktila in February-March 1945 was sped by both air supply and air reinforcement.[65] Slim consulted Fergusson about air supply prior to these operations and Mountbatten was unambiguous on how the technique originated:

> [N]o one would claim that Wingate invented Air Supply because it was well known. But what he did was to prove that military ground forces could operate with no other form of supply at all, other than air supply. And these lessons were taken up with practically the whole of the 14th Army on air supply, of which Wingate was the pioneer.[66]

This was re-emphasised at a lecture to the Royal United Services Institute in May 1945, by Air Marshal Sir John Baldwin, Deputy Air Officer Commanding-in-Chief, India, who commented that:

> I consider that the air is the key to any operations across northern Burma. Burma is a sea of tropical jungle and has in itself been regarded as a barrier to any movement from West to East in so far as ground troops are concerned, but it does afford the shortest and quickest route by which we have a chance of hitting the Jap where it hurts most… I feel that the lessons we have learned in the Wingate operations have shown us how it is possible to overcome this… barrier and to develop a combined air and ground attack against the Japanese.[67]

However, while certain techniques used by Special Force became standard in subsequent SEAC operations, there was less enthusiasm about the whole concept of Long Range Penetration itself. A memorandum prepared by Headquarters, 11th Army Group, on Special Force, post-*Thursday*, noted that: 'In general, the Long Range Operations of 3 Indian Div from March to May had a comparatively limited effect compared to the effort deployed.'[68] But, it noted, the actions of *Galahad*, on Stilwell's flank, and 23rd Brigade at Imphal 'both paid considerably greater dividends by directly assisting the advance of the main forces, which alone are capable permanently of securing the advantages gained by LRPGs.'[69] It went on to describe the perceived shortcomings of LRP Groups:

> LRPGs, which could more logically be called 'penetration groups', are detachments; their use therefore should accord with the same principles applicable to other detachments i.e. sufficiently strong and mobile to avoid defeat in detail, but otherwise their strength should be kept to a minimum... Their reliance on mobility forbids their use where the enemy has good communications. Lack of heavy weapons makes them unsuitable for attack on fortified positions or for prolonged operations in any one area against growing enemy opposition.[70]

The Chindits should, therefore, be limited in future to 'medium range penetration operations in conjunction with the main forces for limited periods', including harassing enemy communications, protecting the flanks of larger formations, seizing or constructing airstrips for air transit troops, and attacking key enemy installations or headquarters.[71] This is a far cry from the decisive role Wingate envisaged for them, and the emphasis upon 'mobility' suggests misgivings about operations based upon Strongholds.

Lentaigne and Tulloch knew about these feelings. Lentaigne commented in a letter of 13 April 1944 to Major General CE Wildman Lushington, Assistant Chief of Staff, SEAC that there was a 'definite feeling' at GHQ Delhi that LRP Brigades should be attached to normal divisions 'to be used in a parochial manner as Divisional Cavalry'; Lentaigne argued that 'We are, I feel, essentially GHQ troops and should never be grouped at a level lower than an Army.'[72] Likewise, in September 1944, Tulloch also expressed the view that 11th Army Group was planning to decentralise control of LRP Groups to corps or divisions, arising from over-emphasis in assessments of 'lessons learned' from the 1944 battles upon 23rd Brigade and, indeed, Tulloch did not help his case with GHQ India or 14th Army by referring to Imphal-Kohima, which had seen three Japanese divisions destroyed, effectively crippling the entire Japanese position in Burma, as a 'strategical success' and 'tactical victory' *for the Japanese* on the basis that no ground had been taken by the British.[73] This suggests either that Tulloch had misunderstood Slim's intentions entirely, or that he was viewing the battle through the filter of a highly personal agenda. Tulloch proposed that all troops in India should be trained to operate under air supply – which they were, largely, by the time he wrote this letter – with Special Force being kept 'for more ambitious roles' and was confident that Slim backed him in this.[74]

The reality is that there were no more LRP operations, and in January 1945 surviving elements of Special Force were absorbed into the newly-raised 44th (Indian) Airborne Division.[75] Mountbatten proclaimed 'There is no more need for Chindits. We are all Chindits now', and an argument could be presented that the extensive use of air supply and air movement by all formations of 14th Army had relieved Special Force of its 'special' nature, thereby rendering it redundant.[76]

Chapter Ten

Orde Wingate and the Twenty-First Century Refined

Parting Shot: the Birth of Modern Warfare?

We opened with an argument that Orde Wingate may have things to say to twenty-first-century soldiers, and have presented some reasons why this might be so. While rejecting the idea that there can be 'lessons' of history, we close with a discussion of the *messages* Wingate might send to commanders of the post-2001 period, along with some speculation on what he may have thought of their operations, were he to observe them.

To begin with, counterinsurgency. Wingate's Night Squads continued the British tradition of deploying small, specialist units combining regular troops with local irregulars inside insurgent-controlled areas and using the insurgents' own methods against them. Moreover, they were not 'Special Forces' *per se*, but soldiers from line infantry battalions and Jewish irregular policemen. It would not be difficult to assign infantry or even local militia units to interdict insurgent supplies or reinforcements, to carry out pre-emptive attacks on lightly-held insurgent bases, or simply to 'visit' those likely to misbehave. This probably reached its apotheosis in Oman in the 1970s, and British and American forces performed some of these tasks in Afghanistan and Iraq in operations following September 2001.[1] However, it would be facile to suggest that any conflict could be resolved by a few 'quick fixes' in tactics or troop organisation, although this does not prevent many 'experts' from trying. The aim of insurgency is to use the duration of the conflict as a weapon, demoralising the counterinsurgent forces and the civilian general public supporting them, and subverting disaffected elements to get them to join the insurgency. Modern democracies are particularly vulnerable to this kind of attack, given the 'resonant mass' of the electorate influencing decisions at the highest levels, a free and unfettered mass media shaping the opinions of this 'resonant mass', and an entire legal, media and political sub-culture willing to pounce on even the suggestion of impropriety. Moreover, after September 2001, the USA and its allies claimed to be waging a global war *against* terrorism in which their forces were deployed in Iraq and Afghanistan as part of an ostensibly 'liberating' mission aimed at replacing brutal, despotic regimes with liberal democratic ones respectful of the rule of law.[2] Misconduct towards civilians or prisoners can undermine faith in this mission, perhaps less in the countries concerned than in the intervening forces' home countries, as reactions to the My Lai, Bloody Sunday and Abu Ghraib episodes indicate. That the British Army, and Jewish political leadership, were concerned that Arab insurgent 'atrocity stories' might tell as propaganda and that the behaviour of certain units was encouraging this, has been discussed already, as have the misgivings about the Night Squads' impact on inter-communal relations; this, and Wingate's unapologetic advocacy of pre-emption, reprisal and 'counter-terror' are matters of record – a lot of it Wingate's own – raising the question of whether a direct revival of the Night Squads concept would be worth the risk politically, whatever its other virtues. A possible illustration of how far times have changed comes from the closest twenty-first-century analogy to the Night Squads, the programme of night raiding by US and British Special Forces carried out in Iraq to accompany the much-hyped 'Surge' of 2007 and in Afghanistan from 2008 onwards. The aim of these night raids was explicitly to disrupt insurgent networks of command and control, and as with the Night Squads, they involved surprise assaults on houses, villages or city blocks believed to be holding insurgent leaders or those involved in organising supplies of money or weaponry.[3] Certain things which would have been inconceivable in Wingate's time have impinged on the night raid programme, which probably played a far bigger part in defeating the insurgency in Iraq than the 'Surge' and yet which ran into problems in Afghanistan: local politicians, most notably Afghanistan's President, Hamid Karzai, complained they were a violation of sovereignty; poor intelligence and deliberate deception by locals may have led to the wrong targets being hit, leading to adverse reports from Western media outlets and Non-Governmental Organisations with axes to grind already (and technological developments meant these reports were around the world, reaching potentially millions, within days) and the involvement of the US Drug Enforcement Agency in targeting led to Special Forces being used in police work which may have had little to do with beating the insurgency and may, indeed, have aggravated it, given the importance of the poppy crop to the Afghan economy. Consequently, in Afghanistan at least, the night raids have been put under a degree of local political and legal oversight which many commanders far more patient and forbearing than Wingate would likely find intolerable.[4]

As to Long Range Penetration, with some creative imagination this might be seen as bridging the 'scallywagging' of the World Wars and the 'Aspin-Rumsfeld Doctrine' of military operations applied in Afghanistan in 2001 and parts of Iraq in the invasion of 2003, which involved regular Special Forces cooperating with local irregulars, reliant on air resupply and with heavy airpower support, being used in lieu of main-force action, a pattern repeated with the NATO intervention in Libya in 2011.[5] However, the differences between his recommendations and how these operations were actually carried out have been touched upon already, and as to the situation faced by allied forces in Afghanistan and Iraq post-2003, Wingate would most likely have commented on how the cultural mores of the West since his time allowed the Taliban and al Qaeda a freedom of action he would never have allowed.

It is vital not to take these arguments too far, particularly as they extract Wingate's ideas from the specific historical context which gave them birth. The Night Squads formed one end of a spectrum of insurgency, that of 'small wars' involving local irregulars and the British Army trying to engage each other in battle, as detailed by Charles Callwell. Certain British military authors recognised already that the nature of resistance to British rule was changing, particularly Charles Gwynn, who argued that this could include also mass civil disobedience and other relatively peaceful action, and H.J. Simson, whose 'sub-war' mixed terrorism with political subversion. The Night Squads come closest to the model of Callwell's 'armed scouts' and, perhaps later, when it began aggressive pre-emption against the insurgents, of Simson's 'G men'. References to Callwell and Simson indicate profound ways in which Wingate was 'of his time and place.' Throughout his papers, there is the implicit but consistent argument that war is a clash of cultures, dialectical and human-centred. This is often expressed in the language of ethnic stereotyping – Arabs were scared of a 'straight fight', Italians were soft and panicky, Japanese were brave but obtuse – and while this may seem flawed and even immoral to twenty-first-century readers, such opinions were common at the time and methods apparently rooted in them proved effective in practice. One such assumption, held by prominent authors such as Callwell and Simson and by some senior military commanders – Dill, Haining, Evetts, and Montgomery – was that insurgency within the Empire should be dealt with summarily and without too much reference to the rule of law because force was the only thing certain cultures understood or respected. Wingate was a lifelong advocate of such 'severity', one role given to the Night Squads being to intimidate the local Arab population of Galilee into obedience, and using 'robust' methods to extract information from captured insurgents; writing on the possible use of local guerrillas in Burma, he argued that Japanese 'severity', in the form of reprisals against the civilian population, would restrict their effectiveness. Given the widespread revulsion at the Amritsar episode and the activities of the Black and Tans in Ireland, as well as high-level misgivings about the behaviour of certain units in Palestine, it may be that Wingate's opinions and actions placed him outside the mainstream in his own time. Yet, as late as 1936–39, when the Night Squads were in action in Palestine, there was an undercurrent of thought in the Army that the only way to deal with rebellion was to get tough with the rebels, sometimes brutally so, and that interference from civilian politicians and administrators prevented this. This may explain Wavell's and Haining's backing for Wingate, which seemed to continue so long as he operated 'under the radar' and was withdrawn when he opened the threat of attracting public attention to what was going on through his open lobbying for the Zionists in London. Even here, he did not set himself apart from his colleagues, as the Zionists had other sympathizers and helpers in the British military in Palestine and, indeed, the Night Squads were just one expression of Anglo-Jewish military cooperation which certain people of both nationalities felt did not go far enough. Alongside cultural change has been technological. Any attempt to carry out the continent-wide LRP offensive envisaged by Wingate post-*Thursday* would hinge on complete and uninterrupted command of the air to secure the aerial routes of delivery and supply, therefore would have to be opened with a major air superiority and counter-air campaign, which in the twenty-first century would involve the destruction not only of the enemy air force, but the neutralisation of possibly extensive air defence systems based on anti-aircraft guns and surface-to-air missiles and coordinated by radar, through a combination of direct attack and electronic and possibly cyber warfare, and the constant suppression of enemy air defences around the Strongholds themselves, to prevent them suffering the fate of Dien Bien Phu. This might be possible were a large, world-class air force committed, but even then, the attackers might not have the luxury that Wingate had, of a large secure base right on the hostile border.

So, in conclusion, in terms of his military ideas, rather than being a 'maverick', Orde Wingate fitted into the British Army of his time perhaps far more than he would the British Army of the twenty-first century. However, he also emerges as having some very important things to say to practitioners of insurgency and counter-insurgency, covert and Special Forces operations and proxy war, all things likely to be with us well into the twenty-first century.

Notes

Introduction

1. Quoted in J Bierman and C Smith, *Fire in the Night: Wingate of Burma, Ethiopia and Zion* (London: Macmillan, 2000), p.379
2. J Thompson, *The Imperial War Museum Book of the War in Burma 1942-1945* (London: Sidgwick & Jackson, 2002), p.62
3. Y Allon, *The Making of Israel's Army* (London: Valentine, Mitchell, 1980), pp.8–10; for Sharon's opinion of Wingate, see BJ Bond, *Liddell Hart: A Study of his Military Thought* (London: Cassell, 1977), pp.247-248; for Dayan's, see M Dayan, *Story of My Life* (London: Weidenfeld & Nicholson, 1976), pp.44-48 and R Slater, *Warrior Statesman: The Life of Moshe Dayan* (London: Robson, 1992), p.47
4. See D Ben-Gurion, 'Our Friend: What Wingate did for us', *Jewish Observer and Middle East Review* No.27, September 1963, LHCMA File 15/3/311; Dayan, *Story of My Life*, pp.45-48
5. Colonel OC Wingate, 'The Ethiopian Campaign, August 1940 to June 1941', several copies held in the IWM Wingate Abyssinia Papers; the best published history of this operation is that by D Shirreff, *Bare Feet and Bandoliers: Wingate, Sandford, the Patriots and the part they played in the Liberation of Ethiopia* (London: Ratcliffe, 1995); see also W Thesiger, *The Life of My Choice* (London: Collins, 1987)
6. Wingate, 'Ethiopian Campaign', pp.1, 4–5, 14-15; Colonel OC Wingate, 'Appreciation of the Ethiopia Campaign', several copies held in the IWM Wingate Abyssinia Papers, pp.3-7, 10, 13-14
7. Vice Admiral the Earl Mountbatten of Burma, *Report to the Combined Chiefs of Staff by the Supreme Commander South-East Asia 1943-1945* (London: HMSO, 1951), Section A, Para.5, Section B, Para.36
8. Christopher Sykes, *Orde Wingate, A Biography* (New York: World Publishers 1959); Trevor Royle, *Orde Wingate: Irregular Soldier* (London: Weidenfeld & Nicholson 1995)
9. 'SAS "Smash" squads on the ground in Libya to mark targets for coalition jets', http://www.dailymail.co.uk/news/article-1368247/Libya-SAS-smash-squads-ground-mark-targets-coalition-jets.html, accessed 20 July 2011; 'Libya: SAS veterans helping Nato identify Gadaffi targets in Misrata', http://www.guardian.co.uk/world/2011/may/31/libya-sas-veterans-misrata-rebels, accessed 20 July 2011
10. 'SAS on Ground during Libya Crisis', http://www.bbc.co.uk/news/world-africa-16624401, accessed 27 April 2012
11. Richard Clarke, *Against All Enemies: Inside America's War on Terror* (London: Free Press 2003), pp.247–277; George Friedman, America's Secret War (London: Little, Brown 2004), pp.151–155, 160–165, 178–182; Bob Woodward, *Bush at War* (London: Pocket Books 2003), pp.251–267
12. George Steer, *Sealed and Delivered: A Book on the Ethiopian Campaign* (London: Faber & Faber 2009), pp.161–162; Simon Anglim, *Orde Wingate and the British Army* (London: Chatto & Pickering 2010), pp.140–141
13. Major General S Woodburn Kirby et al, *History of the Second World War, The War Against Japan, Volume III: The Decisive Battles* (London: HMSO, 1961) [hereafter *OHJ3*]; Field Marshal Sir W Slim, *Defeat Into Victory* (London: Cassell, 1956)
14. Slim, *Defeat into Victory*, pp.218-220; 'LRP Groups – Comment on note of DSD by Colonel OC Wingate', IWM Wingate Chindit Papers, Box I
15. Helmet currently displayed in the Imperial War Museum, London; see also Wingate to Central Command, Agra, of 15 August 1942, IWM Wingate Chindit Papers, Box I; Dayan, *Story of My Life*, p.47; P Stibbe, *Return via Rangoon* (London: Leo Cooper, 1995), p.19; Author's interview with Sir Douglas Dodds-Parker, of G(R) and Special Operations Executive, and Wingate's Staff Captain in East Africa, 25 August 2004; W Burchett, *Wingate's Phantom Army* (London: Frederick Muller, 1946), p.43; JRM Calvert, *Fighting Mad: One Man's Guerrilla War* (London: Jarrold, 1964), p.113; Stibbe, *Return via Rangoon*, pp.20-21; Sykes, *Wingate*, p.249; Thesiger, *Life of My Choice*, p.320

210 Orde Wingate

16. See Wingate, 'Appreciation of the Ethiopia Campaign', p.16, where he refers to General Sir Alan Cunningham as a 'military ape'; see also S Bidwell, *The Chindit War: The Campaign in Burma 1944* (London: Book Club Associates, 1979), pp.38-44; Slim, *Defeat into Victory*, pp.218-219, 220; Thesiger, *Life of My Choice*, pp.319-320, 330, 332-333, 336, 349-350
17. Anonymous, 'Narrative of Events: May to November, 1941', IWM Wingate Abyssinia Papers, Box II
18. T Segev, *One Palestine, Complete: Jews and Arabs under the British Mandate* (London: Abacus, 2000), pp.430, 587–588

Chapter 1
1. Moshe Dayan, Story of My Life, p.47
2. Slim to Fergusson of 19 April 1956, Churchill Archives Slim Papers, File 5/1c
3. R Rhodes James, *Chindit* (London: John Murray, 1980), pp.90-91; C Sykes, *Orde Wingate* (London: Collins, 1959), p.378, 380, 436, 442-443
4. Mountbatten quoted in Peter Mead, *Orde Wingate and the Historians* (Braunton, Devon: Merlin 1987), p.86; Wavell quoted, Foreword to Bernard Fergusson, *Beyond The Chindwin* (London: Collins 1951), p.13; Sir Robert Thompson, *Make for The Hills* (London: Leo Cooper 1989), p.76
5. Down quoted, Major Victor Dover MC, *The Sky Generals* (London: Cassell 1981) p.99; Slim quoted in Ronald Lewin, *Slim: The Standardbearer* (London: Pan 1978) p.143; Pownall quoted in Mead, *Wingate and the Historians*, p.90
6. Major General S Woodburn Kirby et al, *History of the Second World War, The War Against Japan, Volume III: The Decisive Battles* (London: HMSO, 1961) [hereafter *OHJ3*]; Field Marshal Sir W Slim, *Defeat Into Victory* (London: Cassell, 1956)
7. See www.awm.gov.au/korea/faces/burchett.htm
8. Burchett, *Wingate's Phantom Army*, pp.45-48, 49
9. Mosley, *Gideon Goes to War*, pp.46–49, 52-54, 72
10. Mosley, *Gideon*, pp.58–59, 75–77; Segev, *One Palestine*, pp.429–432
11. Ibid, pp.97-110
12. Quoted in Mead, *Wingate and the Historians*, pp.190–191
13. Slim, *Defeat into Victory*, pp.162, 218-220
14. Ibid, p.162
15. Ibid, p.218
16. Ibid, pp.162-163
17. Ibid, pp.218-219
18. Ibid, pp.547-548
19. Major General S Woodburn Kirby CB CMG CIE OBE MC and others, *The Official History of the War against Japan*, Volume II (hereafter *OH2*), Volume III (hereafter *OH3*) (London: HMSO 1959 and 1962) pp.243–244 of *OH2*
20. *OH2*, pp.324–329
21. Kirby, *OHJ3*, p.219
22. Ibid, , p.219
23. Ibid, p.221
24. Ibid, p.221-222
25. Ibid, p.222
26. Ibid, pp.442-443
27. Rooney, *Wingate and the Chindits*, p.238–239; Bierman & Smith, *Fire in the Night*, p.386
28. C Rolo, *Wingate's Raiders* (London: George Harrap, 1944), pp.18, 25. The author has no idea of what a 'brass hat' might be.
29. BE Fergusson, *Beyond the Chindwin: Being an Account of the Adventures of Number Five Column of the Wingate Expedition into Burma, 1943* (London: Collins, 1945)
30. Brigadier BE Fergusson DSO, 'Behind the Enemy's Lines in Burma', *Journal of the Royal United Services Institute*, August 1946, p.357
31. BE Fergusson, *The Wild Green Earth* (London: Collins 1947), especially pp.139-146
32. David Rooney, *Mad Mike: A Life of Brigadier Michael Calvert* (Barnsley: Pen & Sword 1997), pp.77–78, for a brief account of the Pagoda Hill action
33. Ibid, pp.93–111
34. Many of his papers will be cited in what is to come.
35. Michael Calvert, *Prisoners of Hope* (London: Jonathan Cape 1952), pp.68, 94–95, 166

36. Calvert, *Prisoners of Hope*, p.283
37. See especially Ibid, pp.12, 97
38. Calvert, to his credit, made no attempt to conceal this or evade blame. See, for example, Rooney, *Mad Mike*, pp.110–111, 119, 144–146
39. Ibid, especially pp.139–145; Tony Geraghty, *Who Dares Wins: The Special Air Service, 1950 to the Gulf War* (London: Little, Brown 1992), pp.327, 336–337
40. Rooney, *Mad Mike*, pp.146–154
41. Ibid, pp.167–171
42. Ibid, pp.184–186
43. Ibid, pp.194–199
44. Ibid, p.160
45. Ibid, p.136; John A Nagl, *Learning to eat soup with a Knife: Counterinsurgency Lessons from Malaya and Vietnam* (Westport: Praeger 19——), pp.194–195; Sanderson is not named in any published source, but his name can be inferred from Army Lists.
46. I am indebted to Mark Baillie, formerly of 7th Gurkha Rifles and a graduate of the Army Jungle Warfare Course, researching a PhD on the Malayan Emergency at the time of writing, for sharing the results of his detective work on this case – Calvert makes these allegations in his recorded interviews in the Archives of the Imperial War Museum, Cat No.9989, while Sanderson's subsequent record has been pieced together from *The Army Lists, The London Gazette*, and David Erskine's history of the Scots Guards.
47. Quoted in Bernard Fergusson, 'The Wingate "Myth"', *RUSI Journal* Volume LXVII, September 1972, p.75; see also Rooney, Mad Mike, pp.182–184 for Fergusson's measured response
48. Derek Tulloch, *Wingate in Peace and War: A Portrait of the Chindit Commander* (London: Macdonald 1972), p.9
49. Mead, *Wingate and the Historians*, pp.18–19
50. Tulloch, *Wingate in Peace and War*, especially pp.149-174
51. Ibid, pp.194-195, 256, 259
52. Mead, *Wingate and the Historians*, p.19
53. Ibid, p.14
54. Ibid, pp.143-144
55. Ibid, pp.163-178
56. Ibid, pp.115-116, 152-153
57. R Thompson, *Defeating Communist Insurgency: The Lessons of Malaya and Vietnam* (New York: Frederick A Praeger, 1966)
58. Thompson, *Make for the Hills*, p.73
59. Mead, *Wingate and the Historians*, pp.19-20, 179-184, 195-196
60. Thompson, *Make for the Hills*, pp.71-72
61. Ibid, p.76

Chapter 2

1. J Kiszely, 'The British Army and Approaches to Warfare Since 1945', in Major General JJG Mackenzie and B Holden Reid (Editors), *Central Region vs. Out of Area: Future Commitments* (London: Tri-Service Press, 1990) p.185
2. Quoted in D French, *Raising Churchill's Army: The British Army and the War against Germany 1919-1945* (Oxford: Oxford University Press, 2000), pp.12-13
3. TR Moreman, '"Small Wars" and Imperial Policing: The British Army and the Theory and Practice of Colonial Warfare in the British Empire, 1919–1939', in Brian Holden Reid (Editor) *Military Power: Land Warfare in Theory and Practice* (London: Frank Cass, 1997), pp.106–107, 112–113
4. See Major General CW Gwynn KCB CMG DSO, *Imperial Policing* (London: Macmillan, 1939), pp.34–64; PA Towle, *Pilots and Rebels: The use of aircraft in unconventional warfare* (London: Brassey's 1989), pp.35, 40,43. Dyer was actually a substantive Colonel, local acting Brigadier General.
5. Anonymous, 'The Burmese Rebellion 1931', *Journal of the United Services Institute of India (JUSII)* Volume LX 1932, pp.146-150, 153-154; 'MFC', 'Raids and Reprisals on the North-West Frontier', *JUSII* Volume LIV, 1922, pp.383-392
6. Callwell, *Small Wars*, cited already
7. Ibid, pp.71-108; *FSR 1929(ii)*, pp.204-207; Moreman, 'Small Wars', p.110
8. Gwynn, *Imperial Policing*, pp.3-5, 34-64

9. HJ Simson, *British Rule, and Rebellion* (Edinburgh and London: William Blackwood, 1937), p.36
10. Ibid, especially pp.36–52
11. Slim, *Defeat into Victory*, pp.17-18, 121, 143, 221, 368, 380, 537
12. Colonel CE Callwell, *Small Wars: Their Principles and Practice* Bison Books Edition (Lincoln and London: Bison, 1996), pp.29-32, 49-50, 289, 348-349
13. DP Marston, *Phoenix from the Ashes: The Indian Army in the Burma Campaign* (Westport & London: Praeger, 2003), pp.13–14, 32–33, 218–219
14. Brigadier AP Wavell CMG MC, 'The Training of the Army for War', *RUSI Journal* Volume LXXVIII, 1933, pp.258-259
15. Callwell, *Small Wars*, p.72
16. Ibid, pp.76-78
17. Simson, *British Rule*, pp.6–11, 14, 16–18, 22, 32–35
18. Ibid, p.41
19. Ibid, pp.41-42, 147-149
20. Ibid, p.148
21. Gwynn, *Imperial Policing*, pp.14-21, 23–24, 99-100
22. PRO WO141/93, 'Record of the Rebellion in Ireland in 1920-21 and the part played by the Army in dealing with it, Volume I – Operations', pp.22, 24, 26 30-31, 33–35; PRO CJ 4/152, 'The Black and Tans', pp.1-2; C Townshend, 'The Anglo-Irish War', unpublished paper presented to the Institute for National Strategic Studies, Foreign Policy Institute, Johns Hopkins School of Advanced International Studies, pp.12, 14–15, and *Britain's Civil Wars: Counterinsurgency in the Twentieth Century* (London: Faber & Faber 1986), pp.57–58
23. Simson, *British Rule*, pp.48–49, 61–62, 68–98
24. Ibid, pp.118–130
25. Anonymous, 'The Burmese Rebellion', pp.157-161; Captain W St J Carpendale, 'The Moplah Rebellion 1921-22', *USII Journal* Volume LVI 1926, pp.79, 82, 86-87; Captain CMP Durnford, 'The Arab Insurrection of 1920-21', *USII Journal* Volume LIV, pp.188-189; Towle, *Pilots and Rebels*, especially pp.20–23, 29, 41–45
26. General Sir A Skeen, *Passing it On: Short Talks on Tribal Fighting on the North-West Frontier of India*, reprinted as *Lessons in Imperial Rule* (London: Frontline, 2008), pp.121–129; Moreman, 'Small Wars', pp.118–119
27. 'MFC', 'Raids and Reprisals', p.391
28. AF Perrott, Inspector General of Police, Northwest Frontier Province, to Major General R O'Connor of 18 October 1938, LHCMA O'Connor Papers File 3/2/1
29. 'Burmese Rebellion', pp.155-157
30. Ibid, pp.155-156; Appendix C to PRO 191/88, 'History and notes on operations; disturbances in Palestine', 1936-1939; O'Connor to Major General DK McLeod of 21 May 1939, LHCMA O'Connor Papers, File 3/4/54; Simson, *British Rule*, pp.102–104
31. See PRO WO32/3522; PRO WO32/4148; PRO WO191/75, Preliminary Notes on lessons of Palestine Rebellion 1936, February 1937, especially Para.26 and the whole of p.10; PRO WO191/88, History and Notes on Disturbances in Palestine, 1936-39, pp.2-3; PRO WO32/9401, Disturbances, 1936, p.4; Townshend, *Britain's Civil Wars*, pp.64–65
32. Carpendale, 'Moplah Rebellion', pp.77-78; Durnford, 'Arab Insurrection', pp.186-188; Townshend, *Britain's Civil Wars*, p.64
33. Callwell, *Small Wars*, especially pp.108-114, 135-136, 140, 290-291, 362
34. Skeen, *Passing it On*, especially pp.25-33
35. Ibid, pp.25–79, 103–109
36. Callwell, *Small Wars*, pp.125-149
37. Ibid, pp.80–81, 142 150-194, 171–172
38. Townshend, *Britain's Civil Wars*, p.64
39. PRO WO141/93, Record of the Rebellion in Ireland, Volume I, pp.32, 43-44; Volume IV Part I – 5th Division, pp.16-17; Townshend, 'Anglo-Irish War', pp.33-35, and *Britain's Civil Wars*, p.64
40. Durnford, 'Arab Insurrection', pp.186-189
41. Carpendale, 'Moplah Rebellion', pp.82-86, 88-89, compare with Callwell, *Small Wars*, pp.130, 133-135, 141; see also Gwynn, *Imperial Policing*, pp.98-100; Moreman, 'Small Wars', pp.122–124
42. Moreman, '"Small Wars" and Imperial Policing', pp.119-120; 'Shpagwishtama', 'The Changing Aspect of Operations on the North-West Frontier', *JUSII* Volume LXVI 1936, pp.103-104
43. Skeen, *Passing it On*, pp.22, 101, 130-131

44. Towle, *Pilots and Rebels*, p.14
45. Ibid, pp.13–27
46. Major LVS Blacker OBE, 'Modernised Mountain Warfare', *JUSII* Volume LXI 1931, pp.89-95
47. Skeen, *Passing it On*, pp.23–24, 131
48. PRO WO32/3522, pp.3, 7, 16-17
49. PRO WO32/4148, pp.4–5, 6–7, 9; 'Shpagwishtama', 'Changing Aspect of Operations on the NW Frontier', p.109; Skeen, *Passing it On*, p.135
50. Ibid, pp.2-3, 11, 14; 'Shpagwishtama', 'Changing Aspect of Operations on the NW Frontier', pp.105-107
51. Skeen, *Passing it On*, pp.131–136
52. Callwell, *Small Wars*, pp.144, 339-345, 350-351
53. India – Northwest Frontier Force Corps Troops – Corps of Gurkha Scouts, War Diary, 1919 May-1919 August, in PRO WO95/5390
54. PRO CJ4/152, p.1; PRO WO141/93, Volume I, p.24; PRO WO141/93 Volume IV, pp.68-69; Townshend, 'Anglo–Irish War', pp.15, 17, and *Britain's Civil Wars*, pp.58–59
55. Townshend, *Britain's Civil Wars*, p.58
56. Anonymous, 'Burmese Rebellion', pp.160-161
57. Simson, *British Rule*, pp.37–38
58. *Notes from the Theatres of War No.1 Cyrenaica* (London: HMSO 1942), p.4; PRO WO106/2290, pp.43–48; Wavell's War Communiqués of 14 and 19 December 1940, in PRO WO106/2136, and 7 April 1941, in PRO WO106/2088
59. PRO WO106/2290, p.47; Wavell's Daily Sitreps of 21 and 22 April 1941, in PRO WO106/2088; Wavell's Daily Sitreps of 30 November 1940 and 29 January 1941, in PRO WO106/2088; Major General ISO Playfair, *The Official History of the War in the Mediterranean and the Middle East, Volume I* [hereafter OHM1] (London: HMSO 1954), pp.397, 399
60. Wavell's War Communiqués of 27 January and 6 February 1941, in PRO WO106/2136; Major General RJ Collins, *Lord Wavell: A Military Biography* (London: Hodder and Stoughton 1948) p.396
61. PRO WO32/11434, Para.ii).6; Telegram from CinC ME to War Office of 14 June 1941, in PRO WO106/3073, Iraq: Operations April-May 1941; Report from Wavell to the War Office of 27 July 1941, in PRO WO201/174, Plan 'Exporter', June 1941; Wavell's Sitrep of 30 June 1941, in PRO WO106/2089
62. *Notes from Theatres of War No.1*, pp.6–7; Bidwell & Graham, *Fire Power*, pp.224, 250
63. *Notes from Theatres of War No.6: CYRENAICA, November 1941/January 1942* (London: War Office 1942) in PRO WO106/2223, p.3
64. J Connell, *Wavell: Soldier and Scholar* (London: Collins, 1964), p.396 ; Colonel JW Hackett DSO MBE MC, 'The Employment of Special Forces', *RUSI Journal* XCVII 1952, pp.29–30; Sir F Maclean, *Eastern Approaches* (London: Jonathan Cape, 1949), pp.193, 205–206
65. Wavell's Sitrep of 16 January 1941, in PRO106/2088, and War Communiqué of 12 April 1941, in PRO 106/2136
66. PRO WO218/173, L Detachment SAS Brigade (later 1 SAS Regt.) formation, training and report of operations in the Mediterranean area, May 1941–July 1942; Maclean, *Eastern Approaches*, pp.190–195
67. Barnett, *Desert Generals*, pp.338-342; Bidwell and Graham, *Fire Power*, pp.226–227, 233, 238–239; see also Dorman-Smith's correspondence with Liddell Hart in the Liddell Hart Centre at King's
68. Moreman, 'Small Wars and Imperial Policing', pp.116–120
69. PRO WO106/2290, p.44
70. PRO WO201/297, 'Abyssinia and Eritrea: Operational Dispatch by Lt Gen. Sir William Platt', Part IA, p.5
71. Ibid, Part II, pp.5–14; PRO WO106/2290
72. PRO WO106/3073, Syria, Operations Summaries, May-July 1941

Chapter 3

1. 'Paper by Lieutenant OC Wingate RA, Subject "B" – Strategy in Three Campaigns', The British Library (TBL) Manuscript File 2313 – The Wingate Palestine Papers, p.1
2. '77 Infantry Brigade: ROLE', 22 September 1942, IWM Wingate Chindit Papers, Box I, p.1
3. Wingate, 'Strategy in Three Campaigns', p.1

4. Ibid, p.2 It would be interesting to ponder on what Wingate and, indeed, many of his contemporaries would have made of the 21st century academic industry aimed at producing 'principles of strategy'.
5. Ibid, pp.6-8
6. Ibid, pp.6-8
7. Ibid, pp.6-9
8. Ibid, p.17
9. Sykes, *Orde Wingate*, p.51
10. Ibid, pp.53-56
11. PRO WO106/6104, 'Summary of events during Arab revolt in province of Hejaz', 1918, pp.12-15; TE Lawrence, *Seven Pillars of Wisdom* (London: Jonathan Cape 1935), pp.58, 62, 111-113; E Kedourie, *In the Anglo-Arab Labyrinth: The McMahon-Hussein Correspondence and its Interpretations 1914-1939* (London: Frank Cass, 2000), especially pp.12-13, 42-44, 46-47, 51-52, 149, 161
12. Sykes, *Orde Wingate*, pp.56-57
13. Royle, *Orde Wingate*, p.48
14. Mosley, *Gideon Goes to War*, p.22 – there is absolutely no evidence that Wingate was theorizing on guerrilla warfare before his arrival in Palestine, almost ten years later.
15. Royle, *Orde Wingate*, p.68
16. Ibid, pp.62-63, 69-70; Sykes, *Orde Wingate*, pp.68-69
17. Dayan, *Story of My Life*, p.46
18. Colonel BT Wilson DSO RE, 'The Sudan of To-Day', *RUSI Journal* Volume LXXIX, 1934, p.538
19. Brevet-Major JEH Boustead OBE MC, 'The Camel Corps of the Sudan Defence Force', *RUSI Journal* Volume LXXIX, 1934, p.548
20. Ibid, p.552; Sir Douglas Dodds-Parker, interview with the author of 24 August 2004
21. Boustead, 'Camel Corps of the SDF', p.553
22. Ibid, pp.554-556; Wilson, 'Sudan', p.541
23. Boustead, 'Camel Corps of the SDF', pp.556-557
24. Dodds-Parker Interview of 24/8/2004; Sykes, *Orde Wingate*, p.65
25. Harold G Marcus, *A History of Ethiopia* (Berkeley, Los Angeles and London: University of California Press 2002), pp.120-121
26. Mosley, *Gideon Goes to War*, p.98
27. *FSR 1929*(ii), pp.205, 207; see also Callwell, *Small Wars*, pp.34-42, 85-107
28. *FSR 1929*(ii), p.205
29. Ibid, pp.205, 211-212
30. Boustead, 'Camel Corps of the SDF', pp.556-557; Wilson, 'Sudan', pp.543-544
31. Sykes, *Orde Wingate*, p.65
32. Dodds-Parker Interview of 24/8/2004
33. *Bimbashi* OC Wingate, 'Report on DINDER Patrol carried out by two sections of No.2 Idara EAC from 11/4/31 to 26/4/31', Copy No.3, IWM Wingate 'Early Life' Papers, Box III, p.1
34. Ibid, p.3
35. Ibid, pp.4-6
36. Ibid, pp. 1, 4, 5
37. OC Wingate, 'Report on No.11 patrol EAC 1932', IWM Wingate 'Early Life' Papers, Box III, p.1
38. Ibid, p.6
39. 'No.4/EAC/0/1-1/32 Note on Game Protection on Dinder and Rahad Rivers by El Bimbashi OC Wingate EAC', IWM Wingate 'Early Life' Papers Box III, p.1
40. Ibid, p.1
41. Royle, *Orde Wingate*, pp.60-61
42. Ibid, pp.61-62
43. Mosley, *Gideon Goes to War*, pp.12-13
44. See Leo Amery's diary entry of 10 December 1939, in J Barnes and D Nicholson (editors), *The Empire at Bay: The Leo Amery Diaries 1929-1945* (London: Hutchinson, 1988), pp.576-577, wherein he compares Wingate favourably with Lawrence; Liddell Hart to Wavell of 12 December 1948, wherein he comments on Wavell's piece on Wingate for *The Dictionary of National Biography* and that Wingate 'was clearly casting himself for the role of a second TE', LHCMA Liddell Hart Papers Files LH 1/730-733, Pt.3; Weizmann, *Trial and Error*, p.389
45. See particularly WO106/6104, pp.6, 12-15; L James, *The Golden Warrior; The Life and Legend of Lawrence of Arabia* (London: Weidenfeld & Nicholson, 1990), pp.114, 147-149, 161

Notes   215

46. James, *Golden Warrior*, pp.322-325, 360; see also C Cruise O'Brien, *The Siege: The Story of Israel and Zionism* (London: Weidenfeld & Nicholson, 1986), p.158
47. Wavell, *Good Soldier*, pp.57-61
48. For a summary of Wingate's views on Arabs, see Captain OC Wingate, 'Palestine in Imperial Strategy, HMS Dorsetshire 6/6/39', TBL Wingate Palestine Papers, Manuscript Number 2313, pp.1-4. Wingate's views of the Bedouin are probably shared by the majority of their fellow Arabs.
49. Ibid, pp.6-7
50. Colonel OC Wingate, Commanding British & Ethiopian Troops Employed, 'Appreciation of the Ethiopian Campaign, GHQ ME 18.6.41', several copies held in IWM Wingate Abyssinia Papers, pp.2-4
51. See, for instance, Liddell Hart's manuscript, 'Lawrence of Arabia – The (Almost) Free Man', in the LHCMA Liddell Hart Papers, File 9/13/27
52. PRO CO732/81/3, 'Note on the possibility of concerted military opposition from the Arab peoples to HM Government's policy in Palestine', 1938, pp.2-3; for a historical perspective on this issue, refer to M Hughes, 'What did the Arab Revolt Contribute to the Palestine Campaign? An Assessment', *Journal of the TE Lawrence Society*, Volume XV No.2, Spring 2006, pp.75-87
53. PRO WO106/6104, pp.3, 12
54. High Commissioner for Egypt to Foreign Office of 6 January 1917, in PRO FO141/825
55. PRO CAB37/161/9, Para.11
56. BJ Bond, 'Ironside', in Keegan (Ed), *Churchill's Generals*, pp.17-18
57. Ironside to Wingate of 8 June 1939, TBL Wingate Palestine Papers, Manuscript 2313
58. Quoted in Sykes, *Orde Wingate*, p.250
59. Lawrence, 'Guerrilla', p.881
60. Lawrence, 'Guerrilla', p.881
61. Ibid, pp.882-883
62. Ibid, pp.881-882
63. Lawrence, *Seven Pillars*, pp.197-198
64. Lawrence, 'Guerrilla', p.882
65. Lawrence, *Seven Pillars*, p.200
66. Lawrence, 'Guerrilla', p.884
67. Ibid, pp.47-48
68. Lawrence, 'Guerrilla', pp.886-888
69. Telegram from Foreign Office to High Commissioner for Egypt of 1 September 1916, Telegram from CinC Ismailia to High Commissioner for Egypt of September 1916, both in PRO FO141/462; PRO CAB 37/161/9, 'War Cabinet, 1st Meeting' Minutes Signed 9 December 1916, Paragraph 11
70. Lawrence, 'Guerrilla', pp.886, 888-890
71. Lawrence, *Seven Pillars*, p.201
72. Lawrence, 'Guerrilla', p.890; Captain TE Lawrence to the Right Honourable Arthur Balfour of 29 July 1917, in PRO FO141/825, wherein he suggests a possible 'doctrine' for the Arab Revolt
73. Lawrence, *Seven Pillars*, pp.200-201
74. TE Lawrence, entry on 'Guerrilla Warfare' in the *Encyclopaedia Britannica*, reproduced in G Chaliand (Editor), *The Art of War in World History* (Berkeley, CA: University of California Press 1994), pp.886-889; *The Seven Pillars of Wisdom* (London: Jonathan Cape 1935), pp.197-201
75. PRO WO106/6104, pp.3-4, 5, 7, 10, 12; TE Lawrence, *Encyclopedia Britannica* entry on 'Guerrilla Warfare', reproduced in G Chaliand (Editor), *The Art of War in World History* (Berkeley: University of California Press 1994), p.888-889; Hughes, 'Arab Revolt', pp.75-77
76. Wingate, 'Appreciation', p.6
77. Holland's Reading List is in PRO HS8/260, 'MI(R) Progress Reports, 1939-1940'; Brigadier A Smith, BGS HQ ME, to General Sir W Platt, GOC East Africa, of 28 September 1939, in PRO WO201/2677, especially Para.2
78. Sykes, *Orde Wingate*, pp.98-103
79. Index No.8, Paper No.2, Question No.2 (b), 'The importance of Palestine and Trans-Jordan to the Empire', IWM Wingate Early Life Papers Box 3, p.1
80. Ibid, p.2
81. Index No.8 Paper No.2 Question No.3, 'What is to be discussed?', IWM Wingate 'Early Life' Papers, Box 3, p.1
82. Ibid, pp.1-2
83. Ibid, p.2

84. Ibid, p.3
85. Ibid, p.3
86. Tulloch, *Wingate in Peace and War*, p.43
87. Bierman & Smith, *Fire in the Night*, pp.59-64; Mosley, *Gideon Goes to War*, pp.34-38, 71-72, 74-78; Royle, *Orde Wingate*, pp.97-99; Sykes, *Orde Wingate*, pp.104, 110

Chapter 4
1. PRO WO32/9497, 'Operations in Palestine, 20 May-30 July 1938', pp.6–7
2. 'Remarks of GOC 10/7/39', TBL Wingate Palestine Papers, File 2313
3. D Leebaert, *Dare to Conquer: Special Operations and the Destiny of Nations, from Achilles to al Qaeda* (New York and Boston: Little, Brown, 2006), p.491
4. See, for instance, Robert Eisenman, 'Who killed Orde Wingate?', *Huffington Post*, 24 June 2011, http://www.huffingtonpost.com/robert-eisenman/post_2154_b_884195.html
5. Allon, *Making of Israel's Army*, p.93
6. *Ha'aretz*, 2 April 1944; I Erlich, 'On Wingate', *Hatzofeh*, 5 April 1944, facsimiles of both are in the IWM Wingate Chindit Papers, Box III
7. *Ha'aretz*, 2/4/44; J Nadwa, 'Wingate, the Modern Gideon', unpublished paper in IWM Wingate Chindit Papers, Box III
8. *Hazman*, 2 April 1944, IWM Wingate Chindit Papers, Box III
9. Ibid, p.3
10. Burchett, *Wingate's Phantom Army*, p.45
11. Ibid, p.46
12. Mosley, *Gideon Goes to War*, pp.46–49, 52–54, 72
13. Sykes, *Orde Wingate*, pp.109-110, 121-125, 135-137
14. Rossetto, *Orde Wingate*, pp. X-XI
15. Ibid, pp. X-XII, 28-30
16. Royle, *Orde Wingate*, pp.128–130; Sykes, *Orde Wingate*, pp.154-155
17. Royle, *Orde Wingate*, pp.134-138
18. 'Anti Ahmaddiya Movement in Islam, 26 January 1999' (www.alhafeez.org); 'Assasinating [sic] for Peace in Palestine and Ireland', *Irish Political Review*, Sept 2002 (www.atholbooks.org); 'Darbyism in Israel: Ariel Sharon', *Executive Intelligence Review* (www.larouchepub.com).
19. The most prominent of the 'new historical' works are B Morris' *Righteous Victims: A History of the Zionist-Arab Conflict 1881–2001* (New York: Random House 1999), Segev's *One Palestine, Complete* and A Shlaim's *The Iron Wall: Israel and the Arab World* (London: Penguin 2000), while the explicitly military dimensions of Israel's self-image as 'a community under siege' are criticised by Michael Handel in 'The evolution of Israeli Strategy: the psychology of insecurity and the quest for absolute security' in W Murray, M Knox and A Bernstein (Editors), *The Making of Strategy: Rulers, States and War* (Cambridge CUP 1994). For an introduction to the 'new' historians and their intellectual opponents, the 'new-old historians', see M Hughes' review of Avi Shlaim's *The Iron Wall: Israel and the Arab World* on the Institute of Historical Research Website, http://www.history.ac.uk/reviews
20. Segev, *One Palestine*, pp.430-431; see also Oren, 'Friend under Fire', p.3
21. Ben-Gurion, 'Friend', pp.15-16; Segev, *One Palestine*, p.431
22. Quoted, Oren, 'Friend', pp.3, 12
23. H Strachan, *The Politics of the British Army* (Oxford: Clarendon Press 1997), pp.169, 171; C Townshend, *Terrorism: A Brief Introduction* (Oxford: OUP 2002), p.125
24. O'Brien, *The Siege*, pp.87-90, 125; Segev, *One Palestine*, pp.36-39
25. See, for instance, P Mansfield, *A History of the Modern Middle East* (London: Penguin 2003), pp.159–164, Shlaim, *Iron Wall*, pp.5–11
26. Abdul Wahhab Said Kayyali, *Palestine: A Modern History* (London: Third World Books, 1978), pp.174–175; Major EW Polson Newman, 'Britain's Position in Palestine', *RUSI Journal* Volume LXXXI 1936, p.866; PRO CO733/410/11, 'The Strategic Importance of Palestine', 1939
27. O'Brien, *Siege*, pp.166-167; Simson, *British Rule*, pp.157–169
28. O'Brien, *Siege*, pp.167-168, 196-200; Simson, *British Rule*, pp.166–168
29. O'Brien, *Siege*, pp.202-203; D Ben-Gurion, 'When Bevin Helped Us', *Jewish Observer and Middle East Review*, 4 October 1963, LHCMA 15/5/311, p.18; O'Brien, *Siege*, p.209; Segev, *One Palestine*, p.212; Simson, *British Rule*, p.159
30. Simson, *British Rule*, p.203-205

31. Lt Colonel Anthony Simonds, 'Pieces of War', unpublished memoir held in the Department of Documents in the Imperial War Museum, p.55
32. Kayyali, *Palestine*, p.156
33. Ibid, p.180;Segev, *One Palestine*, pp.359–363; O'Brien, *Siege*, p.209
34. Kayyali, *Palestine*, pp.181–182; O'Brien, *Siege*, p.212
35. Kayyali, *Palestine*, p.178
36. Ben-Gurion, Op.Cit, p.18
37. Cutting from the *New York American* of 8 October 1936 detailing contemporary attitudes to the land issue, in PRO CO733/316/1, 'Interests and opinions of the USA on the situation in Palestine', August-December 1936; Kayyali, *Palestine*, pp.156–160, 178–180
38. Allon, *Israel's Army*, p.7; Ben-Gurion, Op.Cit, p.18; O'Brien, *Siege*, pp.378–381
39. Letter of 2 April 1938 from MacMichael to WGA Ormsby-Gore, Principal Secretary of State for the Colonies, in PRO CO733/384/9
40. Kayyali, *Palestine*, pp.156–157, 178–179
41. Note on the Peel Report in PRO CO733/346/9, 'Division of Palestine into Two Separate States', 1937; Press cutting (newspaper and date unknown) in PRO CO733/384/9
42. Extract from District Commissioner, Galilee and Acre District's Monthly Administrative Report for November 1938, in PRO CO733/372/18, 'Situation in Palestine: district commissioner's reports for 1938', p.2
43. Palestine (Defence) Order in Council, Regulations made by the High Commissioner under Article 6, in PRO CO733/384/9
44. PRO WO191/70, pp.1–2, 22–23, 159–161; Kayyali, *Palestine*, pp.189–191
45. Kayyali, *Palestine*, p.197; Segev, *One Palestine*, p.363; Towle, *Pilots and Rebels*, p.46
46. PRO 191/70, pp.1–2, 160; Kayyali, *Palestine*, pp.198–199; Simson, *British Rule*, pp.249–250
47. Cutting from the *New York Times* of 16 October 1936, in PRO CO733/316/1, 'Interests and Opinions of the USA on the situation in Palestine', August-December 1936; see also Townshend, *Britain's Civil Wars*, p.106
48. Ibid, and see Appendix B to PRO WO191/88 for 'Damascus FSR'; 'Documents and Portraits', TBL Wingate Palestine Papers, File 2313, pp.10–16: Kayyali, *Palestine*, p.199; Simson, *British Rule*, pp.191–192, 199
49. Kayyali, *Palestine*, pp.190–191, 198–199
50. Folios 7a, 32a, 40a, 41b, 55a, 57g in PRO WO191/86, 'Report of Palestine Royal Commission: events preceding and following publication', June-September 1937; Telegram from Clark Kerr to FO in PRO CO733/348/9, cited above; 'Documents and Portraits', pp.10–12, 14; Kayyali, *Palestine*, p.198; Simson, *British Rule*, pp.245–246, 248
51. Weapons, see PRO WO191/70, pp.148-149; Propaganda, see PRO WO32/4562, 'Hostile propaganda in Palestine 1938: unfounded allegations against behaviour of British troops', 1939, and Appendix D to PRO WO33/1436, 'Information for Commanders of reinforcing troops in Palestine', 1936; 'Documents and Portraits', p.14; see also M Williams, 'Mussolini's Secret War in the Mediterranean and the Middle East: Italian Intelligence and the British Response', *Intelligence and National Security* Volume 22 Number 6, December 2007, pp.891–896
52. M van Creveld, *The Sword and the Olive: A Critical History of the Israeli Defence Force* (New York: Public Affairs 2002), p.34
53. Annex F to PRO WO33/1436; PRO WO191/70, p.161; PRO WO191/75, 'Preliminary notes on lessons of Palestine rebellion, 1936', Paras.26-29; Townshend, *Britain's Civil Wars*, pp.105, 108
54. PRO WO32/4176, 'Palestine Disturbances: Policy Adopted', 1936, especially pp.3-4
55. PRO WO32/4500, 'Notification to Parliament of calling out of Section "A" Army Reserve to form Palestine re-enforcements', 1936; 'A Correspondent in Jerusalem', 'Service Problems in Palestine', *RUSI Journal* Volume LXXXI 1936, pp.805-807; Simson, *British Rule*, pp.252–255; Townshend, *Britain's Civil Wars*, p.107
56. Army Council Instruction of 7 September 1936, Folio 7a in PRO WO32/4174, 'Army Council Instructions to Lieutenant General JG Dill regarding the command of the Palestine Armed Forces', 1936
57. The Palestine Martial Law (Defence) Order in Council 1936, and other papers in PRO WO32/9618, 'Palestine Disturbances, Martial Law Policy', 1936-1938; M Hughes, 'The Banality of Brutality: British Armed Forces and the Repression of the Arab Revolt in Palestine, 1936–39', *English Historical Review* Vol.CXXIV, No.507, March 2009, pp.346–349

58. PRO WO32/4562, pp.9-11; M Hughes, 'The Meaning of Atrocity: British Armed Forces and the Arab Revolt, 1936–39', unpublished paper of 2007, especially pp.21–22, 'Banality of Brutality, pp.316–317; Towle, *Pilots and Rebels*, pp.46–47; Townshend, *Britain's Civil Wars*, pp.105–106, 109–110
59. PRO WO191/75, 'Military Lessons of the Arab Rebellion in Palestine, 1936', February 1938, pp.1–2, 10, 22–23, 159–161;PRO WO33/1436, Paras.15-36
60. PRO WO191/75, p.29; Callwell, *Small Wars*, pp.376, 398–400
61. Simson, *British Rule*, pp.266–267; Towle, *Pilots and Rebels*, pp.49–51; Townshend, *Britain's Civil Wars*, p.108
62. Kayyali, *Palestine*, pp.201–202; O'Brien, *Siege*, pp.218–219
63. PRO WO191/90, 'Development of the Palestine Police Force under military control', 1939, pp.9-10; 'Section III: Frontier Protection, posts and roads', in PRO CO733/383/1, 'Police Reorganisation, Sir C Tegart's Mission to Palestine', 1938; Townshend, *Britain's Civil Wars*, pp.111–112
64. Townshend, *Britain's Civil Wars*, pp.91–92, 99–100
65. 'A Rural Mounted Police', in PRO CO733/383/1, pp.1-2
66. Ibid, p.2
67. Unattributed handwritten comment on p.5 of Ibid.
68. Appendix C to WO PRO191/88, 'History and notes on operations: disturbances in Palestine', 1936-1939; Major General Richard O'Connor to Major General DK McLeod of 21 May 1939, LHCMA O'Connor Papers, Folio 3/4/54
69. PRO WO191/88, p.2
70. Ibid, pp.2-3
71. PRO WO32/9401, 'Disturbances, 1936', p.4
72. PRO WO191/88, p.4
73. Hughes, 'Banality of Brutality', pp.320–327
74. PRO WO32/4562, pp.3-4; PRO WO191/88, pp.4-5; 'Kidnappers in Palestine – The Terrorists' Technique', *Daily Telegraph* 28 December 1938, in LHCMA File 15/5/297
75. PRO WO32/4562, p.4; Simonds, 'Pieces of War', pp.19–20, 142
76. Ibid, p.4
77. Ibid, pp.1-2; Kayyali, *Palestine*, pp.211–212; Townshend, *Britain's Civil Wars*, p.108
78. PRO WO32/9497, 'Operations in Palestine, 20 May – 30 July 1938', pp.1-2
79. PRO WO32/9497, p.6
80. Enclosure Ic to PRO CO733/383/1, 'Police Reorganization, Sir C Tegart's Mission to Palestine'
81. Simson, *British Rule*, pp.235–236
82. PRO 32/9497, pp.2, 7; PRO WO191/88, 'History and notes on operations, disturbances in Palestine', p.4
83. PRO WO32/9498, 'Operations in Palestine 1 Aug – 31 Oct 1938', p.5
84. Stuart Emeny, 'Arabs gain control over large areas in Palestine', *News Chronicle*, 12 October 1938, LHCMA File 15/5/297
85. PRO WO32/9498, p.2
86. PRO WO 191/88, p.5
87. PRO WO191/90, 'Development of the Palestine Police under military control', 1939, pp.3-4; Hughes, 'Banality of Brutality', pp.325, 331–335; AJ Sherman, *Mandate Days: British Lives in Palestine, 1918–1948* (Baltimore and London: Johns Hopkins University Press, 1997), pp.107–109, 113–117; Simson, *British Rule*, pp.172–173
88. PRO WO191/90,pp.5–6, 27–28; PRO WO191/88, pp.4–5; PRO WO32/9498, p.3
89. PRO WO191/90, pp.6, 9-14
90. C Weizmann, *Trial and Error* (London: Hamish Hamilton, 1949), pp.484, 488–489; Letter from Political Secretary, Presidency of the New Zionist Organisation, to Secretary of State for War of 25 November 1937, in PRO WO201/169
91. Kayyali, *Palestine*, p.191; Segev, *One Palestine*, pp.383–384; Sykes, *Orde Wingate*, p.108
92. V Jabotinsky, 'The Iron Wall (We and the Arabs)', first published in *Rasviyet*, 4 November 1923, published in English in *The Jewish Herald*, 26 November 1937, online copy available at http://www.marxists.de/middleast/ironwall/ironwall.htm, last accessed 10 January 2010
93. PRO CO733/349/19, 'Memorandum by New Zionist Organisation on the Defence of Palestine', 1937, pp.6–15

94. D Ben-Gurion, 'Britain's Contribution to arming the Hagana', *Jewish Observer and Middle East Review*, 20 September 1963, in LHCMA 15/5/304, p.12
95. David Ben-Gurion, 'Jabotinsky scorns Beigin', *Jewish Observer and Middle East Review*, 11 October 1963, LHCMA 15/5/311, p.14
96. Ibid, pp.14–15
97. Ibid, pp.14–15
98. PRO WO32/4176, p.3; Van Creveld, *The Sword and the Olive,* pp.35, 38
99. Allon, *Israel's Army*, p.7; Ben-Gurion, 'Britain's Contribution', p.13 and *'Rechesh* and *Ta'as –* Arms for the Hagana', *Jewish Observer and Middle East Review*, 27 September 1963, pp.17–18; Van Creveld, *The Sword and the Olive*, p.43
100. Van Creveld, *The Sword and the Olive*, pp.34–35
101. Ibid, pp.34–35
102. Ibid, pp.35, 39
103. Segev, *One Palestine*, pp.382–383
104. Allon, *Israel's Army*, pp.9–10; Sykes, *Orde Wingate*, p.170
105. Van Creveld, *The Sword and the Olive*, pp.40–41
106. H Eshed, *Reuven Shiloah, The Man Behind the Mossad: Secret Diplomacy in the Creation of Israel* (London: Frank Cass 1997), pp.25-26
107. See Bierman & Smith, *Fire in the Night*, pp.70-71; Royle, *Orde Wingate*, pp.106-108
108. Eshed, *Shiloah*, p.27; Simonds, 'Pieces of War', pp.129, 152
109. Ibid, p.27; Air Commodore G Pitchfork, *Shot Down And On The Run: The RAF And Commonwealth Aircrews Who Got Home From Behind Enemy Lines 1940-1945* (London: National Archives 2003), pp.151-154, 158, 164; Sir Douglas Dodds-Parker expressed admiration for Simonds in his interview with the author of 24/8/2004
110. PRO WO32/4174, p.7, cited already
111. CRPal/10126/G, Dill's Report on events in Palestine to the WO, from 15 September to 30 October 1936, in PRO WO32/9401, 'Disturbances, 1936', Para.6
112. Précis of Dill's Dispatch No CR/Pal/1026/G, in PRO WO32/9410, Para.17; Telegram from High Commissioner, Palestine, to Secretary of State for the Colonies, 10 September 1936, Folio 39a in PRO WO32/4176; Folios 43b-57b in PRO WO32/4176; Memorandum of Comments by the High Commissioner on General Dill's report on events in Palestine from the 15th September to the 30th October, 1936, in PRO WO32/4178, 'Respective Functions of High Commissioner and General Officer Commanding the Forces', 1937, Paras.23, 34
113. Townshend, *Britain's Civil Wars*, p.110
114. CR/Pal/10126/G, PRO 32/9401, Para.20
115. Ben-Gurion, 'Britain's Contribution', pp.13-14; PRO WO191/70, p.118
116. PRO WO191/70, p.30
117. Letter from Wauchope to Dill of 15 December 1936, in PRO WO32/4178; Wauchope to Secretary of State, 26 January 1937
118. Letter from Colonial Secretary to Officer Administering, the Government of Palestine, Folio 30b in PRO WO32/4178, Part 1, Paragraph a)
119. Ibid, Part 1, Paragraph a)
120. Ibid, Part 1, Paragraph b)
121. Ibid, Part 1, Paragraph b)
122. Ben-Gurion, 'Britain's Contribution', p.14
123. Ibid, pp.13-14
124. WO 33/1436, Part IV, 'Present Intelligence System', p.1
125. Ibid, pp.2-3; IWM Thomas Interview, pp.19-20
126. 'Appreciation by Captain OC Wingate, of Force HQ Intelligence on 5.6.38 at NAZARETH of the possibilities of night movements by armed forces of the Crown with the object of putting an end to terrorism in Northern Palestine' (hereafter 'Night Movements'), in the papers of Major General HEN Bredin, IWM, pp.3-4
127. Ibid, p.6; 'The Plan' – a three-page manuscript on Wingate's recces of the Jordan, is held in TBL Wingate Palestine Papers, File 2313
128. Sykes, *Orde Wingate*, p.141
129. Wingate, 'Night Movements', pp.12-13
130. Even the best of Wingate's biographers have fallen for this one – see Royle, Orde *Wingate*, p.117; Sykes, *Orde Wingate*, pp.142–143

131. Wavell, *Good Soldier*, p.62
132. Ibid, p.62
133. Patrick Cosgrave, *The Lives of Enoch Powell* (London: Bodley Head 1989), p.81
134. Letter from Wavell to Evetts of 4 January 1939, LHCMA Evetts Papers, File 2
135. See Boxes 3–4 of the LHCMA Evetts Papers
136. PRO WO191/70, p.147
137. Annex F to PRO WO33/1436, p.2
138. Callwell, *Small Wars*, pp.304-305, 486-487
139. Annex F to PRO WO33/146, p.2
140. Ibid, p.2
141. PRO WO191/70, pp.147–148
142. Sykes, *Orde Wingate*, p.111
143. Quoted, David Ha'Cohen, 'The Story of a Historic Friendship', *Jewish Observer and Middle East Review*, 17 October 1969, LHCMA 15/5/315, p.15
144. Wingate told Thomas they would both be serving in the 'Jewish Legion' 'before long', IWM Thomas Interview, p.27; see also Sykes, *Orde Wingate*, p.113
145. Ben-Gurion, 'Our Friend', p.15; Ha'Cohen, 'Friendship', pp.14-15
146. O'Brien, *The Siege*, pp.223-224
147. MacMichael to Ormsby-Gore, 2 April 1938, in PRO CO733/384/9, pp.1–4; Cutting from the *Palestine Post* of 24 March 1938, in PRO CO733/384/9
148. WO 191/70, p.119
149. Ibid, p.119
150. Ibid, p.119
151. Sykes, *Orde Wingate*, pp.146–147
152. Sykes, *Orde Wingate*, pp.146–147
153. Mosley, *Gideon goes to War*, pp.57-58
154. Sykes, *Orde Wingate*, pp.146–147
155. Ibid, pp.147–148
156. Barr, *Line in the Sand*, p.163
157. Ibid, p.119
158. PRO WO32/9401, pp.4, 15-16
159. Vera Weizmann, *The Impossible Takes Longer* (London: Hamish Hamilton 1967), p.164
160. PRO WO33/1436 Part II Para.8; PRO WO190/70, p.131
161. Ben-Gurion, 'Britain's Contribution', p.14
162. Wingate, 'Night Movements', p.1
163. Ibid, p.1
164. Ibid, p.1
165. Ibid, p.2
166. Ibid, p.2
167. Lt R King-Clark, 'Special Duty', *Manchester Regiment Gazette*, date not known, p.2
168. Ibid, p.3; see also 'Organization and Training of Special Night Squads' (different document from that cited elsewhere) in TBL Wingate Palestine Papers, File 2313
169. Wingate, 'Night Movements', pp.4-5, 11
170. Ibid, p.6
171. Ibid, pp.13, 16
172. Ibid, pp.15-16
173. Ibid, p.3
174. 'Reconnaissance of Ghor Beisan'; Report of Operation by Special Night Squad at (unreadable) JURDIEH (unreadable) on night 11/12 June 1938, TBL Wingate Palestine Papers
175. Ben-Gurion, 'Friend', p.15
176. Ibid, p.15; Slater, *Warrior Statesman*, p.48; Sykes, *Wingate*, p.149
177. PRO WO191/90, p.18
178. Eyal, 'Arab Revolt', p.33
179. Wingate, 'Night Moves', p.17
180. Wingate to King-Clark, 17 July 1938, in the King-Clark Papers, IWM; Appendix to Captain OC Wingate, 'Organisation and Training of Special Night Squads (SNS), HQ 16 Inf Bde No.1127/1 August 1938', p.4
181. Wingate, 'Organisation and Training', Appendix p.2

182. Ibid, Appendix p.2
183. Ibid, p.3
184. King-Clark, PERSONAL DIARY, pp.2-5, 6-7
185. Ibid, pp.1, 6, 21
186. Israel Erlich, 'On Wingate', *Hatzofeh* 5 April 1944, facsimile in IWM Wingate Chindit Papers, Box III
187. King-Clark, PERSONAL DIARY, p.1
188. Lieutenant HEN Bredin, 'Impressions of Wingate', in Collection 81/33/1, the papers of Major General HEN Bredin, IWM, p.1
189. Allon, *Israel's Army*, p.11
190. Quoted, Ben-Gurion, 'Friend', p.16
191. Ibid, p.16
192. 'Principles governing the laying of ambushes and night movements of armed forces, with effect from 7/4/38', TBL Wingate Palestine Papers
193. 'In Wingate's Company – Commander and Friend', *Haboker* 7 April 1944, facsimile in IWM Wingate Chindit Papers, Box III
194. Captain OC Wingate, 'Organisation and Training of Special Night Squads, HQ 16 Inf Bde No. 1127/1, August 1938, pp.1-2
195. Captain OC Wingate GSI, 'Principles Governing the Employment of Special Night Squads', Nazareth 10.6.37 (although Wingate refers to events on later dates), p.1
196. Ibid, p.1
197. Ibid, p.3
198. Ibid, p.3
199. Ibid, p.4
200. Ibid, pp.4-5
201. 'Wingate avenges the death of Sturman and his comrades', *Ha'aretz*, 21 April 1942, transcription in IWM Wingate Chindit Papers, Box V
202. 'Report of Operation by Special Night Squad at [unreadable] JURDIEH [unreadable] on night 11/12 June 1938', TBL Wingate Palestine Papers, File 2313; Sykes, *Orde Wingate*, p.151
203. Wingate, 'Principles', p.3
204. Ibid, p.5
205. King-Clark, 'Diary', p.2
206. King-Clark, 'Special Duty', p.1
207. Segev, *One Palestine*, pp.587-588
208. Ibid, p.430
209. Ben-Gurion, 'Friend' p.15-16
210. King-Clark Diary, p.4
211. Bierman & Smith, *Fire in the Night*, pp.115-116; King-Clark Diary, pp.13, 17
212. O'Connor to his wife of 2-3 November 1938, LHCMA O'Connor Papers 3/1/18
213. Haining to Montgomery and O'Connor, undated of December 1938, LHCMA O'Connor Papers 3/2/8
214. Covering note to Ibid, LHCMA O'Connor Papers 3/2/8
215. Wingate, 'Principles', p.6
216. King-Clark Diary, pp.11-12
217. King-Clark Diary, pp.7-8
218. King-Clark, 'Special Duty', p.2
219. Captain OC Wingate OCSNS, 'Report of Operation carried out by Special Night Squads on the Night of 11th/12th July 1938', LHCMA Liddell Hart Papers, p.1
220. MacMichael to MacDonald of 2 July 1938, in PRO WO32/4176, Para.2
221. Ibid, Paras.2-3
222. Ibid, Para.2
223. Ibid, Para.5
224. MacDonald to MacMichael of 22 August 1938, in PRO WO32/4176
225. Wingate, '11/12 July', pp.2-3; King-Clark Diary, p.27
226. Wingate, '11/12 July', p.3
227. Quoted, Maurice Samuelson, 'Return to Ein Harod: Major-General HEN Bredin describes the Night Squads', *Jewish Observer and Middle East Review*, October 17 1969, p.20
228. Ibid, p.20

229. Sykes, *Orde Wingate*, p.151
230. King-Clark Diary, p.28
231. Ibid, p.26
232. Ibid, p.27
233. Wingate, '11/12 July', p.3
234. R King-Clark, Acting OC SNS to Brigade Major 16 Inf Bde of 27 July 1938, TBL Wingate Palestine Papers
235. Captain OC Wingate, 'Note on the Development of Special Night Squads, RAF Hospital, Sarafand, on 14.7.38', pp.1-3
236. Ibid, p.3
237. Ibid, p.2
238. Ibid, p.2
239. Ibid, p.2
240. Sykes, *Orde Wingate*, p.168
241. Allon, *Israel's Army*, pp.9, 11-12
242. PRO WO32/9497, pp.6-7
243. Quoted in Townshend, *Britain's Civil Wars*, p.110
244. Commander 16th Infantry Brigade's Memo CR/Pal/8336/17/G of 12 September 1938, TBL Wingate Palestine Papers, File 321
245. Ben-Gurion, 'Friend', p.16
246. Ben-Gurion, 'British Contribution', p.14
247. MacMichael to MacDonald of 11 September 1938, in PRO WO32/4176, p.1
248. Captain OC Wingate, 'Addition to Standing Orders for SNS, 3/8/1938'
249. Quoted, Samuelson, 'Bredin', pp.20-21
250. PRO WO32/9498, pp.1-2
251. 'Wingate avenges the death of Sturman [sic] and his comrades', *Ha'aretz* 21 April 1944, facsimile held in IWM Wingate Chindit Papers, Box III
252. Quoted, Bierman & Smith, *Fire in the Night*, pp.114-115
253. Ibid, pp.113, 115; Sykes, *Orde Wingate*, pp.169, 177
254. Sykes, *Orde Wingate*, pp.178-179; Royle, *Orde Wingate*, pp.142-143
255. Sykes, *Orde Wingate*, pp.180-181; Royle, *Orde Wingate*, pp.143-144
256. Sykes, *Orde Wingate*, p.180
257. Sykes, *Orde Wingate*, p.180
258. PRO CO733/386/23, pp.2-3; Kayyali, *Palestine*, p.211, 217
259. Montgomery to Adam, 4 December 1938, in PRO WO216/111 'Major General BL Montgomery, 8 Division Palestine: demi-official correspondence', November 1938-February 1939, p.1-3; see also Townshend, *Britain's Civil Wars*, pp.112–113
260. PRO WO216/46, 'Brief notes on Palestine by Major General BL Montgomery', 1939, p.3; Instruction No.1 issued to 8th Division by Montgomery, 25 November 1938, LHCMA O'Connor Papers, 3/4/4
261. Montgomery to Adam, 4 December 1938, p.5
262. Montgomery to Adam, 1 January 1939, in PRO WO216/111, p.2
263. 16th Infantry Brigade Intelligence Summary No.44, 9 May 1939, in PRO WO201/2134, 'Palestine Intelligence Summaries: 16th Infantry Brigade Operations', 1939-1940, p.1
264. 16th Infantry Brigade Summary', 5 September 1939, in PRO WO201/2134
265. Wingate met informally with members of the commission during its investigations; see Sykes, *Orde Wingate*, pp.160–166
266. D Ben-Gurion, 'Table Talk with Lord Lloyd', *Jewish Observer and Middle East Review*, 13 December 1963, LHCMA 15/5/311, p.14
267. Ibid, pp.15-16
268. Amery's Diary Entry of 4 November 1938, in Amery, *Empire at Bay*, p.534
269. Letter from Liddell Hart to Churchill of 11 November 1938, LHCMA 15/5/30; BH Liddell Hart, *The Second World War* (London: Cassell, 1970), pp.382–383
270. Sykes, *Orde Wingate*, pp.192-193
271. Burchett, *Wingate's Phantom Army*, p.46
272. Sykes, *Orde Wingate*, p.190

273. The written order confirming this, issued by the War Office in 1940, has not survived in the public domain, but Douglas Dodds-Parker had a sighting of it in Wingate's Personal File upon Wingate's arrival in Khartoum in 1940; the Order was apparently signed by Brigadier (later Field Marshal Lord) Gerald Templer. Dodds-Parker interview of 24/8/2004, and cited in Sykes, *Orde Wingate*, p.232
274. 'Annual Confidential Report by Officer's Immediate Commander'; 'Extract from Army Form B.194 in respect of Captain OC Wingate DSO, Royal Artillery, covering the period 1.11.38 to 30.4.39'; 'Remarks of GOC 10/7/39', all in TBL Wingate Palestine Papers, File 2313
275. Wingate's 'Complaint to the Sovereign', which runs to eighteen pages, and its eight-page annexure, are in TBL Wingate Palestine Papers, File 2313
276. Quoted in Wingate to Haining of 31 January 1939, TBL Wingate Palestine Papers, File 2313
277. Ibid
278. PRO WO 191/88, pp.8-9
279. PRO WO 32/9500, 'Operations in Palestine 1 Apr-30 July 1939', pp.1-4
280. PRO WO 201/169, 'Dispatches on operations in Palestine by Lt Gen Barker', Aug 1939-Sept 1940, p.3
281. R King Clark, Acting OC SNS to Brigade Major, 16 Infantry Brigade, of 29 July 1938, TBL Wingate Palestine Papers, File 2313; King Clark reported that in the two weeks since Dabburiya, not a gang was encountered, despite extensive patrolling, nor were there any instances of sabotage on the pipeline.
282. PRO WO32/9498, pp.2-5
283. Asprey, *War in the Shadows*, pp.425–427, 639, 1126–1127; A Geraghty, *Who Dares Wins: The Special Air Service 1950–1992* (London: Little, Brown, 1992), pp.187–188, 198–203, 325, 331, 333–334, 336–338
284. Segev, *One Palestine*, pp.430–431
285. Ibid, p.431
286. Haining to General Sir Henry Pownall, undated of December 1938, enclosing extracts from articles in German press accusing British troops of atrocities, LHCMA O'Connor Papers 3/2/8
287. Simonds, 'Pieces of War', pp.145–146
288. Hughes, 'Banality of Brutality', pp.336–339; Simonds, 'Pieces of War', p.148
289. O'Connor to Brigadier HC Wetherall of 22 January 1939, LHCMA O'Connor Papers, 3/4/19; Report by District Commissioner Buxton of 16 March 1939, LHCMA O'Connor Papers, 3/4/44; Hughes, 'Banality of Brutality', p.329
290. AF Perrett, Deputy Inspector General of Police, Northwest Frontier Province, to O'Connor of 18 October 1938, LHCMA O'Connor Papers 3/2/1; Simonds, 'Pieces of War', p.145
291. Segev, *One Palestine*, pp.414, 430
292. IWM Thomas Interview, pp.18–21
293. 'Annual Confidential Report by Officer's Immediate Commander, by Wingco AP Ritchie RAF, 18/11/38', TBL Wingate Palestine Papers, File 2313
294. Major OC Wingate, 'Chronology of events following a proposal to establish a special type of unit to deal with penetration of enemy units behind lines, either by tanks, by parachutists or air-borne troops', IWM Wingate Abyssinia Papers, Box I, p.1
295. Oren, 'Friend under Fire', pp.10–11
296. I have also had to turn down invitations from Zionist organisations who presume my interest in Wingate means I must share his political agenda.
297. RE Harkavy and SG Neuman, *Warfare in the Third World* (New York: Palgrave, 2001), pp.202–205
298. Ibid, pp.201–202, 230–232
299. Shlaim, *Iron Wall*, pp.598–599
300. Ibid, p.599
301. For the impact of such attitudes on Israeli politics, see C Coker, *Empires in Conflict: the Growing Rift between Europe and the United States* RUSI Whitehall Paper Number 58 (London: RUSI, 2003), p.31
302. Quoted, Segev, *One Palestine*, p.430
303. Slater, *Warrior Statesman*, p.4; Dayan, *My Life*, p.47; Bond, *Liddell Hart*, pp.247–248; D Ben-Gurion, 'Our Friend: What Wingate did For Us', *Jewish Observer and Middle East Review*, 27 September 1963, LHCMA Liddell Hart Papers, File 15/3/311, p.16; Bierman & Smith, *Fire in the Night*, p.390; Segev, *One Palestine*, p.470
304. Quoted, Allon, *Israeli Army*, p.10

305. Segev, *One Palestine*, p.379
306. For an excellent discussion of this see Handel, 'The evolution of Israeli Strategy', throughout
307. PRO WO106/2018A, Third Part; PRO WO191/70, p.30; PRO CO733/316/1-2; Townshend, *Britain's Civil Wars*, pp.85–87
308. PRO WO33/1436, Chapter ii, Para C (i)
309. Simson, *British Rule*, particularly pp.151–169
310. Minutes of a meeting between Macdonald and Haining at the Colonial Office on Sunday, 20 August 1939, in PRO CO733/389/18
311. Ben-Gurion, 'Britain's Contribution', p.14
312. O'Connor to Keith-Roach, undated of January 1939, LHCMA O'Connor Papers, 3/4/10
313. Simonds, 'Pieces of War', p.153

Chapter 5

1. Quoted in Shirreff, *Bare feet and Bandoliers*, p.212
2. Thesiger, *Life of My Choice*, p.320
3. D Rooney, 'Command and Leadership in the Chindit Campaigns', in G Sheffield (Editor) *Leadership & Command: the Anglo-American Military Experience since 1861* (London: Brassey's, 1996), pp.142-143; see also Mosley, *Gideon Goes to War*, especially pp.137-138, Shirreff, *Bare Feet and Bandoliers*, pp.150-153, 178, 285–286, 293; Thesiger, *Life of My Choice*, pp.433-434; the high regard in which Wingate is held in Ethiopia is clear from communication the author had with the son and granddaughter of the patriot leader, Ras Mesfin, in 2003-2008
4. Ibid, p.286
5. Rossetto, *Orde Wingate*, pp.70-72
6. Colonel OC Wingate, Commanding British & Ethiopian Troops Employed, 'Appreciation of the Ethiopian Campaign', GHQ ME – 18/6/41, several copies in IWM Wingate Papers, Appendix D, pp.3-5, 9-10
7. See Colonel OC Wingate DSO, 'The Ethiopian Campaign, August 1940 to June 1941', several copies in the IWM Wingate Abyssinia Papers, p.2, for Wingate's first use of this term.
8. Appendix A to Aide-Memoiré on the Co-Ordination of Subversive Activities in the Conquered Territories, in PRO HS8/259, MI(R), Strategic Appreciations, 1940
9. Brief for DMO for COS Meeting of 7/6/40, in PRO HS8/259, p.1
10. For German activities in Austria and the Sudetenland, see AJP Taylor, *The Origins of the Second World War* (London: Hamish Hamilton, 1961), pp.8, 51, 112–115, 176–179, 214. Although they suspected such an organisation existed, the Allies could not confirm the existence of *Brandenburg* until after the war; for what they suspected about German special forces in 1940, see FO Miksche, *Paratroops* (London: Faber & Faber, 1943), p.65; PRO WO208/2998, 'Enemy Air-Borne Forces', pp.10, 25; for an introduction in English, based on original German documents and interviews with former operatives, see J Lucas, *Kommando: German Special Forces of World War Two* (London: Cassell, 1985), especially pp.15–27, 43–52, 71–76
11. See GW Rendel, British Ambassador to Sofia, to Lord Halifax of 17 May 1940, and British Air Attaché, Bucharest to PBB Nichols of the Foreign Office of 13 May 1940, in PRO CAB 21/1181
12. Review of German Organisation, Auxiliary to Traditional Machinery, built up to assist in the achievement of German strategical and political aims, in PRO HS8/261, MI(R), Operational Reports, 1939-1940; JP(40) 253, Minutes of War Cabinet Joint Planning Sub-Committee of 17 June 1940, in PRO CAB84/15; 'Chronology of events following a proposal to establish a special type of unit to deal with penetration of enemy units behind lines, either by tanks, by parachutists or air-borne troops', Box I, p.1
13. War Cabinet Joint Planning Sub-Committee, Directive to Lieutenant-General Bourne, Report by the Joint Planning Sub-Committee submitting a draft directive, in PRO CAB84/15, Para.2, Draft Directive attached, Paras.1-2, 8
14. Draft Directive in Ibid, Paras.4, 10; JP(40) 363 of 31 July 1940, in PRO CAB84/17
15. Draft Directive, Para.4; 'Development of Parachute Troops', in PRO AIR2/7239, Para.1; JP(40) 421 of 14 June 1940, in PRO CAB84/15; Otway, *Airborne Forces*, p.21
16. 'Provision of Air-Borne Forces – Air Ministry Aspect', 25 December 1940, Para.1, Draft COS Paper – Policy as regards Air-Borne Forces, 19 January 1941, both in PRO AIR/7470; Otway, *Airborne Forces*, pp.22-23
17. Churchill, *Second World War*, pp.299–300; J Thompson, *War behind Enemy Lines*, pp.4, 5, 11

18. COS (40) of August 1940, Strategy, in PRO CAB84/17, Paras.3, 4–7
19. Ibid, Paras.19-24, Annex Paras.163, 173, 178; COS (40) of August 1940, Annex, Paras.203–205; COS (40) 27(O) of 25 November 1940, Subversive Activities in Relation to Strategy, in PRO CAB121/305, Para.6
20. COS (40) of August 1940, Paras.8, 19–24, 189, 191–193, Annex Paras.51-56, 196-198; 'Subversive Activities', Paras.4–5, 7–8; CP (40) 271 Home Defence (Security) Executive Special Operations Executive – Memorandum by the Lord President of the Council, 19 July 1940 Paras.a-d, f, g in PRO CAB 121/305
21. COS (40) August 1940, Paras.196–199
22. Ibid, Para.197
23. Ibid, Para.198
24. MIR War Office, Report on the Organisation within the War Office for the conduct of para-military activities, 25 August 1940 in PRO HS8/260, MI(R) Progress Reports 1939-1940, p.1
25. Colonel Holland to Brigadier Wyndham (undated) in PRO HS8/258 MI(R), Functions and Organisation, 1940, details policy.
26. 'Report on Organisation', p.1
27. Quoted, Mackenzie, *SOE*, pp.8-9
28. GS (Research) – Report for DCIGS No.8, Investigation of the possibilities of Guerrilla Activities, 1 June 1939, in PRO HS8/260, p.1
29. Ibid, pp.1–2; Holland's reading list is in PRO HS8/261
30. Report No.8, pp.1-2
31. Ibid, pp.4, 6-7; Mackenzie, *SOE*, pp.44–46
32. Appendix C to DMO Briefing for 7/6/40, Para.1
33. DMO Briefing for 7 June 1940, p.5; JP(40) 363, Minutes of War Cabinet Joint Planning Committee Meeting of 31 July 1940, in PRO CAB84/17; Mackenzie, *Secret History of SOE*, pp.53–54
34. Memo from Holland to MI1 of 6 April 1940, and Appendix I of 'Report on Organisation', both in PRO HS8/260; Mackenzie, *Secret History of SOE*, pp.52–54
35. Calvert, *Fighting Mad*, pp.45–46
36. Ibid, pp.53–58; Calvert, *Prisoners of Hope*, pp.10–12; Mackenzie, *SOE*, p.46; DMO Briefing of 7 June 1940, Para.2
37. Calvert, *Fighting Mad*, pp.46–52
38. Appendix C to DMO Briefing of for 7 June 1940, Paras.1–2
39. Seaman, 'A new instrument of war', pp.10–11
40. Lieutenant Colonel C McV Gubbins, *The Art of Guerrilla Warfare* (London: MI(R) 1939)
41. 'Appreciation of the Possibilities of Revolt In Certain Specified Countries by March 1941' in PRO HS8/259, pp.1-2; Dodds-Parker interview of 25/8/2004
42. Dodds-Parker Interview of 28/8/2004
43. Gubbins, *Art of Guerrilla Warfare*, pp.1-3
44. Ibid, p.3
45. Ibid, p.1
46. Ibid, p.4
47. Ibid, pp.6–7
48. Ibid, p.7
49. Ibid, p.7
50. Ibid, pp.9, 16–17
51. 'An Appreciation of the Capabilities and Composition of a small force operating behind the enemy lines in the offensive', 7 June 1940, in PRO HS8/259, p.1
52. Ibid, p.1
53. Ibid, pp.1-2
54. Ibid, p.2
55. Ibid, pp.3–4
56. Lias, pp.1–4
57. 'Report on para-military activities', p.5; Minute Sheet No.2, Register No. MIR No.309/40, in PRO HS8/258; CinC Middle East [Wavell] to War Office of 4 June 1941 and 16 June 1941, both in PRO HS3/146
58. Appendix G to 'Report on Para-Military Activities'; Briefing for DMO for COS Meeting of 7 June 1940

59. Bidwell & Graham, *Fire Power*, p.186; BJ Bond, *British Military Policy Between the Wars* (Oxford: OUP 1980), pp.197-8, 207-8, 257-8, 202-63
60. Bond, *British Military Policy*, pp.261-4
61. Forty, *British Army Handbook*, p.75; PRO WO365/105, Air Defence of Great Britain: Approximate Strengths, 1939-1940
62. Memo AAC/2/1000/G, in PRO WO199/1565, Air Defence of Great Britain, Organisation, September 1936-January 1940
63. PRO WO106/2795A, Anti-Aircraft Command, Provisional Mobilisation Instructions, August 1939, pp.201
64. Ibid, p.26; Captain OC Wingate DSO RA, 'Organisation of Light AA Defences in ADGB in Time of War', 18 November 1939, IWM Wingate Abyssinia Papers, Box. I, pp.2-3; Memo AAC/2/693/G in PRO WO199/1565; Forty, *British Army Handbook*, p.4
65. PRO WO106/2795A, pp.26-27
66. Captain OC Wingate, undated Draft Paper on Light Anti-Aircraft Artillery Defences, IWM Wingate Abyssinia Papers, Box. I, pp.2-3
67. Memorandum No.8/56/71/84 by Captain OC Wingate for Brigadier, Commander 56th Light AA Bde, RA, of 7 November 1939 – Training of Newly Raised Light AA Troops, 1pp, IWM Wingate Abyssinia Papers, Box I; Wingate's Draft LAA Defences Paper, p.3
68. Ibid, pp.3-4
69. Ibid, pp.3-4
70. Ibid, p.8
71. Wingate's Paper of 18 November 1939, p.8
72. See Ibid, p.8; quotation from Captain OC Wingate, 'The Theory of Siting LAA Artillery Defences', 1 April 1940, Box I, pp.3-4
73. Handwritten P/S on final page of 'Theory of Siting'
74. Circular WO Memo 79/HD, in PRO WO199/1565
75. Circular WO Memo 79/WE/106 (AG1 (PA)), 9 October 1939, in PRO WO199/1565
76. Circular WO Memo 3/General/474 (AA2 (a)) of 9 December 1939; Notes on the Agenda for the 40th Meeting of the War Office AA Standing Committee, 25.1.1940, both in PRO WO199/1565
77. Ibid, p.216
78. Appreciation by Captain OC Wingate DSO RA at RA Drill Hall, Sidcup, Kent, 7 October 1939, Box I
79. See Sykes, *Orde Wingate*, pp.84, 481, 538
80. Newspaper clipping, date and paper unrecorded, in PRO CO733/384/9
81. Sykes, *Orde Wingate*, pp.222-3
82. Bierman & Smith, *Fire in the Night*, pp.139-40; Sykes, *Orde Wingate*, p.227
83. D Ben-Gurion, 'Ironside Supports Jewish Army', *Jewish Observer and Middle East Review* November 15 1963, copy in LHCMA Liddell Hart Papers File LH15/5/311 pp.18-19
84. Ibid, p.19
85. Ibid, pp.19-20
86. Ibid, p.20
87. Appendix C to Brief for DMO for COS Meeting of 7.6.40, Para.8; Review of German Organisation, Auxiliary to traditional machinery, built up to assist in the achievement of German strategical and political aims, in PRO HS8/261 Covert Operations, 1939–42; R Thurlow, 'The Evolution of the Mythical British Fifth Column, 1939–46', *Twentieth Century British History*, Volume 10 Number 4, 1999, pp.481–489
88. Wingate, 'Chronology', p.1
89. Ibid, p.1
90. Ibid, p.1; Royle, *Orde Wingate*, pp.165-166
91. 'Chronology', p.1
92. Ibid, p.1
93. Ibid, p.2, on which references to specific regiments are crossed out, but still legible, one reference clearly being to the al Bassa incident
94. Alanbrooke's Diary Entries of 13 and 17 February 1941, in A Danchev and D Todman (editors) *War Diaries, 1939-1945* (London: Weidenfeld & Nicholson 2001), pp.140-1
95. 'Chronology', p.2
96. Ironside to Wingate of 9 June 1940, Box I

97. 'Chronology', p.2
98. Ibid, p.2
99. Thurlow, 'Fifth Column', pp.489–491
100. Quoted, Royle, *Orde Wingate*, p.166
101. Wavell, *Soldier*, p.62
102. Sykes, *Orde Wingate*, p.230
103. Ibid, p.231; Bierman & Smith, *Fire in the Night*, p.141
104. Sykes, *Orde Wingate*, pp.231-232
105. The original document does not appear to be available in the public domain, but Sir Douglas Dodds-Parker, who had a sighting of it, says it was signed by Brigadier Gerald Templer: interview with the author of 24 August 2004; Sykes, *Orde Wingate*, p.232; Bierman & Smith, *Fire in the Night*, p.142
106. See Wavell's Sitrep of 24 September 1940, in PRO WO193/956
107. Burchett, *Wingate's Phantom Army*, p.47
108. Ibid, p.48
109. Mosley, *Gideon Goes to War*, pp.97-110
110. Sykes, *Orde Wingate*, pp.236-237
111. Ibid, pp.240-251; Royle, *Orde Wingate*, pp.178-202
112. A Mockler, *Haile Selassie's War: The Italian-Ethiopian Campaign, 1935-41* (New York: Random House 1984) especially p.285
113. Shirreff, *Bare Feet and Bandoliers*, pp.22-28, 68
114. Foot, *SOE*, pp.251-264
115. Professor HG Marcus, 'Ethiopian Insurgency against the Italians, 1936-1941', unpublished paper, 1997, pp.7-8, 11-12
116. 'Extent of MIR Activities in the Past, At Present, and Possibilities for the Future' in PRO HS8/258, pp.6-7; Cipher Telegram No.341 to Sir M Lampson (Cairo) Foreign Office 26th April 1939, in PRO CO323/1670/4, Abyssinia: coordination of arrangements to foster rebellion, 1939; Dodds-Parker interview, 25/8/2005
117. Whalley to ED Cavendish-Bentinck of 21 February 1939, in PRO FO371/23377
118. Major Mallaby, WO, to Cavendish-Bentinck of 27 April 1939, PRO FO371/23377
119. MI(R) Report No.2: Progress Up To date and Action if War Breaks Out Early, in PRO HS8/260, pp.16-17; Major General Arthur Smith to HQ RAF Middle East of 10 April 1940, in PRO WO201/2677
120. Held in PRO WO201/2677
121. Shirreff, *Bare Feet and Bandoliers*, pp.4-7. Sandford's home in Charlotteville, Guildford, is still called 'Sandford House'
122. Wavell to Platt of 29 September 1939, in PRO WO201/2677
123. List in PRO WO201/2677, Paras. 2, 4; Report by Colonel Elphinston, G(R), on visit to Khartoum, PRO WO201/2677, Para.4; Cablegram from Khartoum to DMI of 25 May 1939, in PRO WO201/2677; D Dodds-Parker, *Setting Europe Ablaze: An Account of Ungentlemanly Warfare* (London: Springwood 1983) p.57
124. Smith to Platt of 28 September 1939, in PRO WO201/2677, Para.2
125. Ibid, Para.2
126. Ibid, Paras.2, 5-6
127. Ibid, Paras. 2, 7
128. Ibid, Para.2
129. General AP Wavell's Dispatch on East African Operations, in PRO CAB120/471, p.1; *OHM1*, pp.391-392
130. Shirreff, *Bare Feet and Bandoliers*, pp.23-26
131. Ibid, pp.26-28; Dodds-Parker, *Setting Europe Ablaze*, p.57
132. GHQ Middle East Operation Instruction No.1 – 10/6/1940 in PRO HS8/261, Para.2
133. Ibid, Para.4
134. Ibid, Para.9
135. Appendix B to Operational Instruction No.1, Paras.1-2
136. Ibid, Para.4
137. Quoted, Shirreff, *Bare Feet and Bandoliers*, p.30
138. Major EA Chapman-Andrews, 'Abyssinia', in PRO FO371/24639, pp.1-2; Attachment to Sandford's Dispatch of 20 November 1940, in PRO CAB106/934; *OHM1*, p.403

139. Chapman-Andrews, 'Abyssinia', p.3
140. See, for example, Sir Ernest Thompson's internal memorandum of 29 August 1940, in PRO FO371/24635, or PRO CAB106/356, pp.8-9, 12 or Haile Selassie's telegram to Churchill of 23 August 1940, intercepted by the FO and now in PRO FO371/24635
141. Wavell, 'East African Operations', pp.1-2
142. *OHM1*, p.392
143. Ibid, p.404
144. 'Record of Meeting held at the Palace, Khartoum, on the 29th October 1940 – The Abyssinian Revolt', in PRO FO371/24639, pp.1-2
145. Ibid, p.7
146. Ibid, p.7
147. GHQ ME Operational Order No.1, Para.10
148. Amery, *Empire at Bay*, p.603
149. Amery to Haining of 24 August 1940, in Churchill Archives Amery Papers File AMEL 2/1/31
150. Haining to Amery of 24 August 1940, in Churchill Archives Amery Papers File AMEL 2/1/31
151. Wavell, *Good Soldier*, p.62
152. Platt to Haile Selassie of 10 November 1940, Box I
153. Dodds-Parker interview of 25/8/2005
154. Colonel OC Wingate DSO, 'The Ethiopian Campaign August 1940 to June 1941', p.13. Several copies held in the IWM Wingate Abyssinia Papers.
155. Ibid, p.5
156. Ibid, p.5
157. Ibid, p.5
158. Ibid, p.5
159. Thesiger, *Life of My Choice*, pp.318–320
160. Wingate, 'Ethiopian Campaign', p.5
161. Wingate, 'Appreciation', Appendix D, p.1
162. Chapman-Andrews, 'Abyssinia'
163. Wingate, 'Ethiopian Campaign', p.5
164. Wingate, 'Appreciation', Appendix D, pp.1–2
165. Wingate, 'Ethiopian Campaign', pp.5-6; 'Appreciation', p.3; Sandford's Dispatch of 1 December 1940, in PRO CAB106/3050, Paras.9-11
166. Sandford's Dispatch of 1/12/40, Para.10
167. Colonel DA Sandford, 'Notes on Plans for Abyssinian Campaign', 10 November 1940, in PRO CAB106/3050
168. Shirreff, *Bare Feet and Bandoliers*, pp.61–62; Thesiger, *Life of My Choice*, p.328
169. Wingate, 'Ethiopian Campaign', p.6
170. Ibid, p.6
171. Wingate, 'Appreciation', Appendix D, p.6
172. Wingate, 'Ethiopian Campaign', p.7
173. Ibid, p.7
174. Ibid, p.7
175. Shirreff, *Bare Feet and Bandoliers*, pp.61–62; Thesiger, *Life of My Choice*, p.328
176. Wingate, 'Lectures', p.4
177. Ibid, p.4
178. Wingate, 'Appreciation', pp.9-10
179. Wingate, 'Ethiopian Campaign', p.7
180. Thesiger fought at Gallabat with the SDF, *Life of My Choice*, pp.315-318; see also Shirreff, *Bare Feet and Bandoliers*, pp.52-53; Field Marshal Sir W Slim KG GCB GCMG GCVO GBE DSO MC, *Unofficial History* (London: Cassell 1959), pp.125–148
181. Wavell, 'East African Operations', p.2
182. Ibid, p.2
183. Ibid, p.2
184. *OHM1*, pp.397-399, 407-408
185. PRO WO106/2290, pp.40-42; PRO WO201/297, p.3
186. Wingate, 'Ethiopian Campaign', p.9
187. PRO WO201/297, p.3
188. Wingate's 'Notes on Sandford's Dispatches', 17 November 1940, Box II, Para.5

189. Undated letter from Wingate to Platt in Box II
190. Minutes of a Conference held at HQ Tps in the Sudan, 12 February 1941, Box I, Paras. 2, 3(a)-(e); Wingate, 'Ethiopian Campaign', pp.9–10; Shirreff, *Bare Feet and Bandoliers*, p.88
191. Wingate, 'Appreciation', pp.9–10
192. Ibid, p.10
193. Wingate quoted in PRO WO201/308, 'Abyssinia: Guerrilla Warfare in the Gojjam by WAB Harris MC', p.28
194. Ibid, pp.28–29; PRO WO201/297, 'Abyssinian and Eritrea: Operational Dispatch by Lt. Gen. Sir W. Platt', pp.10–11
195. PRO WO291/297, p.11
196. Simonds to Wingate of 12/2/41, Box II
197. PRO WO178/36, 'War Diary, 101 Mission, Northern Section', compiled by Major AWD Bentinck, entries of 15 and 19 September 1940, 24 and 25 November 1940; see also Report by Major Neville, commanding Mission 107 in southern Ethiopia, in PRO WO201/91
198. Boustead to Wingate of 5 and 6 March 1941, both in Box I of the IWM Wingate Abyssinia Papers; Wingate to Sandford of 7 March 1941, in Box II; Avram Akavia's Diary Entry of 6 March 1941, in PRO WO217/37; Wavell's Dispatch of 9 March 1941, in PRO WO106/2088; Wingate, 'Ethiopian Campaign', p.10; Shirreff, *Bare Feet and Bandoliers*, pp.91, 109–111; Thesiger, *Life of My Choice*, p.335
199. PRO WO291/297, p.11; PRO WO201/308, pp.44-47; Simonds to Wingate of 12/2/41; Thesiger, *Life of My Choice*, p.331; PRO CAB106/952, pp.62-63, 93–94
200. Dodds-Parker interview of 25/8/2004
201. Wingate to Lieutenant Colonel Terence Airey of 4 April 1941, IWM Wingate Abyssinia Papers, Box II; Simonds to Wingate of 12/2/41
202. Thesiger to Wingate of 7 April 1941; Boustead to Wingate of 9 April 1941, both in IWM Wingate Abyssinia Papers, Box I; Thesiger, *Life of My Choice*, p.339
203. Wingate, 'Ethiopian Campaign', p.9; undated from Wingate to Platt in Box II; Minutes of a Conference held at HQ Troops in the Sudan, 12 February 1941, Box II, Paras.2–3
204. Wingate to G(R) of 7 February 1941, Box II
205. Wingate to Boustead of 8/2/41
206. Wingate, 'Appreciation', p.8
207. Green to Wingate of 14 December 1940, Box II
208. For example, Simonds to Wingate of 12/2/41, Box II
209. Wingate to Sandford of 9 March 1941, Box II, Para.3
210. Sandford to Wingate of 18 March 1941, Para.5, Box.II
211. Colonel OC Wingate, 'Notes for Lt.Col. Airey, Dambatcha, 11 March 1941', Box II, Para.4; Wingate, 'Appreciation', Appendix A, p.4, 'Ethiopian Campaign', p.10; Edmund Stevens, 'Writer on the Storm: Memoirs of a Correspondent at War', unpublished manuscript in IWM Department of Documents, pp.65-66
212. Wingate to Sandford of 7 March 1941, Box II; Wingate, 'Ethiopian Campaign', p.10; Wavell's Dispatch of 9 March 1941, Folio 385 of PRO WO106/2088; PRO WO201/297; Thesiger, *Life of My Choice*, pp.335–336, the latter being the most honest account of the battle from an eyewitness
213. Wingate, 'Appreciation', p.3
214. Wingate, 'Ethiopian Campaign', p.10
215. Gideon Force Operational Order No.2, 13 March 1941, Box II
216. Wingate to Airey of 31 March 1941, Box II
217. Communiqué, Commander, British and Ethiopian Forces, GOJJAM, calling DEBRA MARKOS, 30 March '41, Box II
218. Dodds-Parker, *Setting Europe Ablaze*, p.63, and interview of 25/8/2004
219. Commander, British and Ethiopian Forces, to the Commander, Italian Forces between Addis Derra and Agibar, 19 May 1941, Box II
220. Shirreff, *Bare Feet and Bandoliers*, p.206
221. Report on Operations at Debra Tabor – HQ Frontier Battalion, 29th May 1941, Box II, Paras.11-13; Thesiger, *Life of My Choice*, p.348
222. CinC ME to WO of 12/4/41, PRO WO193/379
223. Wingate, 'Appreciation', p.4
224. Ibid, p.4
225. Ibid, pp.4–5

226. Ibid, pp.5–6
227. Urban, *Big Boy's Rules*, pp.30–32
228. Galula, *Counterinsurgency Warfare*, p.53
229. TE Lawrence, entry on 'Guerrilla Warfare' reproduced in Gerard Chaliand (Editor) *The Art of War in World History* (Berkeley, CA: University of California Press 1994) p.890; Colonel OC Wingate, Commanding British and Ethiopian Troops Employed, 'Appreciation of the Ethiopian Campaign GHQ ME 18/6/41, several copies held in the Wingate Papers at the Imperial War Museum, pp.5–6
230. Kitson, *Low Intensity Operations*, pp.85–87
231. Kilcullen, *Accidental Guerrilla*, pp.39–40; Tim Pat Coogan, *The IRA* (London: HarperCollins 1995), p.237
232. 'Afghan Taliban says rehearsed attack for two months', *Reuters*, 16 April 2012, http://www.reuters.com/article/2012/04/16/us-afghan-taliban-plan-idUSBRE83F0LX20120416, accessed 17 April 2012
233. Mao Tse-Tung, *On Guerrilla Warfare* (New York; Praeger 1962), pp.79, 82–85; Guevara, *Guerrilla Warfare*, pp.60–62, 80–83 Che's 'M-16' shotgun-mortar would probably be more dangerous to the user, and anyone within fifteen feet, than the enemy, particularly if there was any overhead cover.
234. In the 1960s and 70s, it was taken for granted that the USSR was fomenting insurgency in Western Europe; see Kitson, *Low Intensity Operations*, pp.43–48
235. Ibid, pp.246–262, 443–449; Robert Asprey, *War in the Shadows* (London: Little, Brown 1994), pp.1062–1121
236. Steve Coll, *Ghost Wars: The Secret History of the CIA, Afghanistan and bin Laden, from the Soviet Invasion to September 10, 2001* (London: Penguin 2004), pp.92–93, 97–100; George Friedman, *America's Secret War: Inside the Hidden Worldwide Struggle between the United States and its Enemies* (London: Little, Brown 2004), pp.10–15; For an inside view from the ISI, see Mohammad Yousaf and Mark Adkin, *The Battle for Afghanistan* (London: Pen & Sword 2007)
237. Friedman, *America's Secret War*, pp.249–250, 301–302; Richard A Clarke, *Against All Enemies: Inside America's War on Terror* (London: Free Press 2004), pp.101–104; Ed Blanche, 'Iran's Foreign Legion', *The Middle East*, Issue 449, December 2013, pp.12–16
238. Ibid, p.6
239. Ibid, p.7
240. Ibid, pp.7, 10
241. Ibid, pp.6–7, 13–14; see also Wingate, 'Ethiopian Campaign', pp.4–5
242. Wingate, 'Appreciation', p.6
243. Lawrence, 'Evolution of a Revolt', p.69, 'Guerrilla Warfare', p.890; Wingate, 'Ethiopian Campaign', p.1; 'Notes Relating to Possible Employment', Box II
244. For instance, see Galula's description of the Maoist 'cause' in *Counterinsurgency Warfare; Theory and Practice* (New York and London: Praeger 1964), pp.29–30 while Kitson details the development of subversion in Portuguese Guinea in the 1950s in *Low Intensity Operations: Subversion, Insurgency and Peacekeeping* (London: Faber & Faber 1971), pp.35–37
245. Galula, *Counterinsurgency Warfare*, pp.15–16
246. Wingate, 'Ethiopian Campaign', pp.13–14
247. Lawrence, *Seven Pillars*, pp.200–202
248. Wingate, 'Ethiopian Campaign', pp.14–15
249. Ibid, p.14
250. Ibid, pp.14–15
251. Richard A Clarke, *Against all Enemies: Inside America's War on Terror* (London: Free Press, 2003), pp.47–54; Friedman, *America's Secret War*, pp.11–17
252. Clarke, *Against all Enemies*, pp.52–53, 59, 70, 154; Friedman, *America's Secret War*, pp25–32
253. Clarke, *Against all Enemies*, pp.274–277; Friedman, *America's Secret War*, pp.151–155, 160–165; Woodward, *Bush at War*, pp.251–254, 260, 267, 275, 282
254. Murray and Scales, *Iraq War*, pp.185–195
255. Dodds-Parker, *Setting Europe Ablaze*, p.67
256. Ibid, pp.72–73; PRO HS7/111, SOE Oriental Mission, March 1941–May 1942, pp.30–31
257. Mackenzie, *Secret History of SOE*, pp.603–606 The ISI seems to have continued the ethos and organisation of the Jedburghs.

Notes   231

Chapter 6
NOTE: References to Boxes I, II, III, IV and V in this chapter's notes and the next refer to the five boxes of Wingate's and Tulloch's Chindit Papers, held at the Department of Documents of the Imperial War Museum
1. Fergusson, *Beyond the Chindwin*, p.20
2. Calvert, *Slim*, p.55
3. C Cruickshank, *SOE in the Far East* (Oxford: OUP 1983), pp.163–167, footnote on pp.169–170
4. L Allen, *Burma: The Longest War* (London: JM Dent 1984), pp.4–7; JRM Butler, *History of the Second World War: Grand Strategy, Volume II* [hereafter *OHGS2*] (London: HMSO 1957), pp.328–330
5. 'Note on 204 Military Mission', 7 January 1942, in PRO WO106/2654, p.4; Major General S Woodburn Kirby, *The Official History of the War against Japan, Volume II* [hereafter *OH2*] (London: HMSO 1958), pp.11, 16–18, 20–21
6. CinC FE to WO of 13 April 1941, in PRO CAB121/137
7. Ibid; Calvert, *Fighting Mad*, pp.53–55
8. 'Note on 204', p.4
9. CinC FE to WO of 13 August 1941, in PRO WO106/2629
10. WO to CinC FE of 9 September 1941, in PRO WO106/2629
11. Ibid
12. Calvert, *Fighting Mad*, pp.55–56
13. 'Note on 204', p.4
14. Ibid, p.1, and accompanying map
15. PRO HS7/111, Pt I, pp.1–3, 17–19, 26–27; Cruickshank, *SOE in the Far East*, pp.16, 61–62, 83, 163–164
16. Memorandum by SOE on their Proposed Organisation in India and the Far East, in PRO HS1/202, Para.15; Note by Sir Frank Nelson in PRO CAB121/317; Note on GHQ FE39/2 and draft telegram from MEW to CinC FE, in PRO CAB121/317
17. PRO WO106/2634, Appreciation of the Situation in Burma by General Staff, India on 15th December 1941, Paras.12, 16–18
18. Mountbatten, *Report*, Section A, Para.44
19. Slim, *Defeat into Victory*, p.199; Undated letter from Stilwell to his wife, in *Stilwell Diaries*, p.194
20. Admiral the Earl Mountbatten of Burma GCVO KCB DSO ADC, 'The Strategy of the South-East Asia Campaign', *RUSI Journal*, November 1946, p.471
21. Mountbatten, *Report*, p.246
22. CinC India to CIGS of 26 March 1943, in PRO WO106/3807, Para.6; Allen, *Burma*, pp.7–24; C Bayly and T Harper, *Forgotten Armies: Britain's Asian Empire and the War With Japan* (London: Allen Lane 2004), pp.9–11, 29, 82, 98, 164, 170, 244–252; JRM Calvert, *Slim* (Pan 1973) p.48; *OH2*, pp.245–248
23. PRO HS7/111, pp.21–22; Cruickshank, *SOE in the Far East*, pp.167–168
24. For instance, see PRO WO106/2639, 'Some Points from Burma Campaign 1941/2'; Governor of Burma to Secretary of State for Burma of 8 March 1942, in PRO WO 106/2662; Slim, *Defeat into Victory*, pp.15–16, 39, 116; Stilwell's diary entry of 12 March 1942, in General JW Stilwell, *The Stilwell Papers*, edited by TH White (New York: Da Capo 1973), p.60
25. *Notes from the Theatres of War No.8 – The Far East, December 1941 – May 1942*, in PRO WO208/3108, p.5
26. *OH2*, pp.8, 439
27. Slim, *Defeat into Victory*, pp.39, 44, 46, 52, 56, 61–63
28. Cruickshank, *SOE in the Far East*, p.68
29. *Notes from Theatres of War No.17 – Far East, April-November 1943 [NTW 17]*, in PRO WO208/3108, pp.3–4
30. *Notes from Theatres of War No.12 – SW Pacific, August 1942-February 1943 [NTW 12]*, in PRO WO208/3108, pp.3–4
31. 'Some points from Burma Campaign, 1941/42' in PRO WO106/2639, Para.B
32. Slim, *Defeat into Victory*, p.118
33. *Notes from Theatres of War No.15, SW Pacific January-March 1943 [NTW15]* in PRO WO208/3108, pp.3–4; Fergusson, *Wild Green Earth*, p.204
34. Slim, *Defeat into Victory*, p.119

35. *NTW8*, p.5
36. Slim, *Defeat into Victory*, p.119
37. CinC India to GOC Burma of 6 April 1942, in PRO WO106/2663; *NTW5*, p.12; Slim, *Defeat into Victory*, pp.4–7, 41–42
38. *NTW5*, p.12; 'Some Points', Para.B; *NTW8*, p.18, gives credence to the 'handful of rice' claim
39. 'Aquila', 'Air Transport on the Burma Front', *RUSI Journal*, May 1945, p.203
40. Stilwell's diary entries of 15 and 19 April 1942, *Stilwell Diaries*, pp.85, 89
41. Quoted, Mosley, *Gideon goes to War*, p.185
42. e.g. Fergusson, *Wild Green Earth*, pp.206, 209
43. Slim, *Defeat into Victory*, pp.142–143, 181, 186–187
44. *OH2*, p.382
45. Combined Chiefs of Staff Memorandum for Information No.25 – Japanese Intentions, 8 November 1942, in PRO CAB122/163, Appendix A Para.B; SICTEL No.11 from War Cabinet Offices, 24 June 1943, in PRO CAB122/163, Para.1
46. 'Note by PM and Minister of Defence', Pt.IV, Para.3
47. Churchill to Wavell of 22/1/42
48. *OH2*, pp.379, 387; *OH3*, pp.10–11; CF Romanus and R Sutherland, *The United States Army in World War II: China-Burma-India Theater, Stilwell's Mission to China*, (Washington DC: Department of the Army 1953) pp.12–13, 20–21, 23, 56–57, 323–324, 357–358
49. D Clayton James, 'American and Japanese Strategies in the Pacific War', in P Paret (Editor) *Makers of Modern Strategy from Machiavelli to the Nuclear Age* (Oxford: OUP 1994) pp.709, 721
50. *OH2*, pp.380, 421–424
51. WO to CinC India of 31 March 1942, in PRO WO106/3771; WJ Koenig, *Over the Hump: Airlift to China* (London: Pan 1972); Romanus and Sutherland, *Stilwell's Mission to China*, pp.163–167
52. The 'Peanut's' greed, cronyism and fantasizing are the dominant themes of Stilwell's diaries; the Americans wanted to tie Burma and India into a single command to bind him to the defence of Southeast Asia, see British Joint Staff Mission to Washington to WO of 1 January 1942, in PRO WO106/2662 ; SICTEL No.11, Para.5
53. *OH2*, pp.292–293, 295–297, 305–306
54. Records of Chiefs of Staff (India) Meetings of May 1942– February 1943, in PRO WO106/6110; *OH2*, pp.235–237, 297–298, 369–370, 419–423; Admiral the Earl Mountbatten of Burma GCVO KCB DSO ADC, 'The Strategy of the South-East Asia Campaign', *RUSI Journal*, November 1946, pp.26–30
55. Callwell, *Small Wars*, pp.348–373
56. *MTP52*, pp.68–70
57. Ibid, pp.3–4
58. Ibid, pp.4–5
59. Ibid, pp.4–5, 20, 33–34
60. Ibid, pp.19, 35–38
61. Ibid, pp.7, 19–20, 35–38, 51–52
62. Ibid, pp.20–22
63. Ibid, pp.8–10
64. Ibid, p.23
65. Ibid, pp.24–26
66. *Notes from Theatres of War No.10 – Cyrenaica and Western Desert January/June 1942 [NTW10]* (London: HMSO 1942), pp.9, 13–14; 'Lessons from Operations 14 Sept 41 – 21 Aug 1942, Fixed Defences and the Defensive Battle – Deductions from the Present War' in PRO WO201/538; Barnett, *Desert Generals*, pp.139–141; French, *Raising Churchill's Army*, pp.219–220; Marston, *Phoenix from the Ashes*, pp.107–108
67. Marston, *Phoenix from the Ashes*, pp.107–108
68. Ibid, p.108
69. *MTP52*, pp.6–7; Reginald Dorman-Smith, the Governor of Burma, felt Wingate was mistaken not to include former district commissioners in his LRP force; see R Dorman-Smith to Amery of 3 June 1943, Churchill Archives Amery Papers AMEL 2/3/21
70. Brooke to Amery of 12 January 1942, Churchill Archives Amery Papers, AMEL 2/1/31; Sir Hastings Ismay to Harold Laski of 13 February 1942, IWM Wingate Chindit Papers, Box I, explains why Wingate was sent to Burma; Alanbrooke's Diary Entry of 4 August 1943, *Alanbrooke*

Diaries, p.436; Wavell, *Good Soldier*, p.64; Colonel OC Wingate, 'Record of an attempt to organise long range penetration in Burma during April 1942', Box I, p.1; *OH2*, p.243
71. PRO CAB106/46, 'Draft Narrative of Operations of 77th Indian Infantry Brigade ("The Chindits") commanded by Brigadier OC Wingate, Burma 1943 Feb-June', p.4
72. Wingate, 'Record', p.1; Colonel OC Wingate, 'Appreciation of chances of forming long range penetration groups in Burma by Colonel OC Wingate at Maymyo on 2/4/42', Box I, p.6
73. See Stilwell's diary entries of 11 and 12 March 1942, *Stillwell Diaries*, pp.59–60
74. Calvert, *Fighting Mad*, pp.67–75 and *Prisoners of Hope*, pp.80–81
75. 'Mission 204', p.1
76. Colonel OC Wingate, 'Notes on Penetration Warfare – Burma Command', Box I, p.1
77. Wingate, 'Notes', p.2
78. Ibid, pp.2–4; Accounts of Japanese atrocities are myriad – for a reliable sample, see Slim, *Defeat into Victory*, pp.46, 73, 240, 531; Slim made no secret of using hatred of the Japanese as a means of building British morale.
79. Wingate, 'Notes', pp.2–4
80. See the previous chapter and Wingate's correspondence files in the IWM Wingate Abyssinia Papers
81. See Thomas Parrish (editor), *The Encyclopedia of World War II* (London: Secker & Warburg 1978), p.245, for a brief introduction to the Goumiers, Moroccan Berber tribesmen employed by the French on guerrilla operations, using traditional tribal weaponry and tactics.
82. Wingate, 'Notes', p.5
83. Wingate, 'Notes', p.5
84. Ibid, pp.6–9
85. Ibid, p.9
86. Wingate, 'Record', pp.1–2; 'Appreciation 2/4/42', pp.1–2; for a more flattering account, see Slim, *Defeat into Victory*, pp.44–46
87. Wingate, 'Record', p.2
88. Calvert, *Slim*, p.65. Slim was also kinder about Calvert than Calvert was about him, among other things offering him help on a number of occasions after his expulsion from the British Army.
89. Wingate, 'Appreciation 2/4/42', p.2
90. Ibid, p.2
91. Ibid, pp.5–6
92. Box 1, Folio 1, Letter No.25, from Iris Appleton (a friend of Lorna Wingate) to her parents of 30 March 1942 describes Wingate's arrival at Maymyo and the general situation in Burma, including the large-scale Burmese cooperation with the Japanese; see also Vice Admiral the Earl Mountbatten of Burma KG PC GCSI GCIE GCVO KCB, DSO, *Report to the Combined Chiefs of Staff by the Supreme Allied Commander South-East Asia, 1943–45* (London: HMSO 1951), Part 'C' Paras.10, 55–56, 63; '"OH2"', p.6; Calvert, *Prisoners*, p.297; Tulloch, *Wingate*, p.61. The comment by Alexander is from Chapter VIII, Paragraph 2 of the manuscript of a LRP Training Pamphlet referred to hereafter as 'LRP Pamphlet'.
93. Mr FJ Hill, muleteer in 16 Brigade HQ, interview with the author, 13 June 2000.
94. Ibid, pp.68–69; Asprey, *War in the Shadows*, pp.433–434; Bayly & Harper, *Forgotten Armies*, pp.205–206
95. Cruickshank, *SOE in the Far East*, pp.69–70
96. *OH2*, p.176; Tulloch, *Wingate*, p.60; *Notes from Theatres of War No.15, South-West Pacific January-March 1943 [NTW15]* (London: HMSO 1943), pp.3–4
97. Tulloch, *Wingate*, pp.99, 183
98. Slim, *Defeat into Victory*, p.18
99. Wingate's notebook is held in Box I; amongst Wingate's musings are 'Bushido = Samurai' and, the line below 'Never yet been successful soldier without code.' Both p.50; see also an interview with Wingate in the Report 'Brigadier Wingate's Expedition into Burma', Reuter's New Delhi, 20 May 1943: 'The Japanese are hardworking and methodical, but lacking in imagination. They have a stereotyped way of dealing with situations, rather like the Germans, and they can be caught out…' and in a BBC Telediphone recording from New Delhi of 22 May 1943: 'Although incapable of the sombre and humourless self-immolation of the Japanese, the British soldier can, nevertheless, beat him on his own chosen ground, provided he gets scope for his greater intellectual power and stronger and saner character.' Both from Box I. The quotation is from 'LRP Pamphlet', Chapter XV, Para 2(a)

100. B Tuchman, *Stilwell and the American Experience in China 1911-1945* (London: Macmillan 1970), pp.213-214
101. Slim, *Defeat into Victory*, pp.14-15
102. PRO WO106/4837, *Military Training Publication (Australia) No.23 – Jungle Warfare*, Draft Copy, p.29
103. Brigadier OC Wingate DSO, 'Intruder Mission', *War*, No.48, 10 July 1943, pp.7-8
104. Ibid, p.5
105. Wingate, 'Training Notes No.1', p.5
106. Ibid, p.5
107. '77 Infantry Brigade: ROLE', 22 September 1942, Box 1, File 11, p.1
108. Ibid, p.1
109. Ibid, p.1
110. Ibid, p.1
111. Ibid, p.1
112. 'LRP Pamphlet', Section 153, Para 1(a)
113. '77 Infantry Brigade: ROLE', p.1
114. Brigadier OC Wingate, *Report on Operations of 77th Infantry Brigade in Burma, February to June 1943* (New Delhi: Government of India Press 1943) p.3; Copy No.27 is held in Box I
115. Calvert, *Prisoners*, pp.10–11 and *Fighting Mad*, pp.46–47. Calvert's papers are held in the Department of Documents of the Imperial War Museum, but begin with his period of service in Malaya in the early 1950s and are sparse before his discharge from the Army in 1955. Even thereafter they consist largely of press cuttings and official documents authored by others, Calvert, apparently, not being a great letter writer. Consequently, for Calvert's experiences in Burma the researcher must rely heavily upon his published works and papers held in other collections, the Wingate Papers in particular.
116. *MTP52*, p.42
117. *OH2*, pp.212-214, 241; *OH3*, p.38. Slim was at pains to point out, in his postwar correspondence, that the use of air supply preceded Wingate's arrival: for example, in a letter to Kirby of 24 April 1959, he pointed out that air supply had been used in India in the 1930s and in Iraq in 1941, and that it was only Japanese air superiority which precluded its use in Burma in 1942; Churchill Archives Slim Papers, File 5/3
118. *NTW15*, pp.24, 29-32
119. 'Some Points', Para.B; correspondence concerning the ordering of jeeps and mules for the Light Divisions is in PRO WO106/2678; *OH2*, pp.241-243
120. *OH2*, p.243
121. Wingate, *Report*, p.1
122. Wingate, '77 Brigade', p.2
123. Ibid, p.2
124. *Notes from Theatres of War No.14, Western Desert and Cyrenaica, August/December 1942 [NTW14]* in PRO WO208/3108, pp.40-43; RP Hallion, *Strike from the Sky: The History of Battlefield Air Attack 1911-1945* (Shrewsbury: AirLife 1989), pp.171-172; RJ Overy, *The Air War 1939-1945* (London: Europa 1980), pp.67-68; J Terraine, *The Right of the Line: The Royal Air Force in the European War 1939-45* (London: Hodder & Stoughton 1985), pp.361, 370-389
125. Hallion, *Strike from the Skies*, p.172
126. Ibid, pp.171-172; Overy, *Air War*, pp.67-68; Terraine, *Right of the Line*, pp.379-382
127. LRP Pamphlet, Chapter II, Para.3(b)
128. Ibid, Para 3(b)
129. Ibid, Chapter XI, Section 110, Para.1
130. Ibid
131. '3rd Indian Division Operational Instruction Number 2, to Brigadier BE Fergusson DSO commanding 16th Inf Bde', 28 February 1944, Box II
132. Wingate, *77 Brigade*, p.2
133. Wingate, *Report*, p.11
134. Ibid, pp.11, 14; Calvert, *Prisoners*, pp.46–47
135. Calvert, *Prisoners*, pp.44–45; Fergusson, *Wild Green Earth*, pp.162–163; Wingate, *Report*, pp.5–6
136. Wingate, *Report*, p.16
137. Fergusson, *Wild Green Earth*, pp.234–235

Notes 235

138. PRO HS7/111, p.23; WO to GOC Burma of 24 February 1942, in PRO WO106/2662; Cruickshank, *SOE in the Far East*, pp.70, 163–167
139. Mackenzie, *Secret History of SOE*, pp.388-392
140. PRO HS7/111, pp.19-20; War Cabinet – Chiefs of Staff Committee, Minutes of Meeting Held in Room 240 Combined Chiefs of Staff Building on Friday 21 May 1943, in PRO CAB121/317; R Dorman-Smith to Amery of 3 October 1942, Churchill Archives Amery Papers, AMEL 2/3/1; Bayly & Harper, *Forgotten Armies*, pp.353-354; Cruickshank, *SOE in the Far East*, pp.269–270; Foot, *SOE*, pp.210–211
141. *OH2*, p.192; Cruickshank, *SOE in the Far East*, p.85
142. Slim, *Defeat into Victory*, pp.147-148, 289
143. Minutes of a Meeting Held in DMO's Office on 24.4.42 to Discuss Guerrilla Operations in BURMA, Box I, Paras.1–2
144. Ibid, Para.3
145. Ibid, Para.3
146. Ibid, Paras.3, 4, 6
147. Ibid, Para.5
148. Ibid, Paras.5, 9
149. WO to CinC India of 14 June 1942, in PRO WO106/3771
150. Cruickshank, *SOE in the Far East*, p.165
151. *Notes from Theatres of War No.6 – Cyrenaica, November 1941/January 1942* (London: HMSO 1942), pp.3-4
152. Field Marshal The Viscount Montgomery of Alamein, *Memoirs*, (London: Collins 1958) p.101
153. *Notes from Theatres of War No.14 – Western Desert and Cyrenaica August/December 1942* (London: HMSO, 1942), pp.23-24; Barnett, *Desert Generals*, pp.275-286; French, *Raising Churchill's Army*, pp.237–239; Montgomery, *Memoirs*, pp.87-90, 116-140
154. A Hoe, *David Stirling: The Authorised Biography of the Creator of the SAS* (London: Little Brown, 1992) pp.208-210
155. Hackett, 'Special Forces', p.39; Major General ISO Playfair, *The History of the Second World War: The Mediterranean and Middle East: Volume III* [hereafter *OHM3*] (London: HMSO, 1960), pp.8-9
156. Hackett, 'Special Forces', p.30; Montgomery, *Memoirs*, pp.159-160; *OHM3*, pp.8-9
157. Hackett, 'Special Forces', p.31; Otway, *Airborne Forces*, p.105
158. Hackett, 'Special Forces', p.32; Hoe, *David Stirling*, pp.178-180; Otway, *Airborne Forces*, p.104, 106
159. Otway, *Airborne Forces*, p.106; *OHM3*, pp.358-359
160. JRM Butler, *History of the Second World War: Grand Strategy, Volume II Part II* [hereafter *OHGS3/2*] (London: HMSO, 1964), pp.514-516, 638-642; Hackett, 'Special Forces', pp.32-33; Otway, *Airborne Forces*, pp.101-103
161. Hackett, 'Special Forces', p.32; Hoe, *David Stirling*, pp.209-210

Chapter 7

1. Calvert, *Prisoners of Hope*, p.14
2. Slim, *Defeat into Victory*, p.218
3. Draft of a letter from Wingate to Central Command of 15 August 1942, Box I, IWM; it is not clear what Wingate meant by 'the Imperial point of view'.
4. PRO CAB106/46, pp.6, 8; Fergusson, 'Behind Enemy Lines', p.348; Philip Stibbé, *Return via Rangoon* (London: Leo Cooper 1994), pp.13-15; Wingate, *Report*, p.4
5. Fergusson, *Chindwin*, pp.30-31; PRO CAB106/46, pp.6-7; Wingate, *Report*, pp.4-5
6. Wingate, *Report*, pp.113–114; Tulloch, *Wingate*, pp.63, 73
7. Wingate, 'Intruder Mission', p.5
8. Wingate, *Report*, p.9
9. Wingate, *Report*, p.3-4; Fergusson, *Wild Green Earth*, p.244
10. PRO CAB106/46, pp.6, 8
11. PRO CAB106/46, pp.8-9
12. Ibid, p.6; 'LRP Pamphlet', p.10
13. Fergusson, *Chindwin*, pp.27–29; Stibbé, *Rangoon*, pp.10-30
14. 'LRP Pamphlet', p.9
15. Ibid, p.11
16. Ibid, p.11

17. The beast on the Chindit badge actually resembles a rather stylised Asian Lion more than a true *Chinthey*. One officer remarked rather uncharitably that it looked like a Pekinese contemplated a stein of beer.
18. Fergusson, *Chindwin*, p.21
19. *FSR 1929(i)*, pp.40-41
20. Bidwell, *Chindit War*, pp.39-40
21. Ibid, p.40
22. 'LRP Groups – Comment on note of DSD by Colonel OC Wingate', Box I, pp.1-3
23. Calvert to Wingate of 6 August 1942, Box I
24. Calvert to Wingate of 7 August 1942, Box I
25. Wingate to Calvert of 8 August 1942, Box I
26. Bidwell, *Chindit War*, pp.54-55
27. Wingate, *Report*, pp.4, 25, 29, 31; unsurprisingly, Wingate remains a hate-figure for the Gurkhas, Gurkha histories tending to become splenetic when discussing *Longcloth* in particular
28. Wingate, *Report*, p.4; Masters, *Road Past Mandalay*, pp.156-157
29. PRO CAB106/46, p.8; Wingate, *Report*, p.4
30. Calvert, 'No.3 Coln', pp.1, 10-12, 14
31. Stibbé, *Return via Rangoon*, p.19
32. Wingate to HQ Central Command, Agra, of 15 August 1942, Box I, where he attributes the large numbers of sick in 13th King's to eating cooked food; Mr FJ Hill interview of 13/6/2000; Fergusson, *Wild Green Earth*, p.68; Sykes, *Orde Wingate*, p.515
33. Calvert, *Fighting Mad*, p.113; Stibbé, *Return via Rangoon*, pp.19-23
34. Wingate, *Report*, p.2 and 'Intruder Mission', p.5; CinC India Sitrep of 15 February 1943, in PRO WO106/3807, Para.3; *OH2*, pp.294–295, 300–303, 309–310; Tulloch, *Wingate*, p.64
35. *OH2*, p.11
36. Wingate, *Report*, pp.28–29
37. Ibid, pp.28–29; *MTP52*, p.3; Fergusson, *Beyond the Chindwin*, p.87 and *Wild Green Earth*, pp.149–169
38. Slim, *Defeat into Victory*, p.163; Sykes, *Orde Wingate*, p.442
39. Wingate, *Report*, pp.24–25; PRO CAB106/46, p.17
40. '3 Coln WAR DIARY', pp.1, 4, and , 'No.5 Coln, 77 IND INF BDE Operations in Burma Feb-Apr 43, Preliminary Outline Report', Paras.1, 3, 5, 21, several copies of both in the IWM Wingate Chindit Papers; Fergusson, *Chindwin*, pp.62–68, 109–110
41. Wingate, *Report*, pp.29–30; CinC India Sitrep of 15 February 1943, in PRO WO106/3807, Para.3; *OH2*, p.315
42. Wingate, *Report*, pp.46–47
43. Ibid, p.47; *OH2*, p.320; 'No.3 Coln', pp.14–15
44. 'No.5 Coln', Paras.19–21; Wingate, *Report*, pp.50–54
45. Wingate, *Report*, pp.50–54
46. Ibid, pp.54–55
47. Allen, *Burma*, p.167
48. Ibid, p.167
49. Fergusson to Slim of 11 April 1956, Churchill Archives Slim Papers File 5/1c; see also Fergusson's *Wild Green Earth*, pp.186–190
50. Fergusson to Slim of 11/4/56; Fergusson, *Wild Green Earth*, p.95
51. Fergusson, *Chindwin*, p.241
52. Calvert, *Prisoners*, p.9
53. Slim, *Defeat into Victory*, p.215
54. PRO WO106/4827, Para.13
55. Ibid, Para.13; *OH2*, pp.329, 428-430; *OH3*, pp.73-75
56. Sykes, *Orde Wingate*, pp.433-437, 442
57. Ibid, p.442
58. Mountbatten, *Report*, Section A, Paras.62–63
59. Slim, *Defeat into Victory*, p.163
60. Stillwell's summary of the conference is in the *Stillwell Diaries*, pp.204–206, Brooke's in the *Alanbrooke Diaries*, p.404
61. *OH2*, pp.379–381

62. Summaries of Chiefs of Staff Meetings of 9 May 1942 and 10 February 1943, in PRO WO106/6110; Brooke's diary entries of 14–15 May 1943, *Alanbrooke Diaries*, p.403–405
63. *OH2*, p.381
64. Mountbatten, *Report*, Section 1, Para.1; Brooke's diary entry of 21 May 1943, in *Alanbrooke Diaries*, p.408
65. Summary of Chiefs of Staff Meeting of 28 July 1943, in PRO WO106/6110; *OH2*, pp.382–387
66. Sykes, *Orde Wingate*, p.445
67. The issue of Wingate as commander in Southeast Asia is covered in Brooke's Diary Entry of 25 July 1943, in *Alanbrooke Diaries*, p.433; see also Summary of Chiefs of Staff Meeting of 26 July 1943, in PRO WO106/611; Brooke to Amery of 12 January and 21 July 1942, Churchill Archives Amery Papers, AMEL 2/1/31 and 2/1/35
68. Brooke's diary entry of 4/8/43
69. *OH2*, p.399
70. Ibid, p.400; *OH3*, pp.53-66
71. *OH2*, p.399
72. Ibid, p.400
73. Ibid, pp.400-401
74. Ibid, p.401; 'War Cabinet, Joint Staff: Long Range Penetration Groups – Report by the Joint Planning Staff', Box II, Para.1
75. 66689/COS 19 August 1943, in PRO WO106/6110; 'Report by the Joint Planning Staff', Paras.3–8, 11, 13–15; *OH2*, pp.401–403; in a letter to Kirby of 14 December 1959, Slim argued that 70th Division intact would have been worth 'three times its number in Special Force', Churchill Archives Slim Papers File 5/3
76. 'Report by the Joint Planning Staff', Para.14
77. *OH2*, p.421; Brooke's diary entry of 17 August 1943, *Alanbrooke Diaries*, p.443
78. Mountbatten, *Report*, Section A, Paras.1–3, 31, and 'Strategy of the Southeast Asia Campaign', pp.470–471; *OH2*, pp.424–426
79. Mountbatten, *Report*, Appendix A, Paras.21, 40; Appendix I to PRO WO106/6110, Para.44; *OH2*, pp.422–423
80. PRO WO106/6110, Appendix I, Para.4; PRO WO203/1536, Paras.1–2; *OH2*, p.422
81. PRO WO106/6110, Para.37
82. HH Arnold, *Global Mission* (Blue Ridge, PA: Tab Books 1989), p.442; Mountbatten, *Report*, Section A, Para.6, and 'Strategy of the Southeast Asia Campaign', p.472; *OH3*, p.38
83. OC Wingate, Major General Commanding Special Force, 'Considerations affecting the employment of LRP Forces Spring 1944', Box II, Part 5; 'Notes for Supreme Commander 11/1/44', Box II; John Masters, Brigade Major of 111th Brigade on *Thursday*, recalled in his memoir of *Thursday*, 'Equipment – mainly American – descended upon us in torrents...walkie-talkie radio sets, VHF radios, and, blessed above all, K-rations', *The Road Past Mandalay*, p.139; In his August, 2000 interview with the author, Mr. FJ King, who served as a muleteer in the headquarters of the Chindit 16th Brigade on Operation *Thursday*, recalled that most of 16th Brigade HQ carried American M1 carbines; see also Tulloch, *Wingate*, pp.128-129
84. Mountbatten, *Report*, Section A, Para.73; Section B, Para.51; CF Romanus and R Sutherland, *United States Army in World War Two, China-Burma-India Theatre: Stilwell's Command Problems* (Washington DC: Department of the Army 1956), pp.34-36; *OH3*, p.38
85. 'Directive to Colonel Davidson-Houston', Box II
86. Mountbatten, *Report*, Section B Para.51; *OH3*, pp.225-226, 227-229, 292, 295, 399, 401-402
87. Note from Wingate to Mountbatten of 2 September 1943, Box II; Letter No. AC 05 from GE Wildman [Lushington] to Wingate of 2 February 1944, Box II
88. 'Note on Development of LRP Force for use of LRP Representatives at COHQ 11 September 43, Box II, Para.3(d); Wingate's Note to Mountbatten of 2/9/43; Letter 'Welfare 332' of 23 August 1943, summarised in PRO WO106/6110
89. Correspondence held in Churchill Archives Chartwell Collection, File 20
90. Mountbatten, *Report*, Section B, Paras.5-8, and 'Strategy', p.473; *OH3*, pp.11-13
91. Mountbatten, *Report*, Section B, Paras.14-16, and 'Strategy', p.474; *OH3*, pp.54-56
92. Mountbatten, *Report*, Section B, Paras.21-25; *OH3*, p.61
93. Supreme Commander's Personal Minute No. P.27 of 28 December 1943, Box II, Para.1; Mountbatten, *Report*, Section B, Para.23, and 'Strategy', p.475; *OH3*, pp.62, 64

238   Orde Wingate

94. Mountbatten, *Report*, Section B, Para.28(a), and 'Strategy', p.475; *OH3*, pp.66-67
95. Mountbatten, *Report*, Section B, Paras.26, 33–41
96. Mountbatten, *Report*, Section B Paras.49-50; Personal Minute No.P-27, Para.1(b)
97. Mountbatten, *Report*, Section B Para.12; *OH3*, pp.8-9, 61-62; Headquarters Air Command South East Asia Operational Directive No.2, to Major General George E Stratemeyer, US Army, Air Commander, Eastern Air Command, in PRO WO203/3299, Para.4(ii)b
98. 'Headquarters South East Asia Command SAC (43) 109, Note by CinC 11 Army Group, Review of Operations in Upper Burma 1943/44, 5 December 1943', in PRO WO203/3299, Para.1
99. Mountbatten, *Report*, Section A Para.26; 'Review of Operations by CinC 11 Army Group', Para.4
100. Supreme Commander's Minute P-27, Para.1(c); 'Review of Operations by CinC 11 Army Group', Para.4
101. Supreme Commander's Minute P-27, Para.1(a); *OH3*, p.65; 'Operational Directive No.2', Para.4
102. 'Review of Operations by CinC 11 Army Group', Paras.5, 15-20
103. Ibid, Paras.21, 25-26
104. Slim to Giffard of 19 April 1956, Churchill Archives Slim Papers, File 5/1c; Slim to Kirby of 24 April 1959, Churchill Archives Slim Papers, File 5/3
105. Slim to Fergusson of 19 April 1956, Churchill Archives Slim Papers, File 5/1c
106. Handwritten note in Churchill Archives Slim Papers, File 5/5
107. Slim to Kirby of 24/4/59; Slim to unknown of 14 July 1952, 'commenting on book on Ghurkas [sic]', Churchill Archives Slim Papers File 13/2
108. Transcript of interview with Fergusson held in Churchill Archives Slim Papers, File 13/2
109. Marston, *Phoenix from the Ashes*,pp.105–107, 109; Mountbatten, *Report*, Section B, Para.44; Slim, *Defeat into Victory*, pp.188-189
110. CinC India Sitrep of 10 July 1943, CinC India to WO of 17 August 1943, both in PRO WO106/3810
111. Slim, *Defeat into Victory*, p.189
112. Ibid, p.189
113. Ibid, p.142
114. Kirby to Slim of 27 February 1959, Churchill Archives Slim Papers File 5/3; Lewin, *Slim*, pp.70–75
115. Marston, *Phoenix from the Ashes*, p.107; Mountbatten, *Report*, Section A, Paras.53-56
116. JAL Hamilton, *War Bush: 81 (West African) Division in Burma 1943-1945* (Wilby: Michael Russell, 2001), pp.60-164, 197-233, 362-363; Mountbatten, *Report*, Section B Para.89
117. 'Precis of talk to Royal Empire Society on February 6th 1946', Churchill Archives Slim Papers, File 3/2
118. Lewin, *Slim*, pp.185, 200-202
119. Slim to Kirby of 24/4/59
120. Handwritten lecture notes for 'Press Club', Churchill Archives Slim Papers, File 3/2
121. *OH3*, pp.128-127
122. Slim, *Defeat into Victory*, pp.292-293
123. Ibid, pp.293-294; Mountbatten, *Report*, Section B Paras.71-72, 105
124. Slim, *Defeat into Victory*, p.294
125. Romanus and Sutherland, *Stilwell's Command Problems*, pp.196-197
126. Quoted, *OH2*, p.351
127. Minutes of Conference held at HQ Fourteenth Army and Air HQ Bengal, 3 Dec 43, Box II, Para.3
128. Slim's letter of 14/7/52, 'commenting on book on Ghurkas' [sic]; Slim, *Defeat into Victory*, pp.217-218
129. Cruickshank, *SOE in the Far East*, pp.169–170

Chapter 8
1. Letter AX.866 from the Air Ministry to AHQ India, 22 September 1944, Box IV; Minutes of Conference held at HQ Fourteenth Army and Air HQ Bengal, 3 Dec '43, Para.8
2. R Overy, *Why the Allies Won* (London: Pimlico 1995), pp.123–124
3. Bierman & Smith, *Fire in the Night*, p.346
4. Letter AX.866; HQ 14th Army to HQ 3rd Indian Div of 3 March 1944, Box II, Para.8; Otway, *Airborne Forces*, p.361
5. Alison's Foreword to Tulloch, *Wingate*, pp.5–6
6. Tulloch, *Wingate*, pp.156-159

7. Mountbatten, *Report*, Section B Para.56
8. Ibid, Section B Paras.56-57
9. I Dear, *Sabotage and Subversion: SOE and OSS at War* (London: Cassell 1996), pp.111-112
10. *OH3*, p.70; Mead, *Orde Wingate and the Historians*, p.41
11. Tulloch, pp.192-193
12. Mountbatten, *Report*, Section A Para.54
13. Brigadier OC Wingate, 'Special Force Commander's Training Memorandum No.8, "The Stronghold"', Box II, p.1
14. Ibid, p.2
15. Ibid, p.2
16. Ibid, p.1
17. Ibid, p.3
18. Ibid, p.4
19. Ibid, p.4
20. Ibid, p.5
21. No.1 Air Commando Close Support Forecasts – period 14/25th March 1944 – Note by Special Force Commander, Box II; Signal 11, undated, from Mountbatten to General Sir Henry Pownall, COS SEAC, Box II; 'Meeting at Air HQ, 17/1/44'
22. Mountbatten, *Report*, Section A Para.5; 14 Brigade Operational Instruction No.1, 27 Mar 44, Box II, Para.19; PA to BGS, Special Forces Op. Memo No.44, Box IV; Hallion, *Strike from the Sky*, pp.163-179
23. 'Close Support Forecasts'
24. Wingate's Operational Order to Special Force of 2 February 1944, Para.11
25. Wingate to Mountbatten of 27 December 1943, Box II; see also 'Notes for Supreme Commander, South East Asia on LRP Force by Force Commander', Box II, Para.2, wherein Wingate demands RAF officers as forward observers for close air support.
26. Wingate, 'Stronghold', p.5
27. Ibid, p.16
28. Slim, *Defeat into Victory*, p.220; see also Marston, *Phoenix from the Ashes*, pp.138–139
29. Wingate, *Report*, p.112
30. See 'Comment by Commander, Special Force, on Aide-Memoire by Commander-in-Chief, 11th Army Group No.10012/OPs/1 Subject -OPERATIONS IN BURMA: SPRING 44', Box 2, File 9, Folio 11, especially p.3
31. Tulloch, *Wingate*, p.207
32. 'Directive to Lt.Col Herring, Commanding DAH Force, of 29 February 1944', Box II; Cruickshank, *SOE in the Far East*, pp.164–165
33. Fergusson, *Wild Green Earth*, pp.92-95
34. Calvert to HQ Special Force (A Wing) of 18 November 1943, p.1
35. Ibid, p.2
36. Ibid, p.2
37. Ibid, pp.2-3
38. Masters, *Road Past Mandalay*, pp.139-140; Lentaigne to Tulloch of 28 July 1944, Box II
39. Masters, *Road Past Mandalay*, pp.139-140
40. Ibid, pp.143-145
41. Ibid, pp.157-158; Slim, *Defeat into Victory*, pp.217-218

Chapter 9

1. *Gideon goes to War*, p.241
2. *OH3*, pp.170-171
3. Aide Memoiré for CinC 11th Army Group Reference Supreme Commander's Personal Minute No.P27 of 28 Dec '43, Box II
4. Comment by Commander Special Force on Aide Memoiré by Commander-in-Chief, 11th Army Group No.10012/OPS/1, Subject:- OPERATIONS IN BURMA SPRING 44, Box II
5. Major General, Commanding Special Force, 'Considerations Affecting the Employment of LRP Forces, Spring 1944', IWM Wingate Chindit papers, Box II; *OH3*, pp.170-171
6. For example, Wingate to Mountbatten of 27/12/43; 'Notes for Supreme Commander, 11/1/44'; 'Notes for Supreme Commander by Commander Special Force'; 'Notes for Supreme Commander on Army Commander's Conference, 4/1/44'

7. OC Wingate, Major General, Commanding Special Force, 'Appreciation of Situation in NORTHERN BURMA by Commander Special Force', Box II, p.1
8. Ibid, p.1
9. Ibid, p.1
10. Ibid, pp.3–5; see also *OH3*, p.171
11. Tulloch, *Wingate*, p.194
12. Ibid, pp.194–195
13. Slim's Operational Instruction to Wingate of January 1944, Box II, Paras 1, 3, 6
14. Wingate's Operational Instruction of 2 Feb 1944, Box II, Para.9
15. Fergusson, *Wild Green Earth*, p.75
16. Wingate's Operational Instruction of 2 Feb 1944, Paras.10–11
17. Calvert, *Prisoners of Hope*, p.27
18. Ibid, pp.3–5; see also *OH3*, p.171
19. *OH3*, pp.177–180; Fergusson, *Wild Green Earth*, pp.40–49
20. *OH3*, p.178; Fergusson, *Wild Green Earth*, pp.72–76; Tulloch, *Wingate*, pp.180–181
21. See 'Note by Commander LRPGs for General STRATEMEYER, Commanding General, Eastern Air Command' on 10 February 1944, IWM Wingate Chindit Papers, Box II, for details of Wingate's bombing plan; *OH3*, pp.205–206
22. *OH3*, pp.179–182; Calvert, *Prisoners*, pp.21–33
23. *OH3*, pp.181–182; Tulloch, *Wingate*, p.215
24. *OH3*, pp.181–182; Tulloch, *Wingate*, pp.216–217
25. *OH3*, pp. 181–182, 205–206; Fergusson, *Wild Green Earth*, p.98
26. *OH3*, p.206; Slim, *Defeat into Victory*, p.267; Calvert, *Prisoners*, pp.105–117
27. *OH3*, pp.207, 208, 214, 216–219; Fergusson, *Wild Green Earth*, pp.96–117
28. *OH3*, p.185
29. Ibid, pp.185–186
30. See Allen, *Burma*, pp.191–315; Marston, *Phoenix from the Ashes*, pp.138–154
31. Review of Special Force Ops Feb-May 1944', Box III, Para.8; Mead, *Wingate and the Historians*, p.256; Mountbatten, *Report*, Section B Para.125; Slim, *Defeat into Victory*, p.267; *OH3*, pp.207–208
32. Mountbatten, *Review*, Section B Para.127
33. *OH3*, pp.208–210; Slim, *Defeat into Victory*, p.268
34. Tulloch, *Wingate*, pp.209–210
35. Ibid, p.210
36. Ibid, pp.211–212; *OH3*, pp.208–209, 219
37. BGS to Commander of 14 March 1944, Box II
38. Wingate to Tulloch of 16 March 1944, Box II
39. BGS to Commander of 17 March 1944, Box II
40. Fergusson, *Wild Green Earth*, p.98
41. Rear HQ 3 Indian Div to SACSEA 21 March 1944, for transmission to PM, IWM Wingate Chindit Papers, Box II
42. Ibid
43. Message from SACSEA to Adv 3 Ind Div, 23 March 1944, Box II; Personal Telegram from Mountbatten to Churchill of 23 March 1943, Churchill Archives Chartwell Collection, File 20/160
44. Ibid
45. GOC in C Fourteenth Army to CinC Army Group, 22 March 1944, Box II, p.1
46. GOC in C Fourteenth Army's of 22/3/44, pp.1–2
47. Ibid, p.2
48. Ibid, p.2
49. Signal from Slim to Giffard of 23 March 1944, Box II
50. Ibid
51. Prime Minister to Admiral Mountbatten of 23 March 1943, Churchill Archives Chartwell Papers, File 20/160
52. Tulloch, *Wingate*, p.225
53. Mountbatten, *Report*, Section B Para.126–127; *OH3*, p.219; 14 Bde Operational Instruction No.1, 27 Mar 44, Box II, Paras. 3–3A, on Wingate's intention and enemy lines of communication, states clearly that 14th Brigade should attack Japanese 31st Division's lines of communication.

54. Major General OC Wingate, 'Appreciation of the prospect of exploiting Operation Thursday by Commander Special Force at Imphal on 10 February 44. For Supreme Commander', Box II, pp.3–4
55. Ibid, p.4
56. 'Note by Major-General OC Wingate on LRP Operations against Siam and Indo-China, 11th February 1944, Box II, Para 3(b)
57. Mountbatten, *Report*, Section B, Para.115
58. *OH3*, pp.217, 279–281; Fergusson, 'Behind Enemy Lines', p.347
59. *OH3*, p.280
60. Ibid, pp.281–282
61. Ibid, pp.283–287
62. Ibid, p.286; Mountbatten, *Report*, Section B, Paras.148–159
63. Ibid, Section B, Para.199
64. 'Aquila', 'Air Transport', p.206
65. Lewin, *Slim*, pp.179-183, 199-200, 216-217, 222-224, 228-229, 233; Sykes, *Orde Wingate*, pp.528-529
66. Transcript of interview with Fergusson in Churchill Archives Slim Papers, File 13/2; Lewin, *Slim*, pp.193-194; Mountbatten quoted in Mead, *Orde Wingate and the Historians*, p.193
67. Air Marshal Sir J Baldwin KBE CB DSO, 'Air Aspects of the Operations in Burma', *RUSI Journal*, May 1945, p.189
68. Main HQ Army 11 Group SEAC, 'Note on Special Force, 27 July 44', in PRO WO203/1495, Para.1
69. Ibid, Para.2
70. Ibid, Paras.3–5
71. Ibid, Paras.8–9
72. Lentaigne to Wildman Lushington of 13 April 1944, Box II
73. Tulloch to Perowne of Sep 44, Box III
74. Ibid
75. PRO WO203/3736, p.5
76. quoted, Royle, p.318

Chapter 10

1. George Friedman, *America's Secret War: Inside the Worldwide Struggle between the United States and its Enemies* (London: Little, Brown, 2003), pp.309–313; Christian Jennings, *Midnight in Some Burning Town: British Special Operations Forces from Belgrade to Baghdad* (London: Cassell 2005), pp.195–211
2. For example, see Tommy Franks, *American Soldier* (New York: Regan, 2004), pp.419–425; George Packer, *The Assassin's Gate: America in Iraq* (London: Faber & Faber, 2005), pp24–99
3. Mark Urban, *Task Force Black: The Explosive True Story of the SAS and the Secret War in Iraq* (London: Little, Brown 2011) covers these operations in some detail.
4. See, for instance, 'Afghan Forces take control of controversial night raids', *France 24*, 8 April 2012, http://www.france24.com/en/20120408-afghan-forces-usa-oversee-controversial-night-raids-special-forces-taliban-insurgents-isaf-nato, accessed 13 October 2013; "Afghan Forces take control of controversial night raids', *France 24*, 8 April 2012, , accessed 13 October 2013; 'US, Afghanistan sign key "night raids" deal', CNN 8 April 2012, http://edition.cnn.com/2012/04/08/world/asia/afghanistan-night-raids/index.html, accessed 13 October 2013
5. Michael Codner, 'An Initial Assessment of the Combat Phase', in RUSI Whitehall Paper No.59, *War in Iraq: Combat and Consequences* (London: RUSI 2003), pp.10–13; Friedman, *America's Secret War*, pp.82–90; Williamson Murray and Robert H Scales, *The Iraq War* (Cambridge, Mass: Harvard University Press, 2003), pp.58, 69–71.

Bibliography

Unpublished Primary Sources
The National Archives, Kew
Departmental Papers
Air Ministry: AIR 2, AIR40
Cabinet: CAB21, CAB37, CAB84, CAB106, CAB120, CAB121, CAB122, CJ4/152
Colonial Office: CO323, CO732, CO733
Foreign Office: FO141, FO371
Special Operations Executive: HS1, HS3, HS7, HS8
War Office: WO32, WO33, WO95, WO106, WO106, WO141, WO178, WO190, WO191, WO193, WO201, WO203, WO208, WO216, WO218, WO217, WO230, WO231, WO291

The British Library
Captain OC Wingate Palestine MSS

Churchill Archives, Churchill College, Cambridge
The Right Honourable Leopold Amery MSS
The Right Honourable Sir Winston Churchill MSS and Chartwell Collection
Field Marshal Viscount Slim MSS

Imperial War Museum, Department of Documents
Major General HEN Bredin MSS
Brigadier JM Calvert MSS
General Sir Robert Haining MSS
Lieutenant Colonel R King-Clark MSS
Simonds, Lieutenant Colonel Anthony, 'Pieces of War', unpublished memoir
Stevens, Edmund, 'Writer on the Storm: Memoirs of a Correspondent at War', unpublished memoir
Major General OC Wingate Early Life, Abyssinia and Burma MSS

Imperial War Museum, Department of Sound Records
Transcript of Taped Interview No.004545/04, with Lieutenant Colonel Ivor Thomas

Liddell Hart Centre for Military Archives, King's College London
Major General E Dorman-Smith (AKA Dorman O'Gowan) MSS
Lieutenant General Sir John Evetts MSS
Major General S Woodburn Kirby MSS
Colonel TE Lawrence MSS
Captain BH Liddell Hart MSS
General Sir Richard O'Connor MSS
Field Marshal Earl Wavell MSS
Captain OC Wingate MSS

Published Primary Sources – Official Publications
Design for Military Operations – The British Military Doctrine *(London: MOD 1989)*
Field Service Regulations 1920 Volume I – Organisation and Administration *(London: HMSO 1920)*
Field Service Regulations 1920 Volume II – Operations *(London: HMSO 1920)*

Field Service Regulations 1923 Volume II – Operations *(London: HMSO 1923*
Field Service Regulations 1929 Volume I – Organisation and Administration *(London: HMSO 1930)*
Field Service Regulations 1929 Volume II - Operations *(London: HMSO 1930)*
Field Service Regulations 1935 Volume II – Operations: General *(London: HMSO 1935)*
Field Service Regulations 1935 Volume III – Operations: Higher Formations *(London: HMSO 1935)*
Gubbins, Lieutenant Colonel C McV, The Art of Guerrilla Warfare *(London: MI(R) 1939*
The Partisan Leader's Handbook *(London: MI(R) 1939)*
Mountbatten of Burma, Vice Admiral the Earl, KG PC GCSI GCIE GCVO KCB DSO, Report to the Combined Chiefs of Staff by the Supreme Allied Commander South-East Asia, 1943–1945 *(London: HMSO 1951)*
Notes from the Theatres of War No.1 – Cyrenaica *(London: HMSO 1942)*
Notes from the Theatres of War No.6 – Cyrenaica, November 1941/January 1942 *(London: HMSO 1942)*
Notes from the Theatres of War No.8 – The Far East, December 1941–May 1942 *(London: HMSO 1942)*
Notes from Theatres of War No.10 – Cyrenaica and Western Desert January/June 1942 *(London: HMSO 1942)*
Notes from Theatres of War No.12 – SW Pacific August 1942–February 1943 *(London: HMSO 1943)*
Notes from Theatres of War No.14 – Western Desert and Cyrenaica August/December 1942 *(London: HMSO 1943)*
Notes from Theatres of War No.15 – SW Pacific January-March 1943 *(London: HMSO 1943)*
Notes from Theatres of War No.17 – Far East, April-November 1943 *(London: HMSO 1944)*
Wingate, Brigadier OC, Report on Operations of 77th Infantry Brigade in Burma, February to June 1943 *(New Delhi: Government of India Press 1943)*

Published Primary Sources – Diaries, Memoirs, Etc
Alanbrooke, Field Marshal Lord, *War Diaries 1939–1945* edited by Alex Danchev and Daniel Todman (London: Weidenfeld & Nicholson 2000)
'Aquila', 'Air Transport on the Burma Front', *RUSI Journal* May 1945
Arnold, General HH, *Global Mission* (Blue Ridge, PA: Tab Books 1989)
Baldwin, Air Marshal Sir John, 'Air Aspects of the Operations in Burma', *RUSI Journal*, May 1945
Ben-Gurion, David 'Our Friend: what Wingate did for us', *Jewish Observer and Middle East Review*, September 1963
'Recesh and Ta'as – Arms for the Hagana [sic]' *Jewish Observer and Middle East Review*, September 1963
'Britain's Contribution to arming the Hagana [sic]', *Jewish Observer and Middle East Review*, September 1963
'Table Talk with Lord Lloyd', *Jewish Observer and Middle East Review* December 1963
Boustead, Brevet Major JEH, DSO RE, 'The Camel Corps of the Sudan Defence Force', *RUSI Journal* Volume LXXIX, 1934
Calvert, Michael *Prisoners of Hope* Revised Edition (London: Leo Cooper 1996)
Fighting Mad: One Man's Guerrilla War (Shrewsbury: AirLife 1996)
Churchill, Winston, *The Second World War* Abridged Single Volume Edition (London: Cassell 1959)
Dayan, Moshe, *Story of My Life* (London: Weidenfeld and Nicholson 1976)
Dodds-Parker, Douglas, *Setting Europe Ablaze: An account of ungentlemanly warfare* (London: Springwood 1983)
Fergusson, Bernard, *Beyond the Chindwin* (London: Collins 1945)
The Wild Green Earth (London: Collins 1946)
'Behind the Enemy's Lines in Burma', *RUSI Journal* August 1946
Ha'Cohen, David, 'The Story of a Historic Friendship', *Jewish Observer and Middle East Review* October 1969
Hamilton, John AL, *War Bush: 81(West African) Division in Burma 1943–1945* (Wilby: Michael Russell 2001)
Hickson, Captain JGE, 'Palestine Patrol', *Army Quarterly* Volume 40, 1940
King-Clark, Lt R, 'Special Duty', *Manchester Regiment Gazette*, date not known
Lawrence, TE, 'The Evolution of a Revolt', *Army Quarterly*, Volume I Number I, 1920

―― *Revolt in the Desert* (Ware: Wandsworth Editions 1997)
―― *The Seven Pillars of Wisdom* (London: Jonathan Cape 1935)
Liddell Hart, BH, *Memoirs* Volume I (London: Cassell 1965)
Masters, John, *The Road past Mandalay* (London: Michael Joseph 1961)
Montgomery of Alamein, Field Marshal the Viscount, KG, *Memoirs* (London: Collins 1958)
Mountbatten of Burma, Admiral the Earl, GCVO KCB DSO ADC, 'The Strategy of the South-East Asia Campaign', *RUSI Journal* November 1946
Rhodes James, Richard *Chindit* (London: John Murray 1980)
Slim, Field Marshal Sir William, GCB GCMG GCVO GBE DSO MC, *Defeat into Victory* (London: Cassell 1956)
Steer, George, *Sealed and Delivered: A Book on the Ethiopian Campaign* (London: Faber & Faber 2009)
Stibbe, Philip *Return via Rangoon* (London: Leo Cooper 1995)
Stilwell, General Joseph W, *The Stilwell Papers* edited by Theodore H White (New York: Da Capo 1991)
Thesiger, Wilfred, *The Life of My Choice* (London: Collins 1987)
Thompson, Sir Robert, *Make for the Hills* (London: Leo Cooper 1989)
Tulloch, Derek, *Wingate in Peace and War* (London: Macdonald 1972)
Wilson DSO RE, Colonel BT, 'The Sudan of To-Day', *RUSI Journal* Volume LXXIX, 1934
Wavell, Field Marshal the Earl, *The Good Soldier* (London: MacMillan 1948)
Weizmann, Chaim, *Trial and Error* (London: Hamish Hamilton 1949)

Interviews
Brigadier Sir Douglas Dodds-Parker, Grenadier Guards, 1939; G(R) and Special Operations Executive 1940–45; Colonel Wingate's General Staff Officer 2, 1940–41
Mr FJ Hill, Muleteer, Headquarters 16th Infantry Brigade, Special Force, Operation Thursday, 1944
Mr Thomas, RAF Clerk, Headquarters Special Force, Operation *Thursday* 1944

Unpublished Secondary Sources
Hughes, Matthew, 'The Meaning of Atrocity: The British Army and the Arab Revolt, 1936–41', unpublished paper presented to Institute of Historical Research, November 2006
Marcus, Professor Harold G, 'Ethiopian Insurgency against the Italians 1936–41', unpublished essay of 1997
Townshend, Charles, 'The Anglo-Irish War', unpublished paper presented to the Institute for National Strategic Studies, Foreign Policy Institute, Johns Hopkins School of Advanced International Studies, year unknown

Published Secondary Sources – Books And Monographs
Allen, Louis, *Burma: The Longest War* (London: Phoenix 1994)
Allon, Yigal, *The Making of Israel's Army* (London: Valentine, Mitchell 1970
Asprey, Robert B, *War in the Shadows* (London: Little, Brown 1994)
Atkins, Major John, RLC, 'A Model for Modern Nonlinear Noncontiguous Operations: The War in Burma, 1943 to 1945' (Fort Leavenworth: School of Advanced Military Studies, United States Army Command and General Staff College 2003)
Barnes, John and Nicholson, David, (Editors), *The Empire at Bay: The Leo Amery Diaries 1929–1945* (London: Hutchinson 1988)
Barr, James, *A Line in the Sand* (London and New York: Simon and Schuster 2011)
Bayly, Christopher and Harper, Tim, *Forgotten Armies: Britain's Asian Empire & the War with Japan* (London: Penguin 2005)
Barnett, Corelli, *The Desert Generals* (London: Cassell 1983)
Beckett, Ian FW (Editor), *The Roots of Counter-Insurgency: Armies and Guerrilla Warfare 1900–1945* (London: Blandford 1988)
Bidwell, Shelford: *The Chindit War: The Campaign in Burma 1944* (London: Book Club Associates 1979)
Bidwell, Shelford and Graham, Dominick *Fire-Power: British Army Weapons and Theories of War* (London: George Allen & Unwin 1982)

Bibliography 245

Bierman, John and Smith, Colin *Fire in the Night: Wingate of Burma, Ethiopia and Zion* (London: Macmillan 1999)
Bond, Brian *Liddell Hart: A Study of his Military Thought* (London: Cassell 1977)
—— *British Military Policy between the two World Wars* (Oxford: Clarendon 1980)
Burchett, Wilfred, *Wingate's Phantom Army* (London: Frederick Muller 1946)
Butler, JRM *History of the Second World War: Grand Strategy, Volume II Part I* (London: HMSO 1957)
—— *History of the Second World War: Grand Strategy Volume II Part II* (London: HMSO 1964)
Callwell, Colonel CE *Small Wars: Their Principles and Practice* Bison Books Edition (Lincoln and London: University of Nebraska Press 1996)
Calvert, Mike, *Slim* (London: Pan/Ballantine 1973)
Chaliand, Gerard (Editor), *The Art of War in World History* (Berkeley: University of California Press 1994)
Chandler, David, (General Editor), *The Oxford Illustrated History of the British Army* (Oxford: OUP 1994)
Clarke, Richard, *Against All Enemies: Inside America's War on Terror* (London: Free Press 2003)
Clausewitz, Carl von, *On War*, translated by Michael Howard and Peter Paret (London: Everyman 1993)
Coker, C *Empires in Conflict: the Growing Rift between Europe and the United States* RUSI Whitehall Paper Number 58 (London: RUSI, 2003), p.31
Coll, Steve, *Ghost Wars: The Secret History of the CIA, Afghanistan and bin Laden, from the Soviet Invasion to September 10, 2001* (London: Penguin 2004)
Collins, Major General RJ, *Lord Wavell: A Military Biography* (London: Hodder & Stoughton 1948)
Connell, John, *Wavell: Soldier and Scholar* (London: Collins 1964)
Connor, Ken *Ghost Force: The Secret History of the SAS* (London: Weidenfeld & Nicholson 1998)
Cosgrave, Patrick, *The Lives of Enoch Powell* (London: Bodley Head 1989)
Cruickshank, Charles, *SOE in the Far East* (Oxford: OUP 1983)
Dear, Ian, *Sabotage and Subversion: SOE and OSS at War* (London: Cassell 1996)
Dupuy, Trevor N, *The Evolution of Weapons and Warfare* (New York: Da Capo 1984)
Elliot-Bateman, Michael, (Editor), *The Fourth Dimension of Warfare, Volume I – Intelligence, Subversion, Resistance* (Manchester: MUP 1970)
Eshed, Haggai, *Reuven Shiloah, the Man behind the Mossad: Secret Diplomacy in the Creation of Israel* (London: Frank Cass 1997)
Foot, MRD *SOE: The Special Operations Executive 1940–1946* (London: BBC 1984)
Franks, Tommy, *American Soldier* (New York: Regan, 2004)
French, David, *Raising Churchill's Army: The British Army and the War against Germany 1919–1945* (Oxford: OUP 2000)
Friedman, George, *America's Secret War* (London: Little, Brown 2004)
Galula, David, *Counterinsurgency Warfare: Theory and Practice* (New York and London: Praeger 1964)
Geraghty, Tony, *Who Dares Wins: The Special Air Service 1950–1992* (London: Little, Brown 1992)
Gwynn, Major General Charles W, KCB CMG DSO, *Imperial Policing* (London: Macmillan 1939)
Hallion, Richard P, *Strike from the Sky: The History of Battlefield Air Attack 1911–1945* (Shrewsbury: AirLife 1989)
Heilbrunn, Otto, *Warfare in the Enemy's Rear* (London: George Allen & Unwin 1963)
Hoe, Alan, *David Stirling: The Authorised Biography of the Creator of the SAS* (London: Little Brown 1992)
Holden Reid, Brian, (Editor), *Military Power: Land Warfare in Theory and Practice* (London: Frank Cass 1997)
James, Lawrence, *The Golden Warrior: The Life and Legend of Lawrence of Arabia* (London: Weidenfeld & Nicholson 1990)
Jennings, Christian, *Midnight in Some Burning Town: British Special Operations Forces from Belgrade to Baghdad* (London: Cassell 2005), pp.195–211
Jones, Tim, *Postwar Counterinsurgency and the SAS 1945–1952: A Special Type of Warfare* (London: Frank Cass 1997)
Kayyali, Abdul Wahhab Said, *Palestine: A Modern History* (London: Third World Books, 1978)

Kedourie, E, *In the Anglo-Arab Labyrinth: The McMahon-Hussein Correspondence and its Interpretations 1914–1939* (London: Frank Cass, 2000)
Keegan, John, (Editor), *Churchill's Generals* (London: Warner 1991)
Kirby, Major General S Woodburn, CB CMG CIE OBE MC, with Captain CT Addis DSO RN, Brigadier MR Roberts DSO, Colonel GT Wards CMG OBE, Air Vice Marshal NL Desoer CBE, *The War Against Japan, Volume II: India's Most Dangerous Hour* (London: HMSO 1958)
—— *The War Against Japan, Volume III: The Decisive Battles* (London: HMSO 1961)
Kitson, General Sir Frank, *Low Intensity Operations: Subversion, Insurgency and Peacekeeping* (London: Faber & Faber 1971)
Koenig, William J, *Over the Hump: Airlift to China* (London: Pan 1972)
Lewin, Ronald, *Slim: The Standardbearer* (London: Leo Cooper 1976)
Liddell Hart, BH, *The Strategy of Indirect Approach* (London: Faber & Faber 1941)
—— *The Second World War* (London: Cassell 1970)
Lyman, Robert, *Slim, Master of War: Burma and the Birth of Modern Warfare* (London: Constable & Robinson 2004)
Maclean, Sir Fitzroy, *Eastern Approaches* (London: Jonathan Cape, 1949)
Mackenzie, William, *The Secret History of SOE* (London: St Ermine's Press 2000)
Mackenzie, Major General JJG and Holden Reid, Brian, (Editors), *Central Region vs. Out of Area: Future Commitments* (London: Tri-Service Press 1990)
Marston, DP, *Phoenix from the Ashes: The Indian Army in the Burma Campaign* (Westport & London: Praeger, 2003)
Mead, Peter, *Orde Wingate and the Historians* (Braunton: Merlin Books 1987)
Miksche, FO, *Paratroops* (London: Faber & Faber 1943)
Mockler, Anthony, *Haile Selassie's War: The Italian-Ethiopian Campaign 1935–41* (New York: Random House 1984)
Mosley, Leonard, *Gideon goes to War* (London: Arthur Barker 1955)
Murray, Williamson and Scales, Robert H, *The Iraq War* (Cambridge, Mass: Harvard University Press, 2003)
Nath, Colonel Prithvi, VSM, *Wingate: His Relevance to Contemporary Warfare* (New Delhi: Stirling 1990)
O'Brien, Conor Cruise, *The Siege: The Story of Israel and Zionism* (London: Weidenfeld & Nicholson 1986)
Otway, Lieutenant Colonel TBH, *The Second World War 1939–1945, Army: Airborne Forces* (London: Imperial War Museum 1990)
Overy, RJ (Richard), *The Air War 1939–1945* (London: Europa 1980)
—— *Why the Allies Won* (London: Pimlico 1995)
Paret, Peter (Editor), *Makers of Modern Strategy from Machiavelli to the Nuclear Age* (Oxford: OUP 1994)
Pitchfork, Air Commodore Graham, *Shot Down and on the Run: The RAF and Commonwealth Aircrews who got home from behind enemy lines* (London: National Archives 2003)
Place, Timothy Harrison *Military Training in the British Army, 1940–44: From Dunkirk to D-Day* (London: Frank Cass 2000)
Playfair, Major General ISO, *The Official History of the War in the Mediterranean and the Middle East, Volume I* (London: HMSO 1954)
—— *The Official History of the War in the Mediterranean and the Middle East, Volume III* (London: HMSO 1960)
Rolo, Charles J, *Wingate's Raiders* (London: George G Harrap 1944)
Romanus, Charles F and Sutherland, Riley, *The United States Army in World War II, China-Burma-India Theater: Stilwell's Mission to China* (Washington DC: Department of the Army 1953)
—— *The United States Army in World War II, China-Burma-India Theater: Stilwell's Command Problems* (Washington DC: Department of the Army 1956)
Rooney, David, *Wingate and the Chindits: Redressing the Balance* (London: Arms & Armour 1994)
Rossetto, Luigi *Major General Orde Charles Wingate and the Development of Long Range Penetration* (Manhattan: Kansas MA/AH 1982)
Royle, Trevor, *Orde Wingate: Irregular Soldier* (London: Weidenfeld & Nicholson 1995)

Scruton, Roger, *A Dictionary of Political Thought* (London: Macmillan 1996)
Seaman, Mark, (Editor) *Special Operations Executive: A new instrument of war* (Oxford: Routledge 2006)
Segev, Tom, *One Palestine, Complete: Jews and Arabs under the British Mandate* (London: Abacus 2000)
Seymour, William, *British Special Forces: The Story of Britain's Undercover Soldiers* (London: Sidgwick & Jackson 1985)
Shirreff, David, *Bare Feet and Bandoliers: Wingate, Sandford, the Patriots and the part they played in the Liberation of Ethiopia* (London: Radcliffe 1995)
Simson, HJ, *British Rule, and Rebellion* (Edinburgh and London: William Blackwood, 1937)
Skeen, General Sir Andrew, *Passing it On: Short Talks on Tribal Fighting on the North-West Frontier of India*, reprinted as *Lessons in Imperial Rule* (London: Frontline, 2008)
Slater, Robert, *Warrior Statesman: the life of Moshe Dayan* (London: Robinson 1992)
Strachan, Hew, *The Politics of the British Army* (Oxford: Clarendon 1997)
Sykes, Christopher, *Orde Wingate* (London: Collins 1959)
Terraine, John, *The Right of the Line: The Royal Air Force in the European War 1939-45* (London: Hodder & Stoughton 1985)
Thompson, Julian, *The Imperial War Museum Book of War behind Enemy Lines* (London: MacMillan 1998)
—— *The Imperial War Museum Book of the War in Burma* (London: Pan 2002)
Towle, Philip Anthony, *Pilots and Rebels: The use of aircraft in unconventional warfare 1918-1988* (London: Brassey's 1989)
Townshend, Charles, *Britain's Civil Wars: Counterinsurgency in the Twentieth Century* (London: Faber & Faber 1986)
—— *Terrorism: A brief introduction* (Oxford: OUP 2002)
Tuchman, Barbara, *Stilwell and the American Experience in China 1911-1945* (London: Macmillan 1970)
Yousaf, Mohammad and Adkin, Mark, *The Battle for Afghanistan* (London: Pen & Sword 2007)

Published Secondary Sources – Articles And Essays
Anonymous, 'The Burmese Rebellion 1931', *RUSI Journal* Volume LX 1932
Anonymous, 'Tactical Doctrine Up-To-Date: Field Service Regulations, Part II, 1935', *Army Quarterly* Volume 32 No.2, July 1936
Blacker, Major LVS, 'Modernised Mountain Warfare', *Journal of the United Services Institute of India*, Volume LXI, 1931
Blanche, Ed, 'Iran's Foreign Legion', *Middle East*, Issue 449, December 2013
Carpendale, Captain W St J, 'The Moplah Rebellion 1921-1922', *Journal of the United Services Institute of India*, Volume LVI, 1926
Codner, Michael, 'An Initial Assessment of the Combat Phase', in RUSI Whitehall Paper No.59, *War in Iraq: Combat and Consequences* (London: RUSI 2003)
Durnford, Captain CMP, 'The Arab Insurrection of 1920-21', *Journal of the United Services Institute of India*, Volume LIV, 1922
Festing, Major FC, DSO psc RMLI, 'The value of close order drill in training the soldier for war', *RUSI Journal* Volume LXVI, 1921
Hackett, Colonel JW DSO MBE MC, 'The Employment of Special Forces', *RUSI Journal* XCVII, 1952
Hughes, Matthew, Review of Avi Shlaim's *The Iron Wall*, Website of the Institute of Historical Research, http://www.history.ac.uk/reviews/paper/hughesMat2.html
V Jabotinsky, 'The Iron Wall (We and the Arabs)', first published in *Rasviyet*, 4 November 1923, published in English in *The Jewish Herald*, 26 November 1937, online copy available at http://www.marxists.de/middleast/ironwall/ironwall.htm, last accessed 10 January 2010
Liddell Hart, BH, 'The Essence of War', *RUSI Journal*, Volume LXXV, August 1930
'MFC', 'Raids and Reprisals on the North-West Frontier', *Journal of the United Services Institute of India* Volume LIV, 1922
Oren, Michael B, 'Orde Wingate: Friend under fire', *Azure* Issue 10, www.azure.org.il/10-oren.html
Polson Newman, Major E, 'Britain's Position in Palestine', *RUSI Journal* LXXXI 1936

Rooney, David, 'Command and Leadership in the Chindit Operations', in Gary Sheffield (Editor), *Leadership and Command: The Anglo-American Military Experience since 1861*(London: Brassey's 1996)

Samuelson, Maurice, 'Return to Ein Harod: Major General HEN Bredin describes the Night Squads', *Jewish Observer and Middle East Review* October 1969

'Shpagwishtama', 'The Changing Aspect of Operations on the North-West Frontier', *Journal of the United Services Institute of India* Volume LXVI 1936

Internet Sources

'Afghan Forces take control of controversial night raids', *France 24*, 8 April 2012, http://www.france24.com/en/20120408-afghan-forces-usa-oversee-controversial-night-raids-special-forces-taliban-insurgents-isaf-nato, accessed 13 October 2013

'Afghan Taliban says rehearsed attack for two months', *Reuters*, 16 April 2012, http://www.reuters.com/article/2012/04/16/us-afghan-taliban-plan-idUSBRE83F0LX20120416, accessed 17 April 2012

'Anti Ahmaddiya Movement in Islam, 26 January 1999' (www.alhafeez.org)

'Assasinating [sic] for Peace in Palestine and Ireland', *Irish Political Review*, Sept 2002 (www.atholbooks.org);

'Darbyism in Israel: Ariel Sharon', *Executive Intelligence Review* (www.larouchepub.com).

Robert Eisenman, 'Who killed Orde Wingate?', *Huffington Post*, 24 June 2011, http://www.huffingtonpost.com/robert-eisenman/post_2154_b_884195.html

SAS "Smash" squads on the ground in Libya to mark targets for coalition jets', http://www.dailymail.co.uk/news/article-1368247/Libya-SAS-smash-squads-ground-mark-targets-coalition-jets.html, accessed 20 July 2011

'Libya: SAS veterans helping Nato identify Gadaffi targets in Misrata', http://www.guardian.co.uk/world/2011/may/31/libya-sas-veterans-misrata-rebels, accessed 20 July 2011

US, Afghanistan sign key "night raids" deal', CNN 8 April 2012, http://edition.cnn.com/2012/04/08/world/asia/afghanistan-night-raids/index.html, accessed 13 October 2013

www.awm.gov.au/korea/faces/burchett.htm, Accessed July 2001

Index

Page numbers in bold type refer to maps.

Abyssinia *see* Ethiopia
Adam, General Sir Ronald, 110
Afghanistan, 3, 131–2, 135, 205, 206
Afula, 83
Alanbrooke, Field Marshal *see* Brooke, General Sir Alan
Alexander, General Sir Harold, 152
Alexander of Tunis, Field Marshal Earl
Alison, Colonel John, 184
Allon, Yigal, 1, 47, 73–4, 82, 89, 92
Amery, Leo, 86, 107–8, 111, 116, 147
Amritsar, 19, 207
'Aquila' (Author of article on jungle warfare), 143, 203
Arnold, General HH 'Hap,' 5, 144, 175, 176
Auchinleck, Field Marshal Sir Claude, 27, 146
Avigur, Saul, 60

Bagnold, Major Ralph, 26
Baldwin, Air Marshal Sir John, 203
Bardia, 26
Barton, Colonel J.E.B., 9, 10
Ben-Gurion, David, 49, 52, 59, 60, 63, 67, 77, 91–2, 93, 108
Bidwell, Brigadier Shelford, 168
Blacker, Major L.V.S., 24
Boustead, Lieutenant Colonel Hugh, 113, 128, 129–30
Bredin, Major General HEN, 72, 73, 80
Brenner, Zvi, 68, 77, 84
Brooke, General Sir Alan, 110, 147, 173, 174
Brooke-Popham, Air Chief Marshal Sir Robert, 137–8
Burchett, Wilfred, 6–7, 47–8, 54, 87, 94, 111
Burma, 2, 21, 25–6; British thoughts on jungle warfare, 145–7; Japanese weaknesses, 152–4; long range penetration, 154–60; Mission 204, 138, 147–8, 150, 161; Operation *Longcloth*, 169–79; Operation *Thursday*, 191–204, **192**; warfare in Southeast Asia 1940–41, 137–45; Wingate in Burma, 136–7; Wingate's operational models, 147–52

Callwell, Major General Charles, 23, 25, 26, 136, 138, 150, 207; on bayonets, 54, 66; jungle warfare, 145; and 'national characteristics,' 20, 21; recommendations on 'bush warfare,' 33; *Small Wars: Their Principles and Practice*, 19, 20, 121, 206
Calvert, Brigadier Michael, 9, 10, 11–15, 100, 156, 163, 167, 168, 170, 171–2, 189, 194, 196, 201, 202
Cazalet, Victor, 107
Chennault, General Claire, 138, 144, 173
Chetwode, General Sir Philip, 18
Chiang Kai-shek, 139, 144, 169, 173, 177
Chindits, 5, 6, 8, 9–10, 11, 12, 13, 28, 163–6, 169–79, **170**, 182, 189–90, 195, 200–1, 202–3, 204
Churchill, Winston, 1, 5, 9, 10, 24, 36, 86–7, 96, 97, 112, 122, 144–5, 173–4, 177, 199, 200
Cochran, Lieutenant Colonel Philip, 157
Cohen, Tzion, 76–7, 90
Coningham, Air Marshal Sir Arthur, 157–8
Coogan, Tim Pat, 132
Cyrenaica, 26, 27

Dabburiya, 78, 79–81
Dayan, General Moshe, 1, 5, 32, 92
Defeat into Victory (Slim), 4, 6, 7–8, 9, 10, 153, 179, 182
Dennys, Major General L.E., 137, 138, 147
Deverell, Field Marshall Sir Cyril, 43
Dill, Lieutenant General J.G., 55, 61–2
Dodds-Parker, Captain Douglas, 33–4, 100, 112, 114, 116–17, 125, 135
Dorman-Smith, Major General Eric, 27
Down, Lieutenant General Sir Ernest, 5–6, 188
Dyer, Brigadier General Reginald, 19

Eden, Anthony, 111, 115
Emeny, Stuart, 58
Eritrea, 3, 26, 28, 33, 122
Ethiopia, 1–2, 3, 7, 33, 37, **104**; G(R) and resistance in Ethiopia, 111–17; impact of Ethiopian campaign on Wingate's ideas,

130–5; Mission 101, 114–15, 118–19, 120, 127; operational developments, 121–30; Wingate takes charge of operations, 117–21
Evetts, Brigadier John (later Lieutenant General Sir), 54, 57, 65–6, 70, 77, 82

Fergusson, Major General Sir Bernard, 10–11, 15, 136, 143, 152, 166, 170–1, 180, 189, 194, 195, 198, 201, 202
Fleming, Peter, 100
Foot, M.R.D., 112

Gadaffi, Colonel Muammar, former President of Libya, 2–3
Galula, David, 131
Germany, 30, 95–6, 97, 108
Ghandi, Mahatma, 140
Gideon Force, 1–2, 3, 121–30
Giffard, General Sir George, 175, 178, 179, 191, 199
Gojjam region *see* Ethiopia
Graves, Robert, 37
Gubbins, Major General Sir Colin, 100–2, 149
Gwynn, Major General Charles, 19, 21, 207

Haganah, 2, 52, 60–1, 62, 63, 66–9, 72, 74, 77, 82, 88, 91, 92
Haile Selassie I, Emperor of Ethiopia, 1, 7, 94, 111–12, 113, 115, 116, 117, 122
Hailu, Ras, 119
Haining, General Sir Robert, 1, 46, 57, 58, 59, 69, 77, 82, 83, 88, 90, 93, 109–10, 116, 207
Hanita, 67, 68
Harris, Air Commodore Arthur (later Marshal of the Royal Air Force Sir), 62, 82
Hitin, 89, 90
Holland, Lieutenant Colonel J.C.F., 43, 99–100, 156, 172, 184
Husseini, Haj Amin al, 51, 54, 93

Imphal, Battle of, 9, 15, 16, 17, 147, 153, 172, 179, 181–2, 197, 199, 204
Indaw, 194, 195–7, 202
India, 22, 24
Iran, 133
Iraq, 24, 26, 54, 205, 206
Ireland, 21–2, 23–4, 25, 131, 132, 207
Ironside, General Sir Edmund, 38, 84, 96, 108, 109–10, 113

Jabotinsky, Vladimir, 59–60, 91

Kassa, Ras, 124, 129
Keith-Roach, Edward, 93

Kennedy, Major General Sir John, 95–6
Keren, 3, 28, 128
Kilcullen, Colonel David, 131–2
King-Clark, Lieutenant Reginald ('Rex', later Lieutenant Colonel), 71, 73, 76, 77, 80, 82
Kirby, Major General S Woodburn, 4, 6, 9–10, 17, 137, 166, 167, 180, 197
Kiszely, Lieutenant General Sir John, 18
Kitson, General Sir Frank, 131

Lawrence, Colonel Thomas Edward ('of Arabia'), 2, 29, 35–43, 101, 113, 117, 121, 131; compared with Orde Wingate, 37–8, 41–3; military philosophy and views on Bedouin/Turkish conflict, 38–42; Orde Wingate's opinion of, 36–7, 130
Lean, Sir David, 37
Lentaigne, Brigadier W.D.A. ('Joe'), 189–90, 195, 201–2, 204
Lewin, Ronald, 8–9
Lias, Geoffrey, 102, 103
Libya, 2–3, 27, 28, 33, 54, 111, 206
Liddell Hart, Basil, 27, 37, 43, 86, 92

MacMichael, Sir Harold, 52, 53, 56, 67, 79–80, 83
Marlborough, Duke of, 189
Masters, John, 168, 189
Mead, Brigadier Peter, 15–16
Mecca, 38–9
military operations: *Anakim*, 173; *Compass*, 26, 27, 121; *Culverin*, 200–1; *Enduring Freedom*, 3; *Iraqi Freedom*, 135; *Longcloth*, 2, 8, 9, 11, 136, 137, 154, 156, 159, 160, 164, 168, 169–79, **170**, 183, 188; Mohmand operations, 24–5; *Tarzan*, 178; *Thursday*, 2, 9, 11, 12, 15, 16, 136, 137, 146, 159, 160, 164, 172, 174, 177, 182, 183–4, 187, 188–9, 191–204, **192**
Mockler, Anthony, 112
Montgomery, Major General Bernard, 85, 161, 162
Mosley, Leonard, 6, 7, 31, 48, 60, 68, 94, 112, 191
Mountbatten of Burma, Admiral of the Fleet Earl, 5, 15, 97, 139, 140, 145, 173, 175–6, 177, 197, 199, 202, 203, 204
Mufti *see* Husseini, Haj Amin al
Mutaguchi, Lieutenant General Renya, Japanese Army, 172, 193, 197, 202

Nadwa, Joseph, 47
Night Squads, 1, 2, 7, 46, 48, 49, 63–4, 72–84, 92, 205, 206–7
Northwest Frontier, 24, 25

O'Connor, Lieutenant General Sir Richard, 27, 77, 89, 93

Palestine, 1, 7, 44, **50**, 207; Anglo-Jewish cooperation, 61–3; British response to Arab Revolt, 54–6; development of the Arab Revolt 1936-39, 49–53; Jewish responses to the Arab Revolt, 59–61; Night Squads, 63–4; phase four of the Arab Revolt, 85; phase one of the Arab Revolt, 53–4; phase three of the Arab Revolt - guerrilla warfare to terrorism, 57–9; phase two of the Arab Revolt, 56–7
Platt, Lieutenant General Sir William, 26, 28, 38, 94, 114, 122, 123
Pownall, General Sir Henry, 6

Qassam, Sheikh Muhammad Izz al-Din al, 52
Quwuqji, Fawzi al-, 54

Rolo, Charles, 10
Rooney, David, 10, 14, 94, 126
Rossetto, Luigi, 48, 95
Royle, Trevor, 31–2, 112

Sadeh, Yitzhak, 61, 92
Samuel, Sir Herbert, 51
Sanderson, Lieutenant Colonel David, 14
Sandford, Colonel Daniel, 112, 113, 114, 115, 118–19, 123
Scoones, Lieutenant General Geoffrey, 146, 180, 181, 188
Segev, Tom, 48–9, 76–7, 89, 90
Sharon, Ariel, 92
Shirreff, David, 112
Shlaim, Avi, 91
Simonds, Major Anthony, 61, 90, 123, 124, 125, 125–6
Simson, Lieutenant Colonel H.J., 19–20, 21–2, 25–6, 51, 93, 207
Skeen, General Sir Andrew, 22, 23, 24, 146
Slim, Field Marshal the 1st Earl, 17, 20, 121, 136, 140, 141, 142, 147, 153, 154, 156, 172, 193–4, 203; as commander of Fourteenth Army, 175, 180–2; on commanders' mentality, 143; *Defeat into Victory*, 4, 6, 7–8, 9, 10, 153, 179, 182; on jungle warfare, 182, 199; Operational Order for *Thursday*, 193–4; opinion of Japanese, 143–4; opinion of Orde Wingate, 4, 5, 7–8, 163, 173, 179–80, 188, 199; penetration forces, views on, 182; relations with Wingate, 150, 197–8, 200; and tactical overmatch, 179–82; views on special forces, 6, 8, 136
Small Wars: Their Principles and Practice (Callwell), 19, 20, 121, 206

Smith, Major General Arthur, 113
Somalia, 3, 26, 121, 122
Stevenson, Lieutenant Colonel H.N.C., 152, 160, 161
Stibbe, Lieutenant Philip, 168
Stilwell, General Joseph, 12, 140, 141, 143, 153, 160, 173, 176, 191
Strachan, Hew, 49
Sudan, 30–5, 112–14, 121–2
Sykes, Christopher, 68, 112, 172
Syria, 28

Tegart, Sir Charles, 56
Thesiger, Sir Wilfred, 94, 117–18, 129–30
Thompson, Major General Julian, 1
Thompson, Sir Robert, 5, 15, 16–17
Tiberias, 84, 90
Townshend, Charles, 25, 49
Tulloch, Major General Derek, 15, 45, 178, 185, 188, 193, 197, 198, 204

Wauchope, Sir Arthur, 62
Wavell, Field Marshal the 1st Earl, 1, 5, 9, 20, 26, 36, 43, 56, 64–5, 111, 113, 114, 115, 116, 122, 130, 136, 145, 147, 166, 173, 207
Weizmann, Chaim, 46, 49, 59, 67, 108
Whalley, Captain Richard, 112
Wingate, Ethel, 47
Wingate, General Sir Reginald, 31, 37
Wingate, Major General Orde Charles: and air supplied strongholds concept, 184–9, 193, 203; on anti-aircraft defences, 106–7; anti-Arabism, 37, 81, 91; 'Appreciation of chances of forming Long Range Penetration Groups in Burma,' 151; 'Appreciation of the Ethiopian Campaign,' 37, 118, 130, 148, 149, 152; 'Appreciation of the Gojjam Campaign,' 136–7; belief in 'national characteristics,' 20, 30, 129, 207; box system, use of, 146–7, 182, 186, 189, 190; in Burma, 136–7; Churchill's opinion of Wingate, 1, 5, 9, 173–4, 177, 200; on column commanders, 157–8; as commander of Gideon Force, 1–2, 3, 121–30; as commander of Night Squads, 1, 2, 7, 46, 48, 49, 63–4, 74–84, 92, 205, 206–7; as commander of the Chindits, 5, 5–6, 6, 8, 9–10, 11, 12, 13, 28, 94, 163–6, 169–79, 189–90; compared with T.E. Lawrence, 37–8, 41–3; and counterinsurgency, 2, 205; counterinsurgency, views on, 71–2; criticism of, 6–10; death, 201; defence of, 10–17; future of the Chindits, views on, 200–1; and future of warfare, 188, 205–8; guerrilla warfare, views on, 70–1; guerrilla warfare, views on, 120–1,

128, 148–9, 163; and the *Haganah*, 66–9, 72, 74, 77, 82, 91; impact of Ethiopian campaign on Wingate's ideas, 130–5; and the Indian Army, 166–9; influence on Israeli history, 91–2; insurgency, views on, 20, 134, 149–50, 207; Islamophobia, 7; Japanese, views on, 30, 153, 154; as a junior officer, 29–30; Lawrence, opinion of, 36–7; and long range penetration, 1–2, 5, 130, 133–5, 147–8, 151, 152, 154–60, 174–5, 203–4, 206; long range penetration and other Allied penetration forces 1942-43, 160–2; low opinion of staff officers, 44–5; 'Notes on Penetration Warfare , Burma Command, 25/3/42,' 147–8, 150; operational models for Burma, 147–52, 154–60; Operational Order for *Thursday*, 194, 200; opinion of self, 167; parachute troops, opinion on use of, 188; personality, 4, 10, 17, 168–9; and the phony war, 105–11; plans for Operation *Thursday*, 193, 195, 196, 197–8; 'Principles Governing the Employment of Special Night Squads,' 74–5; proxy war, use of, 132; relations with Slim, 150, 197–8, 200; relationship with Wavell, 64–6; scare tactics, use of, 129–30; sets up Night Squads, 72–4; Slim, opinion of, 180; Slim's opinion of Wingate, 4, 5, 7–8, 163, 173, 179–80, 188, 199; special forces, views on, 29, 163, 167–8; staff college papers, 43–5; Sudan Defence Force, 30–5; takes charge in Ethiopia, 117–21; and training, 31–2, 35, 44–5, 65, 69, 73–4, 80, 105–6, 105–7, 120, 164–5, 176, 188; Zionism, 7, 37, 45, 46–9, 66–7, 207

Woodhead, Sir John, 86

Wetherall, Lieutenant General Sir Harry, 94